—

A VERY DIFFERENT COUNTRY
A TYPICALLY ENGLISH REVOLUTION

NICHOLAS FAITH

A
VERY
DIFFERENT
COUNTRY

A TYPICALLY ENGLISH REVOLUTION

SINCLAIR-STEVENSON
LONDON

To C. S-S
without whom not

First published in the United Kingdom by
Christopher Sinclair-Stevenson in 2002
3 South Terrace, London SW7 2TB

ISBN 0-9540476-4-8

Typeset by Rowland Phototypesetting Ltd., Bury St Edmunds, Suffolk.
Printed and bound in the United Kingdom by
St Edmundsbury Press, Bury St Edmunds, Suffolk.

Contents

List of illustrations

The illustrations appear between pages 150 and 151

Introduction

This book is an attempt to make sense of the changes in English society and culture during the Queen's long reign. These changes are so profound that, in my view, they add up to a revolution deeper than any since the Industrial Revolution two hundred years earlier, and the period involved is long enough to allow one to form at least a preliminary judgement. The book is not an orthodox chronological history but an account of what affected people's lives, their attitudes and prospects, social as well as economic, their hopes and fears. In writing it I have tried to confine myself to the ways in which England's history was distinctive during a period when the whole of Western Europe was also changing at a great rate.

The scope of the book is so wide that simplifications are inevitable, and writing it has involved a mixture of the chronological and the thematic, for I treat a select handful of themes within a fairly definite time-span. I believe in the old saying that 'A sixpenny life will give you all the facts' and as a result many important events – the Falklands War, for example – are summarised in a few lines because they have been so often and so exhaustively treated elsewhere. Yet political events obviously matter. Professor Patrick Collinson was not exaggerating (much) when he asserted that 'All social history is necessarily political and . . . politics is equally a social process.'[1] For I have tried not so much to reach the parts that other histories have not tried to reach, but instead to concentrate on the salient themes – social, economic and cultural – rather than on the political events and personalities which have been endlessly chewed over. Above all, the book is designed to explain the – largely non-political – aspects that politically based histories skim over or even ignore and yet include some explanation of major events.

A Very Different Country represents a contradiction of A. J. P. Taylor's belief that 'political history provides the acts of the drama; and the rest – culture, economics, religion and so on – are refreshing interruptions like drinks at the bar during the interval.' Political histories are the result not only of politicians' deluded belief in their central position in any historical narrative but also of the more general assumption that the centre was actually, in Lord Beaverbrook's immortal phrase, 'in charge of the clattering train'. By contrast, for most of the time covered by this book, it emphatically wasn't. As a result, the only politician to receive full-length treatment is Mrs Thatcher, while the others intrude only when they have important roles, positive or negative. The lack of 'politics' is particularly evident in the period from 1956 to 1979 when, virtually all the time, successive Prime Ministers were at the mercy of what Harold Macmillan so rightly described as 'events, dear boy, events'.

The politicians' helplessness is even more evident when discussing economic events. The insistence of orthodox histories of the past fifty years on providing details of every twist and turn of economic policy, down to the smallest movement in interest rates, seems to me profoundly misplaced. The reason is very simple: throughout the post-war era until 1992, after Mrs Thatcher's revolution and after we had regained our economic freedom by leaving the European Monetary System, Britain's economic position was so precarious, its susceptibility to the slightest puff of wind so great, and so often exacerbated by government policies, that no consistent economic policy was possible. As Kenneth Morgan put it, 'Of all the chancellors in the period only Cripps, Butler, Jenkins and (briefly) Lawson seemed to have matters under secure direction'[2] – to which number he could now add Gordon Brown who had the advantage of inheriting an unprecedentedly sound economic situation from his predecessor.

In 1952 there were two strait-jackets. One was social and external. The other was an extension of this and internal, a sort of psychological clamp. Both led to low expectations and narrow, self-imposed limitations on the part of those who felt, and usually were, excluded. At a time when the economic and social porosity, the absorptive power of Britain, which had kept the country so alert and healthy over the previous centuries, seemed to have disappeared, the social structure had, seemingly, frozen. As I worked on this book, it increasingly appeared to me to be a saga of how these constraints slowly melted, largely through the inadequacies, to put it mildly, of the then-ruling classes.

Today Britain is by no means an equal society – in terms of relative incomes it is far more unequal than most other industrialised countries – nor is there anything like total equality of opportunity. It's just that it's freer, there is more of a feeling that anything is possible, than in any other country in Europe. From being one of the most stratified, most frozen, societies in the Western world it has been transformed into one of the most, if not the most, open, and this despite a whole host of residual class distinctions. When the Queen came to the throne the pace (dignified, slow) was set by the over-sixties. Today, for better or worse, the pace is being set by the under-thirties. (In the course of my researches I found a number of excellent books written by thirty somethings or even twenty somethings, an unheard-of phenomenon fifty years ago.)

The young are not the only group who, fifty years ago, were treated as outsiders, as irrelevant, as lesser breeds outside the law. Indeed the 'excluded' made up the majority of the population. Yet, by the end of the Millennium all sorts and conditions of outsiders – women, gays, immigrants and the first generation of their descendants, as well as large numbers of the working and lower middle classes – had broken through, in many cases effectively enough to allow their reactions, their cultural and social habits to influence or dominate national attitudes. At the start of the third Millennium, the 'tent' of those able to 'better themselves', if not as inclusive as Tony Blair would pretend, is infinitely more inclusive than it was back in 1952.

A Very Different Country is also, implicitly, a rejoinder to the increasing number of nostalgists who have made an excellent living these past few years lamenting the supposed – and occasionally very real – virtues of the Britain We Have Lost. One of the virtues was the degree of general knowledge that could be assumed, rightly or wrongly, among a general readership, smaller though it was then than it is now. I fully realise that this is no longer the case (if it ever were: in the late 1960s I remember my then boss Mary Goldring – at the *Economist* yet – laying down that 'our readers were pig higgorant'). Although this work conveys my inevitably and unashamedly personal analysis when looking back over the five decades of my adult life, I was determined from the start that it should not be overly personal, that my own experiences should be included only when truly relevant to the story.

And who am I to write such a book? Well, why not me? 'We all live with history,' wrote the great historian Richard Cobb, 'and we live in history, and the frontiers between history and imagination are very little more than Chinese walls, removable at will. And a historian is a person who walks his chosen itineraries with his eyes open'[3] – as he did so well. Well, I'm a 'veteran' journalist who has written about a vast range of subjects for most of Britain's classier newspapers, and, as they say, a journalist 'is an historian writing fast'. Between 1964 and 1973 I had a successful ten years in senior positions on the *Economist* and the *Sunday Times* – before the arrival of Rupert Murdoch a genuinely great newspaper. I then opted out to help start London Broadcasting, Britain's first commercial radio station, to write books – and to help campaign against Britain's membership of the then EEC. In working for LBC, which was in trouble from the start, and by campaigning against the EEC, I found myself doubly isolated from my contemporaries: in believing in a new and risky venture and in adopting a political stance which put me firmly beyond the pale for most of my friends in the media. But the experience provided me with a degree of independence from received soft radical opinion which I have found immensely useful in writing this book.

I needed a firm conceptual framework, if only because the sources I could have tapped were almost infinite – books, articles in newspapers and magazines, television and radio programmes. Of the thousands of books on the subjects involved, I have been particularly partial to relatively unself-conscious memoirs by such apparently marginal figures as Woodrow Wyatt and Alistair McAlpine. (By contrast, most politicians operate at three levels, and they reveal only the most super-ficial – what they claim they were doing – in their memoirs. The deeper levels – what they thought they were doing and what in reality they were doing – are generally neglected.) But I was also able to draw heavily on my own experiences and the memories of friends of my own age, many of them journalists, who also witnessed the revol-ution. As Tony Judt put it: 'In the writing of contemporary or near-contemporary history, memory is a crucial resource: not just because it adds detail and perspective, but because what people remember and forget, and the uses to which memory is put are the building blocks of history too.'[4] Writing contemporary history is inevitably complicated because of the need – which comes naturally to journalists – to weigh the relative value of a bewildering variety of sources, memories, reports, interviews. I can only hope that I've managed to separate the reliable from the suspect and, as far as my own memories are con-cerned, relied only on the firmest of my recollections.

Notes

1. *London Review of Books*, March 22, 2001.
2. *The People's Peace 1945–1989*, Oxford University Press, 1990.
3. *Paris & Elsewhere*, John Murray, 1998.
4. *New York Review of Books*, December 3, 1998.

1

The Outsider

IT WAS THE EVENTS of the week after the death of Princess Diana which triggered the thoughts underlying the structure of this book. For me – and I suspect for many others – Diana's death made so deep an impact that we remember exactly where we were when we heard the news. In this respect, it was like the assassination of President Kennedy, the departure of Mrs Thatcher from 10 Downing Street or, most recently, the attacks on the World Trade Centre and the Pentagon. But Diana's death was different to a degree. For a start, it was so absurd – a drunk driver late at night transporting a British princess and her lover, the sleazy, druggy son of an Egyptian chancer. And because the event seemed to touch a nerve, the loss was personal rather than public, as it had been in the case of President Kennedy.

The outbreak of grief in the week that followed the death was unprecedented in British history and revealed just how many British people were prepared to abandon their traditional reticence and, more-over to show their feelings in public. It was Father Fayers, a parish priest in South-East London quoted by Monica Furlong[1], who expressed the fundamental point, that the outburst of grief 'was more like something you would see in a Latin country' – Eva Peron's was the name on the lips of many cynics that week. 'For me,' Fayers wrote, 'it seemed like a sacramentalising process – lighting candles, putting down flowers, setting up shrines, weeping, expressing grief instead of keeping it all inside. This can be shallow and many British people will resist it, but the fact that it happened at all is an indication of change.'

Tears in public had been unthinkable for several generations – though the Victorians had wept buckets at the slightest provocation. But during the 1990s the idea had become less unthinkable. It had been the sight of two totally dissimilar figures alike only in the improbability of their expressing open emotions which gave vicarious permission, as it were, to the British public to blub so freely. In the summer of 1990 that epitome of laddism, Paul Gascoigne, wept copious

1

tears when he received a second yellow card which would have prevented him from playing in England's team in the final of the World Cup. The effect was enormous. *Spitting Image*, the satirical television show, created a weeping puppet, wrote Barbara Gunnell, 'whose geyser eyes spouted with greater force by the week. Like yawning, crying proved contagious.'[2] Later that year Gazza's example was followed by Mrs Thatcher. Some years earlier she had wept in public when her son Mark was lost in the Sahara in the course of a motor rally. She also allowed her emotions to show when she left 10 Downing Street for the last time and a few months later she dabbed her eyes in public after she had announced her retirement from the House of Commons.

In the wake of Diana's death the public figure who perfectly grasped the opportunity to speak for the nation, to act in what might be termed a Presidential fashion, was Tony Blair, then in his honeymoon period a mere four months after becoming Prime Minister. His – undeniably brilliant – speech expressed simply and quite genuinely the – equally genuine – sadness felt by the mass of the country and Diana's own family. The most famous phrase he used, that Diana was 'The People's Princess' was in fact suggested by his Press Secretary, Alistair Campbell, who in turn had taken it from the unlikely figure of Julie Burchill, the raucous, brilliant, bisexual defender of the princess and scornful enemy of the royal family.

Blair's feeling for the popular mood was not matched by the majority of commentators. Paul Dacre, who, as editor of the *Daily Mail*, believed in his empathy with the feelings of much of the Great British Public, was in despair because he could not share his readers' deep sense of grief. More obvious was the tacit, unadmitted alliance between worthy left and snobby right characteristic of their attitudes over the past half century towards any new cultural phenomena particularly when the 'common people' were involved. As a result, the self-appointed best and brightest of both ends of the political spectrum made pompous idiots of themselves. To a man they refused to accept the obvious fact that Princess Di – as shown by the diminutive I use automatically – really had touched the hearts of the British people – including many millions who did not openly demonstrate their grief that week – as no member of the royal family had even done before. For Diana was the Queen the British people felt they had never had, a fully paid-up, albeit deeply neurotic, member of the human race and unafraid, at least in her last few years, to exhibit her emotions in public. They forgave her faults, above all her infallible taste in tacky men such as James Hewitt, Will Carling and, above all, Dodi al Fayed.

Yet from the right Simon Heffer huffed and puffed over 'the untimely deaths of an over-indulged woman and her delinquent inamorato'[3]. 'September was not a good month for those who imagined that human society is, or could one day, be governed by reason,' thundered Ian Jack, the editor of *Granta*, icon of the radical chic left[4]. He was joined by the distinguished historian Ross McKibbin, who wrote that 'a democracy which admired her with such intensity is both incomplete and immature'[5].

But the person who showed the most complete lack of understanding, and whose limitations and lack of ordinary human qualities were displayed more fully – and more publicly – than ever before was Her Majesty Queen Elizabeth II. Indeed the week provided an incomparable and unprecedented demonstration of the enormous gulf that had grown between her and her people in the previous forty-five years. Of course she was biased. She and Diana were total opposites. Diana was an openly emotional style goddess, the Queen a dowdy countrywoman – she spent several months of the year at Sandringham and Balmoral – trained to shown no emotion at all in public and personally inclined to show little enough in private.

For at least two years before Diana's death, once Andrew Morton had published the book to which she had contributed anonymously but so effectively, and above all after the ground-breaking *Panorama* interview with Martin Bashir, Diana had been perceived by the Palace as a dangerous loose cannon. We saw the Royal Firm, wrote Julie Burchill, 'in all its over-manned, outdated disarray. And what did they do, as dying monoliths always do when something new and true comes along? They sent in the Heavies.' Diana was prevented from applying for jobs for which she was perfectly suited, such as president of the British Red Cross and head of UNICEF, and when she wanted to deliver the Richard Dimbleby lecture on the subject of Aids, the Palace asked for the invitation to be withdrawn.

The week showed clearly that the Queen had no connection with the Britain as it had evolved during her reign. In her defence it must be said that the Hanoverian dynasty has always had damaging experiences with those of their members – or their spouses – who were fashionable. Although these included her own sister, and obviously Diana, the pace had been set at the end of the eighteenth century by George III's louche son, the profligate Prince Regent, later George IV. As Prince of Wales, the future Edward VII was leader of a 'smart set' which involved itself in every sort of misbehaviour at a time when straightforward adultery didn't count, for the husbands anyway. But the guilty parties the Queen had in mind were her uncle, the Duke of Windsor, and Wallis Simpson, the lady for whom he abandoned the throne. Even sixty years later, the abdication still haunted the royal family, which had refused to allow the Duchess of Windsor to be called Her Royal Highness through fear that she might divorce the Duke or remarry some totally unsuitable person if he died before

her. This ban, although groundless so far as the Duchess was concerned, was not unreasonable in the case of Diana. So she was also
deprived of the title, even though she was the mother to the heir to
the throne and even though it was an accolade still possessed by
eighteen members of the family including Princess Michael of Kent,
correctly described by Robert Harris in the *Sunday Times* as 'a Catholic
foreign divorcee.

Given the disreputable lovers with whom Diana had been associated
once her marriage had become a sham, anything might have happened,
she might even have married Dodi al Fayed. On the surface this seems
a ridiculous idea, given his appalling character, his shallowness,
selfishness, nothingness, not to mention his drug addiction – and the
fact that Diana herself was smitten with a heart surgeon at the time.
But women as insecure and over-exposed to the public gaze as Diana
– or Jackie Kennedy – crave above all security and privacy which
costs a great deal of money, and Fayed, like Aristotle Onassis, could
provide that essential item.

The sheer callousness of the Queen's reaction was shown first and
most obviously within a few hours of Diana's death. That morning
she took her grandsons to church, not for a service of mourning, which
might have helped them cope with their mother's sudden death, but
for a routine service, complete with a jocular sermon by the priest, an
act of unthinking cruelty emphasised by the way the Queen smiled
and waved at spectators on her way to the service. I still cannot
understand how she could have behaved so callously – however much
she had hated her daughter-in-law, why should she have inflicted this
punishment on two teenage boys? His mother's behaviour obviously
proved too much for the Prince of Wales and, probably for the first
time in his life, he disobeyed his mother and flew to Paris to collect
his former wife's body and bring it back to England in a proper royal
style. Moreover, from then on he could afford to be seen in public
showing that he cared about his sons, with his hands on their shoulders,
just like Any Ordinary Dad. In the long-term his ex-wife's death
had a massively favourable effect on the public's perception of him.
According to MORI, in the dramatic week of Diana's death only
two-fifths of the population thought he would make a good king, a
figure which had risen to nearly two-thirds six years later.

A clue to the reasoning behind the Queen's behaviour can be found
when she asked her courtiers to telephone the hospital where Diana
died to recover some jewellery she had taken to Paris with her, a piece
of heartlessness comprehensible only to those who remembered the
arguments concerning the royal jewels at the time of the abdication.
But by the middle of the week following Diana's death it finally
dawned on the mass of British people – and not only those who were

4

placing flowers in the Mall – that the Queen had ceased to represent them in any meaningful way, and even her son was warned that it might be unsafe for him to appear in public in London. As that redoubtable republican Tom Nairn put it[6], that week 'The enchanted glass of Monarchy was irretrievably broken.'

It took five long days for the Queen to make any public comment, and after the by no means heartfelt or convincing broadcast she made that Friday night, twelve hours before the funeral, she turned and said with icy contempt, 'Is that enough contrition?' By then the Spencer family, whose title predated the arrival of the Hanoverians in 1714, were firmly in charge of the arrangements, representing a far deeper threat to the monarchy than the millions piling flowers round royal palaces. For, as Julie Burchill says, the only force likely to abolish 'that monumental blockage in the S-bend of public life we call the British monarchy ... are the aristocracy.'[7]

The first defiant step taken by Diana's younger brother Earl Spencer was to choose Elton John to sing and, moreover, he was not required to choose a hymn – two years earlier the Palace had shown its monumental lack of understanding of popular taste when they chose the ineffable Cliff Richard to sing 'Congratulations' (a song of which no one in the crowd seemed to know the words) at the fiftieth anniversary celebrations of VE Day. John, though deservedly universally popular, was the flounciest of gays; everything about him was a 'taste-free zone'. Nevertheless he was a favourite with the Queen Mother, always, unlike her elder daughter, a friend of trendy show-business gays from Noel Coward on. More relevantly, he had been a close friend of Diana, indeed had been photographed publicly consoling her at the funeral of Gianni Versace. In the event, Elton John sang an especially rewritten 'Candle in the Wind' – originally composed in memory of another icon, Marilyn Monroe – with complete composure.

To emphasise the extraordinary nature of the occasion, it was Spencer's close friend, the brilliant but disgraced Darius Guppy, who wrote the famous speech in which Spencer spoke of Diana's intuition, 'her greatest gift' – and one so obviously denied to any of the members of the family into which she had married, of the 'innermost feelings of suffering that made it possible for her to connect with her constituency of the rejected', of the obvious fact that 'for all the status, the glamour, the applause, Diana remained throughout a very insecure person at heart, almost childlike in her desire to do good for others'. At the time the fact that the words were written by a convicted fraudster and spoken by a dubious sprig of the aristocracy seemed irrelevant. Spencer attacked the press and challenged the royal family over the upbringing of the Princes William and Harry, asserting the priority accorded to the 'blood family'. As he finished speaking his voice broke and the crowds listening outside the Abbey started applauding. The sound of the applause penetrated into the Abbey and the congregation joined in, the most open possible symptom of the complete breakdown of tradition as could ever be imagined, while the Queen sat stony-faced.

Spencer's glory soon ended when it became clear that he wanted to divorce his wife in South Africa rather than Britain to reduce the amount of alimony he would have to pay. The week of panic when outsiders took over did not have a lasting effect, many of the participants obviously treating it like a teenage love affair too embarrassing to recall. But the week showed just how badly the Queen suffered from what Andrew Adonis & Stephen Pollard call 'Windsor sclerosis . . . an uncharacteristic state for the British monarchy. Until the early part of this [the 20th] century, Britain's sovereigns were the best royal adapters in the world.'[8]

Notes

1. *The Church of England: The state it's in*, Hodder & Stoughton, 2000.
2. *New Statesman*, November 22, 1999.
3. *New Statesman*, 28 August 28, 1998.
4. *Granta*, an issue 'Unbelievable', devoted largely to Diana.
5. *London Review of Books*. 2 October 1997
6. *The Enchanted Glass, Britain and its monarchy*, Radius Books, 1988.
7. *Diana*, Orion, 1999.
8. Andrew Adonis and Stephen Pollard, *A Class Act*, Hamish Hamilton, 1997.

2

The Still Centre

In times when nothing stood
but worsened or grew strange,
there was one constant good:
she did not change.

PHILIP LARKIN

THE POET'S TRIBUTE TO THE QUEEN on her Silver Jubilee expressed the general view that she – and to some, like Larkin, she alone – was a stable element in a deplorably shifting society. Because the Queen has remained virtually unchanged in her behaviour and attitudes while all around her the whole country was being transformed, she has become, as it were, a one-person control group to measure the extent of the changes. Everything evolved except her. Indeed her lack of enthusiasm for Mrs Thatcher was partly based on the disturbance Mrs T made, the waves she created, the very opposite of the Queen's wish for a quiet life.

She was, and remains, a still small personage around whom have swirled the waves of successive revolutions. The public image was formed early on by the famous cloaked, dignified waxwork-like portrait commissioned from the Italian artist Pietro Annigoni who, wrote Tom Nairn, 'had already established himself as a master of up-market kitsch'. Annigoni felt that the sittings were 'like a half-dream in which I took part in a light opera'. The result was what Nairn calls 'a piece of meta-grovelling'. Yet, and perhaps unsurprisingly, loyalty to the Queen has remained absolute within the establishment. As civil servants would say when confronted by one of Mrs Thatcher's more outrageous demands, 'At the end of the day our loyalty is to the little lady at the end of the Mall.'

Her attitude towards her role has invariably been reminiscent of that of the House of Peers in Gilbert and Sullivan's *Iolanthe*, who 'Throughout the war / Did nothing in particular / And did it very well'. Such an attitude was not new, for it echoed that of Baron Stockmar,

7

who had been an enormously influential adviser to Prince Albert. 'The proper duty of the Sovereigns of this country,' he had written in 1846, 'is not to take the lead in change, but to act as a balance wheel on the movement of the social body.'

The power of the throne had started to decline with the nervous George VI who could never have intervened as his father had done in backing the formation of the first Labour-led government in 1924. In the words of Ben Pimlott, 'the acceptance of a cypher-monarchy, almost devoid of political independence, began in 1936'[1]. This passivity led her not to query the smooth but dubiously constitutional manner in which Anthony Eden eventually succeeded the ageing Winston Churchill as Prime Minister in May 1955 – and the more tumultuous accessions of Harold Macmillan in 1957 and of Sir Alec Douglas-Home in 1963.

Typically, Jim Callaghan found that, as Pimlott puts it, 'if she approved of a policy she would say so, positively. Disapproval was indicated by a significant refusal to comment' – though I was told that when Mrs Thatcher wanted to shut the London women's hospital named after the Victorian doctor Elizabeth Garret Anderson, the Queen was moved to remark, 'I do hope that the rumours about shutting the Elizabeth Garret Anderson aren't true.' As a result of her passivity, she has never put a foot wrong, in her public persona anyway, but then she has never ventured sufficiently out of her shell to put a foot instinctively, impulsively, humanly right. She has never taken the initiative, even when faced by the 1966 disaster which killed 146 people, most of them children, after a coal tip collapsed onto the village of Aberfan in South Wales. She later admitted that she should have gone immediately, especially as her belated visit and obvious sympathy with the bereaved proved so helpful.

She started with the handicap that she had no one to whom to compare herself, and remained by nature conformist – and that to the standards of the already out of date world inhabited by her mother. The picture of her in *The Little Princesses*, a memoir by her former governess, Marion Crawford, universally known as 'Crawfie', as summarised by Ben Pimlott, remains recognisable to this day. She was 'a reserved, strong-willed, narrow-visioned, slightly priggish child, without intellectual or aesthetic interests, taking what she is given as part of a natural order'. Indeed she has never shown any interest in any form of artistic activity, unlike, say, her mother, who is interested in music and the theatre*, her sister, who is as passionate and knowledgeable about the ballet as was her cousin, the Duke of Kent, about

---

* Before a visit to *The Times* in the 1990s, the Queen Mother had particularly asked to meet two journalists, the racing correspondent and the theatre critic.

music, or another cousin, the Earl of Harewood, who was a successful and forward-looking opera producer and impresario. The Queen's detached attitude was much in evidence when she gave Elizabeth David the OBE and asked her what she did. 'I write cookery books,' David said. 'That must be very useful' was the Queen's only reply.

Even before her accession, she was perceived as a touching, dignified figure, a 'woman alone' as *The Times* put it when she replaced her sick father at a Trooping of the Colour. Yet her youthful glamour conquered even the unimpressionable President Truman. After a royal visit he exclaimed, 'When I was a little boy, I read about a fairy princess, and there she is,' while the world-weary financier Bernard Baruch called her 'the world's sweetheart'. The glorification of the young Queen seems ridiculous now that she is widely perceived as a grumpy, frumpy, totally out of touch figure. But fifty years ago people were naturally touched by the photograph of the vulnerable, solitary, young woman descending the steps of the aeroplane that had brought her home from Kenya after her father's death and being greeted by a group of elderly advisers, headed, of course, by Winston Churchill, who worshipped her. At first she provided an apparently irresistible mix of youthfulness combined with a reassurance that nothing had really changed. 'She was a stunning girl longing to be a young wife without too many problems,' one close friend told Pimlott. But duty – or rather her strict interpretation of the word – soon took precedence.

Unfortunately, such was her passivity that even when her potential for imposing herself was virtually unlimited, she did little or nothing to change any aspect of her role, her court, or the attitudes she and her courtiers had inherited from her father – and indeed her grandfather. In the early 1950s, as Pimlott shrewdly observes, 'the Monarchy wasted its most bountiful years – taking what it was given in boundless admiration as its due.' Changes were insignificant. When Sir Alan Lascelles, servant of four monarchs, retired as private secretary four months after the Coronation, he was replaced by Sir Martin Adeane, as averse as his predecessor to allow any departure from precedent.

Fifteen months after her accession, the coronation – which happily coincided with the news of the conquest of Everest by a British-led expedition – provided an incomparable demonstration of the genuinely worshipful attitude then prevailing towards the young monarch. The enthusiasm was even more intense than it had been for earlier celebrations such as the 1887 Golden Jubilee, which itself did so much to retrieve Queen Victoria's long-lost popularity – a recovery subsequently emphasised by the Diamond Jubilee of 1897 and George V's Silver Jubilee in 1935. Moreover the event itself was superbly stage-managed by the Lord Chamberlain, the Duke of Norfolk – although Sir David Eccles, the Minister of Works, tried hard to get in on the act. As Woodrow Wyatt put it, Eccles was 'famous for congratulating her on being such a good leading lady in the arrangements he made for her coronation, the success of which he mainly attributed to himself'.[2] Royalty even had the best tunes – for nearly fifty years the music and words of Handel's hymn 'Zadok the Priest and Nathan the Prophet anointed Solomon king' have remained embedded in my consciousness.

Nevertheless the street parties, the bunting and the air of festivity in June 1953 were as much a symbol of rejoicing at the apparent end of austerity as a celebration of the event itself. For already shrewd observers could see the reality beneath the mask. She and her speech-writers were overly fond of the word 'dedication', as in 'at my Coronation next June I shall dedicate myself anew to your service'. As Harold Nicolson remarked, 'It was a well-trained young woman manufacturing grace and dignity.' The mask was beginning to take over. Forty years later Woodrow Wyatt wrote: 'The Queen has no feelings. I'd always felt that on the brief occasions I have spoken to her.' But perhaps the Queen simply didn't care for him. In private life the Queen, it is said, can be witty, relaxed, warm. 'She could be a wonderful friend if only she were not Queen,' said one.

Her attitude towards her public persona first emerged in a broadcast she made in early 1947 when she and her parents were touring South Africa. She declared, and clearly meant, that 'My whole life, whether it be long or short, shall be devoted to your service and the great Imperial family to which we all belong.' Two years later, in a speech – significantly to that bastion of moral rectitude, the Mothers' Union – she praised the organisation's emphasis on the sanctity of marriage and urged them not to be afraid of sounding priggish. As Queen she sheltered herself behind ritual, formality, regularity, a cocoon to avoid the painful necessity of change, remaining imprisoned by her passivity, itself a by-product of her overwhelming sense of duty. She accepted her duties without any questioning and objected to any change in the royal routine. 'Sometimes,' a courtier told Pimlott, 'it was difficult to persuade her to do something outside the normal run of things ... Others,' Pimlott continued, 'put it more emphatically: she hated the unexpected. A respect for tradition was at the heart of an hereditary monarchy ... Yet there was a constant danger of clinging to habits present-day citizens could no longer relate to.' This tendency was reinforced by the fact that the traditions to which she adhered dated back to the 1930s.

Duty invariably took precedence over any other feelings. She had burst into tears when she said goodbye to the five-year-old Charles before a six-month tour of the Commonwealth. But tears have remained rare and strictly for private occasions – although she was seen dabbing at her eyes when she welcomed Prince Andrew home from the Falklands War and at the memorial service for the victims of the attacks on the World Trade Centre in September 2001. She had known from childhood days that she must not cry even when hurt: 'We are not bad at concealing what we are feeling' is how one member of the royal family put it. Even on the fiftieth anniversary of VE Day she refused to allow her tears to show and retreated indoors from the balcony of Buckingham Palace to cry.

Her public stoicism was partly inherited from her mother, the most important influence over the Queen throughout her reign. Unfortunately she was a woman who lived in a fairy-tale time warp, totally unwilling to accept, or indeed absorb, any bad news, invariably maintaining an attitude of total denial which the family called 'ostriching', a characteristic inherited by her elder daughter. Most obviously, the Queen Mother always refused to admit her hatred of the Duchess of Windsor (whom, rather than the Duke, she blamed for imposing the crushing and indeed fatal burden of the crown on her husband), or much later, that there was anything wrong in the Wales's marriage, or that the Queen was not overly fond of Thatcher or Thatcherism.

None the less the Queen Mother had an instinct for the appropriate gesture denied to her daughter, although she had never seen the need for anything as vulgar as public relations. Indeed, the one and only interview she has ever given dates back to 1923 just before her marriage. This distaste for publicity was reinforced by the publication in 1950 of the book by Marion Crawford, 'Crawfie', who as governess to the two girls was probably closer to them in their formative years than their own parents. The Palace had been consulted over the book and had seen the proofs but, for its own bizarre reasons, expressly declared that it did not want the book serialised in the *Ladies' Home Journal*. The fuss over what seemed even then as a piece of gush was the first demonstration of some of the themes that were to dominate the attitude of the Palace over the following half-century. The Palace displayed its ruthlessness and its total out-of-touchness. It also realised the potential financial profit to be made by exploiting the public appetite for royal revelations.

The Queen herself had been brought up in the 1930s in a world dominated by traditions and assumptions that dated back to before World War One and she has never been able to escape from them. As a result, her education had been sketchy, for she spent only a couple of hours a day in the school room and the Queen Mother was very conscious of the fact. It was an all too accurate remark by Crawfie that she did not bother overmuch with her children's education that triggered the royal fury at the woman who had brought up her daughters, a rage that even extended to a refusal to send flowers to her

11

funeral. The Queen's upbringing was based on the concept of a carefree childhood leading to a happy marriage, the recipe followed by the families of the Queen Mother's own aristocratic youth. Even Crawfie had been engaged, notes Pimlott, 'to help the princesses become lady-like not monarchical', for the Queen Mother, like most aristocratic ladies of her generation, was terribly afraid that her daughter would develop into a bluestocking.

Only the Queen's grandmother, Queen Mary, who came from a different background, tried to insist on her reading some serious books. After her father's accession she did take lessons in constitutional history from Sir Henry Marten and French lessons which enabled her to speak the language fluently. This fact leaves one wondering how much more effective she would have been if properly educated in other subjects. As Pimlott says, she had 'greater mental capacities than any close member of the family cared to appreciate'. But she was not so much educated for her future job but apprenticed, learning by watching. Not surprisingly, given her natural intelligence and awareness of her poor education, she was unnecessarily nervous of meeting intellectuals – although after she had been reigning for a few years those who met her other than on formal occasions were surprised at her grasp of public affairs.

Above all, throughout her life she felt isolated. While he was painting her portrait (occasions when she was notoriously chatty), Pietro Annigoni was told that she had spent many hours in her childhood looking out of the windows at the people and cars in the Mall: 'They all seemed so busy. I used to wonder what they were doing and where they were all going and what they thought about outside the Palace.' Later she told Barbara Castle that the only time she had been able to test her capacities against those of other girls of her age came at the end of the war during the few months when she was learning to drive and maintain vehicles as a junior subaltern in the ATS. She watched a great deal of television, but the events and personalities on the screen bore no relation to her own experience, as if coming from another, to her alien and irrelevant, world.

The loneliness was reinforced by the fact that before 1914, and even up till 1939, the royal family had been only *primus inter pares*, for there were a dozen or more aristocrats as rich as they were, owning London town houses of some splendour. Yet, as Anthony Sampson points out, 'taxation cut down all the other palaces . . . but the Sovereign's allowance remained exempt from the tax commissioners and royal palaces remained the sole relic of the old order, with Buckingham Palace at the centre. The isolation of the palace has transformed the social role of the monarch. ''Before it was like a pyramid,'' explained one courtier, ''now it is more like a bumpy plain, with an island in the middle.'' '[3]

One must not make too much of this isolation – the fact that Prince Charles has moved in rather wider circles has not helped his understanding of his country and its people. His mother – typically of her class – believed that she was not 'well orff', even though she is extremely wealthy, and this justified her life-long, systematic meanness to her staff – which further helped to limit the social background from which they were recruited to those with substantial private incomes. Yet the person closest too her for the first forty years of her reign was a Scots lady, 'Bobo' Macdonald, of lowly birth but forceful character, who was nominally the Queen's dresser but in fact her fierce and fiercely devoted confidante. The Queen herself, like many an aristocratic countrywoman, has always had little of the normal feminine interest in her appearance. To her, wrote Sarah Bradford, 'clothes are props, a part of the job'.[4] The unremarkable clothes and even more the terrible hats and handbags which she normally wore and carried were chosen by Bobo – in 1974, when Macdonald broke four ribs just before the Queen was going on a Pacific trip, she wrote to Hardy Amies how 'my journey is going to be a very much more wearing affair as I really will have to think out clothes for myself this time'. By contrast, she inherited her father's interest in uniforms and went on a diet to ensure that she could fit into the uniform she wore for the Trooping of the Colour.

Until his early death at the age of fifty one in 1975, the only countervailing influence to Bobo was the witty, elegant, assured Patrick Plunket – but then it is obviously easier for homosexuals to fit in at court, not only because of their lack of domestic ties and the nonsexual, unthreatening nature of their relationships with a female monarch, but also because, like Lord Plunket, they tend to be more stylish, more aware of the importance of appearances, than their heterosexual equivalents.

In theory, her marriage to an outsider should have helped. Philip was the only man in her life, she had almost certainly fallen in love with him at their first meeting in 1939 when she was only thirteen and he was already a dashing naval officer. Unfortunately he couldn't provide the stability she needed, and even if he could have, her sense of superiority would have prevented her from allowing him to perform the same role, of guide and counsellor, that Prince Albert had performed for the young Queen Victoria, who generally, if often reluctantly, accepted her husband's ideas.

The Duke wasn't Phil the Greek* as he was nicknamed – indeed,

* There was a lot of fuss about his naturalisation, though it was later discovered that he had been born British because he was a descendant of the Electress Sophie of Hanover, mother of George I.

he had left Greece in his infancy and spoke no Greek – but Phil the Schleswig-Holstein-Sonderburg-Glucksburg, the real name which clearly spelled out the complexity of his background, was not a catchy sobriquet. He was the neglected son of a gambler who soon deserted his family and a mother who, after suffering psychological problems, became a nun. He was rather Phil the outsider who never belonged. He was too abrupt and rude – and well, Teutonic – for the courtiers, too impatient of formality for the court, and not even an old Etonian.

Before his marriage, he had introduced a welcome element of raffishness into Buckingham Palace, but was soon relegated to the role of house-husband, a role (and a description) then virtually unheard of. The limits of his power were shown when he wanted his children to carry his family name but was overruled, partly because of irritation at the overweening ambition of his 'uncle Dickie', Lord Louis Mountbatten. Instead they were to be called Windsor after their mother. 'I am the only man in the country not allowed to give his name to his children,' he said with understandable bitterness.

But the perception that the Queen, her husband and her children were both royal and a family was vital. As Simon Schama put it, it was important that a monarchy should appear as 'the family of families, at once dynastic and domestic, remote and accessible, magical and mundane.'[5] The cosiness of the royal family was first publicised in the portraits painted by Zoffany in the 1760s and 1770s of George III, Queen Charlotte and their numerous offspring. Even more numerous were the images of Queen Victoria and Albert and their – equally numerous – children by Winterhalter in the 1840s and 1850s. These two examples established the model of the royal family as essentially bourgeois. So it seemed natural to portray the Queen as an idealised young mother devoted to her people and her children. In the official souvenir issued at the Coronation, the historian G. M. Trevelyan wrote how the king – and thus his daughter – 'appeal ... to the simple, dutiful human instincts which he and his own family circle represent'. As Pimlott points out, ' "family" had come in the dozen years since George V's death to encroach still further on the other aspects of Monarchy.' But 'the reduction of the royal Family to picture-book iconography did not diminish public enthusiasm: indeed by removing all remaining partisan elements, it enhanced it.'

It would have been ridiculous to expect that she might be a modern mother, let alone one who was affectionate towards her children in public. But most Britons of a certain age remember when the young Prince Charles, decked out with a velvet collar on his overcoat, gravely bowed and shook hands with his mother when he greeted her on her return from a royal journey. Not taking her children with her may have been normal enough in those days and those families. But the pattern had already been set when she failed to collect her infant eldest son for nearly a week after returning from a trip to Malta when her husband was posted there in 1949. Not surprisingly, Charles found solace with his grandmother, a warmer, more motherly personage, whom he could embrace openly if not publicly.

Like many emotionally detached mothers, she was notoriously reluctant to discipline her children, afraid that they would not obey her. Andrew, her favourite, was specially indulged. The result was disastrous: on his first official tour he even sprayed journalists with paint during a visit to California. He was rebuked by a local consular official who realised that Andrew had never been taught how to behave properly in public. The official declined the subsequent offer to become the Prince's press secretary, itself an incident showing the lack of organisation within the Royal Household.

For, like many another upper-class English lady she is, as a relative told Sarah Bradford, 'not a people person, she's a horse person, a dog person, likes being on her own'. As another put it, 'She finds it easier to relate to horses and dogs than people and has an extraordinary empathy with them.' As a result, the one arena in which she could thrive was the horsy world. Brought up with them, she became not only an excellent horsewoman but also a shrewd judge of horses, as much at ease with them as they were with her. She obviously felt totally at home on a racecourse or indeed anywhere horses were around. She understood horses and could read a race better than all but a few of her subjects. Before the Coronation she was asked if she was nervous. 'Of course I am,' she replied, 'but I'm sure that Aureole [a horse of hers much fancied for the Derby] will win.' Throughout her life, wrote Pimlott, 'news of thoroughbreds, pedigrees, racing personalities, auctions, provided a balm. In later years, when the media offensive against [the] royal family became intolerably oppressive, she would quietly retreat into the comforting columns of *Sporting Life*.'

So it was not surprising that the closest relationship of her life outside her family was with 'Porchy', Henry Lord Porchester, later Earl of Carnavon, who died in September 2001. When she was on tour with her father in 1947 before her marriage, she wrote regularly to him – she could share with him her nostalgia for the sights and sounds of an English autumn. According to the not always reliable Woodrow Wyatt, 'She was much in love with him and wanted to marry him. But he wouldn't marry her.' So close were they that there were rumours that the physical resemblance between him and Prince Andrew was, as they say, more than coincidental – an absurd idea, based on the false assumption that the word 'intimacy' implies a sexual element in the relationship. But he remained her racing guru and from 1970 her racing manager – though not a very successful one. Moreover he caused a scandal in racing circles when she allowed him to sack her long-term royal trainer, Dick Hern, when he fell ill. Her concern for animals extended to those notorious doggies, her Corgis, who were allowed to pee freely on the precious rugs at Windsor Castle. After her mother's Corgis had killed one of her own, she wrote a six-page letter to a by no means close friend, full of talk about 'not blaming the dogs', which revealed the depth of her feeling.

The one public relationship where she has been able to exert a long-term influence has been an improbable one: the Commonwealth, which includes very diverse nations, many of them republics, with rulers who were even more diverse, a 'family' to which the Queen has clung tenaciously throughout her life. Indeed, one of the few occasions on which she has been stirred into positive action was in 1957 when Harold Macmillan was nervous about a visit to Ghana and she overruled him. Twenty-six years later the same phenomenon occurred with her open fury at President Reagan's failure to inform the British before the American invasion of Grenada – a British possession. She fought Mrs Thatcher over sanctions against South Africa, an occasion when she kept the Commonwealth together; indeed, it might well not have survived without her continuing involvement. To her the role of 'mother' of the Commonwealth was always primordial and welcomed as such by the many and various Commonwealth leaders she encountered who found her knowledgeable and relaxed.

Indeed this mixed and sometimes dubious bunch, mostly non-white, adored her. Only with them did she feel that she could escape from her otherwise constricted view of her duties and act on her own initiative, and thus fulfil a role that was hers and not an inherited duty. In other words, when acting as a supremely dutiful Queen of Britain she was cribbed, cabined and confined but as Queen of the Commonwealth, a role she invented for herself in an institution born only during her reign, she could relax and demonstrate the intuitive, intelligent and sympathetic aspects of her character which could have proved so useful in her other roles and transformed the public perception of this still enigmatic woman.

Notes

1. *The Queen*, HarperCollins, 1998.
2. *The Journals of Woodrow Wyatt*, Macmillan, 1998.
3. *The New Anatomy of Britain*, Hodder & Stoughton 1971.
4. *Elizabeth – a biography of HM the Queen*, Heinemann, 1986.
5. *Journal of Interdisciplinary History*, Summer 1986.

3

The State We Were In

England
Was so poor! Was black paint cheaper? Why
Were English cars all black – to hide the filth?
Or to stay respectable, like bowlers
And umbrellas?
London a morgue of dinge – English dinge.
Our sole indigenous art-form – depressionist!
And why were everybody's
Garments so deliberately begrimed?
Grubby-looking, like a camouflage? 'Alas!
We have never recovered,' I said, 'from our fox-holes,
Our trenches, our fatigues and our bomb-shelters.'
    'The Beach' from *Birthday Letters* by TED HUGHES[1]

THE AMERICAN POET SYLVIA PLATH was being relatively
restrained when she used the word 'dinge' to describe her first sight
of Britain in the early 1950s. I remember it as worse than that, above
all appallingly polluted. The Thames was so dirty that anyone falling
in would be given an immediate anti-tetanus jab, while there were
palls of acrid chemical smoke hanging low over much of East London,
and regular fogs, one of which killed 12,000 old people from bronchitis
in the winter after the Queen's accession. Of course, much of the
'dinge' was a hangover from the damage caused by the war. But large
parts of Continental Europe had been devastated, and by the early
1950s in many of the worst-affected countries – above all, in what
was then West Germany – there was a determination at work, a confidence that life could be made better which was absent in Britain. By
contrast, in Britain the wreckage seemed to symbolise the thick grey
blanket that lay over the social as well as the physical fabric of the
country at the time.

Recently a number of writers such as Peter Hitchens and Roger
Scruton have lamented Old Days which they find to be golden. Yet the

reality was quite otherwise. Writing of the mid-point of the twentieth century, the distinguished sociologist A. H. Halsey, by no means a Thatcherite or an unquestioning admirer of the new, observed that it was by no means a golden age of traditionalism. 'Material deprivation, and inequality between the classes and the sexes were integral to British society. There was no Utopia. There was cruelty, a double standard of sexual morality, incest and child abuse; savage treatment of unmarried mothers, desertions and separations. Nevertheless the traditional family system was a coherent strategy for the ordering of relations in such a way as to equip children for their own eventual adult responsibilities.'[2] But even this qualification ignores the almost invariably limited horizons available for most of the people of Britain.

It is difficult to convey the sheer bleakness of life at the time. The gloom was intensified by a Puritanism which was worst in England. The blankness of the English Sunday had to be experienced to be believed – it was worse in Wales and Scotland, where there was a greater religious justification for the restrictions*. Although church attendance in England had been declining since the turn of the century, nevertheless a basic strand of Puritanism ensured that Sundays were devoid of any amusement except the pubs and cinemas, and their opening hours were very strictly limited. A thick veil of hypocrisy hung over sex, a subject which was unmentionable in public and publicly assumed to be a generally undesirable activity, and , moreover, one which was, as far as women were concerned, designed not for pleasure but solely for procreation and then, of course, solely within marriage. The very virtues, of rulers and ruled, were typically negative ones. The British were phlegmatic, undemonstrative, decent, showed a proper sense of decorum, and even these carried their own limits. But the key to the situation – which was in many ways worse for people on the Continent – was the lack of hope that things would change or become other than marginally more agreeable.

Where Britain differed most obviously from the rest of Europe was the sense of inevitability about the prevailing state of affairs, a resigned assumption that nothing could be changed. Worse, the prevailing mindset was firmly based on a widespread delusion about Britain's position in the world. 'Led during the war by a master of rhetoric,' wrote Noel Annan, 'Britain now became the victim of her own rhetoric. She fondly imagined she had won the war. She had not. America and Russia had won the war. Britain had in her finest hour not lost it.'[4] But the

---

* Only in 1999 was the last dry corner of Wales converted to allow drinking on the Sabbath, and at least one island in the Hebrides remained dry into the twenty-first century.

overriding impression was that there was no need to change because we had been victorious, so we could return to a 'normality' defined as the pre-war status quo – an attitude unthinkable anywhere else in the world. Nevertheless the ruling elite was safe as long as the great mass of the British public accepted the delusion that Britain had won the war. Having 'a good war' mattered, as did the rank you had reached – for two decades after 1945 MPs such as Brigadier Enoch Powell or Majors Edward Heath and Denis Healey were referred to by their military rank.

Most importantly, and notably unlike that of any other European country, the British ruling class had not been discredited and so felt entitled to continue on its bad old ways, for both the social and the politico-economic elites had survived unscathed. By contrast, in Germany, Italy and France, the social elite had lost most of its political power well before the war and the political elite had been totally discredited by its collaboration with Hitler, Mussolini or, as in the case of the French, with the German occupiers. Only in Britain, as Ross McKibbin noted, 'those who had authority in 1918 still had it, more or less, in 1951, despite the fact that the Second World War significantly recast social relationships. Furthermore they retained it in a society with a greater potential for conflict than contemporaries were prepared to admit.'[3] Yet the early 1950s, as demonstrated most obviously in the 1955 election, marked the final blossoming of that peculiarly British phenomenon, the working-class deference vote, distilled in the immaculate, apparently trustworthy and totally upper-class figure of Sir Anthony Eden, who appealed, in particular, to an astonishingly large number of working class-women.

The moral bank balance resulting not so much from the war as from the experience of other European countries was perfectly reflected in George Orwell's famous essay *The Lion and the Unicorn*, written in 1943. Yes, he agreed, 'England is the most class-ridden country under the sun. It is a land of snobbery and privilege, ruled largely by the old and silly', but, looking at them 'merely from a liberal, *negative* [his italics] viewpoint', they 'had their points. They were preferable to the truly modern men, the Nazis and fascists' – and, he could have added, the Communists. Inevitably, however, Orwell's attitude, legitimate though it was in the 1940s, became increasingly outdated as France, Germany, Italy and, from the mid-1970s, even Spain proved that democracy was not incompatible with a rate of economic progress far greater than that possible in Britain. Nevertheless the delusion of wartime glory, together with a healthy scepticism towards involvement with the continent of Europe, was widespread enough to have survived in the sub-conscious of the Great British public to this day, as can be seen in the continuing popularity of war films.

19

The rulers' superiority complex bred an aura of smugness, a spiritual fog similar to the physical variety that so often afflicted London and other major cities. As a result, not only was there seemingly no need to change, but also a positive disincentive to do more than respond to the vague communal feelings expressed in the 1945 Labour landslide, to nationalise some basic industries, improve pensions and unemployment benefits and introduce the National Health Service. Yet, as Kenneth Morgan pointed out: 'It was the middle classes who knew best how to exploit the National Health Service and other social benefits of the post-war years.'[5] For the supposedly radical changes introduced by the Attlee government not only did nothing to alter the relationships within the British class system, they perpetuated the adversarial relationship between employers and employees, and indeed during the 1945–51 period the 'them and us' feeling grew stronger.

As Morgan points out, the rulers' self-satisfaction was boosted by the fact that 'all the fashionable symbols of identity – the Crown, the Commonwealth, the "mother of Parliaments", the City, the ascendancy of Oxford and Cambridge – ministered to national self-esteem and self-sufficiency. If Britain emerged in the years after 1945 as "one nation", it was a feeling rooted not only in accepted social collectivism at home but also in a spirit of complacent nationalism towards a wider world.' There was a total absence of doubt as to British superiority. 'One of the striking characteristics of the 1950s,' wrote Bogdanor and Skidelsky, 'was the absence of any major intellectual challenges to the dominant political assumptions.'[6] The American sociologist Edward Shils made the point even more forcefully: 'Deeply critical voices became rare. In 1953, I heard an eminent man of the left say, in utter seriousness, at a university dinner, that the British constitution was "as nearly perfect as any human institution could be", and no one even thought it amusing.'[7]

The prevailing sense of unreality ensured that Britain continued to pretend that, for instance, sterling was a 'reserve currency'. Devaluation was therefore unthinkable and sterling had to be supported, at whatever expense to the British economy. A totally unjustified overconfidence meant that our rulers felt able, indeed obliged, to take on the task of defending the Empire – and the Free World – at a cost second only to that borne by Russia. But whereas much of Russia's spending was employed in consolidating its (profitable) grip on Eastern Europe ours was largely devoted either to the unsustainable retention of our Empire or assuming an unfairly large proportion of the expenditure required to defend Western Europe against the 'Soviet menace'.

As a result defence spending accounted for a tenth of the country's national product and a third of the government's income, while the trade surplus of £300 million or more all went on overseas military expenditure. This overwhelming burden inevitably limited more productive expenditure, and nowhere more so than in Britain's pride and joy, the National Health Service.

This had been introduced with a – largely justified – fanfare as the cornerstone of the Welfare State, unmatched anywhere else in the world. But the cracks immediately started to show. For a start, the demand had been grossly underestimated and the costs soon escalated. In the first year they were two fifths above the original estimate and had risen by a further quarter within a couple of years. Moreover it was abundantly clear that they would continue to soar. 'Short-term action to provide false teeth, spectacles and hearing aids on a massive scale,' wrote Charles Webster, 'was merely the first step towards a hugely expensive long-term programme of modernisation.'[8] This was particularly needed in general practice. A report by *The Lancet* in 1950 reported, controversially but accurately, that all too often GPs had 'poor premises and equipment, deficient organisation and declining morale'. Resources tended to be concentrated in the better-off regions of the country, an imbalance which has not been properly remedied in the following half-century. Already sceptics were suggesting that the NHS 'constituted such a drain on resources that the economy would be wrecked', a cry that is still being heard fifty years later. In 1950–51 the Labour government was shaken to the core with the resignation of three cabinet ministers, led by Aneurin Bevan, the father of the NHS, in protest against the introduction of charges for prescriptions, an impost due to the increased defence budget required to finance the Korean war. The arrival of the Tory Party in power merely made matters worse. In 1951 the NHS had absorbed about 4 per cent of national resources, a proportion which went down to 3.5 per cent in the following few years during a decade in which the Minister of Health remained outside the Cabinet, a clear indication of the low priority accorded to the NHS.

Of course the economic burden of defence expenditure would have been infinitely less and the possibilities of improving public services far greater over the years if Britain's economy had performed at anything like the rate of comparable Continental countries. But it didn't, growing on an average of a mere 2.3 per cent during the golden years from 1951 to the onset of the first oil crisis in 1973. Britain's stuttering progress was inevitably marked by repeated crises over the balance of payments and inflationary pressures, meaning that it was a period of 'stop-go', involving periodic restraints on public spending and on economic growth. Although the most common explanation of Britain's relative failure was excessive expenditure on defence or welfare, or both, it owed even more to the inadequacies of the educational and economic infrastructure. The sheer unreality of our rulers' outlook

21

could be summed up in one remark, when Harold Macmillan remarked that 'exporting is fun'.

The prevailing mood inevitably led to an atmosphere of nostalgia, even among the young, an attitude perfectly caught by Nigel Dennis in his absurd, and absurdly funny novel *Cards of Identity*. At their favourite pub, the Coat and Cymbals, his characters – all young – met a fine cross-section of those 'who nowadays find unusual means of spiritual recapitulation. A number of them, for instance, went in for various kinds of medieval calligraphy, puzzling the postman with their renascent addresses. All wore hats; but some wore small, curved bowler hats and arrived at the pub, whatever the weather, in touring cars that had been built in the 1920s; they drank their beer out of old moustache cups. Many were gardeners, and would grow only roses which had not been seen for some centuries.' This sounds absurd, but not in the context of a Chancellor of the Exchequer who could scold the nation in his 1954 Budget speech for living 'too long on old port and overripe pheasant'.

The Chancellor involved was R. A. Butler, one of the many members of an elite who had cashed in so successfully on their war record but did not deserve much of the credit. Indeed, as a minister at the Foreign Office, he had been one of those quite prepared to do a deal with Hitler until well on into the summer of 1940. Moreover, the elite's role in the Allies' victory – one to which, after the United States and Russia had entered the war, Britain's own contribution was never as important as they had made out – was markedly less than that of the outsiders. The most obvious example was Winston Churchill himself, half-American, wholly impossible, a typical aristocratic Whig, a former Liberal without the narrowness of outlook typical of the party he led, and until 1939 an outcast from the party that came to worship him. Other important outsiders included the Labour members of the War Cabinet such as the former docker Ernest Bevin and many others, among them Churchill's friends, the appalling Canadian Lord Beaverbrook, the dubious Irish adventurer Brendan Bracken and Churchill's principal scientific adviser, Freddy Lindemann, Lord Cherwell, the German-born scientist nicknamed Baron Berlin, all of whom held important positions during the war.

This acceptance of wartime glory was not, however, shared by a substantial proportion of the working classes. Indeed the fond delusion that Britain emerged from the war a united nation was precisely that, a delusion largely confined to the middle classes. A Gallup Poll carried out in 1943 asking which country was doing most to win the war showed that only 42 per cent of the sample said that it was Britain, 5 per cent China, a mere 3 per cent the United States, and a full 50 per cent replied, not unreasonably, Russia. For, as if to refute the myth, strikes were frequent during the war, especially in the coal mines and in the engineering industries directly involved in the war effort, as workers whose militancy had been dowsed by mass unemployment before 1939 felt able to exploit the power that came with their new importance. Anyone who believes that the working classes were as loyally patriotic as they were portrayed in British films of the time should read the passage in Bill Deedes's autobiography in which he recounts how the dockers who were supposed to be loading his regiment's armoured cars on their way to Normandy soon after D-Day went on strike for an extra 3d an hour. The troops then had to load the vehicles themselves, and their lack of skill meant that many of the vehicles' suspensions were smashed.[9]

It appeared indeed was unthinkable to challenge authority in any form wherever it was found, in the home, at work, in schools, in society as a whole. It was set in rugged, Philistine concrete. How powerful it seemed to those of us who were young at the time – in 1952 I myself was nearly nineteen – how smug, how impregnable and, above all, how gerontocratic. (The three party leaders at the 1955 election had an average age of 67. By the 1970 election they were twenty years younger, and by 2001 the figure was down to forty-three). This ageism was particularly striking at the first meeting of the Privy Council a few days after the Queen's accession when as Lord Dalton* put it, she faced 'hundreds of old men in black clothes' including 'people one didn't remember were still alive'.

In the words of Jonathon Green, 'In the traditional, pre-1950s society, being mature was what mattered, being young was no more than an unfortunate period through which one had to proceed, best left behind as soon as possible.'[10] Because of the prevailing worship of age, throughout their youth the young were reminded of their second-class status. 'The young were full of good stuff but callow,' wrote Noel Annan about the period, 'they would be all the better for being snubbed and put in their place'. The older brother of the hero of one of Colin McInnes' novels† was 'one of the generations that grew up before teenagers existed . . . In those days you were just an overgrown boy, or an undergrown man, life didn't seem to cater for anything in between'. Adolescence meant simply becoming an adult: 'it was a passage not a status,' as the historian Juliet Gardiner told me 'Teenagers' – and the word has to be put in quotation marks because their existence had not yet been recognised in the 1950s – tended to ape

---

* Hugh Dalton was the son of a Canon of St George's, the royal parish church at Windsor, and had gone on to be a Labour Chancellor of the Exchequer.

† *Absolute Beginners* 1959. This perceptive observer of the outsiders was the son of Angela Thirkell, most correct of bourgeois novelists.

their parents. For me the problem was summed up by the story of my Oxford friend Jeremy Wolfenden, young, openly gay and one of the most intelligent members of his generation. Not surprisingly, he was inevitably doomed to a short life, dying, largely of drink, in his early thirties. Probably only the British Secret Service could accommodate his talents – as he once told me after an interview with MI6, 'And they don't seem to mind me being homosexual.' All these pressures ensured that most of my generation at Oxford – those there in the early 1950s – were underachievers, whatever their speciality, in intellectual, creative or political fields. The idea of automatic, legitimate ambition began with a slightly later generation.

In the week I was called up for National Service in October 1951 the 'hit record' – there was no such thing as an organised hit parade at the time – was Jimmy Young, then what was still known as a 'crooner', singing 'They Tried To Tell Us We're Too Young, Too Young To Really Be In Love.' And, of course, the obligatory two years of National Service was a forcible reminder of the power and apparent permanence of authority. As Trevor Royle put it: 'The army in many ways resembled a well-run, if over-strict boarding school.'[11] I found the two experiences had at least one major element in common: the respect, indeed fear, of authority it instilled, combined with the feeling that even though those put in charge were not necessarily right, they had to be obeyed. Moreover, the two long years spent in the armed services further truncated the possibility of youthful freedom, especially for the working classes, already trapped by going to work at the age of fifteen and by generally early marriage. Royle also noted that 'those who coped best were those who had been working since they were fifteen, or, at the other extreme, had gone to a boarding school . . . the ones who suffered most were those who had led fairly sheltered lives. It was not uncommon for a hard-bitten lad, who had worked previously in a factory or on a building site, to be astonished by the sight of his grammar school-educated neighbour weeping silently in his bed at night – a classic image of social collision between the stoicism of the working-class labourer and the inadequacy of the middle-class pen-pusher.'

There were two contradictory aspects to National Service: for a short time at least it provided those from socially sheltered backgrounds with the shock of seeing how the other 90 per cent of the population lived – and thought and behaved – and of encountering at first hand their narrowness of outlook, their semi-literacy. But within a few weeks the system divided the uncommissionable, almost invariably working- and lower middle-class sheep from the potential officer class. 'The potential National Service officer,' wrote Royle, 'had to possess a good education, social confidence, some previous military training and a certain conceit,' and it was generally agreed, not least by the army, that these qualities were to be found almost exclusively in the ranks of public schoolboys and the products of a handful of elite grammar schools. Nevertheless, a number of future high flyers from the right backgrounds, including Jacob later Lord Rothschild and Andreas Whittam-Smith, founder of the *Independent* newspaper, fell through the officer-quality net.

There were positive aspects to the experience: the inhabitants of the same crowded barrack room learnt the importance of truth and honesty amongst a heterogeneous group. In a generally hostile volume on the experience published by Quartet Books in 1972, B. S. Johnson's *All Bull*, one contributor, John Lawson, made the case in favour in a single phrase. His service in the RAF was, he wrote, a 'crash course in growing up'. Yet National Service provided a plentiful supply of ammunition for a literate and potentially 'Bolshie' minority. David Lodge put it in a nutshell in the introduction to a new edition of his novel *Ginger, You're Barmy*, first published in 1962, about his experiences as a private in the Royal Armoured Corps. The anger behind the book, he wrote, was that of 'a bright, no doubt bumptious young man, who, having sensed exciting possibilities of personal self-fulfilment via education, found his progress rudely interrupted for two years by compulsory enlistment in an institution which he could neither identify with nor defeat.' A later passage will find its echo in the experiences of many other national servicemen – including me. He compares it to 'a very long, very tedious journey on the Inner Circle. You boarded the train with a lot of others, and for a while it was very crowded, very uncomfortable; but after a while the crowd thinned, you got a seat, new faces got in, old faces got out; the slogans on the advertisements got tiresomely familiar, but you sat on, until, after a very long time, you got out yourself, at the station where you had originally boarded the train, and were borne by the escalator back into the light and air.' For me, this remains a perfect description of the inherent meaninglessness of the whole time-wasting experience.

But national service was only for the unconsidered young. The cult of age was distilled in the person of Winston Churchill, who had become Prime Minister for the second time in October 1951 at the age of seventy six. He was obviously not the man who had led Britain in the dark days of 1940, yet even when he finally retired at the age of eighty in April 1955 the aura remained undimmed – I was severely taken to task by a senior army officer for saying that it was 'about time too'. In 1953 Churchill had suffered a severe, incapacitating, stroke. His illness was totally hushed up, for, as the American journalist Bernard Nossiter put it some twenty-five years later, the British elite 'see themselves as guardians of a society that cannot bear too much

25

information, an over-exposure to the truth'. The attitude was summed up in the words of a senior civil servant quoted by the lawyer Geoffrey Robertson in his book *The Justice Game*: 'Government is a contradiction in terms: you can be open or you can have government.' This code of secrecy still overhangs British life, still prevents open discussion of policies and often renders democratic processes powerless. In the mid-eighties the passion for secrecy got the Thatcher government into all sorts of trouble when it tried to prevent the publication of *Spycatcher*, a book by a former MI5 officer, Peter Wright. In a court in Australia the Permanent Secretary to the Treasury, Sir Robert Armstrong, was forced to admit that he had been 'economical with the truth'. Fifteen years later the same obsession with secrecy led to a ridiculous Whitehall campaign against the first woman director of MI5, Stella Rimington, when she published her – largely unrevealing – memoirs.

Like secrecy, gerontocracy was obviously not conducive to democracy. Indeed the very idea of democracy had only started to creep into the Tory party after the war: until the late 1940s a rich man could, effectively, buy himself a seat in Parliament by handing over a hefty donation to the local party. But in the late 1940s, thanks to reforms set out in a report by Sir David Maxwell-Fyfe, contributions were limited to a mere £50 a year, and all election expenses had to come out of constituency funds, not an individuals pocket. Meritocratic Tories were not alone in feeling, as the doctor-turned-politican Charles Hill remarked in his autobiography, that 'now and again – but only now and again – I sensed that within the larger community of the Commons, *as outside* [my italics], there was the smaller community bound together by strong if invisible ties of birth and background and public school to which I did not and could never belong.'[12]

Overall, our rulers resembled nothing so much as the members of a primitive, if successfully war-like, tribe who had succeeded in imposing their will by sheer brute force, through cunning, character and willpower rather than intelligence. This was a deeply suspect attribute. After a brilliant speech by Harold Macmillan to the 1922 Committee which brings together all Conservative MPs, Harold Nicolson remarked to the Chief Whip: 'What a pity it is that now we have the most intelligent Prime Minister of the century, he has to conceal his intelligence from the public for fear that they will suspect it.' The Chief Whip agreed that only the elite could appreciate his mind. Only in Britain could a politician be despised as 'too clever by half', the sobriquet applied to Iain Macleod, while Mrs Thatcher's faithful Number Two, Willie Whitelaw, would cheerfully admit that he deliberately concealed his intelligence and adopted the disguise of a loveable old buffer. In Britain the very word 'intellectual' has a distinctly alien ring about it and it did not help the cause of applied intelligence that after 1945 the intellectuals and academics who had done so much for the war effort retreated into their ivory towers. The cult of anti-intellectualism was all-pervasive, for whereas French intellectuals participated in and sometimes dominated public life and serious intellectual discussion was the norm, in Britain intellectuals have virtually always been mere technicians, living apart in their academic ghettos, and creating what James Walvin calls 'that anti-intellectualism of British life which raises its head whenever social problems are publicly debated in words of more than two syllables'.[13]

In downplaying the role of intelligence in public life, the classically educated could have found a parallel in the way the Spartans had vanquished the more civilised, if less war-like, Athenians. But the rulers' sense of superiority brought with it a domestic version of the old Imperial White Man's burden. As Edward Shils put it, the class system 'demanded a lot both from those who were its obvious beneficiaries and those who were its obvious victims'.[14] Like the Spartans, the British elite accepted a severe self-discipline in the acceptance of rules. For behind the myth of the English upper class was the reality of power and all it entailed. 'The myth,' wrote Malcolm Muggeridge in the *New Statesman*, 'has been an instrument, supple and effective, for impeding the process of putting down the mighty from their seats and exalting the humble and meek, of filling the hungry with good things and sending the rich empty away.' In Dr Sally Taylor's words, 'Hypocrisy, and a willingness to pay lip service to the status quo, led to institutionalised mediocrity, and not rocking the boat was the path to success. On the surface everyone was following the rules; beneath it the same ruthlessness that had informed every other age reigned supreme.'[15] For even the much-trumpeted British tolerance was very easy to exaggerate. As Professor John Gray described old-fashioned Tories: 'They could be tolerant and open-minded but this was founded on a view of hierarchy and inequality, and emerged from a feeling of unchallengeable social power.'[16]

It did not help that both socially and educationally Britain had been hopelessly unready for the twentieth century, an incapacity to cope that became steadily more apparent in the second half of that century. Before the war, the backward-looking nature of British life, as perceived by the British themselves, had been summed up in Britain's pavilion at the 1937 International Exhibition in Paris. Other countries boasted – the Americans paraded achievements such as TVA dams and Hollywood villas – while the British had a bar called a buttery (as college bars were called at Oxford and Cambridge). The result, as Piers Brandon wrote, was that 'ironically genteel leisure was depicted as the main occupation in what had once been the workshop of the world. Life there now seemed to revolve around a permanent country-house weekend. Britain presented itself as largely pastoral and "entirely upper-class".[17]

The country was also incredibly insular – the defeat of the England football team by the United States in the 1950 World Cup passed virtually unnoticed. However, three years later the hammering the team underwent, at Wembley of all holy places, at the hands of the magic Hungarian team under Ferenc Puskas, jolted the whole country – though not the football authorities. Two years later they refused to allow Chelsea to play in the embryonic European Cup. For in sport, as in other activities, British was Best, foreigners were beastly as well as inferior, for the famed British tolerance certainly did not extend beyond the British Isles. Racism was all-pervasive – the Holocaust had not removed a genteel, very British form of anti-semitism. After lunching with the Rothschilds, even the relatively liberal Harold Nicolson wrote to his wife how they were 'crushed and saddened by the woes of Israel and they sat down and wept, hanging up their harps in the counting-house'. The awareness of a – largely unspoken – anti-semitic undercurrent in British society afflicted even the most successful Jews. 'One day,' Sir Freddy Ayer told Anthony Grayling, his last graduate student, 'someone is going to point the finger at me: "You are a fraud. You got into Eton and Christ Church, you were an officer in the Welsh Guards, you became Wykeham Professor at Oxford and you secured a knighthood. But underneath you are just a dirty little Jew-boy."'[18] In this atmosphere it was not surprising that my (middle-class Jewish) parents thought it best to have me baptised before sending me to Harrow, where I spent nearly five years masquerading unhappily as a Christian. As late as 1954 a brilliant Jewish banker, Jeremy Raisman, was told that it 'was not time for a Hebrew to become chairman of a joint-stock bank' – in this case Lloyds – and the job went to Lord Franks, a charter member of the Great and the Good, a former British ambassador to Washington and someone who knew precisely nothing about banking. And Franks's reaction to the invitation? 'If you can run an Oxford College, you can run anything.'

For it was a time when British society, which in the past had proved sufficiently absorptive of newcomers – immigrants as well as the lower orders – to neutralise the idea of revolution, had become unusually impermeable to new ideas as well as to newcomers. Yet the English have always been a mongrel race, systematically infiltrated for two thousand years by the Celts with whom they share the island as well as by waves of refugees from religious and political persecution and other newcomers. This was fully understood by Daniel Defoe, best known for *Gulliver's Travels*. His *True-Born Englishman* published in 1701 contains the immortal lines:

In between rapes and furious lust begot,
Between a painted Briton and a Scot . . .
From whence a mongrel half-bred race there came
With neither name nor nation, speech or fame
In whose hot veins new mixtures quickly ran
Infus'd betwixt a Saxon and a Dane
While their rank daughters, to their parents just,
Receiv'd all nations with promiscuous lust
A True Born Englishman's a contradiction!
In speech and irony! In fact, a fiction!

Over the past half century much of the new blood has been of a different colour, brown or black and thus more noticeable, easier to attack and more difficult to absorb than earlier immigrants. Yet the same absorptive capacity has long applied to the English language, with its double Latin and Germanic parenthood and notoriously hospitable to words of other origins – and now, increasingly, to words from other English-speaking countries. As Roger Scruton points out, even colours are, as it were, colour-blind: 'Black and white are Anglo-Saxon, violet is French, purple Latin, red and green are German while crimson is the Turkish krimizi and azure the Arabic for blue.'

But there was little colour about in the early 1950s. Puritanism was triumphant – typically, the Labour minister Dr Edith Summerskill was a fervent opponent of the importation of French cheeses, and the whole government revolted against the New Look introduced by Christian Dior in 1947, mainly because it involved a wastefully large amount of cloth. The 'rationing mentality' was deeply ingrained throughout British society long after its final remnant, the rationing of meat, disappeared, and that was as late as 1954. Three years later I remember laughing at the idea of *Madame Express*, the style section of the then radical French magazine. At the time, and indeed until well into the 1960s, it seemed incredible that there could be such a phenomenon as *Madame New Statesman*, so Puritan was the British left. There were a few exceptions to the general rule that socialism and Puritanism were inseparable: it was a staunch socialist, Raymond Postgate, who founded the *Good Food Guide* in 1951. Yet Aneurin Bevan was mocked as a 'Champagne socialist' or 'Bollinger Bolshevik', twenty years later Roy Jenkins was attacked because of his love of good claret and Anthony Crosland was out on a limb when he declared that 'I have never been able to see why high consumption and brotherly love should be incompatible.'

British food, of course, was universally ghastly; indeed, it is difficult to recreate the horrors of English cooking at the time. These were the result not only of a lack of decent ingredients but of a general attitude of indifference, amounting to contempt, for the pleasures of the table. This was not a new phenomenon. Things had been pretty bad before the war. After a year spent in Exeter Margaret Halsey, wife of an American lecturer, wrote of British soup as 'thin dark and utterly savourless. It tasted as if it had been drained out of the umbrella stand'.[19] Rationing and the imposition of standard foods merely made matters worse. In August 1954 the French-born gastronomic writer André Simon wrote in his editorial to *Wine & Food* how 'the housewife looks upon cooking as a chore and a bore; she prepares without any pleasure meals which are eaten without any pleasure, without any complaints if bad and without a word of praise if good'. A painter friend of Julian Barnes recalls his mother saying 'eating for me is like cleaning my teeth'[20].

In her first detective novel, *Cover Her Face*, P. D. James echoes Halsey's description with an account of a post-war landlady noted for her 'good plain cooking and plenty of it' – a phrase which rings ominously true for anyone brought up before 1960. James writes of 'tinned peas larger and shinier than any peas that had ever seen pod. They tasted of soya flour . . .' and of an apple and blackberry pie 'in which neither of the fruits had met each other nor the pastry until they had been arranged on the plate by Mrs Piggott's careful hand and liberally blanketed with synthetic custard'. These attitudes persist even today. In his charmingly idiosyncratic way, the arch-nostalgist Roger Scruton regarded such food as one of the 'least celebrated triumphs' of the English – 'a cuisine in which ingredients were systematically deprived of their flavour, so that everything tasted roughly the same and manly stoicism prevailed over sensory enjoyment.'[21] It was no surprise that some of the first, none too appealing, initiatives to introduce foreign cooking came with Indian and later Chinese restaurateurs who alone were prepared to stay open after the pubs closed.

In this 'Spartan' society it was not surprising that Philistinism was systematic and ingrained. When the future prime minister Ted Heath first entered Parliament in 1950, he felt he had to give up his musical activities, including conducting choirs, since they were not the sort of activities approved of by the party or his constituents. Worse, one of the first actions of the incoming Churchill government was an unparalleled act of cultural vandalism. Sir David Eccles, supposedly its most civilised minister, deliberately destroyed virtually every major building of the Festival of Britain – even though there was considerable interest in preserving some of its many exciting structures such as the elegant Skylon, which in the event was chopped up and used to make ashtrays. There could have been no more potent symbol of the government's determination to turn its back on the future.

Culture was narrowly elitist. When the Third Programme was set

30

up in 1946, no-one seemed to have worried about the size, or even the existence, of its possible audience. The idea that communication involves people other than those communicating never seems to have occurred to anyone. But the 'Third' was an exception, since it was at least new and forward-looking. Elsewhere culture, such as it was, was, as so often, backward-looking – the audience at Covent Garden was deeply shocked when Benjamin Britten's offered as his contribution to the Coronation celebrations *Gloriana*, a relatively realistic opera about Queen Elizabeth I. Sir Alfred Munnings, the long-serving President of the Royal Academy, went out of his way to ridicule any modern artist, most especially Picasso – a favourite hate symbol amongst the majority of the establishment. 'Don't you think,' he said at one Royal Academy banquet, 'if we could meet him somewhere in the dark we should kick him in the pants?'

What the younger of Britain's best and the brightest could achieve when not shackled by class and the cult of age was clearly apparent in the British Occupied Zone in Germany after the war, when men such as Noel, later Lord, Annan and Hugh Carleton Greene, the future Director-General of the BBC, helped create the institutional framework for the so-successful German Republic of the post-war years. In Britain itself the narrowness of the ruling elite – and for once that over-worked term is perfectly justified – now seems unbelievable, verging on the ridiculous. One survey of 'Top People' – typically a phrase later coined by a copywriter advertising *The Times* – showed that the majority of the Cabinet, company chairmen, judges and so on were Etonians – indeed, the one exception was that only one in five of senior civil servants had been pupils at one of the major six public schools. After the 1955 election up to a quarter of Tory MPs had been to Eton and most of the rest to a handful of major public schools. As late as 1962, nine members of the Cabinet including the Prime Minister, Harold Macmillan, were descendants of a mere four Victorian peers. And there were, on average, more Etonians in his cabinets and those of Eden and Douglas-Home than ever before in British political history.

All these dignitaries had been boarders at school, often from the age of seven, invariably from thirteen to eighteen, and thus deprived for fully two thirds of the year of the company of their parents and of female company of their own age. History is usually the prerogative of the victors, but in the case of public schools, most of it has been written by vociferous critics of these institutions who, like me, were, or feel themselves to have been, the losers, the victims of the experience. Yet even the most ardent supporters of the public school will now admit that its effects were pretty nefarious. For this was a regime that relied upon an almost compulsory Philistinism, inculcated an automatic dishonesty towards authority, which was perceived to be arbitrary and often unjust, and fostered a wide-spread homosexual atmosphere, something that obviously created difficulties in establishing normal relationships with the opposite sex throughout later life.

Corporal punishment of children was legitimised in both public schools and in religious establishments, notably those run by the Catholic Church. As a result some boys were subject to experiences like that described by Paul Foot, one of the many victims of Anthony Chevenix Trench, once a star headmaster, who enjoyed flogging boys across their naked bottom, preferably while they were draped over his marital bed. Trench was only exposed, to coin a phrase, in the early 1970s when, as headmaster of Eton, he started to punish sons, not of the bourgeoisie but of the aristocracy. They complained to their noble parents, who soon got rid of him (naturally without any publicity).

Despite all these horrors, it seemed perfectly reasonable for grown men to dream again of the days when they were cock of the walk – particularly if they had been members of the select group known as Pop at Eton – and recall them as the best days of their lives. A far greater proportion regarded their years at Oxford or (less so) Cambridge as the high spot of their lives. This extraordinary perception naturally reduced the chance of their ever aspiring to create something new, or to depart from the – usually Victorian – attitudes they had absorbed at school. But, wherever they were educated, they aspired to be all-rounders, capable of tackling the most varied tasks, in the private as well as the public sectors, for specialist knowledge was deemed to be the mark of the inherently inferior, of the other ranks rather than of the officer class. The career of Lord Waverley was a striking example in this regard. As Sir John Anderson, he had been a brilliantly successful senior civil servant in both India and Britain and then, during the early years of the war, Home Secretary – a post in which he was far less successful because of a natural incapacity to understand or take account of the feelings of ordinary people – before becoming Chancellor of the Exchequer. He was the archetypal member of what we would now call the Great and the Good. After the war, he was considered to be the natural choice for positions as varied as chairman of the Royal Opera Covent Garden and the Port of London Authority.

Any effort at change was stifled by the all-pervasive British class system which seeped into every pore of the English consciousness, dominated every aspect of British life. Class, it was said, was 'a life sentence, as inescapable as any caste system'. It was a series of gradations composed of innumerable sub-classes, each with its own attributes, expressed in nuances of speech and vocabulary instantly and universally recognisable. The similarity between the English class system and the many castes in India was no doubt one of the reasons why the English felt so at home there. Another was the fact that the

English rulers felt they had rather more in common with the Indian aristocracy, the Rajahs and Maharajahs, than they did with their own lower orders. In India, it was, of course, impossible to change the caste into which you had been born. In the Britain of the early 1950s, things really weren't all that different: any attempt to change your precise, seemingly God-given, social status was only greeted by suspicion and sneers from those above.

The frozen nature of the caste system was well put by the sociologist Michael Young: 'Until well on into Elizabethan times family succession to jobs was much more common in the lower than in the middle classes. In London or Liverpool the docker's son followed his father's occupation, despite every blandishment of his mistress [no male teachers?] at school, because he had the absurd idea that it was the finest calling in the world. So did coal miners' sons in Durham villages, farm-workers' sons in distant parts of Somerset, steel-men at Corby and Scunthorpe.'[22] The caste system within the working classes was unique in the world. Even in Australia, where the unions were even stronger than in Britain, the battle was virtually exclusively with the bosses and not with members of their own class.

Phrases such as 'People like us' or 'Not one of us' were used quite unself-consciously and it was axiomatic that any accent rather than that of 'received standard' used on the BBC was unthinkable in polite society. The result was what Edward Shils condemned as a 'constriction of spirit' which fostered a national character 'frowning on enthusiasm, distrusting spontaneity and regarding soundness and steadiness as the highest of human virtues'. These attitudes, the 'puritanical suppression of feeling and imagination', Shils argues, contributed to 'a restraint on aspiration', thus preserving social hierarchies. The dominance of class as a factor in social, economic and cultural life was a largely English phenomenon, for Wales was deeply democratic and class was replaced in Scotland and above all Ulster by racial and religious bigotry. Indeed, the strength of the Tory Party in Scotland (and in Liverpool) can be largely explained by the association of the Labour Party with the Catholic Church whose members were still overwhelmingly of Irish origin.

The gulf between the classes actually widened in the immediate post-war years, because of the growing – and largely unjustified – fear amongst the aristocracy and the middle classes that their positions were threatened by the atmosphere of egalitarianism, the social changes, the levelling-down, the 'we're all in it together' atmosphere of wartime and immediate post-war Britain. The fear lingered on into the 1950s with the increasing prosperity of some sections of the working class, partly because their wages – especially if they were on piece-work, or other systems of payments by results – were less firmly tied to rigid salary structures than those of their social superiors. So the middle classes invented the theory that the proles were unable to spend their money properly – hence the oft-repeated canard that miners, confronted by baths in the home for the first time, used them to store their coal.

Even in the business world status was all – a new steelworks built in the 1960s boasted thirteen separate canteens and dining rooms. Indeed the concern with status remains alive and well today in company car parks where the type of car allocated to an executive remains a matter of far greater importance than in any other major industrialised country. Lower down the ladder, receiving a salary (paid monthly into your bank account) rather than a mere wage (paid weekly in cash) assumed an importance which grew greater as wages of skilled workers rose to rival, or even exceed, those paid to the country's increasing number of clerical workers. Within the working classes your status was defined very early on by whether you could aspire to skilled employment. As Ernest Bevin once put it, at the age of sixteen he knew that he could never be a boiler-maker, but that did not stop him becoming Foreign Secretary.

Bevin's problem exposed the heart of Labour's fundamental incapacity to reform British society because it was ridden with so many divisions of its own. As Bevin, the leader of the Transport & General Workers Union, representing largely unskilled workers, knew only too well, the basic division was between different occupations within a given industry. This gave rise to the demarcation disputes that formed the biggest single source of British industrial conflicts. As a German immigrant, Ralf Dahrendorf, pointed out, 'Demarcation disputes often reflected merely the solidarity of smaller groups' over 'the boundary of the unit within which the rules of solidarity hold.'* Confronted by the power of the union barons involved, the Trades Union Congress was never strong enough to separate the warring parties before any damage was done.

Thus class divisions were, one might say, classless, and ran right through British life. Musically the working classes, especially those in the North of England, listened to mass choirs singing a limited range of oratorios, above all *Messiah*, and to the brass bands attached to most coal mines† and major factories in the North of England – a form of music which has never been accepted by the culturocracy, has never received any support from the Arts Council. Middle-class taste

* In *On Britain*, BBC Books, 1982. Dahrendorf enjoyed a distinguished career in his adopted country, culminating in his directorship of the London School of Economics.

† A good player was guaranteed an easy job and a house. Standards were maintained by the all-powerful bandmaster. If you displeased him you were stuck in a lousy job down the pit.

34

was summed up by the long-running series on the BBC's Home Service (the predecessor of Radio 4) featuring a decorous orchestra recorded, with perfect appropriateness, in the lounge of the Grand Hotel East-bourne, most genteel of seaside resorts.

Naturally, the class divide extended to pubs with their snugs, lounges, saloon and public bars. But 'boozers', the principal leisure haunt of the British working classes, were – and, in all too many cases still remain fifty years later – pretty unappealing. Despite the nostalgia still associated with the old-fashioned British pub with its supposedly ever-jolly, invariably welcoming landlord the underlying reality was well described by Colin McInnes: 'The service is slow and slovenly ... will they never wipe the counter, as they do in every civilised country? The food (unless the pub is Jewish) is a disgrace (withered pork pies and leaden sausages are a luxury; the best you can usually hope for are potato crisps, peanuts, aspirins and breath-pills), and you can't get a coffee so that your wretched non-drinking companion has to drench himself in fruit and vegetable juices ... these places are like branches of a bank that happens to sell liquor: hideous, respectable, and unwelcoming, with inconvenient opening hours'.[24]

Other than the pub, the only real escape for the majority of the British people – and not only the working classes – from the all-pervading, almost institutionalised joylessness of life lay in a handful of radio pro-grammes – the majority banal beyond belief but a handful genuinely funny even today like *Take It From Here* and *Where Ignorance is Bliss* – and, for the men weekly visits to a football match and, sometimes more often, to the cinemas, temples of glamorous unreality. Holidays were short (the miners only got a second week in 1953) and, so far as the working classes were concerned, virtually entirely confined to grim boarding houses. As John Betjeman put it in his poem *By The Seaside*:

> Our lodging-house, ten minutes from the shore.
> Still unprepared to make a picnic lunch
> Except by notice on the previous day.
> Still nowhere for the children when it's wet
> Except that smelly, overcrowded lounge.
> And still no garage for the motor-car.
> Still on the bedroom wall, the list of rules
> *Don't waste the water. It is pumped by hand.*
> *Don't throw old blades into the WC.*
> *Don't keep the bathroom long and don't be late*
> *For meals and don't hang swimsuits out on sills*
> *(A line has been provided at the back)*
> *Don't empty children's sand-shoes in the hall.*
> Don't this, Don't that[25]

35

Class was also dominant in Britain's all-important sporting life. In cricket the division between amateurs ('Gentlemen') and professionals ('Players') was total, and until 1962 celebrated in an annual match between the two classes at Lords. There was an obvious contrast between the classy-sounding County Championship and the grittier-sounding, purely professional, Lancashire League where outsiders like the great West Indian cricketer Learie Constantine had been welcome even in the 1930s. When Tom Graveney, a leading professional, went so far as to say 'Well played, David' to the amateur David Shepherd, his captain apologised for what he called 'Graveney's impertinence', adding, 'I think you'll find it won't happen again.' The whole situation was riddled with hypocrisy. By the mid-1950s counties were desperate to find an amateur who was a good enough player to justify inclusion in the team and thus, automatically, take on the captaincy. It was well-known that the 'gentlemen' often made a good living out of the game – in the 1960s the English captain Ted Dexter ran a flourishing public relations business and the great Surrey bowler Jim Laker once asked if he could turn amateur to earn more money.

Similarly, the strictly amateur rugby union was classier – if even more violent – than the professional, proletarian rugby league, which was confined to the north of England. Moreover few of the middle classes would ever have dreamed of attending a professional soccer match. In the early 1950s Pegasus, the (strictly amateur) side composed of Oxbridge undergraduates and graduates, could attract crowds of 100,000 spectators (how they would have shuddered to be called fans . . .) to the Amateur Cup Final. Even in the late 1960s, it remained a major event despite the inevitably mediocre quality of the football. Even the gentle pastime of fishing was – and still is – firmly divided. Coarse fishermen are, well, coarse, while fly fishermen are richer and posher. But in sport, as in so many aspects of life at the time, Scotland and Wales were exceptions. In Scotland, the birthplace of golf, the game was democratic, as was rugby football in Wales, where there were plenty of jobs in friendly insurance companies and the like for retired sporting heroes.

In every walk of life professionals who had risen from the ranks were simply not considered suitable when it came to filling the top jobs. Right into the 1980s, it was inconceivable that even the ablest chief general managers of the clearing banks such as Arthur Chester-field at the Westminster and Deryk Van der Weyer at Barclays, could be considered as potential chairmen – in the case of Barclays, well into the 1990s this post was automatically filled by a descendant of one of the handful of Quaker families which had founded the bank in the early nineteenth century.

The same applied to the police, for the Chief Constables of most

36

of the country's large number of police forces were not, usually, professional policemen but retired army officers. Attitudes towards the police also varied between different classes. Much has – rightly – been made of the fact that the British police, virtually alone amongst those of other civilised countries, went about unarmed. Most commentators then go on to attribute this to the general feeling of respect for the police, that they were 'on our side'. This perception, as so often, was that of the middle classes – and in any case this lasted only until the 1960s when they felt the heavy hand of the law themselves when they committed motoring offences, or when their children were accused of possessing drugs. But in the 1950s the situation was very different. The police themselves lived a life apart, their values and attitudes usually formed by their experience in the armed forces. They were harsh on the working classes, 'fitting up' suspects, and particularly disliked because they systematically harassed anyone engaged in betting, one of the working classes' few pleasures yet one which was largely illegal away from race tracks until 1961, when the Betting and Gaming Act came into force and legalised betting shops. As McKibbin puts it: 'Relations between the police and the working classes were usually, at best, only an armed truce. Many young working-class men [today, read young black people] especially were deeply suspicious of the police, and their neighbours and families usually took their sides.' Not surprisingly, the middle classes felt that the police existed largely to protect them from the lower orders.

The image of the police was greatly enhanced by an extraordinary public relations coup by the Metropolitan Police. In 1950 it seemed that everyone from the commissioner down was helping to produce a film, *The Blue Lamp*, about a certain PC Dixon, who was stationed at a police station called Dock Green (in reality Paddington Green in West London, the scene of a much more accurate portrayal of police work forty years later). In 1955 the BBC took up the theme in *Dixon of Dock Green*, also starring the comfortable, avuncular figure of Jack Warner in the title role, a series which provided millions of viewers with an idealised, heavily sanitised version of policing in London.

The reality, and image, of the police reflected the extraordinary rigidity of the social scheme of things, its apparent immobility, a state of affairs reinforced by 'proletcult', the refusal of left-wing intellectuals to challenge the prevailing worship of working-class values which, in reality, were narrow, negative and based largely on loyalty to a small group. There was a harsh political reality behind the attitude: the fact that over two-fifths of Labour MPs – the same proportion as those from working-class origins – were financially supported by trades unions. But they, like the class they represented, were not ambitious. In Dahrendorf's words, 'There is something strangely passive about working-class values. "Live and let live" is after all not a principle of active progress ... The group works ... against the idea of progress.' McKibbin takes the point further. The workers, he noted, 'were much attached to the workplace, but ruled by group opinion, seemingly without ambition and deeply suspicious of and often hostile to management and the technological changes management were always thought to be promoting ... A "fair day's work" meant that a man should do his stint and not shirk; but no more. And he should do nothing which might threaten a mate's job. Nor, therefore, should he ever compete with his mate. This ... produced not only an introverted and defensive working class, but a culture which was defeatist and fatalistic.'

The workers' attitudes fully justified the bitter comment of Keir Hardie, one of the founders of the Labour Party, that 'the tragedy of the working classes is the limited nature of their ambitions'. As a result, continues McKibbin, 'many working-class men and women held to a kind of folk-Marxism quite independent of actual party-political allegiances. They believed their own work was the source of all value; the only work that mattered. Without it society would not exist. Clerical workers "did nothing". The very strength and, above all, the rigidity of the Labour movement denied the workers the means of their own empowerment'. They were not helped by the profoundly condescending attitude of the – often upper middle-class – leaders of the Labour Party. In the late 1950s Denis Butt, a long-dead friend, pointed out, quite rightly that 'the whole idea of social justice [the catchphrase of the day] is essentially patronising'. In fact the working class, and its socialist partners, inhabited the same cloud-cuckoo land as the right-wing establishment. Michael Young, author of the Labour manifesto in 1945, was totally, if typically, wrong when he imagined how, looking back from 2034, 'without the ferment of socialist agitation, the working man would have remained sunk in apathy, lacking sufficient drive to take advantage of his great new chances'.[22] Precisely the opposite was true, for it was the structure and nature of the Labour party and 'socialist' organisations like the unions that formed the biggest single obstacle to the aspirations to a greater choice in their lives for millions of British working people.

The reality was admirably summed up by Anthea Symonds in a recent letter to the *New Statesman*: 'The so-called Labour heartlands consisted of the monopoly of one industry on communities that were based upon a largely educationally unqualified but relatively well-paid male workforce'.[23] This workforce, due to the power of the trade unions, who were anxious to exclude other workers, especially women, managed to keep wages relatively high until the late 1970s. Women's only jobs were 'in low-paid sweatshops, but this was never a concern for the "boys" of the Labour heartlands'. In the heart felt words of the poet Tony Harrison in *Punchline* when he was writing about his father:

> Revolution never crosses your mind!
> For the kids who never made it through the schools
> The Northern working class escaped the grind
> As boxers or comedians, or won the pools.

This general acceptance of the status quo was natural enough because for nearly a century the Labour Party operated as an uneasy alliance between middle-class intellectuals and proletarian barons, cosily ensconced in the unions and in the town halls of most of Britain's major cities. They, far more than the country's industrialists or the landed gentry, ensured that the workers remained in their place. To reinforce the system there was a – generally implicit – bargain to be had from voting Labour and then being given a council house, for the vast majority lived in flats and houses owned by Labour-controlled local councils. The system was most obvious in purely proletarian enclaves such as mining villages or communities clustered round docks. These resembled the tribal reserves so beloved of Imperialist Britons which, under a system known as Indirect Rule, allowed some privileged tribes thought of as Noble Savages, like the Masai or the Pathans, a considerable degree of independence.

In *Weekend In Dinlock* the radical American writer Clancy Sigal provided a vivid description of the terrible strains imposed on a young miner, Davie, because he is also a talented painter. His book vividly demonstrated the gulf between art and working-class reality as well as the appalling narrowness of life in a mining village like his fictional Dinlock. 'If you live in Dinlock,' Sigal wrote, 'you must make Dinlock your life and you cannot live in Dinlock and be accepted by the core if you have a real means of escape.' He disturbed his British socialist friends by painting a vivid picture of the grind of daily work relieved only by periodic visits to the two working men's clubs (which provided only limited facilities for women, and then only after battles with the old guard) or to one of the two pubs in the village (the other was reserved for non-miners) and of the lives of the women, there to breed, to take care of the children – and grow old only too quickly. In this environment there was no room for any advancement. As Hilary Mantel put it in her description of a fictional mill village in her novel *Fludd*: 'There was a spirit abroad in the village that discriminated so thoroughly against pretension that it also discriminated against ambition, even against literacy.'

Even within the industrial proletariat, there was a clear distinction

39

between the classic slums, with their wife-beating, child neglect and all the other social ills associated with the 'undeserving poor', and the classic working-class neighbourhoods where such terms as 'keeping up standards', 'workmate', neighbour, housewife meant something and where doors were indeed left unlocked (although this may have had something to do with the fact that until television sets and washing machines became a normal phenomenon, there was very little worth stealing in the average working-class home). But either way women bore the brunt of the problems. In his introduction to his television series *Talking Heads*, Alan Bennett, a former satirist-turned-Poet Laureate of English nostalgia, writes how 'a common woman was likely to swear or drink . . . to get all dolled up and go out leaving the house upside down and make no bones about having affairs. Enjoy herself possibly, and that was the trouble; a common woman side-stepped her share of the proper suffering of her sex.'

Whatever their sex or status, the members of the British proletariat were much more 'proletarian' than their European counterparts. Despite the number of mutually owned trustee savings banks and building societies, the activities of these institutions were less wide-ranging than those catering to the needs of the working classes than in most industrialised countries, while the great Co-operative Movement was already showing signs of the managerial rigidity which was to doom its ability to compete with the private sector over the next decades. Only in South Wales did a substantial proportion own their own houses, so it was not surprising that in local government the Tories often called themselves Ratepayers* (hence, too, Mrs Thatcher's desire to replace rates with the Poll Tax). There was a sharp class distinction between manual workers whose wages were 'paid' weekly and white collar workers whose 'salaries' were 'credited' monthly to their bank accounts. So there was a double rigidity, that of the toffs, solidly entrenched behind the delusion that they had won the war, and the workers, unable to break out of a state of urban deprivation, kept in their place by assumptions which seemed natural and indeed noble to the guilt-ridden sentimentalists of the Labour Left. It was to take over forty years to break up the system. For the working class inhabited the same cloud-cuckoo land inhabited by their superiors.

Service and the service trades were even more looked down on, if only because the very word 'service' was associated with the domestic service which employed millions of working-class women before the war. One of the more extraordinary aspects of proletcult was its scorn for service, as opposed to manufacturing industries. In the 1980s, when

* The then form of local taxation, 'the Rates' was levied only on privately owned accommodation.

40

the photographer Colin Jones returned to the native Tyneside he had left twenty years earlier, he remembered 'a different world, where people did proper jobs in the shipyards or making tanks at Vickers. It fascinated me. The huge number of pubs full of men who worked with hot metal. The women out on the streets. The amazing sense of community. There was a terrible sort of innocence to it all.' The disdain for the service industries which were already of growing importance in every industrialised country reached its peak in the Selective Employment Tax introduced by the Labour government in April 1965. This was designed to affect service industries and thus, by an absurd piece of logic, encourage employment in manufacturing industry.

The depth of the gulf between rulers and ruled, not to mention the alienation felt by a substantial section of the population for the industrial proletariat, found its first post-war expression when the coal industry was nationalised. On January 1, 1947, 'Vesting Day', when the collieries' assets were 'vested' in a publicly owned body, the National Coal Board, flags were flown at collieries and the miners proclaimed that 'Today the mines belong to the people.' But it seems never to have occurred to anyone that nationalisation could have brought with it an end to the 'them and us' attitude normal in the mines. In the words of Martin Adeney and John Lloyd, 'the idea of the Coal Board's operations as socialism at work was a myth ... The cult of macho management might have been born, and indeed lived on in many coal fields in ways little different from those of the days of private ownership. Similarly, union distrust of the management did not vanish. A persistent faction in the NUM, highly politicised, argued against "collaboration" from the start.'[26] Typically, when Arthur Horner, the General Secretary of the National Union of Mineworkers, was asked to join the NCB, he replied that he could do more, not only for his members, but also 'for the industry' if he remained where he was and added that 'We always related our demands to the needs of our men and the needs of our industry, but also against the background of the wider needs of the nation.' Yet absenteeism remained at around 10 per cent (face workers failed to turn up on one working day out of eight) despite the country's desperate need for coal.

Horner was a communist, albeit one of those who habitually separated his beliefs from his day-to-day trades unionism. But even after 1956, when the majority of the British Communist Party's most-respected intellectuals left it after the Russian invasion of Hungary and Khruschev's revelations about Stalin, the general alienation of much of the working class ensured the continuing importance of the handful of able and dedicated communists such as Horner who occupied key positions in many unions, or who, like Jack Dash in the London docks and 'Red Robbo' at Longbridge, exercised a total, if

41

generally unofficial, domination over their domain, often with disastrous effects. They were sometimes encouraged by the bosses: Leonard Lord of the British Motor Corporation was grateful that Red Robbo could deliver the workers' votes and Lord Beaverbrook sided with Richard Briginshaw of NATSOPA, the union representing unskilled workers in the newspaper industry, even awarding him a doctorate from his tame university, to use him to drive up costs so that Beaverbrook's financially weaker rivals would suffer. The Communist Party's influence even survived when, later in the 1950s, Woodrow Wyatt, Labour MP and future fan of Mrs Thatcher, provided an early example of television investigative journalism as he revealed the extent of ballot-rigging in the communist-dominated Electrical Trades Union.

Proletcult inevitably bred its own hypocrisy, best illustrated by that archetypal figure Harold Wilson. As a young Cabinet minister, he had made a speech worthy of the famous Monty Python sketch in which each person claims to have had the most deprived childhood ('We slept in cardboard boxes'; 'You were lucky' etc). In what became known as his – widely derided – 'barefoot speech' Wilson claimed that half his school friends in Huddersfield had been shoeless (this sort of claim persisted: in the late 1960s I remember hearing Harold Evans, then editor of the *Sunday Times*, talking in much the same vein). Even when Prime Minister, Wilson would advertise his predilection for HP Sauce and was inevitably photographed with a pipe, whereas in reality his tastes were more for cigars and large quantities of brandy. He was not alone in his two-faced attitudes. When politicians were 'at home', as it were, in the House of Commons, it tended to be the Labour members who would go for that most bourgeois of drinks, gin & tonic, while the Tories in a display of mock-proletcultery would drink Federation Bitter, an excellent beer brewed for the Federation of Working Men's Clubs. The cult reached an apogee of absurdity in the 1970s when a leading left-wing Labour politician, Michael Meacher, sued the political journalist Alan Watkins for writing, quite correctly, that he was not of working-class stock.

To an astonishing extent, the spokesmen of the Labour Party fiercely defended their habits, however socially primitive they seemed even then. One was that the male head of the household did not tell his wife how much he had earned. When the then Archbishop of Canterbury, Dr Fisher, by no means a progressive figure, told an audience – typically when opening a domestic science college – that marriage was 'a partnership' and that 'the man ought always to let his wife know what his earnings were and they should arrange mutually how much should be given to the wife for housekeeping', all hell broke loose. Cassandra, the most influential columnist of the day, informed the millions of readers of the *Daily Mirror* that such an arrangement would 'destroy the harmony of every working-class household'. The attitude persisted for a quarter of a century, delaying the introduction of child benefit, which was to be paid directly to the child's mother and was therefore opposed tooth and nail by the TUC. So, to put it mildly, the Labour Movement could not offer any help for women, who, in Britain as in the United States, had been returned to their dependent status after a period during the war during which they had been able to demonstrate their intellectual and managerial potential as never before.

But the biggest difference between the British working classes and their continental European equivalents, the biggest obstacle to a more egalitarian society, was education. A relative handful of children were brilliantly educated but there was virtually no opportunity for technical or vocational education except for apprenticeships, a handful of which, like those at Vickers or Rolls-Royce, provided as good a technical training as anywhere in the world. The situation was not improved by the general lack of respect for education amongst rulers and ruled alike, resulting in a general contempt for teachers – 'Those who can, do, those who can't, teach'. Most of the male working class – and virtually all its female members – remained largely untouched by modern education or the aspirations which spring from it (a notable contrast with France or the United States). The Labour Movement had, effectively, acknowledged the size of the holes in the educational net by founding Ruskin College. This unique establishment was based on the assumed need for an institution to compensate for the lack of normal educational possibilities, albeit in only a small measure – and then for a purely practical purpose, to train future trades union leaders. Socialists even rejoiced in the miners' libraries and working men's institutes where they should have been ashamed of the need for such initiatives since the intelligent workers who frequented them ought to have received a proper education in the first place.

The lack of adequate educational opportunity was not confined to schools. It existed, too, at graduate and post-graduate level. In the nineteenth century the Germans used to describe Britain, somewhat unfairly, as 'a land without music'. More reasonably, and well into the twentieth century, it could have been described as a land without learning. Before 1914, for instance, many of the country's pitifully few post-graduate students went to Germany to do their doctorates (and even in the 1950s you had to be able to read German if you wanted a serious degree in chemistry). There were far fewer students than in Europe, partly because British universities were, and indeed remain, costlier than their Continental counterparts, for other British academic institutions aped the Oxbridge example and felt they had to provide student accommodation whereas those attending their European counterparts lived (and still live) at home.

The problems of British education, which have provided so many headaches over the post-war period, date back a long way. As McKibbin points out 'throughout the inter-war years, in fact, higher (i.e. secondary) education was closed to the vast majority of English school-children.' Historically, the British ruling classes had survived through their ability over the ages to accept and absorb a steady, if measured, flow of newcomers from the middle and lower classes filtered through an elitist educational system whose key component was the grammar schools catering for bright, socially or financially disadvantaged youngsters. But this system left the vast majority of the young working classes condemned by the 11-plus examination to an education in secondary modern schools which, though better than their predecessors, left them with severely limited learning opportunities.

During the war the Fleming Report had recommended that public schools take 25 per cent of their pupils from state schools, but this would never have worked since the former took pupils at the age of thirteen or fourteen rather than eleven. Inevitably, as McKibbin notes, 'Two of the institutions most central to working-class life, the public and grammar schools, emerged unscathed, despite their doubtful democratic status and the unquestioned, and growing, advantage they gave to the non-working classes' – though the public schools were, and remain, irrelevant to the working classes. By 1950 about 60 per cent of the children of the professional and business classes could expect to win grammar school places compared with 10 per cent of working-class children. Furthermore, 'the differential proportion of working- and middle-class boys and girls who stayed in secondary school beyond the age of seventeen-plus was hardly affected by the 1944 Act' – which thus perpetuated a degree of discrimination unheard-of in comparable European societies. And, McKibbin adds, 'as a system of recruitment, university entrance discriminated in two ways; against girls of all social classes and against working-class boys'. Even though an increasing number of working-class children did find their way to university in the 1950s through grammar schools, the Act, as McKibbin says, 'by entrenching the grammar schools at the expense of the modern schools, arguably increased the "wastage" of ability for which the pre-1939 system had been so criticised'. In addition, the results of the 1944 Education Act were distinctly uneven: the criteria varied wildly – some schools set written tests while others preferred to rely on 'personality tests'. As a result there was a grammar school intake of 12 per cent in Surrey compared with up to 45 per cent in Merioneth in Wales, a part of the country where, as in Scotland, education had always been more highly valued than in England.

The 1944 Act also failed to introduce a system of technical schools, a third alternative used by the Germans in particular to ensure a supply of apprentices who were treated as fully the equal of university graduates. A handful of MPs and the National Association of Labour Teachers condemned successive Labour secretaries of education, notably Ellen Wilkinson, for what Kenneth Morgan describes as 'their blank resistance to the idea of the multilateral [i.e. comprehensive] secondary school, and their tenderness toward the social and intellectual elitism of the grammar school of which Wilkinson was a proud product. But to no avail . . . the broad range of opinion felt confidence that, even in the post-war austerity years, the government was giving a new priority to public education. At last criticisms of Britain's educational deficiencies by contrast to other European countries were being met. Levelling or social engineering could wait until later' – a perfect summary of the – totally unjustified – moral smugness of the post-war years.

Not surprisingly, within education there was a definite hierarchy typified by the existence of six unions for teachers according to the schools at which they taught (primary, secondary, grammar etc). The hierarchy echoed that prevailing at Oxbridge where the practical sciences were decidedly at the bottom of the totem pole (in the mid-1950s I remember one particular college being derided as 'full of Northern chemists'). The contrast in status between Britain and the rest of Western Europe was particularly noticeable in the historically poor status accorded to engineers. In general, education with a practical purpose – even that enjoyed by budding doctors and lawyers – was thought of as mere training; 'real education' had, by definition, to be pure, irrelevant to any future career. By contrast, in France the Polytechnique, one of the most highly rated of all higher education institutions, was devoted to turning out engineers, and in Italy the term 'ingenieri' was a high compliment. The results were disastrous, summed up by the novelist and scientist C.P. Snow as The Two Cultures, scientific and the humanities. So, because our senior civil servants were never scientists or engineers, they were unable to decide on the best solutions to essentially engineering problems. Hence the construction of three types of V-bombers to carry our atom bombs and of three types of nuclear reactors.

The mood was summed up in the words of an aeronautical engineer who had emigrated to the United States and was living in the 'cultural wilderness' of the Pacific North-West. 'Deep down we all prefer England, its way of life, its people . . . but to be an engineer in England is to live on the edge of existence,' treated as 'just a factory worker. The poor image of the engineer in England results in poor pay . . . In America we [the engineers] are on more equal terms with the other professions . . . an engineer is respected in America.'[27] It was even said, with some justice, that in Britain the middle and upper classes

45

would do anything to help British manufacturing industry except work in it. Throughout the twentieth century, as Martin Wiener put it, 'engineering was left to the sons of the skilled working class'.[28]

This lack of a solid industrial educational basis for our technical successes – like the early computers, the Comet airliner and the cars, speedboats and aeroplanes which held world records in the 1950s – meant that they could never be translated into deep-seated industrial strength. For in general the country was technologically backward, a fact symbolised for me by the flyover in Chiswick in West London, built in 1957 and, amazingly, the first in the country, and the second Blackwall tunnel under the Thames. The flyover was built of brick, not the concrete invariably used in advanced countries*, while the second Blackwall tunnel, dug in the mid-1960s, had exactly the same dimensions as the first, built in 1887 for horse-driven traffic and therefore totally unsuitable for large lorries.

As David Caradog Jones, writing about Liverpool, puts it, the dominant metaphor of 'the ladder of opportunity' was only too apposite because 'it is characteristic of a ladder that, although a number of persons may mount up it, they can do so only one or two at a time'. The result throughout the past half century has been that the smug sense of superiority formerly possessed exclusively by the alumni of the public schools has come to be shared by 'Our Generation', those who had come through grammar schools and the better universities. This phenomenon represented a considerable broadening of opportunity – especially for girls – but did not remove, indeed intensified, the feeling of 'them and us' if only because the new elite could feel that those below them had been excluded, not because of the lowliness of their birth but because they were simply not bright or studious enough. Yet, as A.H. Halsey points out, members of the working-class displayed remarkably little resentment at the poverty of their lot, having no aspirations and comparing themselves 'in the traditional way with those near to them in the factory and the neighbourhood . . . Relative deprivation was in fact more likely to be felt by middle-class than by working-class people.'

The narrow, unambitious nature of the attitudes generated by this rigidity was most obvious when children from a working-class background got into a grammar school. In his grammar school uniform, Geoffrey Nicolson was attacked because 'only stuck-up puffs wore uniform, because only stuck-up puffs went to the posh grammar school. The fact that we lived on the same council estate as they did made no

---

* When the contractor raised the issue, no minister would attend the opening and the flyover was opened by Jayne Mansfield, the bustiest Hollywood star of the time. Needless to say, the contractor didn't get any more official contracts.

difference. Stuck-up puffs deserved a good hiding. QED'.[29] It was Richard Hoggart in *The Uses of Literacy* who expressed the dilemma of the 'scholarship boy' most touchingly. In the communal living room 'Mother is ironing, the wireless is on, someone is singing the snatch of a song or Father says intermittently what comes into his head. The boy has to cut himself off mentally, so as to do his homework, as well as he can.' As he – for very very few working class girls had the same opportunity – grows older, he ceases to be part of the world into which he was born while remaining uneasy within the world to which he was aspiring: 'he has left his class, at least in spirit, by being in certain ways unusual; and he is still unusual in another class, too tense and overwound'.[30]

But lack of ambition was not by any means an exclusively working-class phenomenon. 'The experience or memories of capitalism's cataclysm, the depression,' wrote Noel Annan, 'ate into the consciousness of Our Age. We wanted a job that was secure. So government service, teaching and the professions were our first choice. Satirical employers used to complain that those they interviewed did not ask what their prospects were but what their pension was likely to be. Collectivism seemed to be a way of making life safer for everyone and less susceptible to the roulette wheel of the market.' By the end of the war, said the expatriate Donald Horne, quoted by Wiener, 'kindness, tolerance and love of order become snobbery, woolliness and love of the past. Effortless ease becomes the ease of not making any effort to do anything. Gentlemanly intuitive wisdom becomes the inability to make up one's mind. Doing the decent thing comes to mean that there should be no sharp clash of attitudes, no disagreeable new beliefs that might disturb someone. The sense of fairness becomes the belief that competition is unfair. As a result, no one seemed able to imagine any good coming out of novelty. Enthusiasm was frowned on, sloppiness assumed, competence and hard work signs of, well, vulgarity. 'She's frightfully competent' was a typical insult. There remained more than a hint of the historic worship of the Great British Muddle, like a compost heap dating back over the centuries capable of producing some unique flowers as well as a profusion of weeds. Today hard, continuous work is taken for granted, and it could be said that the most important change has been from a country where the managing classes were under-worked and essentially amateur into one where professionalism (and endemic overwork) is assumed and respected.

In 1951 *The Manager* magazine reported a conference speech by a leading manager which perfectly reflected the mood of the times. 'A top-level executive's life' he reassured the gathering, 'was to apply to himself a balanced cultivated life – about half his time should be spent directing his business and the other half in business activities outside, and he should, as far as his working life is concerned, confine that to the minimum. He should have long weekends ... he should play golf ... he should garden ... he should play bridge*, he should read, he should do something different.'

Whatever the attractions of such a way of life, it was not conducive to a competitive economy. But worse was the situation in some major factories. A reporter visiting the Morris plant at Cowley in the mid-1950s remembers that the managers were drunk from mid-morning on. As one Irishman observed, 'The English word for *manana* is delivery date.'

In the City of London the situation was, if anything, worse. An apprentice at a merchant bank recalls: 'By Thursday afternoon at four, one of the senior partners would come across to the juniors and say, "Why are we all still here? It's almost the weekend."'[31] But then the City in the post-war years was a desert – physically much of it was still composed of picturesque, weed-strewn bomb-sites. Its many businesses were still feudal, their activities confined by natural lethargy as well as a mass of financial restrictions on the foreign trade that had been its lifeblood before the war. The situation was so bad that one of the early post-war Lord Mayors, Sir Denys Lowson, was even known to be a shady operator – he died in 1975, just after receiving a summons to answer an indictment for fraud. He got the job largely because no-one else could afford it. On the stock market itself, the insistence that someone's word was their bond was guff and anyway applied only to insiders, who took anyone outside the magic circle as merely suckers. Insider trading was the normal practice. At bankers' weekends, guests would find application forms for particularly promising new issues on the hall table, thus guaranteeing a handy short-term profit. Even secretaries would be let into the magic circle if they had to work late on an issue. The historian of the City, David Kynaston describes how a dealer would ask, ' "Girls, do you want to buy some Rank rights?" and they would ask, "Do we?" and he would reply, "Yes, you do" ... a few days later the same routine would be gone through only this time they were told to sell, at a handsome profit.'

Nor was the financial system geared to helping new or small companies. When a leading merchant banker proposed that the major clearing banks should provide funds other than overdrafts for industrial expansion – a key element in the post-war success of Continental economies – he aroused only fury in his audience. To make matters worse, the overdraft system encouraged imprecise financial thinking. In other countries either it was illegal to exceed limits or banks pro-

---

* Right through the 1960s, senior Treasury officials managed to find time for a rubber or two at their club (the Reform) after lunch.

vided money in loans for specific sums, precise objectives and clearly defined periods of time. In Britain, loans were the exception and overdraft limits were, in general, applied either too laxly or too strictly. There was simply no real agreed framework for smaller companies. Not surprisingly the effect on the British economy was disastrous.

For overall the prevailing ethos was deeply uncommercial. The only way to make big money, or so it seemed for a long time, well into the 1960s was through property development. This was considered as a purely Jewish, down-market and slightly sleazy business – as indeed much of it was. For the rest, the situation remained much as it had been in 1939. Then, wrote Wiener, 'the prevalent form of organisation in the British economy was uncompetitive private enterprise in partnership with the state'. This mentality helped produce a total lack of the 'animal high spirits' which Keynes so rightly identified as the mainspring of economic success under capitalism. The sniffy, superior, attitude of the Indian Civil Service towards commerce pervaded even the civilians in the occupying forces in Germany who declined to allow British companies to take any advantage of the situation of their former German competitors. Virtually the only exception was the late Robert Maxwell, who contrived to buy up one of the world's best scientific publishers, Pergamon Press, which formed the basis of his future fortune. (When Maxwell was forced to sell Pergamon just before his death forty-five years later, you knew he was in a bad way.) The failure to grasp what might be called 'the managerial/commercial nettle' was reflected in attitudes towards the many basic industries such as coal and steel that had been nationalised under the Attlee administration. The Labour Party's intellectuals had assumed that the mere act of nationalisation would itself be enough to result in flourishing industries. Yet nationalisation had created a problem which was to cripple the performance of the country's basic industries over the next generation – indeed until they were privatised at prices far lower than if their finances had been properly managed.

It was simply that the Treasury held a monopoly of power over all matters economic. This was unusual: in most industrialised countries, there were two separate departments of state, one, the more important, concerned with the economy as a whole, the other with the finances of the public sector. An experiment in the late 1940s separating the two roles had ended when the minister, Sir Stafford Cripps, moved into the Treasury, taking his planners with him. Unfortunately the Treasury was institutionally incapable of looking beyond the next financial year, an attitude bound to cripple industries – most obviously the railways – which required long-term investment (we are still living with a network, in England anyway, which was largely completed in 1852). Although the Treasury, and indeed Whitehall as a whole, was always called a 'Rolls-Royce', it often appeared that the motor involved had only one forward gear and was happiest in reverse. The only major shifts happened in response to political pressure and so were largely unplanned.

Even outside the civil service, bureaucratic, not economic or commercial, attitudes prevailed. Money was still unmentionable in polite society: it was assumed that the quantity of money was finite, that they weren't making it any more, and that in any case it was vulgar even to think in commercial terms. Few graduates went into business. Even then they doubted their role. In 1955 the Minister for Economic Affairs at the American Embassy was struck by 'a sense of doubt concerning the social utility of industry and the legitimacy of profits, a sort of industrial inferiority complex often suffered by business leaders themselves . . . In the extreme, some British industrialists seem almost ashamed of their vocation, looking on their jobs as a necessary evil or – in the case of family businesses – an inherited ''white man's burden''.'

Inevitably, when graduates, at least those of the 'ancient universities', did venture into the economic world they avoided harsh commercial realities as far as possible by joining cosy bureaucratic corporations like Shell. These were the sort where they have 'leave' rather than 'holidays', a sure sign of a corporate rather than a business culture. In industry, as in so many other spheres of British life, there was a cult of age. Charles Handy, later an influential management guru, was early recognised by the top management at Shell as a high-flyer but, while still in his twenties, was told that he really could not expect any further promotion before his fortieth birthday. The general refusal to hope for increased personal prosperity engendered the willingness to tolerate ridiculously high levels of personal taxation for the thirty-five years after the war. Indeed, when Conservatives talked about 'punitive taxation' they were right – it could even have been described as confiscatory since at one time it reached up to 98 per cent in the case of large unearned incomes and, inevitably, the yield from the upper end was negligible.

There were a handful of exceptions, companies able to recruit, and even more importantly to retain, intelligent young graduates. One was United Steel, whose alumni formed the core of the management group which saved British Steel in the 1980s. Another was Cadbury, a firm headed by a member of the founding family until well into the 1990s and which appointed the first non-family members to the board only after 1945. Nevertheless the firm recruited its first graduates – including a handful of women – in the 1920s and in the 1930s sent one or two members of the staff to Cambridge, an approach to management which helped ensure that it was only one of a handful of major British companies to have remained flourishing and independent until the twenty-first century. But Cadbury was an exception. It was Jewish refugees, generally scorned or despised, who provided most of the country's few industrial successes in the early post-war period. This can be seen in industries as varied as textiles (Miki Sekers) or publishing where refugees such as André Deutsch and George Weidenfeld demonstrated a mixture of cultural and business acumen not possessed by their British equivalents. Less culturnik was Paul Hamlyn, scion of a distinguished intellectual Jewish family from Berlin, whose offerings, aimed at the 'leisure' market were sneered at as 'coffee-table books for council houses'. The only alternative was American-owned companies – above all Ford, which was the nursery for an abnormally high proportion of the business talent that spread across British industry in the 1960s.

The uncommercial, unambitious mentality was accepted as the norm, an important part of the bland assumption of the superiority of the 'British exception'. 'Your real problem,' the American economist J. K. Galbraith told an interviewer from the BBC – itself an institution worshipped partly at least because it was profoundly uncommercial, 'is that you were the first of the great industrialised nations, and so things happen here first. You are living out the concern for some more leisurely relationship with industrial life that the other people have been discussing for fifty years or more.' There was the underlying thread: that Britain had for so long and so increasingly been dependent on the double crutches of the Empire – which took its goods, however primitive – and on trade and finance capitalism that there was none of the fundamental industrial tradition of France and Germany. Naturally, British society and its educational institutions were geared to serve a double purpose to provide bankers, civil servants and governors for the Colonies.

For their part, British manufacturers' reliance on this tied Imperial market was exacerbated after the war when the Labour government 'blocked' the 'sterling balances', money owed to the colonies by the British government. In doing so, they had, as Trevor Lloyd put it, 'created a slightly artificial market in countries which held sterling and could not do anything with it except buy British goods'.[32] The French were in much the same situation until the creation of the Common Market in the late 1950s forced their industrialists to compete on increasingly equal terms with their – generally far more sophisticated – German equivalents.

As so often throughout the period, the established right was joined by the supposedly radical left in expressing a basically conservative viewpoint, in this instance a scorn for 'mere' economic growth. Typical, and powerful, was the voice of the venerable radical writer J. B. Priestley who coined the term 'admass', which he described as 'the whole system of an increasing productivity, plus inflation, plus a rising standard of material living, plus high-pressure advertising and salesmanship, plus mass communication, plus cultural democracy and the creation of the mass mind, the mass man ... it is better to live in admass than to have no job, no prospects of one, and see your wife and children getting hungrier and hungrier. But this is about all that can be said in favour of it'. His words were echoed by Richard Hoggart, who believed that working-class people 'number several vices among their occupational attitudes, but not those of the "go-getter" or the "live wire"' – and I don't believe that he was being ironic in using the word 'vice'. This was perfectly expressed by the refusal to believe in economic advancement either at the national or personal level if it were to be accompanied by anything as vulgar as advertising.

Inevitably, there was virtually none of the interaction between university and business that had been one of the major secrets of the German industrial success since the middle of the nineteenth century. For, as Anthony Sampson pointed out: 'In general the less practical scientists are, the higher is their prestige. For their part few British companies encouraged research.'[33] According to the great scientist Sir Patrick Blackett there were only 12,000 scientists and engineers doing research funded by private industry in post-war Britain. And by far the biggest centres of research were linked to the needs of the Ministry of Defence.

The fault lay on both sides. The attitude of academics towards industry was well summed up by C. S. Lewis. 'How I hate that man,' he wrote of Lord Nuffield, a major benefactor to his university, in a classic demonstration of the Oxbridge capacity to sneer at a hand that was feeding the university so lavishly. Oddly, although Cambridge, far and away the country's leading academic centre of science and engineering, remained as aloof as Lewis, Oxford showed signs of accepting industry. But at Oxford the science departments, backward and largely amateurish before the 1930s, were largely staffed by immigrants many invited by one of their number Freddy Lindemann, Lord Cherwell, who had woken up the Clarendon Laboratory. British-based scientists had failed to patent penicillin and had to pay royalties to American firms which had devised ways of mass-producing the miracle drug. But when Edward Abraham discovered another antibiotic, cephalosporin, Oxford got the message and still benefits from the royalties. And Nicholas Kurti of the Clarendon was highly enthusiastic when Martin Wood went to him with ideas for exploiting the specialised electrical magnets he was making, leading to Wood's foundation of Oxford Instruments.

If the major universities were smug, the Church of England 'as by law established' was even more hidebound and still very powerful, even though attendance at the churches of all Protestant denominations had been declining at a steady rate of 10 per cent for every decade since the 1920s. Not for nothing was it known as the Tory Party at prayer – as witness the comment made by the Archbishop of Canterbury, Dr Fisher, after a visit to South Africa in 1955 that 'All men are not equal in the sight of God though they are equal in the love of God'. The church was class-based not only because there was a far higher proportion of churchgoers in rural and middle-class areas but also because priests were of a type designed to serve them. Typical was the ordination in 1955 of David Shepherd, captain of the England cricket team the previous year, although he turned out to have a far broader social vision than was typical of the priesthood at the time. It was no surprise that the chairman of the house of laity, the most senior layman, was the Earl of Selborne. Looking at distinguished figures lay and clerical such as Dorothy L. Sayers and C. S. Lewis, Adrian Hastings remarked, perhaps too benevolently, that they were 'seldom reactionary but rather reassuringly conservative'. Nor were their thoughts subversive. Possibly the most important books written by clerics in the 1950s were the Reverend William Awdry children's books about Thomas the Tank Engine and C. S. Lewis's popular works, none of them likely to stir the populace to revolt.

Nor was Churchill himself likely to disturb the status quo, the sleepy consensus of the time. Never a 'true Tory' – after all he had spent over twenty years of his long political life as a Liberal – in his last four years in office between 1951 and 1955 he took good care not to upset the changes instituted by the Attlee government in the six years immediately after the war. There was little privatisation and a generally co-operative attitude towards the trades unions. The 'reactionary' elements of his administration were confined to a generally repressive social atmosphere. Yet, as Peter Wilby noted, 'The 1950s were remarkably liberal with respect to drink-driving, to violence in the home against both women and children, to sadistic teachers, to aggressively racial language. Would we prefer a world where it is acceptable to call a man a "dirty nigger" to one where you can say "fuck" on television?'[34]

The general mood was perhaps best reflected in the acts and attitudes of a key group which included Archbishop Fisher. They were reflecting a moral world which, as Jonathon Green put it, 'at least as far as the Statute Book was concerned, was barely altered from that of a century earlier'.[35] The most public face of reaction was the Lord Chief Justice, Rayner, Lord Goddard*, who openly believed in the deterrent effects

* Goddard was so dominant that when he was attacked by the journalist Bernard Levin the lawyer members of the Garrick Club ganged up to blackball Levin's application for membership

of hanging, and, more unusually for the time, in flogging as well. Indeed a contemporary at Marlborough remembers* that when Goddard was a new boy, he had to submit to a ritual of having to sing. The sound was so awful that he preferred to recite. 'His choice? The striking and solemn words of the death sentence.'

Notes

1. Faber & Faber 1998.
2. *Change in British Society*, Oxford University Press, 1995.
3. *Our Age*, Weidenfeld & Nicolson, 1990.
4. *Classes and Cultures, England 1918–1951*, Oxford University Press, 1998.
5. *The People's Peace*, OUP 1990.
6. *The Age of Affluence*, edited by Vernon Bogdanor and Robert Skidelsky, Macmillan, 1972.
7. *Intellectuals and the Powers*, University of Chicago Press London 1972.
8. Charles Webster, *The National Health Service, A Political History*, Oxford University Press, 1998.
9. Bill Deedes, *Dear Bill*, Macmillan 1997.
10. Jonathon Green, *All Dressed Up, The Sixties and the Counter-culture* Jonathan Cape 1996.
11. *The Best Years of their Lives*, Michael Joseph, 1986.
12. Charles Hill, *Both Sides of the Hill* Heinemann 1963.
13. James Walvin, *Football and the Decline of Britain* Macmillan 1986.
14. *'Britain Awake'* in *Labour's New Frontiers*, Andre Deutsch, 1964.
15. S. J. Taylor, *The Reluctant Press Lord*, Weidenfeld & Nicolson London 1998.
16. *New Statesman*, December 18, 1998.
17. *The Dark Valley*, Jonathan Cape, 2000.
18. *London Review of Books*, July 15, 1999.
19. *With Malice towards Some,* Simon & Schuster, New York, 1938.
20. *New Yorker*, September 21, 1998.
21. *England: An Elegy*, Chatto & Windus, 2000.
22. *The Rise of the Meritocracy, 1970–2033*, Thames & Hudson 1958.
23. *New Statesman*, August 7, 2000.
24. *England, Half English*, Macgibbon & Kee 1961.
25. *Collected Poems* John Murray.
26. *The Miners' Strike, 1984–1985*, Routledge and Kegan Paul, 1986.
27. David Dimbleby & David Reynolds *An Ocean Apart*, Hodder & Stoughton 1988.
28. *English culture and the decline of the industrial spirit, 1850–1980*, Cambridge University Press, 1980.
29. *The Guardian*, April 17, 1999.

* Recorded by Patrick Higgins, *Heterosexual dictatorship*, Fourth Estate 1996.

30. *The Uses of Literacy* Chatto & Windus 1957.
31. David Kynaston, *The City of London, A Club No More*, Chatto & Windus, 2001.
32. *Empire, Welfare State, Europe*, Oxford University Press, 1993.
33. *The New Anatomy of Britain,* Hodder & Stoughton 1971.
34. *New Statesman*, June 19 2000.

4

Shaking the Foundations

'It is the loss of one more element of civilisation . . . we used to trust our colleagues absolutely.'

HAROLD NICOLSON

THE MOMENT AT WHICH 'Britain-as-we-knew-it' started to crumble can be dated with some precision. It was on Friday May 26, 1951, nine months before the Queen came to the throne, when Donald Maclean, a senior diplomat and his disreputable, if well-connected friend Guy Burgess left England on their way to Zurich and thence to Moscow. Their flight provided by far the most shaking event of the first years of the 1950s, the first intimation that All Was Not Well, the first of the many events through which the British Establishment committed suicide over the following fifty years. In terms of national security, the flight's importance was more symbolic than real; in some respects, it even resembled an upmarket undergraduate lark. Burgess followed Maclean out of loyalty not the need to escape – it was Maclean who was due for questioning by MI5. Moreover their plans were sketchy in the extreme, and one of Burgess's main concerns was to ensure that he took with him a precious possession, the works of Jane Austen.

Nevertheless the shock was enormous. Robert Cecil, a friend of Maclean's and his deputy and successor in the American department of the Foreign Office, told Patrick Higgins how 'the defection plunged Whitehall into a state of shock, in which nobody, Ministers included, grasped the need to recognise what had happened and limit the damage. Instead, all hopes were pinned on recapturing the defectors and repressing all information. It was an understandable reaction, but it resembled that of a driver who, after a fatal accident, walks away from the scene, trying to convince himself that it was a nightmare that will eventually go away. The Diplomatic Service with its links to the throne had always gone on the assumption that its loyalty was irrefragable; that its status and tradition set it apart from, and above, the rest of the Civil Service . . . At one blow this whole framework of mutual confi-

56

dence and trust had been shattered . . . Two intelligent men from the right class had been practising disloyalty for sixteen years.'

The flight naturally reinforced Our Rulers' obsession with 'soundness' rather than intelligence, let alone originality. Moreover Burgess was well-known to be homosexual. Inevitably homosexuals felt no loyalty to a society which persecuted them. So the term 'homintern' for Burgess, for another homosexual traitor, Sir Anthony Blunt, and for the bi-sexual Maclean was not inappropriate. Their sexual tendencies had certainly been appreciated by the KGB. The agent who recruited them was a psychologist who had worked with William Reich, a famous expert in matters sexual.

For Britain was unique amongst civilised nations in its treatment of male homosexuals, who were deemed to be criminal if any homosexual act were committed, even between consenting adult males*. Some homosexuals even made a virtue out of necessity. John Sparrow, the Warden of All Souls, thought that the two things essential to homosexual pleasure were the sense of guilt and the dangers of disgrace and imprisonment.

Until their activities were legalised in 1967, there were, broadly, two alternative routes for homosexuals, neither very appealing: either they flaunted their homosexuality, knowing that they would routinely be described as fairies, queens or pansies, or, as was far more often the case, they could conceal their inmost feelings and spend a tortured life pretending not to be 'that way'. Not that homosexuals were necessarily outcasts. As one of Nigel Dennis's characters in *Cards of Identity* put it: 'I am a well-to-do revered and powerful figure. The establishment which we call England has taken me in: I am become her Fortieth Article.† I sit upon her Boards, I dominate her stage, her museums, her dances and her costumes; I have an honoured voice in her elected House. To her – and her alone – I bend the knee, and in return for my homage, she is gently blind to my small failings, asking only that I indulge them privately.'

Some homosexuals, like Noel Coward, became courtiers to royalty, most obviously to the Queen Mother, and to a middle-class audience – right up until his death in 1970 Coward refused to admit his homosexuality in public even after it had been legalised, because it would put off his natural audience, the 'Aunt Ednas'. This was the term coined by another homosexual playwright, Terence Rattigan, to describe the comfortable middle-class, usually suburban, audience for the West End

---

* I have always understood that the failure to extend the legislation to lesbians derived from the unwillingness of the Home Secretary of the day to explain the nature of their activities to Queen Victoria.
† The Church of England had 39 Articles of Faith.

theatre of the day. In the original version of his play *Separate Tables*, first performed in 1954, the retired major's offence which so shook the small seaside hotel in which the play is set was not molesting women in cinemas (in the end tolerance prevails and he is allowed back) but importuning male persons on the esplanade at Bournemouth. But Rattigan would not use this version because he didn't want his mother to know he was homosexual.

The pace of persecution (there really is no other way to describe what was happening) accelerated in the early 1950s. Prosecutions for gross indecency, the most common accusation against homosexuals, which had run at about 800 a year before the war, had risen to 2,300 in 1953 – although part of the increase was due to a change in the way that the statistics were collected: after 1949 every offence counted, whereas previously they had been lumped together. The police used handsome young constables as agents provocateurs in public lavatories where homosexuals would go 'cottaging' – it has been proposed that the public lavatory in North London frequented by the playwright Joe Orton should be adorned with one of the blue plaques awarded to places associated with important figures. Nevertheless, as Patrick Higgins says, 'the Met tolerated the homosexual subculture in the West End'[1] partly because they did not want to offend too many influential people. Moreover the Met was decidedly corrupt, as open to bribes from leading homosexuals as it was to those from pimps and pornographers – although the Commissioner of the Metropolitan Police himself was a stern supporter of prosecution.

More important was the attitude towards homosexuals, and indeed the death penalty, shared by Lord Goddard and two successive Home Secretaries. Sir David Maxwell Fyfe, later Lord Kilmuir, described as 'a Scot on the make at Oxford', was a former disciple of Neville Chamberlain and had been clever enough to have got the better of Goering at the Nuremberg trials: he had called for a new drive against 'male vice' – although he apparently left the Cabinet table whenever the subject was discussed. He was followed by Gwilym Lloyd George, son of David Lloyd George. Both men were backed by their permanent secretary, Sir Frank Newsam, once portrayed as a 'handsome womaniser and reactionary', and Sir Theobald Mathew, a strict Roman Catholic, who had been the Director of Public Prosecutions since 1944.

Much of the increased pressure was due to Mathew. He was immensely influential and the fact that he spent most of his leisure time hob-nobbing with policemen ensured that they backed his ideas. A real prig, he had refused to act for Mrs Simpson in her divorce case but his campaign against homosexuals had a major redeeming feature, for it was largely based on a desire to stamp out the abuse of adolescents which was a major feature of school life, especially in the private schools which then housed a great many homeless children. Indeed, in the 1950s about three quarters of the cases at assizes involved children under the age of sixteen. Mathew persuaded the Department of Education to keep a blacklist of convicted homosexual offenders and the Home Office issued a circular to all institutions housing children and young people instructing managers to record even the smallest instance of homosexual behaviour. Nevertheless he did not distinguish between cases involving the young and those between consenting adults.

The ministers and their officials were supported by supposedly reputable journals like *The* [Medical] *Practitioner* which explained that sexual vice meant 'the slow death of the race', a view echoed by the ineffably named Captain Athelstan Popkiss, Chief Constable of Nottingham, who was speaking for his fellow policemen. They were joined by editorialists like John Gordon, the sulphurously right-wing editor and columnist of the *Sunday Express*, which then enjoyed a circulation of over three million. An even more prominent, and at first sight improbable, ally, was Hugh, later Lord Cudlipp, overlord of the most faithful Labour supporters in the press, the *Daily Mirror* and its Sunday partners the *People* and the *Sunday Pictorial*. Cudlipp, wrote Patrick Higgins, 'played a major part in the development of a tradition which vilified homosexuality ... what is more he has boasted of the fact.'

In 1952 Cudlipp had just returned to the *Sunday Pictorial* as editor and was anxious to make an impression. He was lucky to find an informer who described the appalling practices involving pupils at the fashionable London Choir School and at the end of May 1952 he opened his campaign with a three-part series entitled 'Evil Men', the first major examination of what Cudlipp called 'the homosexual problem'. This, like so many irresponsible press campaigns throughout the ages, was framed as a courageous breaking of 'the last taboo' – in this instance any serious discussion of homosexual problems. As Higgins says, this 'great scoop ... presented a completely negative and hostile picture of male homosexuality' – in whatever form it might take – 'and was intended to titillate and terrify the readers of the newspapers, to promote ignorance, intolerance and hatred.'[2] The only editorial voice against this attitude was that of the *Observer*, whose editor David Astor described Gordon and the others as speaking 'in the rabble-rousing tone of the witch-hunt'. In 1955 the *New Statesman* joined in, publishing an article by the homosexual novelist E. M. Forster pointing out the futility of trying to prosecute homosexuals.

The impact of the persecution varied wildly. The many homosexuals in the theatrical profession were protected by an informal – and almost certainly corrupt – understanding between the police and 'Binkie'

Beaumont, the homosexual theatrical impresario who dominated the London theatrical scene. One bi-sexual actor, the late Sir Alec Guinness, had managed to escape prosecution when caught 'cottaging' by giving his name as 'Herbert Pocket', the name of the Dickensian character he happened to be playing in a film at the time. Virtually the only important theatrical victim of the law was Sir John Gielgud, caught by the police in a public lavatory while in a mood of depression. He was so innocent, so ashamed of being caught, that he gave his name as 'Gielgud', did not tell his close friend Beaumont and was fined; his offence was noted even though he had called himself a 'clerk' (he was betrayed by the unmistakable sound of his voice). He was shattered by the experience – even though his first appearance on stage after the incident was greeted with rapturous applause.

The single most prominent victim of the law was Lord Montagu, who went to jail after he had been caught at a notorious weekend party in the summer of 1953 in a beach hut he owned near Beaulieu in Hampshire. The arrests were made on a Saturday, thus providing the Sunday press with suitably sensational headlines. Montagu was there with a brilliant young journalist, Peter Wildeblood, and a group which included a Dorset landowner, Michael Pitt-Rivers and a couple of RAF servicemen. 'The party which followed,' wrote Wildeblood, 'has achieved more notoriety than any other since the days of Nero but I feel bound to confess that it was, in fact, extremely dull.'[3] Wildeblood was described as 'an adult man who has chosen a homosexual way of life [and] has done so because he knows that no other course is open to him . . . One of the charges often levelled against homosexuals is that they tend to form a compact and exclusive group. They can hardly be expected to do anything else, since they are legally excluded from the rest of the community.'

The servicemen confessed, although only after very lengthy interrogations. Montagu, Wildeblood and Pitt-Rivers faced a number of charges including 'conspiracy to incite acts of gross indecency'. This was the first time this charge had been used since the trials of Oscar Wilde. Patrick Higgins believed that the prosecution lawyer had studied some of the accounts that had been appearing at the time. Their conviction relied less on the evidence of the airmen as on the shock of finding that gently-born persons could have a romantic attachment with the lower orders. 'Class, as much as sexual prejudice,' wrote Philip Hoare, 'secured their conviction . . . The lower-class servicemen were deemed to be far more guilty than their upper-class partners, part of whose guilt was to associate with the lower orders.'[3]

Although those involved in the Montagu trial survived more or less intact, quite a number of homosexuals committed suicide after they had been 'outed'. The most spectacular case was that of Alan Turing.

The circumstances of Turing's death had haunted me for some years before I started work on this book and had already rid me of any regrets I might have had over the passing of the England of the 1950s. To me Turing's story is the perfect example of a tragedy that distils the low, narrow, unforgiving, hypocritical meanness of the Britain of the early 1950s. For he combined, as did no other twentieth-century Englishman except John Maynard Keynes, three qualities: he was an original genius in his own field of intellectual enquiry; he was able to translate his theories into practice; and he performed outstanding wartime service for his country.

Turing was handsome*, though he did not think he was, and a notable athlete – probably only a leg injury prevented him from a place in the 1948 British Olympic team. Already at Sherborne, where he had spent much of his time studying Einstein's theory of relativity, he had been labelled as a 'genius' by a perceptive teacher. Yet he never thought of himself as superior despite his superior intellect, though he hated anything 'phoney', a favourite term. He could be friendly but as a younger colleague, Peter Hilton, said, 'You always felt there was lots more you did not know anything about.' Even at school he had demonstrated his delight that, as Alan Hodges put it, 'a mathematical formula could actually work in the physical world'.[4] He duly won a scholarship to King's College Cambridge, where he felt at home for the rest of his life, for it was not so much tolerant of homosexuals as largely composed of them. This was a major disadvantage since this holy innocent took it for granted that everyone in the world outside King's took his sexual preferences as normal. Unfortunately they didn't.

By the end of 1933 he was striving to relate the abstract and the physical, with an astonishing result. In 1936 he published a paper, 'On computable numbers', which laid the foundation of the science and practice of computing. In envisaging what has been called ever since a Universal Turing Machine, he separated out the two functions: the programming and storage of information and what we would now call the number-crunching phenomenon. In doing so he redefined the word 'computer' not, as it had been previously understood, as the person doing the sums but as a machine. 'He had argued,' wrote Hodges, 'that anything performed by a human computer could be done by a machine. So there could be a single machine which, by reading the descriptions of other machines placed upon its ''tape'' could perform the equivalent of human mental activity! An electronic brain! . . . His machines offered a bridge, a connection between abstract symbols,

* Hence a college rhyme: 'Turing / Must have been alluring / To get made a don / So early on.'

61

and the physical world. Indeed his imagery was, for Cambridge, almost shockingly industrial.'

During the war he was the unquestioned intellectual leader – 'the Prof' as he was affectionately known – at Bletchley Park, the code-breaking centre which played so vital a role in Britain's war effort. He was one of the four scientists who protested directly to Churchill about the lack of resources (they got results within twenty-four hours). Only at Bletchley did he find the perfect combination, 'getting to the heart of something, abstracting its meaning and connecting it with something that worked in the physical world'. As he did so, his was the key role in abstracting the meaning of the most impenetrable and in many ways most vital codes, those used by the German U-boats. But, characteristically, once the problem had been solved, and having no interest in organising the results, he let the British chess champion, Hugh Alexander, take over and moved off to Hynslope, 'a remote station of the new Sigint empire, working with one assistant in a small hut, and thinking in his spare time, an English homosexual mathematician had conceived of the computer'. By the end of 1945, working in one of the intense bursts that characterised his intellectual progress, he had come up with the basis for ACE, the Advanced Computing Engine. The last nine years of his life were an anti-climax. Bureaucracy prevented the creation of a real-life ACE when he worked at the National Physical Laboratory, and he was never part of the key group that produced the world's first real computer while he was at Manchester University. By then he had, characteristically, moved on to use the machine to study problems of life itself

But then Turing foolishly and innocently reported to the police a robbery involving a friend of a young working-class lover. As a result, he was convicted of indecent behaviour, and although not imprisoned, he was put on probation and forced to take hormones to 'cure' him of his 'disease'. On the evening of June 7 1954 he committed suicide by injecting an apple with cyanide. He had always suffered from fits of depression, especially after a major burst of intellectual activity. In the 1930s, indeed, he had thought of a scheme for ending his life involving an apple and electrical wiring – the deadly potential of the fruit had always appealed to him ever since he had seen *Snow White* in which the witch dangled an apple on a string into a boiling pot of poison muttering:

> Dip the apple in the brew
> Let the Sleeping Death seep through

He was cremated privately, in the presence of his mother, his brother and a single friend, his ashes scattered near those of his father. Nearly fifty years later there is still no monument to him, as if the British were so ashamed of his fate that they prefer not to be reminded of him, or of his enormous contributions to his ungrateful country in peace as well in wartime.

Nevertheless, as so often was the case in that supposedly inert period, the early 1950s, the seeds were being sown of future change. In 1953 the Church of England Moral Welfare Council set up an enquiry resulting the next year in a liberal document, *The Problem of Homosexuality*, suggesting that homosexuality was a matter for the individual liberal conscience. The same year a mission from that temple of political incorrectness, the Home Office, was despatched to the United States to learn about policy towards prostitution and that other live contemporary subject, parking meters. It was led by Philip Allen, later as Sir Philip the Permanent Secretary, and it was his report, to which homosexuality was added, which led to a departmental committee on the two (consideration of parking meters came later). This in turn set in motion the Wolfenden Committee on Prostitution and Homosexuality, which itself opened the subject to public debate. In his report in 1957 Wolfenden rejected the idea in that homosexuals menaced national stability. As Jeffrey Weeks put it: 'Wolfenden expressed at the same time 1950s moral anxieties and [provided] a blueprint for the "permissive" legislation of the 1960s.' A plea in a letter to *The Times* for immediate implementation led to the foundation of the Homosexual Law Reform Society.

The general pattern of obvious injustice caused by the intemperate zeal of a handful of officials was backed by a public mood in which a combination of police casualness, to put it mildly, the blind faith of the judiciary in their probity, combined with racial prejudice, could easily lead to appalling miscarriages of justice. In 1952 a simple-minded Somali, Mahmood Mattan, described by his defence lawyer as 'a half-child of nature, a semi-civilised savage', was hanged in Cardiff for a murder he clearly had not committed – he had four witnesses providing an alibi, while four others had failed to identify Mattan in an identity parade. The key prosecution witness was paid to give evidence and in 1969 was jailed for life for trying to kill his daughter. It took until 2001 for the Home Office to award £1.4 million compensation to Mattan's family.

With the death penalty, as with homosexuality, individual cases could lead to a change in public attitudes. One that helped to turn the public against the death penalty was that of Christopher Craig and Derek Bentley. Craig had killed a man, but he escaped the hangman because he was only sixteen at the time. The mentally subnormal Bentley was hanged even though he had been armed only with a knife and a knuckle-duster and his only role had been to encourage Craig with a cry that condemned him to the gallows of 'Give it to him, Chris'. Decisions about the death penalty appeared to be somewhat arbitrary. Lloyd George had reprieved a woman who had murdered a lady of eighty-six by battering her head in with a spade but no such mercy was shown to Bentley or to Ruth Ellis, the last woman to be executed in Britain, who was hanged for murdering a faithless lover.

Lloyd George later told an interviewer that he had allowed the execution to go through because some of the bullets she had fired had missed and, he said, 'I was determined to ensure that people could use the streets without fear of a bullet.' This implied, absurdly, that had she been a better shot she would have got off. But perhaps the most pathetic and telling aspect of the whole affair was that, although Ellis thought she was perfectly justified in shooting her lover – and indeed wanted to demonstrate this to the court and the public – she thought she should hang. Why? Because, she told the police, 'she was born humble and had tried to rise above her station in life'. As I found when on holiday in France at the time, the French were shocked by the idea that a woman should be hanged, or even punished at all severely, for so eminently comprehensible a *crime passionel*.

That same year, 1954, another, much more clear-cut, case revealed that British justice, and above all the death penalty, could lead to disaster. That year it became abundantly clear that Timothy Evans, a Welsh van driver with an estimated IQ of a mere 70, was innocent of the murder of his wife and small daughter for which he had been hanged four years earlier. Their house, 10 Rillington Place in West London, became notorious when another tenant, John Christie, confessed that it was he who had killed them as well as six other women. The case remains famous, or rather infamous, to this day as a reminder of the barbarity of life in Britain in the early 1950s. The next year a bill abolishing the death penalty, proposed by the campaigning Labour MP Sidney Silverman, passed the House of Commons, despite its Tory majority, but was defeated in the House of Lords. Nevertheless in the decade before the death penalty was finally abolished hangings became increasingly infrequent.

In the curious atmosphere, not so much of change, as of a general restlessness within the overriding smugness, even the Coronation in June 1953 was a pointer to the future. To the royal court and the elderly adherents to the much-publicised, totally ridiculous quasi-religious idea of the New Elizabethan Age, it was a sign of the power of royal religion, an 'act of national communion' by 'one great national family'. At the time of the Coronation of this apparently vulnerable, obviously devout and dutiful Queen, surrounded by much, much older men, the notion did not appear altogether ridiculous. There was indeed, as the Annual Register put it, 'a religion of royalism'.

The occasion itself may have been 'a shining moment of brilliantly stage-managed unreality', but the decision to televise the ceremony – taken on the insistence of the Queen and the Duke of Edinburgh after much hesitation and early opposition from Churchill and the government – marked the end of royal seclusion. From then on the public felt entitled to be admitted to any major royal event. For ironically this, the most traditional event of the second half of the twentieth century, marked the start of its most profound cultural revolution, the arrival of television. Before the Coronation even broadcasters sneered down on television from on high. As Trevor Lloyd put it, within the BBC 'the Third Programme absorbed too much of the energy of the Corporation and led it to neglect television as something that should be regarded as subordinate to sound broadcasting'. In 1946 Robert Barr*, a former war correspondent, moved from radio to television. When he returned to Broadcasting House, a senior sound producer ran into him at the door. ' "Good Lord, I thought you were dead." "No, I'm not," said Barr, "No? Ah yes, gone to television; same thing old chap." '[5] Behind the condescension was a load of apprehension. 'Television will abolish newspapers, cinemas, the stage and reading,' wrote Harold Nicolson in his diary, 'and is the *deinotatos* [the Greek for most powerful] force ever invented.'

The boost given to television by the Coronation changed all that. Even more fundamentally, the Coronation greatly helped the idea of commercial television. Within three months, three fifths of the public was in favour of it, the same percentage as had favoured the continuation of the BBC monopoly before the event – a degree of dissatisfaction probably caused by the dreariness of the BBC's normal television programmes, interrupted as they often were by intervals showing a potter's wheel and other sleep-inducing images. The arrival of independent television two years later was the first sign of a new phenomenon, the intrusion of – by definition vulgar – commercialism in British public life and the arrival of a mass of outsiders into positions of ever-increasing influence. Its importance was immediately perceived by George Thomson, then as a Labour MP an opponent of commercial televison but later chairman of the Independent Television Authority, who saw the project raising an issue 'at least equal to, and, it seems to me, possibly of greater importance than the death penalty'.

It was Selwyn Lloyd, a future Foreign Secretary and Chancellor of the Exchequer but then a backbencher, who had started the ball rolling in 1949 in a minority report for the Beveridge Committee which had proposed the continuation of the BBC monopoly, suggesting a new channel paid for by advertisements or sponsorship. As the

* He later went on to write Z Cars

proposals became clearer they were seen to have three objectives 'to introduce an element of competition and to enable private enterprise to play a fuller part, to reduce the financial commitments of the state to a minimum and to proceed with caution to safeguard against "the lowering of standards." '[6] The whole system would be supervised by a controlling authority reporting to the Postmaster-General. Its name, the Independent Television Authority, was suggested by Norman Collins in the course of a dinner, appropriately enough in the Reform Club.

Collins was the real begetter of the whole idea. He was a popular novelist and the inventor of the Light Programme, the first breach in the basic Reithian concept that all the BBC's programmes should combine education and entertainment. Until October 1950 he had been controller of BBC Television but resigned because George Barnes, the former 'Director of the Spoken Word' – a truly BBC job description – had been appointed to the new role of Director of Television. Collins saw this as an indication that the BBC's 'vested interest in sound broadcasting' would limit the growth of television. His first step was to form High Definition Films, recruiting many of the key figures, above all the engineers, who were to ensure that ITV became a reality. A combination of his unique experience in TV and his personal crusade made him the key figure in the fight, especially after he had joined forces with C.O. Stanley, the boss of Pye Radio, and an important industrialist, Sir Robert Renwick.

In the ensuing conflict the battle-lines were not clearly drawn – even the Radio Industry Council did not fight for the introduction of commercial television and some of Collins' own family were horrified at the idea. This was not only because it was commercial. It was also perceived to be, indeed was, the only aspect of British life that was classless, hence the long-entrenched attitude of so many 'intellectuals'. The opposition was often linguistic, as in the use of the term 'Goggle-box' to diminish the status of television as a whole, or calling the new idea 'commercial' rather than 'independent' television.

But the basic attitude of 'people of superior mental constitution', as Sir Robert Fraser called them*, was that 'in their hearts they despise popular pleasures and interests' and that as a result they will naturally 'be angrily dissatisfied with television' – and above all the commercial variety. 'But,' he added, 'it is not really television with which they are dissatisfied. It is with people.' As Trevor Lloyd put it, 'Traditionalists had calculated the situation fairly accurately when they tried to

---

* In an address to the Manchester Luncheon Club in 1960. Fraser was the first Director-General of the Independent Television Authority. He was Australian and a socialist, although, unlike his British counterparts, free from any anti-commercial bias.

resist commercial television. It promoted a view of society which was much more like a market place than the orderly system of deference to one's betters which the traditionalists had hoped to see re-established, and it challenged the idea that some affairs of State were too important to be discussed in public which had been one of the strengths of the system of deference.'

The attitude of what was soon to be called The Establishment came out in a letter at the time of the Coronation to *The Times* which was inspired by Christopher Mayhew, broadcaster and Labour MP, and included as its signatories such ultra-establishment figures as Lady Violet Bonham Carter – an influential woman, the daughter of Earl Asquith and a friend of Churchill. The cause of their lobby, the National Television Council, had been greatly helped at the Coronation by the frolickings of a chimpanzee named J. Fred Muggs who featured in the advertisements which had interrupted the ceremony when it was shown on American TV. The opposition to commercial television included a mix of the established like Lord Derby, later the chairman of a regional TV consortium and Conservative MPs such as Ronald Symms as well as oddballs such as the script writer Ted Kavanagh, the comedian Gillie Potter, the cricketer Alec Bedser and the veteran novelist Somerset Maugham – an unprecedentedly mixed *galère* but the prototype for many such lobbies in the future. Nevertheless, as Lord Brabazon of Tara observed, 'When you look at this coalition of *The Times*, their friends, the Archbishop and the Labour Party it cannot be right; there must be something "phoney" about it.' More fundamental was the worry over the creeping advent of consumerism. 'There is now.' wrote J. B. Priestley, 'a vast crowd that is a permanent audience waiting to be amused . . . cash customers screaming for their money's worth, all fixed in a consumer's attitude. They look on at more and more, and join in less and less.'

One argument, that sponsored programmes inevitably implied a more direct control by the advertisers, was deflated by the Postmaster General, Earl de la Warr, when he confirmed that 'the station not the advertisers [would be] responsible for the programmes'. Moreover the proponents of the idea could use the words of a former Joint Director-General of the BBC, Sir Frederick Ogilvie, who pointed up just how useful it was for the government to have the BBC at its disposal as a monopoly broadcaster, 'a powerful efficient instrument which has all the appearance of independence but which by the existing provisions of the Charter and licence it can control at will'. Further-more, 'no matter how efficiently it is run, the BBC, good as it is, would gain vastly by the abolition of monopoly and the introduction of competition.'

The passage of the Bill to establish commercial television in the

House of Commons was greatly assisted by the fact that the government had a majority of only sixteen, so the relatively small group of 'Libertarians' had more influence than they would have done if the government had enjoyed a more substantial majority. The debate, wrote Sendall, 'represented the fullest and most conscientious examination of broadcasting policy by the elected representatives of the British people that has taken place at any time before or since.' It was also by far the most contentious and revolutionary measure debated in Parliament during the otherwise placid first five years of the decade. In the end it went through by 302 to 280. The debate did, however, contain some lighter moments notably in the discussion about balance – an obsession of all those in authority – when a young MP, Anthony Wedgwood Benn, as he then styled himself, observed that 'a Liberal must never be allowed to talk about bee-keeping without a Tory talking about fish'.

But the arguments underlying the idea were best expressed in a two-day debate in the House of Lords at the end of November 1953, a debate whose first day extended until the unprecedented hour of 11 pm. All the speakers were agreed that, as the Archbishop of Canterbury put it, 'television is an instrument of immense influence upon the social life and habits and thoughts of the people'. The debate was opened by a lengthy oration – for once an appropriate use of the word – from the late Lord Hailsham, quoting extensively from the Bible and everyone from Milton to P. G. Wodehouse without providing much enlightenment.

The arguments against were largely based on an extreme condescension to the supposed childishness of the British people. The distinguished courtier, Viscount Esher, stated that 'the Government propose to let down the Elizabethan Age . . . I find it shameful for Parliament itself to undermine the improving standards of our young [!] democracy by giving sanction and prestige to a project based on nothing but money. Surely it is shameful also to plunge the innocent people of this country into a planned and premeditated orgy of vulgarity.' 'We should not,' said Lord Ammon, a veteran Labour stalwart, ' "give the people what they want", but rather seek to educate them and guide them in the same manner that the BBC has done for so long.'

Moreover, opined that pillar of the Establishment, Viscount Waverley, advertising might well encourage people to demand more goods: 'the purpose of advertisers is . . . to promote domestic consumption mainly, I should think, of non-essentials . . . I am profoundly apprehensive . . . more and more entertainment in present circumstances may mean less and less productive effort' – it seems never to have occurred to the Noble Viscount that people might actually work harder to earn the money to buy these 'non-essentials'. However, he had touched a nerve which was destined to twitch for the rest of the century: that the new consumerism ushered in by ITV was reprehensible in itself and resulted in excessive power being transferred to the world of advertising – to which later was added the public relations profession or the Hidden Persuaders as they were termed in an influential American book published at the time. Anyone with any knowledge of advertising will simply laugh at the idea given the failure of advertising, however powerful, to foist onto the British (or any other public for that matter) any product they did not like, want or need. The classic case must be Smash, the artificial mashed potato launched with one of the most memorable advertising campaigns of all time, with little aliens laughing at us earthlings peeling potatoes and uttering the catch-line, 'For Mash read Smash'. The product was awful – and failed utterly.

But the arguments in favour seem to have been more down to earth, more closely related to the British way of life, than those of the opponents. Typically, Lord Gifford made two shrewd points: that the BBC was not averse to transmitting sponsored material – Shell, for instance, had paid for a film about 'the Italian road race known as the Mille Miglia', and that it was notoriously mean in its payments to artists, like actors 'who were barely making a living because of the very limited employment open to them . . . if you [referring to writers] displease your sole employer, you are out'. Lord Foley added that many of the BBC's most-watched programmes were either American or, like *What's My Line*, based on an American original. The BBC's 'brute force of monopoly' in Lord Reith's words, had, as Lord Balfour of Inchrye pointed out, also prevented critics of the government – like Winston Churchill before the war – from being heard.

But the most startling speech came from the Marquess of Salisbury, head of a family which had been the guardian of the conservative conscience in Britain since his grandfather had been prime minister for over a decade at the turn of the century. So he was uniquely qualified to pour scorn on the conservatism of the opponents, quoting Hilaire Belloc's famous lines:

> And always keep a hold of nurse,
> For fear of getting something worse.

He went on to say how such feelings were 'found far more acutely among the old than among the young . . . is it right that we sexagenarians, septuagenarians and octogenarians should seek to impose the dead hand of age upon the youthful majority in favour of competition?' Here was the first public expression, from a most unlikely source, of the idea that the old had no right to dictate to the young.

Thanks to such support, the essentials of the idea were preserved and the final result provided Britain with what was – at least until the Thatcher reforms of the late 1980s – the best television services the world has ever seen, enjoying a unique independence from government and commercial interests alike. The controlling body, the Independent Television Authority, was left with powers that were real but expressed in deliberately vague terms, and its impartial attitude was boosted by a non-commercial approach, for the ITA never asked for a levy or royalty on the contractors' incomes profits, a demand which could have brought in a major bonanza to the government. It was not even pressured to provide quotas of British programmes (what, asked a Tory MP, would the authority decide about the *Marriage of Figaro*, 'an Austrian composer's score for the Italian adaptation of a French dramatist's play about a Spanish nobleman and his servants'?).

Nevertheless a feeling, almost universal amongst the Establishment, remained that the barbarians had entered the gates, an attitude not greatly softened by the presence of Sir Kenneth Clark, the former director of the National Gallery, as the first chairman of the ITA. Clark, who was booed when he entered the dining room of the Athenaeum Cub, then the London sanctuary of bishops, professors and their like, was an ambiguous figure. As Sendall puts it, 'he was a Jekyll and Hyde ... there was the Jekyll who launched ITV and saw it through its initial difficulties with brilliant success', then left after only three years saying that he hated to go – and promptly applied to Lew Grade for a job presenting arts programmes, the start of a career that was to culminate twelve years later in his mammoth series, *Civilisation*. Then there was the Hyde who had said that 'popular taste was bad taste, as any honest man with experience will agree' and who, less than a decade later, presented disparaging and destructive evidence to the Pilkington Committee (*see pp. 118–19*).

The first franchises were defined by the reach of the original transmitters and covered three major regions: London, the Midlands, and Lancashire and Yorkshire (which needed two transmitters, one each side of the Pennines). The service would be provided by four contractors, two serving London and the North from Monday to Friday evening, one for the Midlands during the week and London at the weekends and one serving both the Midlands and the North at the weekend. No-one involved could possibly have imagined what a bonanza these contracts would prove to be – which goes some way to excusing the cold feet displayed by so many well-placed persons during the birth pains of ITV. When it looked at candidates, it was inevitable that the ITA would prefer to rely on existing companies and their proprietors, above all the 'press lords'. In the event there were two separate waves of investors, with the second, which included some real outsiders, arriving after the more 'established' pioneers had lost their nerve.

The whole process showed clearly the generally gutless nature of the British corporate establishment. The London weekday franchise was originally awarded to a group which brought together Lord Rothermere's Associated Newspapers, which owned half the shares, and two companies, Rediffusion and British Electric Traction, both with radio experience (including relay and commercial radio) which had a quarter each. The station was run – commanded would have been a better word – by the extraordinary (and in principle totally unsuitable) figure of Captain Tom Brownrigg, RN. 'He was said,' commented Sendall, 'to have commanded A-R as if it were a battleship. Quite possibly the company was none the worse for it.' Certainly the creation and equipping of the studios – like the siting and construction of the transmitter network within a few months by the ITA itself – were extraordinary achievements totally alien to the lethargic pace of 1950s Britain and typical of the new dynamism represented by ITV.

Lord Kemsley, owner of a major regional chain of newspapers and of the *Sunday Times*, was the force behind the group founded by a former band leader, Maurice Winnick, which bid for the weekend franchise for the Midlands and the North of England. But, even before the contract was awarded, Kemsley ducked out after the ITA had given him time – far too much because of his importance – to make up his mind. His cowardice allowed in Associated British Pictures, the country's second-biggest cinema chain, even though its vice-chairman, Eric Fletcher, was a Labour MP and thus, in theory anyway, bitterly opposed to the whole idea. More importantly, it was part-owned by Warner Brothers and thus introduced a major foreign shareholder into what was supposed to be a wholly British operation.

The London Weekend-Midlands weekday franchise saw the dilution of Norman Collins's unspoken, though not unreasonable, hopes of becoming the uncrowned king of commercial television. Unfortunately his company, Associated Broadcasting Development, lacked adequate financial backing* and was forced to introduce a group called Incorporated Television. ITC, headed by the showman Prince Littler, brought into the equation not only the *Daily Mirror* but, more prominently, the Littlers and the Grades, kings of show business as agents, promoters and owners of such important variety theatres as the London Palladium. Outsiders, also Jews (as were their bankers S. G. Warburg), they represented precisely the sort of barbarians of whom the establishment was so afraid. The result was that Collins was sidelined in favour of

---

* It was said that it was 'Pye in the sky', a reference to its major backer, C. O. Stanley of Pye Radio.

the showman Val Parnell and the agent-turned-magnate Lew Grade, his only consolation the fortune he made from his shares

The only franchise that went to the original applicant was that for the North during the week. This was awarded to Granada, a cinema chain chaired by Sidney Bernstein, the most remarkable, most creative, most innovative figure in British broadcasting since Lord Reith, though there could have been no greater contrast than between the two: Reith, the austere, forbidding, self-doubting Scottish puritan, and Bernstein, the son of an Orthodox Jewish immigrant. He looked like a boxer with a nose flattened by an operation which gave him a not entirely misleading pugnacious look. He was the very model of the left-leaning. flairful, demanding, autocratic, simultaneously generous and petty-minded Jewish cultural entrepreneur with an obsessive desire to control every tiny detail of a concern he ran as a family company even when it had become a major organisation.

By his background, personality and previous career, he was an ideal candidate. Bernstein was a complex character, irascible and impatient but also good at being a peacemaker – though not nearly as good a negotiator as his brother Cecil. He was a loner, hating ceremony and the enforced social life normal in show business. He had inherited a small chain of cinemas and a variety theatre. In the 1930s he built up a chain of super-cinemas named after the Spanish city where he happened to be on holiday, while at the same time being an active supporter of the Film Society, devoted to showing uncommercial films. He also built a theatre – the Phoenix in Charing Cross Road – campaigning the while for a national theatre. During the war he was deeply involved in Britain's successful use of film for propaganda purposes before going to Hollywood and producing five of Alfred Hitchcock's most innovative albeit least successful films, most notably *Rope*, which was filmed in one long, continuous take.

Originally – like many of those in ITV – he had been against the idea in principle but, somewhat disingenuously, defended his decision to go in for a contract by saying that, with the entry of bigger businesses, he had no alternative but to do so. He first showed the originality of his approach in choosing the Northern franchise. As he later explained, this was based on two maps: one of population (large) and the other of average rainfall (high). His left-leaning sympathies nearly prevented him getting the franchise. Clark recounted how 'government circles put a good deal of pressure on the ITA to turn down the application.'[7] But Clark knew Bernstein well from his days at the Ministry of Information. He had asked MI5 for their opinion, and, according to his account anyway, threatened to resign it Bernstein were turned down. Like all the other pioneers, Granada had a bad start, exacerbated in his case by the fact that the Yorkshire transmitter did not start up for several months after Granada started broadcasting while at the same time ABC was offering attractive advertising packages round the north (and the Midlands) for showing at weekends. Fortunately Bernstein had cannily hedged his bets through a secret profit-sharing arrangement with Associated Rediffusion which proved to be an expensive insurance policy but preserved his independence.

At the outset, the hours in which commercial (or independent) television could transmit were limited, notably on Sunday with a closed period (the 'God slot') at the time of evensong*. In addition, any programme broadcast on Sunday afternoon would have to be designed for 'adult viewing' (in those innocent days a term which emphatically did *not* mean pornography) so that children would not be tempted to stay away from Sunday School. Another limitation was that, after a strike even before transmissions had started, the contractors agreed to employ their technical staff on the same rates and conditions as applied to those working on feature films†.

Despite these problems – and the BBC's spoiling tactic of killing off Grace Archer on the opening night – when ITV first burst on the scene in September 1955, it soon captured 80 per cent of the audience. Nevertheless the first year was nerve-racking enough for Lord Rothermere – a vacillating playboy at the best of times – to lose his nerve and sell out in possibly the single most costly commercial decision of the decade, seventeen months after broadcasting began and just before the station moved into ever-increasing profit – a decision made despite the death-bed pleadings of his brilliant managing director, Stuart MacLean.

By then the system was settling down. Among its key early decisions was the abandonment of much of the high-minded – but largely irrelevant and unappealing – programmes with which they applicants had tried to impress the ITA. Programmes began to feature an increasing proportion of quizzes and game shows like *Double Your Money*, compered by an irrepressible Canadian, Hughie Green. It was all part of what Sendall describes as a 'retreat from culture'. As Roland Gillett, the first (and short-lived) Programme Controller at Associated-Rediffusion put it rather tactlessly: 'the public likes girls, wrestling, bright musicals, quiz shows and real-life drama. We gave them the Hallé Orchestra, Foreign Press Club, floodlit football and visits to the local fire station. Well, we've learned. From now on, what the public

---

* 6.15–7.30 pm, in case you didn't know.

† These became more onerous in 1957 after Sam Spiegel had transported the crew shooting *Bridge On the River Kwai* to and from Ceylon (as it then was) on a cargo plane. The distinguished technicians involved were so angry that their union, the ACTT, decided that in future all such flights should be first-class, an enormous additional cost, especially for current affairs programmes.

wants, it's going to get.' Real barbarian stuff which the ITA was powerless to prevent, given the cash drain being suffered by the contractors – who, at the time, looked more like fledgling dot.com companies than the golden geese they were shortly to become. It did not help that, as Sendall points out, although the retreat lasted months rather than years 'the damage it did to ITV's reputation amongst the opinion-forming minority was much less speedily repaired. The chickens persisted in coming home to roost.'

ITV had its greatest success among the increasingly-affluent working classes. In the 1950s the lesser breeds started to indulge in an increasing variety of consumer durables – like the televisions bought in their millions and the cars bought in their hundreds of thousands. Moreover in the 1950s the wages of adolescents were rising faster than those of other age groups – by 1959 they had an estimated £830 million to spend, for they had few aspirations, they assumed that they had no prospects of advancement and would be confined for the rest of their lives to routine jobs so saw no reason not to spend all the money they earned. These youngsters could afford to rebel against their parents, indeed had no reason not to show their dissatisfaction with the prevailing order. Hence the first of the successive waves of working-class archetypes which repelled and fascinated their (social) betters. These were the Teddy Boys – 'young thugs who dressed in Edwardian style clothes' and imitated their social superiors for whom this was a retro-fashion for a time in the early 1950s, In fact, the Teds were the only rebellious group to take their sartorial clue from the upper classes – although they modified it with the addition of flick knives and other accoutrements. Their hair was worn long. As Nik Cohn says, 'the effect was one of heroic excess, garish, greasy and quite magnificent'.[8] To Cohn they were the start of everything 'the whole concept of a private teen life style, separate from the adult world'. By contrast, the Mods, wrote Jonathon Green, 'were more middle-class, often Jewish, the sons of middle-management, small businessmen or some equivalent.'[8]

Naturally, neither Teds nor Mods were welcome, introducing as they did a long-lasting fear of hoodlums and the creeping Americanisation of British cultural life – although they provided the original inspiration for a succession of purely British pop cults. After a handful of violent incidents, they were refused entry to many dance halls and duly condemned as 'deviant young people of unsound mind' by a 'family doctor' in the London *Evening News*. In 1955 the impact of this declaration of independence by a section of the working-class young was boosted by the arrival of rock, or more precisely 'Rock around the Clock', featuring Bill Haley & the Comets, the theme music for the film *Blackboard Jungle*. This set off what were known as the 'rock and roll riots' and very tame they appear now, with a mere 108 incidents, none of them truly violent. Later some of these young thugs were heavily involved in the Notting Hill race riots. They were, wrote Paul Rock and Stanley Cohen, 'a useful scapegoat for respectable British society to cover up its own failures and prejudices in dealing with its immigrant population'.

The general feeling of possible – if not actual – change was reflected even in Oxbridge. In early 1956, amidst scenes which passed for great excitement in those peaceful days, Harold Nicolson was defeated by W. H. Auden for the largely honorific Professorship of Poetry at Oxford, a good indicator of the intellectual mood of the times. The whole affair was hopelessly over-publicised and considered frightfully daring, what with photographs of Jeremy Wolfenden sitting on Auden's knees. Nicolson bemoaned the fact that he was considered the candidate of the 'reactionaries, the old school, the traditionalists'. Of course he was. When these undergraduates left university, they no longer felt that they were necessarily obliged to enter a profession. There were worlds elsewhere. Geoffrey Wheatcroft believes, quite rightly, that the first half of the 1950s at Cambridge marked a crucial development in post-war Britain. 'It was a time,' wrote Alan Watkins, 'when there was a decisive shift in the terms of trade between politics and journalism'[9] – the first of many such shifts which was to lead the vast majority of the potential best and brightest into the theatre, television and news-papers, a far higher proportion than anywhere else in the world.

Above all, there was the lure of an awakening London. Alan Bennett recalled that in January 1955 as a young undergraduate he visited the Diaghilev exhibition organised by Richard Buckle. This seminal event introduced a whole generation to the idea of luxury, of style, of deca-dence – scent had even been sprayed in one of the rooms. 'The exhi-bition had been sponsored by the *Observer*,' wrote Bennett, 'at that time peopled with fabled beings like Kenneth Tynan, Edward Crankshaw and C. A. Lejeune, a socially and intellectually glamorous world . . . but of course London itself was beginning to seem glamorous then – the Coffee House in Northumberland Avenue, the Soup Kitchen in Chandos Place, films at the Academy on Oxford Street and suppers at Schmidts in Charlotte Street* or Romano Santi's in Soho.'[10] It was indeed fun to feel that one was watching a great city awake from a grey, dreary, bomb-drenched slumber. All of a sudden it seemed that anything was possible, even anarchic comedy. In its modern guise this traditional English art-form had been born with Michael Bentine's comedy act involving a chair leg which he used to accompany his

---

* At the time a favourite German restaurant, famed for its lavish portions and its appallingly rude waiters, but now long gone.

rendition of Hamlet, a performance I saw at the London Palladium in 1949. But it flowered with the *Goon Show* written by Spike Milligan, whom Eddie Izzard describes as 'the godfather of modern comedy' and which Jonathan Miller compares with *Alice in Wonderland*.

But the salient cultural feature of the times were the Angry Young Men, who could be described as the 'come-off-it generation' – provincial almost all of them. As Kenneth Allsop pointed out[11], they were 'dissentients', not dissenters, for that would imply an organised bloc, whereas dissentient implied merely 'to disagree with majority sentiments and opinions' – 'whatever it is I'm against it', in the words of Groucho Marx. They were also disgusted at the world of the New Elizabethans during a period when, as Allsop says: 'The rich who had taken to the hills while Attlee's hunting party amateurishly stumbled about came out of hiding, sniffed the air, then scampered back to the old watering-holes where the society columnists were waiting to welcome them ... the Season and the marriage market clicked smoothly into motion, again as if it had been kept ready oiled and polished.'

But it was a good time to protest. As Allsop went on to say, the Angry Young Men benefited greatly from the budding star system, the cult of the personality engendered by ITV and the expansion of the size of newspapers following the end of paper rationing (Allsop also mentions the, generally high, incomes of many of the Angries, another new phenomenon, since young writers had hitherto been associated with poverty rather than wealth). What they had in common was a rejection of the affected, world-weary, attitude of their elders, a pose summed up in the famous phrase of Cyril Connnolly in 1950 in the last number of his magazine *Horizon*: 'It is closing time in the gardens of the West and from now on an artist will be judged only by the resonance of his solitude or the quality of his despair.'

In the beginning was the now largely-forgotten novel *Hurry On Down* by John Wain, published in 1953, followed the next year by three totally original novels: *Lord of the Flies* by William Golding, *Under the Net* by Iris Murdoch and, most famously, *Lucky Jim* by Kingsley Amis. Not all the writers of the period were 'angry' – not even Murdoch, even though she had been a member of the Communist Party for a time – and nor were distinguished novelists such as Angus Wilson, V. S. Pritchett, C. P. Snow and L. P. Hartley (often recognisable by their initials).

Lucky Jim was different – although probably less remarkable as a novel than the other two. But it was the last novel to make a major social impact, for by the 1960s the role was being filled by films and television programmes. Amis's (anti)-hero Jim Dixon was holding up two fingers against pretension, social as well as intellectual, and in the process – and even more unforgivably, his enemies would say – making us laugh out loud. Amis himself was not a typical 'angry' (if there ever had been such an archetype), just an original talent going his own way – the first thing I heard about Amis was that he conducted his tutorials in a *pub*, for God's sake, a habit unimaginable in the Oxford of 1954. His general attitude was summed up in a letter refusing to contribute to a joint statement of revolt published as *Declaration*. 'I hate all this pharisaical twittering about the state of our civilisation,' Amis wrote, calling the projected book 'a valuable addition to the cult of the Solemn Young Man', a piece of 'dismal self-advertising'. He was not far wrong.

But he certainly got under people's skins. The sense of fear engendered by the novel (another barbarian was entering the gate . . .) was obvious from many of the reviews. In the *New Statesman* of all places, Colm Brogan described Lucky Jim as 'a loafer, a sycophant, a vulgarian, who has taken advantage of state bounty to secure a university post when he is mentally and morally unfit to be a school janitor'. This attitude was echoed by that of the octogenarian Somerset Maugham towards the Angries: 'They are scum'. Indeed he hated all of them because they were evidence of the rise of the 'white collar proletariat'. In choosing *Lucky Jim* as his book of the year, he analysed Dixon's faults and worried that some of his like 'will become schoolmasters and form the young, or journalists and form public opinion. A few will go into Parliament, become Cabinet ministers and rule the country. I look upon myself as fortunate that I shall not live to see it.'

That same crucial year, 1954, another small but significant change occurred, not in the theatre itself but amongst the critics when Ivor Brown, the totally established theatre critic of the *Observer*, was replaced by the twenty-something Kenneth Peacock Tynan. As the illegitimate son of a Midlands retail magnate named Peacock, he had been an outsider since birth and had emerged as a brittle, self-consciously Wildean-witty star at Oxford. For the previous few years the commercial theatre had been largely in the hands of a homosexual clique centred round the impresario Binkie Beaumont. Within a few years the heteros had taken over. But at the time, as Tynan put it, the characteristic play on the London stage had nothing to do with real life. It was set in 'Loamshire . . . where, except when someone must sneeze or be murdered, the sun invariably shines . . . the inhabitants belong to a social class derived partly from romantic novels and partly from the playwright's vision of the leisured life he will lead after the play is a success – this being the only effort of imagination he is called upon to make . . . And so grim is the continuity of these things that the foregoing paragraph might have been written at any time during the last thirty years.'

Tynan was being slightly unfair, there were signs of life – I particularly remember *The Prisoner*, a superbly intelligent play by Bridget Boland about a Communist commissar from an aristocratic background trying to break the will of a Cardinal – played by Alec Guinness – from a working-class family. But in general he was right given the popularity of such offerings as the pretentious mimsy-whimsy of N. C. Hunter and the affectations of Christopher Fry. Ironically the archetypal play of the time, *The Reluctant Debutante*, was written by William Douglas Home, brother of the future Prime Minister. Douglas Home had been a genuine rebel during the war and had indeed been imprisoned for refusing to shell Le Havre, a deed far more courageous than anything attempted by any of the Angries.

But all this was irrelevant to the opening night of *Look Back in Anger* in June 1956, surely the defining cultural moment, not just of the period before Suez, but of the whole 1950s. It is important to emphasise the term 'cultural' because a whole school of theatrical intellectuals are now pointing out, quite rightly, that other playwrights, notably Pinter, Brecht and Beckett, were far more original, and that the actual structure of Osborne's plays was relatively conventional. For Osborne was not a theatrical innovator, but represented a crucial cultural social phenomenon, the end of a theatre which Arthur Miller rightly described as 'hermetically sealed off from public life'. It introduced the dread term 'relevance' to the West End theatre from which it had been absent since the days of Harley Granville Barker at the same theatre, the Royal Court, where Jimmy Porter burst onto a startled world.

Theatrical originality seems irrelevant when looking at the general cultural impact of what Allsop describes as Jimmy Porter's 'creeping barrage of vituperation' against 'the [posh] papers, then Christianity, the English Sunday, the American Age, the upper classes and his wife, [all] are raked over with rapid fire' – though, as Allsop points out, his father-in-law, a colonel, attracts grudging respect. Not so his chinless son, termed the 'platitude from outer space', fully aware that 'he and his pals have been plundering and fooling everybody for generations' while the family will 'kick you in the groin while you're handing your hat to the maid'. In a single outburst, wrote Christopher Booker, 'Osborne had broken through all that stifling atmosphere of socially deferential conservatisms which had settled over Britain since the early 1950s.'[12] Just as important is the attraction of Jimmy's wife, the insider Alison, for the outsider Jimmy, a type of revolt in favour of people whom women rightly perceived as hurt and vulnerable which was to become commonplace.

Fundamentally Porter is a nihilist, declaring, famously, that there were 'no good brave causes' – this a mere couple of years before the

Campaign for Nuclear Disarmament reared its courageous head. For, as Christopher Hollis wrote in the *Spectator* at the time, Osborne at least was 'not protesting about war, economic conditions, Communism or anti-Communism'. His was a general cry of pain and despair. 'The whole,' wrote Allsop, 'was like a Oxford Group public confessional, leaving a whole generation coming away purged of guilt at their oh so horrid but previously unexpressed, indeed unexpressable feelings. Even if we did not share Porter's actual hates, we felt and shared the feelings behind them, for we were not used to seeing our concerns our language on the stage. And it didn't half frighten the horses.'

But the most obvious demonstration of how seriously the intellectual establishment had been thrown off balance, had lost its nerve, was the reception accorded to Colin Wilson's book, *The Outsider*. For a few weeks in the summer of 1956 this was taken absurdly seriously by reviewers as distinguished as Cyril Connolly ('this extraordinary book . . . one of the most remarkable first books I have read for a long time') and Philip Toynbee ('an exhaustive and luminously intelligent study of a representative theme of our time') who should have known better. Wilson was described by Allsop as a 'guerrilla philosopher' campaigning 'against the present high priests of Western civilisation'. The book even launched a game of 'Insider or outsider'. In fact it consisted largely of quotations, many of them inaccurately transcribed, a potpourri 'of a certain ill-defined tradition', defined by D. E. Cooper as the 'anti-rationalist and nihilist-cum-existentialist-cum-mystical.'[13]

The reason was obvious. Wilson was uneducated, an auto-didact, who had lived rough, sometimes on Hampstead Heath (how chic . . .) and so was himself an Outsider, which mattered more than mere talent. In mitigation it has to be said that the book was the genuine reaction, a cry of pain, of someone who represented very well the feelings of the – well – Outsider. Within a year, however, poor Wilson had gained a reputation, as a 'self-important bombast' in Allsop's words. His second book was badly received ('a deplorable piece of rubbish,' wrote his erstwhile fan, Philip Toynbee) and he has never recovered any sort of reputation, intellectual or popular, in any of the more than two dozen books he has written since.

Wilson was a butterfly flapping its wings for a summer moment, showing the fragility of the establishment. Somehow the mere coining of the term 'the establishment' made it legitimate to attack it – or at least provided a legitimate target for attack. The term had been coined by Kingsley Martin, the editor of the *New Statesman*, in 1952, but was popularised two years later by the journalist Henry Fairlie. This caught the toffs on the raw. In his Diary, Harold Nicolson attacks Fairlie's notion that John Sparrow, Lady Violet Bonham Carter and Sir William Haley were 'cardinals' of the establishment: 'Three more disparate people I cannot conceive and I suppose that ''Establishment'' means scholarship as opposed to red-brick technology.' He was wrong, for Fairlie had hit the nail on the head.

As a corollary to discussion of the establishment came the often-hilarious debate involving the proper usage of the language, 'U and Non U', terms which really summed up the exclusivist attitudes of the ruling minority (Us and somehow Not Us). The debate had been initiated by an academic, Alan Ross, with the observation that the members of the upper class were no longer 'necessarily better educated, cleaner or richer than someone not of that class' so only linguistic distinctions remained. These were not confined to accents but also included usages – John Betjeman even wrote a poem called *How to Get On in Society*, using exclusively 'non-U' terminology:

> Phone for the fish-knives, Norman
> As cook is a little unnerved;
> You kiddies have crumpled the serviettes
> And I must have things daintily served
>
> Are the requisites all in the toilet?
> The frills round the cutlets can wait
> Till the girl has replenished the cruets
> And switched on the logs in the grate.

The resulting discussion of what was acceptable or not entertained the literate in 1954–55, providing useful tools for everyone who felt excluded and, more importantly, a major step in opening the mystery of the elite to the common view. The U-speakers were stoutly defended by Nancy Mitford, who rather gave the game away by defining them as 'the sensible men of ample means who generally seem to rule our land'.

Just as much fun, and just as significant, was a foretaste of the satire boom generally associated with the 1960s. It came from an unlikely source, *Punch*, through an explosive mix of two prodigiously gifted journalists, one, the editor, Malcolm Muggeridge a right-wing anarch-ist, the other, Claud Cockburn, a maverick – and almost equally anarch-ist – former member of the Communist Party. Above all they fought wittily against the culture of '*cela ne se dit pas, et surtout cela ne s'ecrit pas*' which still prevails in France. As Muggeridge's friend and biographer Richard Ingrams pointed out: 'It was typical of Malcolm that he should decide to break the silence and state what most people felt but nobody liked to say: that Churchill was past it and should retire.'[14] This was done cleverly through a cartoon showing an ageing, dispirited WSC at a desk accompanied by a long mock-Gibbonian caption on the facing page talking of a Byzantine leader called Bellarius who had successfully repelled the barbarians from the gates of the city. There was an uproar. Churchill himself, always prone to the fits of depression known to his family as Black Dog, was in despair, and his son-in-law Christopher Soames was 'grieved to see the depths into which you have dragged *Punch* . . . little did I think that your magazine would be so debased'. This was followed by another cartoon unfairly comparing Eden, then involved in a conference trying to bring peace to Vietnam, to Neville Chamberlain at Munich.

At the time even Muggeridge had not got round to attacking royalty but, as was to happen thirty years later, royalty was quite capable of undermining the foundations of its own support. The first own goal for the Windsors was scored by Princess Margaret, by far the most glamourous figure of the early 1950s. She was very affected by her father's death: 'she did not wish to see any of her usual circle of friends,' one of them told the Queen's biographer Ben Pimlott. She also became increasingly dependent on her father's favourite aide-de-camp, a young war hero called Peter Townsend. Insiders became aware of the depth of her love for him at the Coronation. While she was watching her sister leave the Abbey, wrote Sarah Bradford, 'she flicked a piece of fluff off Townsend's uniform, an obviously protective gesture typical of the care for a loved one'.[18] The affair had a faint but unmistakable echo of her mother's experience. Lady Elizabeth Bowes-Lyon, as she then was, had been in love with the Hon James Stuart, the fifth son of the Earl of Moray, but when the Duke of York fell in love with her, Stuart was despatched to Canada to keep him out of the way (thirty years later the couple got together again in the castle of Mey she had bought on the northern tip of Scotland after her husband's premature death).

Margaret's – fully reciprocated – love for Townsend created all sorts of problems. He was not an aristocrat but a royal servant (as one courtier put it to Pimlott, 'masters do not marry their servants') and, far more important, had been divorced, a status which would have barred him from many royal occasions and which brought up the possibility of the ultimate royal nightmare, a re-run of the Wallis Simpson affair. Fortunately, under the 1772 Royal Marriages Act – which nobody seems ever to have thought of repealing – the Queen could bar her sister's marriage until she was twenty-five, so Townsend was sent off to Brussels as air attaché for two years.

During his absence the royals did not talk about it to anyone – the first occasion on which the Queen indulged in 'ostriching' – refusing to look at the reality of an unpleasant situation, a characteristic she had inherited in full measure from her mother and which continued to have appalling consequences for the family. On Townsend's return in 1955, things soon came to a head. It soon became abundantly clear to the couple what marriage would involve. In a leader, *The Times* stated bluntly that Margaret's marriage to Group Captain Townsend would 'involve withdrawal not merely from her formal rights in the [Royal] Succession established by law' but also 'abandonment of her place in the Royal family.' Neither of them had ever thought through the logical consequences of their love. On his side, this was the consequence of a certain naivety, combined with the sense of loss and dislocation, the alienation inevitable after a painful divorce. In her case arrogance and 'ostriching' were important factors.

The prospect of being cast into outer darkness, of being treated as a normal subject of her sister rather than her seriously spoilt sibling, was not agreeable, to say the least. 'While the Windsors' marriage,' wrote Sarah Bradford, 'had been supported by a great deal of money, the Townsends would have to have lived on his pay, already stretched by the education of his two sons. For a Princess who had once said, "I cannot imagine anything more wonderful than being who I am," the prospect of losing her royal status was unthinkable ... they both knew that they loved each other more than anyone else in the world and they both felt that they had made the right decision.' Bradford adds bluntly, 'It is by no means certain that if she had married Townsend, even keeping her royal position and income, she would have been happy. Marriage without position would have been a disaster.'

But it is important not to be too cynical about Margaret's decision. In her statement she declared that she was above all 'mindful of the church's teachings that Christian marriage is indissoluble and conscious of my duty to the Commonwealth.' At the time it was assumed that she had been got at by the stern figure of the Archbishop of Canterbury, representing the establishment – the first case in which this mythic entity had been called as witness. This was not the case: she needed no prompting. Her religious feelings have often been underestimated. As a young girl, she had attended post-confirmation classes, and after her father's death, a friend told Pimlott, she 'frequently left the Palace early in the morning with her lady-in-waiting to visit unheralded and privately a church'. At the time of the Townsend break-up, her friend Noel Coward expressed the hope 'that she will not take to religion in a big way and become a frustrated maiden princess'.

The whole episode showed the underlying toughness, not only of the Queen and her mother, but of the whole family. The survival of The Firm, as the Duke of Edinburgh famously called them, sometimes demanded more than a hint of ruthlessness. In her memoirs, the Duchess of Windsor remarks that there is 'something inhuman in the monarchical principle'. You have only to remember the way George V had refused to give asylum to his 'beloved cousin' Nicky, also known as Tsar Nicholas II of all the Russias, when the latter was threatened by the Bolsheviks, so afraid was he that the Red fever would spread to Britain.

'The whole affair,' wrote Sarah Bradford, was the result 'of the moral strait jacket into which the royal family was to be confined, trapped by an image of its own creation.' It was also a typical case of looking backwards and playing false analogies – in this case with the position of Wallis Simpson. This tendency was not confined to royalty. Harold Wilson's refusal to countenance the idea of devaluation for three years owed much to his fear of people remembering that it was Labour that had devalued in 1949. In both instances the insiders were hopelessly out of touch with the feelings of the bulk of the British people.

Notes

1. *Heterosexual dictatorship – male homosexuality in post-war Britain*, Fourth Estate, 1996.
2. *Against the Law,* Weidenfeld & Nicolson, 1954.
3. Obituary of Peter Wildeblood, *Independent*, November 25, 1999.
4. *Alan Turing: The Enigma*, Burnett Books, 1983.
5. Leonard Miall, Obituary, *Independent*, January 31 1999.
6. Bernard Sendall, *Independent Television in Britain, Volume 1*, Macmillan, 1982.
7. *The Other Half*, John Murray, 1977.
8. *Independent*, November 1 1999.
9. *A Short Walk down Fleet Street*, Duckworth 2000.
10. *London Review of Books*, January 25 2001.
11. *The Angry Decade*, Peter Owen, 1958.
12. *The Neophiliacs*, Collins 1969.
13. Bogdanor and Skidelsky, op cit.
14. *Muggeridge, the biography*, Harpercollins 1995.

5

So Smells Defeat

'Political parties ... can live down the most appalling errors
when they are in office. The prestige of a class, however, and of
the leadership derived from it, is more difficult to sustain.'

MALCOLM MUGGERIDGE, Diary

AT MIDNIGHT ON NOVEMBER 6 1956, the French and English
forces halted their advance towards Cairo, thus ending the so-called
Suez Adventure. Ever since the summer the whole affair had been a
muddle, with the British, French and Israeli Prime Ministers conspiring
in secret to bring down the Egyptian leader Colonel Nasser. But, apart
from trying to prevent Nasser from nationalising the Suez Canal, they
lacked a clear political aim, hence the complaint by General Sir Hugh
Stockwell, the British commander, that no one in the forces had a 'full
and clear idea as to what they were being sent to do and why'. Hence,
too, the remark of the elderly Winston Churchill that 'I am not sure I
should have dared to start; but I am sure I should not have dared to
stop.'

Suez was the most important single event in post-war British history,
a defeat whose importance it is difficult to exaggerate. In a few short
weeks the whole sham, all the illusions that had sustained the ruling
class since 1945, that We Had Won the War, that We Were Invulnerable, that we could rely on the United States, were shattered. Hugh
Thomas was not alone in feeling that it was 'tragic to see great imperial
countries (especially our own) ending their pretensions in comic style
... This was not the first moment when the power of Britain faltered,'
he added, 'but, more important, when it was shown to have done so.'[1]
The loss of authority was enormous; everything was now up for grabs.
The resulting insecurity provoked a largely hollow defiance, expressed
in our nuclear deterrent, combined with a sense of inferiority towards
the United States and – increasingly – towards Continental Europe.
The defeat also spawned a desperate need to escape to other models,
cultural as well as economic. And until the arrival of Margaret Hilda

Thatcher in power nearly twenty-three years later, politicians were all to remain reactive.

The helplessness, the sheer despair and bitterness engendered by the consequences of the defeat – and the growing realisation that we were becoming the increasingly derided, increasingly (if relatively) poverty-stricken relations of Western Europe – is superbly described by John le Carré, clearly embittered by his experiences when working for MI6, notably in Bonn, the eponymous *Small Town in Europe* of what is to me his finest novel. The whole book is suffused with le Carré's despair at the effects of the poverty and the impotence induced by the realisation that Britain counted for less and less in the world and culminates in an abject approach by British diplomats to a potential führer figure. 'Holy God,' says the disillusioned security officer, 'we're like the rest of them after all ... we're trying to make our number with tomorrow's lucky winner ... All power corrupts. The loss of power corrupts even more. We thank an American for that advice.'

Importantly, the hero of the book is a refugee, the only person at the British embassy in Bonn who knows a potential führer figure's deeply shameful past and who risks his life in defence of democratic decency. He is confronted by weaker souls: one diplomat confesses that 'We are a corrupt nation and we need all the help that we can get. That is lamentable and, I confess, occasionally humiliating. However, I would rather fail as a power than survive by impotence. I would rather be vanquished than neutral. I would rather be English than Swiss.' The staff at the embassy has been cut to the bone and Britain is over-stretched, committed in Rhodesia, Hong Kong, Cyprus. Policy is in flux: 'One minute we were conspiring against the French, the next minute we were conspiring with them. While that was going on we found the energy to scrap three quarters of the Navy and nine-tenths of our independent deterrent.' As another diplomat puts it: 'We are playing a poker game here. With open cards and nothing in our hand. Our credit is exhausted, our resources are nil ... We were bankrupt begging for trade and loans.'

The author's understanding of British diplomatic attitudes at the time emerges from the mouth of a willowy, intelligent diplomat: 'Optimism. That's the trouble with Americans, isn't it really? All that emphasis on the future. So dangerous. It makes them destructive of the present. Much kinder to look *back*, I always think. I see no hope at all for the future, and it gives me a great sense of freedom. And of caring: we're much nicer to each other in the condemned cell, aren't we?' – and he ends with the true tone of pre-Thatcherite Britain: 'Don't take me too seriously, will you?' Thirty years later nature imitated art. In a magazine article, Robert Cooper, one of the brightest sparks in the Foreign Office, argued that irony is at the centre of modern foreign policy-making, Whitehall-style (and I don't think that he was being ironical). 'What else,' he argued, 'is there left for the citizens of a post-heroic, post-imperial, post-modern society? Provided it is tinged with humanity, irony is not such a bad thing. It suggests a certain modesty about oneself, one's values and one's aspirations. At least irony is unlikely to be used to justify programmes of conquest or extermination.'[2] It is also, he notably didn't add, a means of being able to convey – but only to other initiates – one's own and their innate superiority, a point made before the war by sheer power. For its widespread use implies a sense of helplessness in the face of brute strength despite one's innate superiority.

The reality had been spelt out as early as 1949 by Sir Henry Tizard, then the chief scientific adviser to the Ministry of Defence. 'We persist in regarding ourselves as a great Power,' he pointed out, 'capable of everything and only temporarily handicapped by economic difficulties. We are not a Great Power [his capitals] and never will be again. We are a great nation, but if we continue to behave like a Great Power we shall soon cease to be a great nation.' Another sign of the sense of helplessness was a breed of bird which was to emerge in flocks in the following decade, the idea that There Was Something Wrong With Britain. The first sighting came soon after the abandonment of the Suez Adventure in a series of radio discussions called *Our Present Discontents*, chaired by the eminent historian Asa Briggs. This was accompanied by a restless search for outside examplars, for external solutions to Britain's problems, as if the adoption of policies which had been found suitable for other countries would avoid the need for any fundamental re-examination of Britain's own problems. The articles, the books, the television programmes, amounted to a replay of the old Victorian theme The Condition of England, only this time it was concerned with the problem of seemingly inexorable decline and not those of exuberant growth. The first and in many ways the best of all the analyses came from the economic editor of the *Observer*, Andrew Shonfield, in which he pointed out that the key lay in economic growth and that the heart of the problem lay in the importance being attached to symbols such as the value of the pound and on military over-spending outside Britain, compounded by conservatism and complacency at home. Instead he preached 'realism' and 'dynamism'.[3]

There were plenty of similar analyses. In a major article, the revisionist Labour politician Anthony Crosland used terms like 'complacent' 'sluggish', 'obsolete', 'paralysis of will', and 'failure of nerve'. He stated baldly: 'A dogged resistance to change now blankets every segment of our national life. A middle-aged conservatism, parochial and complacent has settled over the country; and it is hard to find a single sphere in which Britain is pre-eminently in the forefront.

Our production and export performance is almost the poorest of any advanced industrial country; and in individual industries one constantly finds that the only dynamic firm is controlled by an American, a Canadian, an Irishman, or a refugee ... No doubt we still lead the world in certain historical spheres ... but whenever innovation is required, we see a frightful paralysis of the will.'[4] By 1963 Arthur Koestler, the ex-communist, was writing a book entitled simply *The Suicide of Britain*.

In the 1960s the television documentary makers joined in. One of their best contributions was the Tuesday documentary *Half-time Britain*, produced by Glyn Jones, in 1964 which asked the question 'Are we a half-time nation, getting half-pay for half a day's work under half-hearted management?' – an echo of the old communist saying 'We pretend to work and they pretend to pay us' or another, 'How many people work here? About half'. Four years later Jones made another thoughtful programme, *What about the workers: are they to blame?* 'If workers appear selfish, aggressive and irresponsible,' he argued, as his obituarist put it[5], 'then that is their response to a society that appears to them to be unequal, selfish and irresponsible.' In the programme workers complained of the depth of the gulf between the treatment accorded to workers and management.

For some observers the rot set in rather later, although the analysis remained the same. 'In the 1950s,' wrote Kenneth O. Morgan, 'Britain had offered the world, many felt, a spectacle of hedonism and insular complacency. Evident defeats like Suez, economic setbacks like the threat to sterling in mid-1957, the crisis of defence policy with the end of Blue Streak in 1960, were publicly presented [albeit only by Harold Macmillan] as "little local difficulties". But from 1961 on this form of genteel evasion was no longer possible or credible. Britain embarked on a traumatic process of self-examination, self-doubt and declining morale, a perception of external weakness and internal decay from which it had yet fully to recover in the late 1980s.'

It was the tariff reformer Joseph Chamberlain – not surprisingly the voice of Birmingham, heartland of British manufacturing – who had been the first figure to point to Britain's industrial decline. In the early years of the twentieth century he preached that unless we started copying the rest of the industrialised world, abandoned free trade, then as now a dogma of the British intellectual establishment, and provided some protection to British industry through tariffs, he foresaw, with considerable prescience, that Britain would go the way of Venice and Holland, both great trading powers fallen into a long decline (though the Dutch, after one final, bloody and unscrupulous attempt to retain their hold over the Dutch East Indies, had accepted the reality of powerlessness far more gracefully than the British were able to do).

The comparisons with Holland and Venice were real enough, but the closest was with Spain after the first effects of New World gold had worn off. Then, as the historian J. H. Elliot pointed out, the ruling class 'lacked the breadth of vision and the strength of character to break with a past that could no longer serve as a guide to the future ... at a time when the face of Europe was altering more rapidly than ever before, the country that had once been its leading power proved to be lacking the essential ingredient for survival – the willingness to change.'

But not all the books and programmes made sense. One of the most influential, and in retrospect most ridiculous, books was *The Stagnant Society* by the journalist Michael Shanks which sold 60,000 copies – even though it was predicated on the continuing success of communist-type planning, a vision of which inspired him after a trip to, for God's sake, Bulgaria. He was not alone: in the early 1960s a great many non-communist radicals assumed that the economic battle between communism and capitalism was by no means decided. Even so intelligent a politician as Richard Crossman was convinced that East Germany might well surpass West Germany.

Intriguingly, there was a strong streak of opinion that opposed the cult of efficiency, some of it from surprising quarters and reminiscent of the opposition to Thatcherism. Christopher Booker, one of the leading lights in the satire movement, was disgusted by Crosland's article in *Encounter*. He hated such terms as 'drastic', 'modernisation', 'innovation', 'change' and, above all, 'dynamic'. Booker called the piece a 'chant of the neurosis which came to be summed up in the years to come under the all-purpose phrase ''What's wrong with Britain?'' ' In reviewing Anthony Sampson's highly influential book, *An Anatomy of Britain*, David Marquand wrote how 'having dissected the odd combination of sloppy amateurism and unadventurous professionalism which bedevils so much of life in Britain today, he goes on to advocate a kind of tough-minded, forward-looking elitism which seems to me almost as unpleasant as the attitudes which prevail now. Mr Sampson's Britain would be much harder, more ruthless and more prosperous than the present one; but I am not sure it would be more democratic or more humane.'[6] Marquand went on to discuss a saying of Per Jacobssen, a legendary director of the IMF, which Sampson had quoted approvingly: 'What would be the good if people were to say that the British are nice people, but they no longer have money?' Marquand's answer was that 'it might be a great deal of good ... The British people might decide to sacrifice a part of their standard of living for the sake of greater leisure or they might deliberately reduce the efficiency of their industries in order to establish a system of industrial democracy.' I have quoted Marquand at length, not only because he represents a major strand in British thinking throughout the post-war era but more importantly because he was a young Turk, a mere thirty at the time and destined to be one of the country's best political philosophers and one who was writing in a paper which was supposed to be at the vanguard of British radicalism.

The official reaction to Suez varied alarmingly between two opposite but equally unrealistic attitudes: defiance of the underlying reality and a panicky self-abasement. The most obvious, and most immediate, reaction was the Defence White Paper published in 1957 which abolished National Service as part of a doctrine of 'small forces, big bangs' aimed at retaining our *bella figura* internationally by clinging onto the trappings of Great Power status. This involved developing the hydrogen bomb and clinging to our expensive military presence East of Suez until finally the Labour government was forced to abandon the pretence in the late 1960s for financial rather than political reasons. The doctrine continued: in the 1970s Harold Wilson asked for a 'little piece of modernisation' for our nuclear armoury which in the end cost nearly a billion pounds, fifty times the original estimate he had given. And while France, too, embarked on a costly nuclear adventure, the country's continuing economic success made it far more affordable.

But the defiance was hollow. Our 'independent nuclear deterrent' relied on American help, one of the signs of the increasing dependence on the United States. This was not new. In the 1930s Sellars and Yeatman had ended their comically accurate history *1066 And All That* in 1918 when America became 'clearly Top Nation and history came to a .'. Nevertheless before Suez Britain retained enough vestiges of self-confidence to welcome, or at least to receive and employ, refugees from McCarthyism. The children of the film-maker Carl Foreman recalled how as late as the early 1960s Churchill asked him to write a film based on his early life. Foreman reminded him how he had been blacklisted. 'Oh, I know all about you. But we don't like political blacklists in England. And speaking for myself, I don't care what a man believed in when he was a boy. My concern is whether he can do the job.'[7]

World War II had obviously altered the balance between the two countries – hence the famous cry that American soldiers stationed in Britain were 'over paid, over-sexed and over here' – and the combination of admiration and envy grew in the post-war years. The Americans' wealth and glamour was emphasised by their rough treatment of Britain after the war. The open humiliation of Britain by the Americans had started a mere nine days after the end of the war against Japan with the cancellation of Lend-Lease, the provision of food and weapons on credit by the Americans. This was replaced by a loan, albeit on relatively easy terms. The next year came the McMahon Act which brutally ended Britain's access to American atomic secrets – the result of a gentleman's agreement which had recognised the pioneering work of British scientists.

By then there was a resigned recognition that we were in thrall to the Americans. As Jimmy Porter put it: 'I must say it's pretty dreary living in the American Age – unless you're an American, of course. Perhaps all our children will be Americans. That's a thought, isn't it?' The process left a legacy of anti-Americanism not only on the left but also on the right amongst such groups as the so-called Empire Loyalists. But one result of the increasing concern with wealth rather than social status over the years made the right increasingly pro-American, so that by the 1990s some rightists were floating the idea of a North Atlantic Free Trade Area to replace our connections with Europe.

Nevertheless Suez did push the relationship even further into a recognition of ever-increasing dependence. It is easy to forget that Suez was also a shock to the Americans. 'At the time of Suez,' wrote Trevor Lloyd, 'both Nixon [then American vice-president] and St Laurent the Canadian prime minister had spoken as though it was only at this crisis that they had realised that England and France no longer dominated the world.' But ours was by far the greater shock. Obviously the first result was to upset the complacent attitude that we could always rely on the Americans. Churchill had said that he would never have gone ahead without consulting the Americans, and it was President Eisenhower, supposedly a friend of Britain's, who had pulled the plug on the Adventure. In his last speech in the 1956 election he said firmly that the United States could not have 'one law for those opposing us, another for those allied with us. There can only be one law or there can be no peace.'* Before Suez, as Lloyd puts it, 'foreign policy was reasonably successful – in one respect too successful: people were able to slip into the habit of forgetting how much the world had changed in the last dozen years.'

Contrary to predictions at the time, the American alliance was not shattered but since then, as Hugh Thomas wrote, 'the British have never been able since to venture on a foreign policy independent of the USA'. We became, and remained, the 'junior partner in the Pax Americana', in the words of Vernon Bogdanor. The relationship could be dressed up as being more dignified than it really was. Harold Macmillan told Anthony Sampson that the Brits were the 'Greeks in the American Empire' and must run it 'as the Greek slaves ran the oper-

---

* A doctrine systematically broken by him and his successors in being prepared to prop up numerous rotten regimes throughout the world in the sacred name of anti-communism.

ations of the Emperor Claudius'[8]. But the reality inevitably involved numerous humiliations. The most public, and accurate, was the famous remark made by Dean Acheson, the former Secretary of State in late 1962 that 'Great Britain has lost an Empire and has not yet found a role. The attempt to play a separate power role – based on a ''special relationship'' with the United States, and on being the head of a ''Commonwealth'' which has no political structure, or unity, or strength . . . this role is about to be played out.' He was less pro-British than the majority of his class, the so-called Best and the Brightest. Unfortunately for Britain, the influence of this generally – if condescendingly – anglophile group steadily decreased in the 1960s as their support for the Vietnam war helped their decline.

The Vietnam war brought forth contrasting reactions. London saw riots against the Americans, Harold Wilson – notably unlike the Australians – refused to allow Britain to get involved or to send troops (though he did send a junior minister in a pathetic gesture to try and help make the peace). But some distinguished Britons, like Isaiah Berlin, rallied to the American cause, offering slavish support for the hardliners. As he wrote in a letter: 'I can see the thin red line, formed by you [Joseph Alsop] and Mac [McGeorge Bundy, a distinguished American government servant] and me, and Chips Bohlen – four old blimps, the last defenders of a dry, and disagreeably pessimistic, tough and hopelessly outmoded position . . . one will perish at least with their eyes open.' After four hours with Bundy, he wrote, 'I have never admired anyone so much . . . his character emerged in such exquisite form that I am now his devoted and dedicated slave.'[9]

After Suez Anglo-American relationships inevitably depended primarily on personalities. Eden's successor, Harold Macmillan, performed miracles. In the words of L. A. Siedentop, he 'prided himself that he knew how to ''handle Americans'' ' – he was, after all, himself half American and he had shown his diplomatic skills when he was Churchill's representative in North Africa and the Middle East during the war, where Eisenhower, in charge of military operations, had learnt to appreciate his abilities. Within a few months, he had re-established Britain's diplomatic position. 'It hardly seemed possible,' wrote Siedentop, 'that leaders who had strongly disapproved of the Suez adventure should so soon be talking of their ''old and trusted ally''.'[10]

Macmillan enjoyed a different, almost avuncular (as he saw it anyway) relationship with Eisenhower's successor, for he and Jack Kennedy shared the same stylistic flourishes, albeit expressed very differently, and shared the credit for the nuclear test-ban treaty signed in Geneva in July 1963. The relationship led to a series of agreements so that the British nuclear deterrent could continue, although inevitably it became and remained dependent on the Americans for a series of missiles – a fact that weighed heavily with General de Gaulle when he rejected our application for entry into the EEC. The influence continued, albeit patchily, through the late 1960s and early 1970s when Henry Kissinger kept the Foreign Office more fully in the picture than he did his own State Department (which wasn't saying much).

But by then the American public regarded Britain as one large stately home. The image was reinforced by a steady flow of television series, most obviously *Upstairs, Downstairs* and *Brideshead Revisited*. But it inevitably centred on the royal family. 'The presence on the Throne of the Queen, with her Dutiful Son and his Beautiful Wife [her capital letters] waiting at his side,' wrote Diana Simonds, 'is the one thing that really stops little England from facing up to this ghastly reality . . . [of being] a small aircraft carrier for the USA.'[11]

Sometimes, and inevitably, reality intruded. One of the most influential forces in urging Britain to join the Common Market was one of the genuinely Bestest of the Brightest, George Ball – a close friend of Jean Monnet, the 'Father of Europe' – when he was Under-Secretary of State in the Kennedy administration. Indeed, during the whole period the Americans treated us like a tiresome, clinging relative who needed to be guided into a suitable institution like the EEC. The proprietorial attitude was also shown in 1976 when the American government interfered in the negotiations between Britain and the IMF (see Chapter 9) pressing for more onerous terms and, at one point, virtually taking control of the negotiations.

Only a few years later came the famous romance between Ronald Reagan and Margaret Thatcher which restored relations to a basis far more nearly equal than they had been since 1956. At times she undoubtedly did have some influence, not just over the president, but, more importantly, over American policy. After all it was she who decided as early as 1985 that she could do business with Gorbachev, and her influence with Reagan helped to end the Cold War. She was also at hand to stop Reagan continuing his dialogue with Gorby in which he had offered to give up American nuclear weapons at Rekjavik the following year. The support could be mutual. As Secretary of State, Kissinger's disciple Alexander Haig provided crucial help during the Falklands War, partly because Haig was pro-British and also because Caspar Weinberger, the Secretary of Defense, was infatuated with a British academic Janet Morgan (who was probably working with MI6).

But there were always limits. The Queen was furious we were not consulted when the Americans invaded Grenada, nominally a British colony. Nevertheless, as one minister told Ben Pimlott: 'We were concerned not to be humiliated by appearing not to have been in the Americans' confidence: at the same time we were torn about whether to keep up the pretence and shelter under the notion of the special relationship.' And three years later Margaret Thatcher, alone of European leaders, allowed American bombers to overfly Britain when bombing Libya. The personal nature of the relationship continued in the 1990s. John Major had provided secret information for the Bush campaign in the 1992 election so was naturally not well received by President Clinton, who speedily established a genuinely warm relationship with Major's successor (it probably helped that both their wives were brilliant lawyers, more intelligent than their husbands).

But the double face of Britain before and after Suez was most amply demonstrated by our relationship with Continental Europe. In trying, as we ended up doing, to curry favour with both the United States and Europe it was as though the British elite had forgotten de Gaulle's famous doctrine that 'a country has no friends, it only has interests'. Winston Churchill's attitude had been set as early as 1930: 'We are *with* Europe, but not *of* it [his italics]. We are linked but not comprised.' He carried this attitude through to his famous speech in Zurich in September 1946, in which he talked of a United States of Europe designed to bring France and Germany together. But, as Hugo Young points out, it 'was the speech of a grandiloquent map-maker who wanted to dissolve the emotional frontiers between warring continental countries, but was rooted in a system that cast Britain as facilitator, even mere spectator of the process.'[12] To Churchill, and to eurosceptics through the years, Britain was at the centre of three concentric circles, involving equal relationships with Europe, the Commonwealth and the United States. His attitude was echoed by Ernest Bevin, for whom any European union had to be purely between sovereign governments.

The ever-growing reality of European unity began with the natural longing of French and German politicians to ensure that their countries never went to war again. The first result was the European Coal and Steel Community, a largely symbolic gesture of cooperation between what became the six founding countries of the EEC, an institution engineered by Jean Monnet and a handful of European-minded statesmen such as Maurice Schuman of France and Paul-Henri Spaak of Belgium. The founders deliberately didn't ask the British to be involved. They might have been the biggest producer of both coal and steel at the time but the founders knew that the British would have tried to abort the exercise, and, in any case, the German chancellor, Konrad Adenauer, never made any secret of his anti-British beliefs. In the event, as Young points out, the ECSC 'did not in reality diminish the economic powers of governments over vital resources . . . the full grandeur of the ECSC's aspiration proved to be rather empty.'

The basic misunderstanding of the formative years of the EEC was compounded by British arrogance and indifference, which ensured that we sent only a middle-ranking civil servant to report on the conference at Messina in Sicily in 1955 which resulted in the Treaty of Rome, the cornerstone of the EEC. Behind the neglect was the assumption that the Continentals could never get their act together, could never threaten British dominance. It was not helped by the fact that, even after Suez, America, in Young's words 'was still Britain's uncontested priority. It was the Entente Cordiale which died over Suez when, as the French saw it, we betrayed them by panicking over the Suez operation.' But, wrote Gladwyn Jebb, a typical Foreign Office insider, Suez proved that our special relationship with the United States was no more, so 'only by forming a greater Western Europe could we continue to wield any substantial influence on world events'. Many years later Anthony Nutting, an anti-Suez minister who had been a victim of the adventure, pointed out that 'British foreign policy was left in a sort of void, really for several years, until we picked ourselves up and said well we have got to go in some direction.'[13]

A defining moment in our relationship with Europe came with the appointment of Sir Frank Lee as head of the Treasury in 1960. He was not outwardly impressive. 'His appearance,' wrote Sir Roy Denman, later a senior official in the European Commission, 'suggested a more than usually dilapidated second-hand suit that had spent the night in a hedgerow. His voice was like the creaking of a rusty gate. But he spoke with force and fire and with an intellectual clarity few could match. To hear him laying down the law to a minister was an experience not easily forgotten.' 'His greatest strength,' wrote Eric Roll, was the strong untypically bureaucratic 'belief in what he considered to be the right solution of this particular problem . . . that we should join the EEC for economic as well as political reasons.'

But still most of official Britain was in two minds. There were the Europeans, and then there were the supporters of its putative rival, the European Free Trade Area which brought together the European countries, most obviously in Scandinavia, left outside the new EEC. EFTA was never a starter, but such was the state of insecurity, of powerlessness, that it never seems to have occurred to anyone that we could have gone it alone, relying on our importance as a market for the EEC countries to effect an acceptable deal with them. It was in 1958–59 that the awful truth dawned on Harold Macmillan. In June 1958 he was still hopeful of staying away from Europe. 'There were three elements who wanted supra-nationalism and who were playing no small part in the [newly created European] Commission . . . the Jews, the planners, and the old cosmopolitan elite.' By the end of 1959 he had concluded that the EEC was 'here to stay' and that it threatened to exclude us 'both from European markets and from consultation in European policy'. At point we became, and remained, beggars at the Euro-table.

But as an official report, completed in 1960, pointed out, 'We cannot join the Common Market on the cheap. Joining means taking two far-reaching decisions. First we must accept that there will have to be a political content in our actions – we must show ourselves prepared to join with the Six in their institutional arrangements and in any development towards closer political integration. Without this we cannot achieve our foreign policy aims (i.e. maximising our influence in world affairs). Second there must be a real intention to have a Common Market . . . and in general we must accept the Common Tariff.' For the author of the report, as for the vast majority of 'Europeans', our entry was a refuge, a necessity. But there was a minority of what one might term 'Old Bolsheviks' for whom it was an ideal. The true believers were headed by Edward Heath, the minister Macmillan chose to head our first negotiations in 1962–63 until they were brutally cut short by General de Gaulle in January 1963. As an undergraduate Heath had gone on holiday to Germany with a Jewish friend. They had attended a Nuremberg rally and had indeed brushed shoulders with the Führer and shaken the hand of Heinrich Himmler ('I remember him for his soft, flabby handshake') – an experience which convinced Heath that Hitler 'was capable of carrying the German people with him into any folly, however mad' and that only a Europe 'united, free and democratic' would be safe from the demons let loose by Hitler in the name of ultra-nationalism. He carried his fervour into Parliament: his maiden speech in late 1950 was about the future of Europe.

But there was one limitation in Heath's attitude. As his former Private Secretary Robert Armstrong put it, 'for him, getting in was an end in itself'; he did not have 'a coherent vision about what to do with it when we were in' – in other words Heath's was a short-term view, which naturally went with a willingness to sacrifice our interests since the future form of the relationship was so much less important than the overwhelming need for entry. The other leading Old Bolshevik was Roy Jenkins. He had been converted to the European cause in the early 1950s as a delegate to the Council of Europe, and was a politician with the guts to stand up and oppose his close friend Hugh Gaitskell immediately after the latter's famous speech at the 1962 Labour Party Conference.

By the time we had finally been admitted – on humiliating terms – it had become established that support for Europe, however fanatical, was somehow the mark of the 'moderate' and that any opposition was the result of backward-looking ultra-nationalism – even though the first British politician to have put forward the idea of European federalism in the early 1950s had been Sir Oswald Mosley.* Europeanism,

* A fact unmentioned by Hugo Young.

95

like communism in the 1930s, became a secular religion for the generation that had come of age around the time of Suez. But the fanaticism, itself at least partly the result of a disgust at British policy, was confined to a single generation. Today's, inevitably much younger, commentators still wonder at the phenomenon. The *Independent*'s Anne McElvoy once shrewdly remarked how, unlike Blair – and herself, 'They are fearsomely ideological – nay theological – in their attachment to The Cause.'

The 'Europeans' shared a surprising number of attributes, not only with the communists but with many other elites, including the Best and the Brightest in the United States. They assumed that they, and they alone, were right, that they were indeed an elite, a constantly recurring label attached to pro-Europeans in Hugo Young's monumental history of our relationship with the EEC, *This Blessed Plot*. As Sir John Hoskyns noted after Sir Michael Butler, a senior foreign office official, had returned after six years as our ambassador to the EU, he had become 'the embodiment of Europhile arrogance and breathtaking condescension to anyone of a sceptical frame of mind'. They were the British equivalent the members of communist parties who saw themselves as the 'vanguard of the proletariat', of the future. As a result, any opposition could not only be mistaken: it was simply ridiculous. I would agree with the words of the Elizabethan poet John Harington:

> Treason doth never prosper: what's the reason?
> For if it prosper none dare call it treason

In this case, as so often, history has been written by the winners, for these self-styled moderates have in fact managed to impose their own version of events, above all that our entry was natural and eminently desirable, indeed essential, whereas in fact it wasn't, and moreover didn't attack the roots of our problems as they assumed it would. Because of their feeling of innate moral superiority, they felt they could behave with an otherwise unthinkable degree of dishonesty. Their attitude is displayed with unself-conscious arrogance by Hugo Young in his book, which is, effectively the Bible of the Euros, for Young, like all the euro-fanatics, is so deeply convinced of the righteousness of his cause that he will cheerfully admit to the dishonesties involved – although he is noticeably reticent in bringing out the cost of our European adventure and in discussing the Common Agricultural Policy, which rates only a handful of mentions in a work of over 500 pages, one which drips with the condescension characteristic of his fellow Europeans towards anyone who dared oppose them.

The Europeans were helped by the mind-set of the Foreign Office. In Anthony Sampson's words, 'the diplomats in London (as one of them put it) tend to see themselves as ambassadors *from* the country they deal with on the desk'[14] – a habit which the Treasury understandably regarded as not altogether patriotic. The most extreme case was John Robinson, the brilliant and devious Foreign Office official in charge of European integration during the dark (for the Europhiles) days of the 1960s after de Gaulle had twice rejected our application for entry. It was he who deliberately leaked the contents of the conversation between de Gaulle and the British Ambassador, Sir Christopher Soames, in which de Gaulle suggested a loosely linked Europe of countries which would have been little more than a free-trade area. By the late 1960s, the Europeans had developed a deadly and deeply effective liaison with senior broadcasters at the BBC which systematically broadcast pro-European programmes as if to educate the audience as to the inevitabilty and desirability of our entry – an attitude in direct contradiction to the Corporation's normally scrupulous even-handedness. According to Paul Lashmar, much of the European campaign was financed by the Foreign Office through the Information Research Department, an ultra-secret group normally devoted exclusively to countering Soviet propaganda.[15]

The Europhiles have been able to present our hesitations in the late 1940s and 1950s before we took the plunge in 1961 as a series of missed opportunities whereas in fact they were perfectly natural hesitations. But they fall into the trap of exaggerating Britain's importance, assuming that, had we been present at the outset, some of the community's more appalling characteristics, most obviously the Common Agricultural Policy, would either not have been introduced or, if they had, would have emerged in a different form. This was obviously untrue since the CAP was the result of the key bargain in the whole affair: support for French farmers in return for opening the French market to the then far more efficient industries of West Germany. In other words, the sheer Alice in Wonderland nature of the CAP was to reward the inefficient.

There was only one sceptic who was a moderate, indeed the king of the tribe, Hugh Gaitskell, the leader of the Labour Party since 1955. At the instigation of his close ally Roy Jenkins, he met Jean Monnet at a private dinner and questioned him closely. But Gaitskell was permanently turned off the whole idea of Europe by what he saw as the Frenchman's mysticism. According to Hugo Young, Monnet's exhausted curtain line was 'Well, we must have faith' to which Gaitskell's reply was simply, ' I don't believe in faith, I believe in reason and there is little reason in anything you have been saying tonight.' Three months after a bitter public clash with Spaak at the Socialist International in July 1962, Gaitskell made his underlying position clear in a monumental speech lasting nearly two hours at the Labour Party

Conference in October 1962. His attitude was uncompromising. Entry into the EEC would 'mean the end of . . . a thousand years of history . . . of Britain as an independent European state . . . the end of a thousand years of history.' The economic equation, which he had previously thought was a balance, was, he concluded, heavily tipped against British entry. The CAP was 'one of the most devastating pieces of protectionism ever invented, so bad that negotiation away of its rougher edges could not meet the case'. The EEC's treatment of the Commonwealth and the government's assurances were 'astonishing' and 'odious'. He ended with a peroration (which Young predictably describes as 'purest demagoguery') describing the idea as 'an odious piece of hypocritical, supercilious, arrogant rubbish'. He received the only real ovation he was ever accorded by a usually sceptical conference – though, as his wife pointed out at the time, 'all the wrong people' – i.e. everyone except the Gaitskellite reformers headed by Roy Jenkins – 'were applauding'. Tragically Gaitskell's death early in 1963 removed the only 'moderate' voice against our entry and for the next thirty-five years left the opposition overwhelmingly to politicians and commentators who could, in most cases, be reasonably be described as right-extremists wedded to an outdated imperialism or leftist believers in 'socialism in one country'.

Gone were the delusions of independence, gone was any belief in ourselves, in the spirit of the summer of 1940 after the fall of France, expressed so memorably in the celebrated cartoon 'Very well, alone'. We were, it was assumed, ineluctably and humiliatingly dependent on any political grouping which would accept us if we were to retain the pretence of importance in the world. No attempt was made to analyse any other possibility – for example, that, most obviously, we could act as an impartial intermediary between Europe and the USA. Moreover our allegiance to 'Europe' was always suspect – and with reason. In September 2001 Tony Blair abandoned the idea of a united European response to the destruction of the World Trade Centre in favour of a unilateral declaration of support for the United States rather than acting through the European Union.

Our eventual entry into the market was made possible after the emollient Georges Pompidou had replaced de Gaulle in 1969. For Pompidou the acceptance of the British case represented a gesture of independence against his predecessor – indeed he had to keep the ultra-Gaullist Quai d'Orsay in the dark during the personal negotiations he conducted with Edward Heath. He further emphasised the contrast by deliberately announcing their agreement in the same room in which de Gaulle had delivered his veto ten years earlier.

The deal meant that the British had to swallow a great deal. As a German official put it, 'an almost inconceivable flood of European law

98

. . . had to be accepted by the candidates'. As Lord Denning remarked at the time, the Treaty of Rome is 'like an incoming tide. It flows into the estuaries and up the rivers. It cannot be held back'. 'To enter the Common Market,' wrote Peter Shore, 'Britain basically abandoned its long-developed food supplies from Canada, Australia and New Zealand and became a second stomach for the high-cost surpluses of French farmers' and, he could have added, the even higher cost foods from their German brethren. 'The institutional structure, the Commission and the European Court of Justice, their voting system in the Council of Ministers, along with the volumes of European legislation – the Directives and regulations enacted since 1958 – all were accepted without amendment.' Because British farming formed so small a part of the economy, the burden on the British taxpayer would have been so horrendous that Heath was granted a steadily narrowing breathing space for the first seven years after our entry. It is not surprising that the Treasury invariably adopted a hostile attitude throughout the negotiations. More minor absurdities included our abandonment of purchase tax in favour of Value Added Tax even though a committee headed by a future Governor of the Bank of England, Gordon Richardson, had advocated its retention. Even the senior civil servant responsible for indirect taxation in France had regretted that his country was not so well organised as Britain and could not impose a consumption tax at the wholesale level like purchase tax.

But by that time we were desperate. In the words of Sir Roy Denman, 'the terms of entry were irrelevant. No sensible traveller on the sinking *Titanic* would have said: "I will only enter a lifeboat if it is well scrubbed, well painted and equipped with suitable supplies of food and drink." ' Even Sir Con O'Neill, that most outspoken and outspokenly Europhile of civil servants, admitted that the terms were unfair: 'We realised that our contribution to the budget would be a very severe strain . . . disproportionate. We realised that we'd be paying more than anyone else.' For it was assumed that we could do nothing in the longer term to lessen the unfair burden imposed by the community budget. 'To keep New Zealand happy, the British were forced to worsen their budget terms,' said O'Neill. The whole deal, wrote Young, automatically disadvantaged a member state which, like Britain, '(a) collected more tariffs and levies on goods imported from outside the EEC and (b) had an efficient agriculture sector' and which 'was therefore rewarded' – surely the right term would be 'punished' – with much lower subsidies from Brussels.

By this stage the Europhiles had taken on a nasty whiff of the attitude of the best and brightest in France after the defeat by the Germans in the summer of 1940. 'We have sinned, we have gone downhill, we are unworthy,' the Petainists felt, and sometimes said, 'therefore we must suffer and above all collaborate closely with the German invader.' Similarly the 'negotiations' and the subservient attitude of British ministers and civil servants after our entry seemed designed to prove that we were the best-behaved boys in the European school (in marked contrast to our 'partners', who invariably fought hard and dirty to defend their own interests). The behaviour was reminiscent of the judgement passed on Austen Chamberlain, a Foreign Secretary in the 1920s and brother of the much tougher Neville: 'He always played the game and always lost it.'

The realisation that we were going to be treated as the poor men of Europe, the losers, the suckers, came a few days before our formal application to join was received. With a haste that was unprecedented in EEC negotiations, the Six had agreed on their first Common Fisheries Policy. In Peter Shore's words, the new policy 'claimed for the Community the newly-agreed 200-mile limit that the United Nations Conference on the Sea had allowed coastal and inland states. It thus brought the great fishing areas of the North Sea, the Irish Sea, the South-West Approaches and the North Atlantic – formerly dominated by UK trawlers – into Community ownership and control, in which the UK was henceforth to be allowed only a quota.' Even Con O'Neill admitted that this was a mistake. In Young's words, 'he and his team ... wholly miscalculated the support which the plight of plucky trawlermen could engender, vastly disproportionate to their numbers or their economic importance'. But the trawlermen were to be sacrificial pawns, in the Great Cause.

The central economic and financial element in the EEC was the Common Agricultural Policy, an agromorass which absorbed three quarters of the Community's budget and, moreover, was the very antithesis of the fundamental belief in free trade that had been the credo of the 'reasonable' classes ever since the repeal of the Corn Laws 125 years earlier. In the early days after entry, it became fashionable in Whitehall to assume that the sensible Germans would not allow the expensive farce to continue and would join with us to revolutionise the system.* Typically, Con O'Neill 'hoped ... agriculture would become less burdensome for the Community as a whole'. Needless to say, there was not the slightest chance of such a change in attitude, if only because German farming was even more fragmented and inefficient than that in France. As a result, well over thirty years since the introduction of the CAP, it still accounts for over half the European Union's budget. In Britain the CAP had a number of ill-effects. It increased the contrast in economic situation between poor hill farmers

* A belief confided to me in 1973 in a confidential interview with the then Permanent Secretary to the Ministry of Agriculture.

and the grain barons of East Anglia and Lincolnshire, and farmers had a further incentive to produce at any cost, to the landscape as well as to the economy, almost as if it were still wartime.

But the over-arching result of our entry was its effect on our capacity to decide our own fate. The 1971 White Paper had stated flatly, and untruthfully, that 'there is no question of erosion of essential national sovereignty' – a phrase explained away by the Europhiles by concentrating on the word 'essential'. Yet in 1961, the Lord Chancellor, Lord Kilmuir, himself a keen supporter of British membership, had emphasised that 'the surrenders of sovereignty involved are serious ones . . . I am sure that it would be a great mistake to under-estimate the force of the objections to them. But these objections ought to be brought out into the open now.' They never were, not directly anyway. As Hugo Young put it, 'The disguising [over the consequences on our sovereignty] was part of an intensely political process' – as though politics automatically involved deception on vital issues. Only by sweetening the truth about national sovereignty, apparently, could public opinion be kept in line.

This deception was the clearest demonstration of the extent of the web with which the 'Europeans' covered the whole exercise, a fact admitted by Young. But nothing about the European Union is democratic; even today, over forty years after the signature of the Treaty of Rome, it suffers from what even its devotees describe as a 'democratic deficit'. The European Parliament is largely impotent, unable even to decide where it can sit* and dependent on a Council of Ministers, who themselves come from democratic countries but have no intention of allowing their voters any say in their decisions.

Since 1973, as Professor Anthony King points out[16], there has been a transformation in the British constitution. From then on supra-national institutions greatly limited the powers of the British government, which, notably unlike say the French or the Germans, automatically obeyed all the enormous number of 'European' rules and regulations. As King says, there is an immense range of subjects, large and small, over which decisions are made in Brussels rather than Britain, adding up to a considerable shift in sovereignty. 'The Common Agricultural Policy, the Common Fisheries Policy, tobacco advertising, metric weights and measures in shops and supermarkets, the quality of British beaches, regional policy, competition policy, labour law, the free movement of labour, fees in higher education, the axle weights of lorries

---

* Because of French pressure it now has two homes, both built at enormous expense, in Brussels and in Strasbourg, symbolically on the historically contested Rhine frontier between France and Germany. The cost of the two buildings, and of the need to transport the whole parliament and its papers and staff between the two is incalculable.

and a great deal else besides.' Entry into the EEC also involved the first referendum in British history and brought the whole idea of direct votes on specific questions out of the constitutional cold in which it had languished since the dawn of constitutional time, allowing it to emerge in many varieties in the 1990s. Thanks largely to our entry into Europe, the position of Britain's judges, a group which had always tried to avoid involvement in political decision-making, was being simultaneously weakened and strengthened. While the authority of the European Court of Justice is a clear net loss to purely British judicial authority, the existence of the European Court of Human Rights led to the 1998 Act which incorporated the European Convention on Human Rights into British law and thus extended the judges' authority into what might be called 'social' areas.

The humiliating way in which we crawled into 'Europe' and behaved when we were inside what became the European Union was sympto-matic of a general lack of confidence in anything labelled 'typically British'. This defeatism spread to every walk of life. It was even reflected in attitudes to English teaching. As Professor Brian Cox wrote in the late 1980s: 'The emphasis on an "English" tradition has come under continuous attack during the last twenty years or so; during their undergraduate training many young teachers of English will have discussed the assumptions that underlie that concern for our cultural heritage. The desire for a national culture is seen as damagingly con-servative, often "racist" and almost inevitably unsympathetic to the rights of women. This may surprise many people who read English literature for pleasure.'[17]

For me the most important victim of the anti-English prejudice was undoubtedly Rudyard Kipling, one of the greatest English writers of the twentieth century. He was a universal man of letters, who distinguished himself as a novelist, a writer of short stories and as a poet. In his introduction to the 1966 anthology, *Nineteenth-century British Minor Poets*, W. H. Auden provides four tests for being a major poet: write a lot; show a range of subject matter; exhibit an originality of style and vision; and have a style and vision that mature over the course of a career. Kipling amply fulfils all these criteria.

Kipling was hated and feared for many reasons. One is the assump-tion that high art must of necessity be elitist. So any work of art, be it musical or artistic or literary, that is appreciated by the plebs cannot by definition be high art. He himself fully understood the dichotomy when he wrote of the Tower of Babel:

They builded a tower to shiver the sky and wrench the stars
    apart,
Till the Devil grunted behind the bricks: It's striking but is it Art?

The primary case against Kipling is that he was an unreconstructed racialist and imperialist, the reason why many departments of English literature do not include his works in their canon. The academics involved ignore the fact that Indians applaud his novel *Kim* as understanding the sub-continent, an accolade they are not prepared to accord to E. M. Forster's politically correct novel, *A Passage to India*. Moreover, as Professor John Carey put it, 'Kipling was no ordinary Imperialist. He cared for the individual caught up in the system . . . Kipling's art reveals what is special about seemingly nondescript people. The implications are democratic . . . Menials and underdogs in these stories repeatedly perform better than those in command . . . Kipling's estimate of the British Army was "brainy men languishing under an effete system." That went for British society too.'[18] Kipling was also a victim of a general, and by no means totally justified, attitude of shame towards the British Empire in general, and the Indian Empire in particular. Indeed for a very long time it was fashionable to admire the China of the murderous Mao Tse-Tung rather than the India of Jawaharal Nehru. But perhaps the oddest twist in all this is that the many academics who hate Kipling as a racist are quite prepared to admire, nay worship, T. S. Eliot, even though he was a devoted disciple of Charles Maurras, the French intellectual of the early years of the twentieth century who was so deeply reactionary as to be near-fascist in his thinking.

But, over the past couple of decades, biographies by younger authors have begun to demonstrate Kipling's true qualities. Typically another poet, Craig Raine,[19] makes a good case that he was not of any time, but experimental (you have only to read the dense later short stories, comparable to Beethoven's last string quartets, to realise the quality of his mind). His virtuosity was also suspect, as was his use of faithfully transcribed dialect which Raine has described as his 'greatest contribution to modern literature – prose and poetry'.

The tendency to ignore or despise typically English artists extended also to composers. In 1999 Edward Elgar was finally portrayed on new £20 notes. Philip Hensher remarked how 'even thirty years ago Elgar would have been a controversial figure to stick on a banknote' because he was so associated with Empire, Pomp & Circumstance, 'but to us' – a younger generation – 'he seems the composer of the Enigma Variations and of the mysterious, spare last works; undeniably English in spirit and voice, but an Englishness which seems veiled and visionary rather than triumphant'.[20]

At least Elgar had become popular again in the 1960s. The same cannot be said of the comic operas of W. S. Gilbert and Sir Arthur Sullivan, which were looked down on by the cognoscenti. The D'Oyly Carte company, which performed them the year round, was left to drift into tattiness and neglected by the Arts Council without arousing any great storm of protest. Yet these are almost certainly the finest comic operas ever written. This is not just a personal belief. It is one that was shared by such American gods as the Gershwin brothers, Yip Harburg, the writer of 'Brother can you spare a dime' and 'Somewhere Over the Rainbow', and Groucho Marx, all of whom revered the pair as their gurus. But in 1999, once British self-hatred had somewhat abated, Mike Leigh, that most fashionable of directors, was able to make *Topsy Turvy*, an affectionate and appreciative film about the couple and their protracted but ultimately triumphant attempts to write *The Mikado*. Thank goodness for the return of a belief in the enduring value of the Best of British in whatever form it was expressed. These are only two examples of a more general 'cultural rehabilitation', indicative of a wider and renascent self-confidence in English culture which spread from our literary to our artistic heritage.

Notes

1. *The Suez Affair*, Weidenfeld & Nicolson, 1967.
2. *Prospect*, December 1998.
3. *British Economic Policy Since the War*, Penguin 1958.
4. *Encounter*, October 1960.
5. Michael Barnes, *Independent*, 22 October 1999.
6. *Guardian*, July 20 1962.
7. *New Statesman*, March 26 1999.
8. Anthony Sampson, *Macmillan*, Allan Lane, Penguin Press 1967.
9. Christopher Hitchens,*London Review of Books*, November 26 1998.
10. In Bogdanor and Skidelsky, op cit.
11. *Princess Di, the National Dish*, Pluto Press, 1984.
12. *This Blessed Plot – Britain and Europe from Churchill to Blair*, Papermac, 1999.
13. Quoted by Peter Shore, *Separate Ways – The Heart of Europe*, Duckworth, 2000.
14. *New Anatomy of Britain*, Hodder & Stoughton 1971.
15. *Paul Lashmar, Britain's Secret Propaganda War*, Sutton, Stroud, 1998.
16. *Hamlyn Lectures: Does the United Kingdom still have a constitution?* Sweet & Maxwell, 2001.
17. *An English Curriculum for the 1990s*, Hodder & Stoughton, 1991
18. *Pure Pleasure: a guide to the twentieth century's most enjoyable books*, Faber & Faber, 2000.
19. *Introduction to Selected Poetry*, Penguin, 1992.
20. *Independent*, June 23 1999.

6

The Death of Deference

BY THE END OF THE 1950s, England's heritage, symbolised by the 'flannelled fools' who had led us into the Suez disaster, was being scorned by opinion-makers and disregarded by the mass of the population. The cloud of deference which had hung so long and so heavily over Britain started to lift as soon as our forces had returned from Suez and Eden had retreated to Jamaica to try and recover, only to resign on his return in January 1957. If you define the 1960s as a more or less organised defiance of authority, then they could be said to have effectively started even while the campaign was still being fought in Egypt, and certainly did so immediately afterwards, so completely had the Suez Adventure upset the natural order of things, the establishment's easy assumption of superiority.

Even during the fighting, Suez had already legitimised dissent within the Overseas Services of the BBC which provided a notably balanced view of the Adventure, much to Eden's fury. Just after Suez the editor of the *Sunday Express*, John Junor, had had to apologise to Parliament for remarking about the petrol rationing caused by the closure of the canal: 'Tomorrow a time of hardship starts for everyone. For everyone? Include the politicians out of that . . . The tanks of the politicians will be brimming over.' His sentiments, which reflected what most people thought, the fact that they were uttered by so right-wing a commentator, and the punishment they incurred infuriated journalists who viewed the affair as a gross abuse of its authority by Parliament.

The new-found lack of respect led to the immediate suspension and equally swift abolition of a restriction which now seems inconceivable – the 'Fourteen Day Rule' which prevented the discussion on the air of any subject which Parliament was going to discuss within the next fortnight. The collapse of the rule followed some farcical incidents (in one programme the journalist Henry Fairlie pointed out that, if ever proceedings in Parliament were to be broadcast, they would be banned under the rule). The establishment was afraid, as Bernard Sendall says, that 'there was a danger that broadcasters representative and unrepresentative, accurate and inaccurate, informed and uninformed, selected ... because of their broadcasting technique and photogenic qualities, may form public opinion and prejudge the issue before Parliament had a chance to get to grips with it.' In the event the government soon gave way. Later Lord Hill, the minister responsible, admitted that the change, of which he was in favour, was made much easier by Suez. It was also Hill who helped the broadcasters – although not the Governors of the BBC, who were all for maintaining it – to abolish the so-called 'Toddlers' Truce' under which no programmes were transmitted between 6 and 7pm to enable parents to put their offspring to bed.

But it was Independent Television News, a subsidiary of the four ITV contractors, that provided the biggest impetus for a generalised lack of respect for authority. ITN was lucky, for until 1961 the BBC equivalent was run by Tahu Hole, most conservative and deferential of editors. Aidan Crawley, ITN's first editor-in-chief, an Old Harrovian, a Kent county cricketer and one of the most surprising members of that eclectic group, the 1945 Labour intake into Parliament, was, like Kenneth Clark, a typical half-way appointment. He – and his deputy, a rather hopeless fellow called Richard Goold-Adams – soon resigned over threats to chop ITN's budget and were succeeded by an experienced journalist, the New Zealander Geoffrey Cox, a former foreign correspondent and assistant editor of the *News Chronicle*. He aimed at positioning ITN somewhere between the tabloids and the broadsheets. Time and again ITN, with a staff of a mere twenty-five, broke and covered properly important events – such as the replacement of Anthony Eden by Harold Macmillan in February 1957 – far more quickly and effectively than their rivals in the BBC. One of their early scoops was an interview with Colonel Nasser in his first contact with Britain after Suez. Cox's news editor Arthur Clifford introduced the idea of 'human interest' stories in the news, normal enough in newspapers but unthinkable to the BBC – the most notable, perhaps, the joy of a Hungarian family when they heard they were to be allowed to settle in Britain. In November 1957 ITN showed that it was going to be more tabloid than broadsheet in its news coverage when it led its evening bulletin for two days running on an appalling train crash at Lewisham in South London – a decision that led to the resignation in disgust of the then deputy editor, Mark Arnold-Forster, a *Guardian* man through and through.

But it was the newsreaders, not Cox himself, a relatively cautious editor, who set the tone of the station. The fact that they were on screen at a time when the BBC's announcers were heard but not seen was one revolution, which swiftly led to the cult of personality which was soon to envelop anyone who appeared regularly on television.

106

Their informality was part of their novelty. They included a number of figures who were to become household names, such as Reginald Bosanquet, the athlete Chris Chataway and Ludovic Kennedy, but the most significant was Robin, later Sir Robin, Day. He was a formidable figure ('those cruel glasses' was the memorable comment of Frankie Howerd) who over the next quarter of a century was to pioneer two significant developments: battling successfully for the broadcasting of Parliament and for a national lottery.

The first indication of Day's lack of respect for authority came in 1957 in an interview with Sir Kenneth Clark. There was talk at the time of cutting ITN's revenue and airtime. According to the former MP Dick Taverne*, 'Day asked him questions about the station's future which dumbfounded colleagues and critics by their directness ... It was unprecedented that the person in ultimate charge should be questioned about his responsibilities by one of his own employees – and the impact was dramatic.' In 1958 Day subjected Harold Macmillan to what one newspaper called 'the most vigorous cross-examination a Prime Minister has been subjected to in public'. The interview had two effects: it made Macmillan into a television personality and it began the transformation of the balance of media power, which soon made television the primary source of political coverage and debate. At first Day was considered a typical rebel. In fact he was a deeply conservative (with a small c) figure. Of the eight records he chose to take with him when he appeared on *Desert Island Discs*, one was Churchill's 'This was their finest hour' speech and another Laurence Olivier's rendering – which now seems terribly mannered – of Henry V's speech before Agincourt in the 1943 film of the play. As was the case with so many of the so-called Angries, the idea that Day was a real rebel sprang from the limitations of an establishment which so exaggerated their differences from the previously accepted norms.

Sidney Bernstein had helped to ensure ITN's independence and, apart from news broadcasting, it was Granada which set the pace for the media's new-found iconoclasm, which, as is almost invariably the case with the media, reflected rather than created the public mood. Bernstein combined show business flair – his office boasted a photograph of Barnum the great American showman – with a genuine drive to widen the field of enquiry. He was also superb at putting the journalistic side forward. A former head of his public relations team once told me how Bernstein would talk only of his prize current affairs programme, *World in Action*, while at the same time he was producing no fewer than eight quiz and game shows, a staple element in the ITV

* Obituary, *Independent*

107

schedule which included give-away quiz programmes like *Beat The Clock, Double Your Money* and so on, almost ad infinitum.

Bernstein gathered round him a team, headed by Denis Foreman, the former head of the British Film Institute, which bore no relation to the gentlemanly norm in the BBC. Together they set the pattern for much of British television over the next quarter of a century. 'We didn't know it at the time,' wrote one disciple, Michel Parkinson, 'but Granada was at the epicentre of a cultural revolution ... I couldn't have got a job as a doorman at the BBC but Sidney Bernstein had decided that Granada should be one long *Coronation Street.*'

Tim Hewat, an Australian journalist from the *Daily Express,* was responsible for a series of programmes on topics as varied, and as previously unthinkable, as euthanasia, homosexuality, coloured immigrants, venereal disease and the pill. Granada's major contribution was the long-running *World in Action*, whose direct, unblinking style had a profound impact on the whole of television current affairs – and on such future luminaries as Jeremy Isaacs, an out of work graduate hired to set up the longest-running series of all, *What The Papers Say.* Hewat, Isaacs said, taught him that TV 'is primarily a mass-audience medium and that one must be understood. He wanted TV programmes to say something' – and, moreover no one at Granada believed in the normally sacred doctrine of impartiality. They were all radicals. As Foreman put it, they were aiming 'to speed up certain processes of social reform'. The only subject they could not touch was freemasonry – for Cecil Bernstein, Sidney's brother, was a freemason and so the brothers remained unexamined until the 1980s.

The knee-jerk iconoclasm of the inhabitants of what Bernstein's publicity machine termed 'Granadaland' inevitably brought the station into conflict with the Television Act – Bernard Levin claimed that one fifteen-minute programme, the night before a murderer was due to be hanged, included seventeen breaches of the act. But such was the mood of the times that both sides enjoyed what became a game. Lord Hill, chairman of the ITA in the 1960s, once said that he particularly appreciated Bernstein's habit of defending a programme 'darting from illogical point to illogical point'. But then it was Hill who also said that it was Granada which provided ITV with 'the feel, the life, the vigour and the excellence of television'.

As a former film producer, Bernstein also encouraged his drama department, scheduling new plays which were both well made and full of – inevitably radical – social content by such noted authors as Lillian Hellman and Arthur Miller (hence the poster 'Who else loves Arthur Miller?' when the playwright was married to Marilyn Monroe). Light entertainment was left to brother Cecil and *Chelsea at Nine* proved that Granada could compete with ATV at its strongest. Cecil's most lasting legacy was the grandfather of all TV soaps, *Coronation Street* – though he was not a great enthusiast for the idea. The Street went on the air on December 9 1960, giving the Great British public its first systematic glimpse of a – more genuine then than it became later – Northern working-class environment. For it dealt seriously and sympathetically with the lives of the working classes, hitherto confined exclusively to supporting, comic roles. Since the start of *Coronation Street* it, and its innumerable imitators, have more or less faithfully reflected changes in British society.

The producer remembers the night they knew its fortunes were made, when in 1962 the Mayor of Blackpool asked for the cast to come and switch on the resort's famous lights. They couldn't get into the town for the crowds. All this was grist to Sidney Bernstein's mill. 'Isn't this exciting?' he would say. His spirit continued to pervade Granada even after he gradually relinquished his formerly tight hold on every detail of the company's business once the Granada contract had been renewed in the 1967 review – a mere formality, as everyone knew it would be.*

It was Bernstein who also revolutionised political broadcasting in 1958 when he organised serious coverage of all the candidates in a by-election in the Lancashire constituency of Rochdale. Although *The Times* wrote cautiously, 'Perhaps things will never be the same again,' Kenneth Allsop in the *Daily Mail* had no doubts that: 'Rochdale has changed the nature of democratic politics . . . Television is established as the new hub of the hustings.' After a high-powered seminar at Nuffield College, Oxford, the rules of election coverage were dramatically altered in time for the 1959 election. At previous general elections there had been an enforced blackout during the weeks between the dissolution of Parliament and polling day. Granada again took the initiative with an election marathon featuring all the candidates in all the constituencies in Granadaland while the BBC followed suit with a series of BBC Hustings. Granada went on to televise party conferences and the annual TUC conference – even though audiences were small, more people saw the conference on television than had attended as delegates during the TUC's entire history.

Throughout television the challenge set by Granada and ITN – to be popular but principled – was taken up, notably by the Canadian Sydney Newman, king of the one-off play, ABC's *Armchair Theatre*. Such executives and producers heralded the first Golden Age of television (there have been several since, their sheen varying according

---

* At that point Granadaland was divided into two seven-day-a-week franchises, with Bernstein taking Lancashire and the newly formed Yorkshire Television taking the east side of the Pennines.

to the viewer's age). Kenneth Clark was not the only heavyweight commentator; there was Dr Jacob Bronowski, the original pop scientific pundit, and A. J. P. Taylor the historian who could mesmerise the viewers by simply talking straight at camera for half an hour. Even religious television ceased to be a backwater – Bill Allenby, the first producer of *About Religion*, divided his creative talents between religion and racing – and the distinguished producer (and later theatrical impresario) Michael Redington started his TV career on the same programme.

ITV's programmes were 'coordinated' through the networking committee in which the big four bargained in an increasingly bazaar-like atmosphere, trying to ensure that as many of their own programmes as possible were networked. They also, and almost incidentally, introduced a new concept, that of scheduling, so that viewers could be confident that their favourite programmes would be screened at the same time on the same days each week. These sessions included both Lew Grade of ATV and Cecil Bernstein, who had already locked horns when they were discussing the fees for artists appearing at Granada's variety theatres. The meetings remained lively affairs – one participant remembers Grade, then well into his sixties, jumping on the table and doing a Charleston, a dance for which he had been famous in his youth, while waiting for everyone else to arrive.

The dominance of the Big Four (five after 1967 with the arrival of Yorkshire Television was not severely cramped by the arrival of nearly a dozen more contractors whose transmitters covered the rest of Britain. These brought in some dignitaries and companies – such as the Earl of Derby and the Rank Organisation – who had either been reluctant to invest in the early days or who had simply lost out in the bidding process. Most prominently, they included Roy Thomson, the Canadian who used the profits from Scottish Television ('a licence to print money' as he so famously – and accurately – remarked) to buy the *Sunday Times* and his regional papers from Lord Kemsley and, in 1966, the *Times* as well, a classic instance of the old establishment giving way to the new.

The late 1950s witnessed a remarkable fight-back by the BBC, which showed a capacity to reinvent itself that seemed surprising at the time though was to prove a feature of its life during the rest of the century. The counter-attack was led by the improbable figure of the then Director-General, Lieutenant-General Sir Ian Jacob. He was a professional soldier (indeed was the son of a field-marshal) who had been the Director of External Services at the BBC but was on secondment as Chief Staff Officer at the Ministry of Defence in 1954 when the BBC post came up after Sir William Haley left to edit *The Times*. Jacob was an archetypal establishment figure but it was he who laid the path for the openness and the willingness to expose society, warts and all, generally associated with his more flamboyant successor, Sir Hugh Carleton Greene – whom in fact Jacob groomed for the job. Jacob was prepared to plan ahead, to expand where Haley had been far too conscious of budgetary restrictions. In the words of Professor Asa Briggs[1], 'he approached his varied tasks methodically and unpretentiously, rather than dramatically, and with a matchless consistency of temperament and purpose' – in other words, he was a great general. But Greene, who succeeded him in 1961, went further. He believed that 'we have a duty to take account of the changes in society to be ahead of public opinion, rather than always to wait on it'.*

The BBC immediately filled the former Toddlers' Truce period with the ground-breaking *Tonight* programme. *Tonight* was produced by a team selected by Grace Wyndham Goldie, one of the outstanding figures in the BBC, and included a future director-general in Alistair Milne as well as a number of journalists escaping from *Picture Post*, the formerly radical current affairs magazine which ceased publication soon afterwards. Moreover, it was the BBC which produced *Z Cars*, perhaps the earliest example of a willingness to look closely and realistically at a symbol of authority through a popular drama series. The aim of a series based on the Liverpool police was 'to use the cops as a key or way of getting into a whole society' portraying the police as 'tough but not yobbish'. Remarkably, for a year or two the series ran parallel to *Dixon of Dock Green*.

Within less than a decade, the way the Met had been allowed to present a totally make-believe world had been replaced by a willingness on the part of the Lancashire police to help show the reality of policing in a big city – although the police authority had withdrawn their co-operation, after the first episode they soon came round to its veracity when they realised that the police were presented as a simple 'set of hearty North Country lads': even Charlie Barlow, the bully of an inspector, was instantly recognisable to the police themselves. The audience leapt from nine to fourteen million in a few weeks as audiences rapidly proved ready to accept that the police were not all fatherly PC Dixon types who always helped old ladies across the road and always had a sweet for a lost child.

Even in light entertainment, where ITV was supposedly unchallengeable, the BBC could exploit a major weakness, that ITV was dominated by agents and producers from the variety stage. The BBC soon gained the critical upper ground with series specially written for television, some of which, like Tony Hancock's *Half Hour*, proved

---

* In a speech in Rome to that notably untrendy gathering, the International Catholic Association for Radio and Television.

immortal. Their initiatives extended even to the improbable field of pop TV, thanks to Josephine Douglas, a BBC staff presenter, and Jack Good, a lower middle-class Oxford contemporary of mine who came up with the first pop TV programme, the fabled *Six Five Special* providing a showcase for the new stars like Adam Faith who were emerging.* Good then decamped to ITV to produce *Oh Boy!* – an early instance of a continuing trend in which the BBC took the initiative only to find the producers and stars lured away by the much larger financial rewards available on the other side. The pop phenomenon spread to the theatre, notably the satirical musical comedy, *Expresso Bongo*, with a witty script by Wolf Mankowitz.

In the late 1950s, although television took a cultural lead it was not to lose for decades to come, George Devine and his successors at the Royal Court continued to build on the success of *Look Back In Anger*. Another great impresario-cum-producer, Joan Littlewood, turned the Theatre Royal in Stratford into a Mecca for theatre-goers – though she never succeeded in attracting the working-class locals. But she did introduce immensely talented new playwrights including Arnold Wesker and the brilliant Irish drunk (and revolutionary) Brendan Behan. Like the producers of *Coronation Street*, both Littlewood and many of the film directors of the time were prepared to take the working classes seriously with the result that many of their efforts were patronised as concentrating exclusively on 'the kitchen sink' (About time too, one might say.) But some plays and films such as Wesker's *The Kitchen*, Shelagh Delaney's *Taste of Honey, Billy Liar,* starring the irresistible Julie Christie, *The Loneliness of the Long Distance Runner, Saturday Night and Sunday Morning* and *This Sporting Life* were both realistic and imaginative. But perhaps the most impressive was *The Servant*, a film directed by Joe Losey, an American refugee from McCarthyism. Starring Dirk Bogarde and from a script by the most original of all the new playwrights, Harold Pinter, it showed a corrupt seedy upper-class ne'er do well being undermined and corrupted by his butler in a stark piece of class war.

Sidney Bernstein had been the first cinema-owner to abolish the custom of playing the National Anthem after the last showing. By the end of the 1950s this had became a joke. Tom Nairn remembers being one of the many cinema-goers sneaking away from a performance of *Kind Hearts & Coronets* but finding that many of them froze on the stairway at the first chords of the anthem and 'turned with exaggerated masochism to honour the scratched screen image of HM on horseback'.

---

* Faith's real name was Terry Nelhans. Deeming this unsuitable for a pop star, Good promptly renamed him after two of his Oxford friends, Adam Fremantle – and Nicholas Faith.

But television, like the press, was still under the thumb of Commander Colville, the Royal Press Secretary, once described by Cecil Beaton as 'ashen-faced and like the wicked uncle in a pantomime' and known as the abominable no-man. Editors were aware that the public did not want 'disloyal' stores and neither ITV nor, more especially, the BBC were going to provide them.

The first attacks on royalty came from three sources. Two – those from John Osborne and Malcolm Muggeridge – came from 'usual suspects' and so were relatively unthreatening. But the third came from the heart of the Establishment – from Lord Altrincham, the son of Churchill's wartime Secretary of War no less.

Over a single weekend in 1957, Osborne wrote a splendid philippic for *Declaration*, a rather self-important collection of radical chic opinion pieces. In it he described the royal family with his customary delicacy as 'a gold filling in a mouthful of decay ... When the mobs rush forward in The Mall they are taking part in the last circus of a civilisation that has lost faith in itself and sold itself for a splendid triviality, for the ''beauty of the ceremonial'' and the ''essential spirituality of the rite''. We may not create any beauty or exercise much spirituality, but by God! we've got the finest ceremonial and rites in the world. Even the Americans haven't got that.' The monarchy's very powerlessness made it invulnerable: 'While commanding a unique position it is protected from ever having to solve a problem or make a choice. It is not merely above criticism, it is above the necessity of having to justify its existence.'

The same year, when the royal couple were visiting the United States, the then important mainstream weekly magazine the *Saturday Evening Post* republished an article by Malcolm Muggeridge – largely about the evils of a consumerist age which had barely begun – which had appeared in *Punch* two years earlier. His description of the Queen as the apex of an undesirably hierarchical social system was compounded by more personal remarks, notably that 'duchesses find the Queen dowdy, frumpish and banal'.

Far more serious, far more to the point, than this knockabout stuff was Altrincham's article the same year in the small-circulation but highly respectable *National and English Review*. He pinpointed the position of the monarchy as the symbol of an unhealthy retreat from reality. 'Britain,' he wrote, 'seemed to be compensating for loss of power in the world by lapsing into a state of collective make-believe, in which the hierarchic aspects of the monarchy were grossly exaggerated and the healthy habit of criticising office-holders was ceasing to apply to the monarchy.' He was also the first to voice what became a regular complaint, that the Queen's friends and advisers came from a limited caste. Looking back much later, in 1992, he added that 'after the

Second World War monarchy reverted to its pre-war routines almost as though nothing had happened'.

But Altrincham also criticised the Queen personally – and prophetically: 'When she has lost the bloom of youth the Queen's reputation will depend, far more than it does now, upon her personality. It will not then be enough for her to go through the motions; she will have to say things which people can remember, and do things on her own initiative which will make people sit up and take notice. As yet there is little sign that such a personality is emerging.' Time, he added presciently, was 'not yet her enemy'. Moreover her style of speaking was 'a pain in the neck'; she sounded like a 'priggish schoolgirl . . . Like her mother, she appears unable to string even a few sentences together without a written text . . . her words and style are stilted . . . Phrases like ''I am deeply moved'' sound very hollow when they are read from a typescript.' This was not inevitable. Although George V's speeches were not written by him, they 'were always in character; they seemed to be a natural emanation from, and expression of, the man.' All true, all relevant, and all the more unforgivable as coming from a Peer of the Realm.

Although Altrincham – who later relinquished his title to become plain John Grigg – remembers that he got more letters in support than against, he was assaulted in the street, even threatened with horse-whipping. When interviewed by the *Daily Mirror*, he showed his exasperation by remarking that when he had written to courtiers, those who had replied had said that ' ''we are only lackeys'' . . . the majority of the Queen's advisers would have been out-dated in the court of Charles II'. The BBC – largely represented by Richard Dimbleby, Their Man For Royal Occasions, and attacked as such by Muggeridge – was still too deferential to provide Altrincham with any publicity, but on ITN he told Robin Day that it was wrong for the Queen to be totally immune from responsibility, and that she, and not her courtiers should be criticised because 'only the boss can get rid of the bad servants'. By then there was a feeling that, as Anthony Sampson put it, 'popular interest in royalty was like a balloon that had broken from its moorings', and that some courtiers 'had an uneasy feeling that the balloon might eventually hit something and explode'.[2] The only journalist to defend the Queen was Dermot Morrah, a romantic figure on *The Times* and later a herald, who argued that the importance of the monarch should lie 'not at all in what she does, but entirely in what she is' – like a Byzantine icon.

Altrincham's opinions, with many of which the majority of the British public, younger courtiers – and Prince Philip – agreed, did have a few, albeit largely cosmetic, effects. The Queen extended her Christmas broadcast from radio to television and ended the practice of presenting debutantes at court. Yet debutantes did not disappear and The Season continued as the sort of marriage market it had always been – demonstrating, perhaps, that social habits would not initially be revolutionised if royalty were to disappear. Ten years later, Christopher Booker pointed to the Altrincham-Muggeridge uproar as a moment of cultural shift occurring just as 'the old social "myths" which had seemed to hold British society together in a great organic whole' were about to lose their force.

The notion that the mood, the forces, the generally iconoclastic atmosphere traditionally associated with the 1960s, were both born and grew up in the last four years of the previous decade is strengthened by the rather farcical story of the Bank Rate Tribunal which opened up the previously secret habits and traditions of the City of London and, in doing so, called them into question. In November 1957, as a result of one of Britain's all too regular economic crises, the Bank rate was suddenly increased from the already historically high level of 5 per cent to an unthinkable 7 per cent. It was obvious from the falls in gilt-edged just before the announcement that some insiders had smelt or known of the jump in advance. A high-powered Tribunal was set up to investigate the leaks. Although it reached only anodyne conclusions, it revealed the anomalous position of directors of the Bank of England who also headed leading City institutions and so would know in advance of changes that would damage their invest-ments. It seemed obvious that at least two directors, Tony Keswick* of the Hong Kong-based Jardine Matheson and Lord Kindersley, had some inkling of what was about to happen and that firms with which they were associated had sold considerable quantities of government stock just before the announcement.

The leading City figures were furious at interrogations which revealed the assumption, as the Labour politician Patrick Gordon-Walker put it, that 'what was good for the City was good for Britain'. For the inquiry marked the beginnings of what was to become a major industry: inquiring into the workings of the British Establishment. Within a year, an analysis of the 'Social background and connections of top decision makers' had been published[3] and by 1962 Anthony Sampson had written The Anatomy of Britain, a best-seller which told the story of Britain's governing class in their own words.

A year after the leak, an unprecedentedly hostile takeover bid, for British Aluminium, set a newcomer, Siegmund Warburg, against the might of the City Establishment. Warburg, scion of a distinguished German-Jewish banking family, was a one-off, described by Peter

---

* Keswick was the author of the splendid reply: 'It would be difficult for me to remember the exact timing of a conversation on a grouse moor.'

Spira, a former director, as 'innovative and cultured, yet ruthless and vicious . . . mercurial, highly emotional, often irrational; hypnotic and impulsive, provocative and conciliatory, prudish yet fascinated by the erotic' – adjectives few if any of which could have applied to any other banker in London at the time. Warburg's contempt for the City was total: it was full of mediocrities, he said, and most of the important people were 'so anxious to avoid unpleasantness that they will knowingly make blunders, with the sole aim of sparing themselves any conflict'. 'He thought the British upper class feared excellence and exertion,' wrote Ron Chernow 'and took refuge in an effete, snobbish gentility, behaving with an arrogance it no longer merited.' He naturally hated mistakes. 'Banking for Siegmund,' continued Chernow, 'involved perpetual self-criticism. At one point he assigned a person to record all mistakes made and the remedies applied. To work for him you had to be as workaholic as he was himself – one of his quirks in the early days was to hold board meetings in his flat at 10 am on Sunday morning, with everyone standing'. Warburg's was known as the 'Night Club' because its staff worked both early and late.

The Great Aluminium Battle which catapulted Warburg into worldwide fame involved rival bids for British Aluminium from the American company Alcoa and from Warburg's clients, the American Reynolds Metals in partnership with the British firm Tube Investments. BA could not have been more established. Its chairman, Lord Portal, had been the Chief of Air Staff during the war – his had been a typical appointment at a time when it was assumed that wartime qualities could be translated into industrial success – while the managing director, Geoffrey Cunliffe, was the son of a former Governor of the Bank of England. At one point Warburg, helped by another self-made banker, Lionel Fraser of Helbert Wagg, faced what *The Times* called 'an array of City institutions never before seen in a take-over battle'. As Chernow pointed out, Warburg the refugee 'now faced twenty-seven indignant men with titles, all lined up behind British Aluminium in a contested take-over battle, itself an almost unprecedented event in the somnolent world of the 1950s City'.

Warburg won because, as he put it, 'we just didn't make any mistakes and the other side did' – most obviously when Portal recommended an offer from Alcoa rather than one nearly a fifth higher from the TI-Reynolds consortium. Warburg fought craftily, once holding a press conference at 7.30 pm on a Friday when he knew full well that his opponents were already ensconced in their country retreats for the weekend. At one point Lord Cobbold, the Governor of the Bank of England, suggested a truce in the old-fashioned City fashion. Warburg, wrote Chernow, 'returned to his office in a fury, outraged at the barefaced cheek of the consortium in instigating Cobbold' – who had naturally patronised the newcomer – 'to take such an unprecedented step.' In the event, Warburg won a match which, as Macmillan said, was Gentlemen v Players. He could rely on the fact that his side's bid was higher – and on the new breed of professional institutional shareholders from the insurance companies. Their involvement was not unprecedented: some years earlier a mild-mannered actuary, announcing himself simply as 'Leslie Brown from Prudential Insurance', had ensured the downfall of one of Britain's most flamboyant industrialists, Sir Bernard Docker of BSA*. But, and typically of many such battles in the future, the BA affair, the first 'modern' take-over battle seen in the City, wasn't very profitable for the winning company. The bid had been so costly that the winners didn't have enough spare capital to invest in BA.

In industry too there was a new generation abroad. This was abundantly clear with the bid that pitted against each other two great rivals in the chemicals and textiles businesses, Sir Paul Chambers, the former tax-expert turned chairman of ICI, and Frank Kearton, a brilliant scientist who fought off ICI's bid for Courtaulds. Equally typical of the new generation was Joe Hyman, the ebullient, self-publicising egomaniacal chairman of the textile firm Viyella. In particular he had a clear strategy: to allow Far Eastern and other countries with cheap labour to dominate the cheap end of the market and to concentrate on what might be described as 'added-value' businesses. Hyman was also, unusually for the time, prepared to air his views in public, notably his objection to the idea 'that top jobs should be the monopoly of the upper middle class'. The media-friendly magnate was born.

But to the general public more important were social, rather than economic, changes. The first sign was the reform of the law on obscenity, which had resulted in five successful prosecutions during the 1950s. The pressure for reform of the legal definition of obscenity (which had been laid down in Victorian times to protect women, children and the feeble-minded) was started in 1955 by Roy Jenkins, then a young backbench Labour MP. 'Rab' Butler, the Home Secretary in the Macmillan government, gave in to pressure from Tory MPs and appointed a committee to review the law but this shiftiest of politicians ensured that the proposals got lost in the legislative pipeline. But then A.P. Herbert, the independent politician and humorist, who had carried through a reform of Britain's divorce laws as long ago as 1937, threatened to stand in a by-election, and a bill proposed by Jenkins went through Parliament ensuring that a work would be considered as a

---

* His wife was even better-known, for her gold-plated Daimler (one of BSA's products) and her famous saying 'I've fallen in love with three men in my life and all of them happened to be millionaires'.

whole – an echo of a ruling by the US Supreme Court in 1957 which allowed a defence of 'redeeming social importance' in cases of obscenity.

So by 1960 the way was open for Penguin to publish *Lady Chatterley's Lover*, one of D. H. Lawrence's most famous – if by no means one of his best – novels, replete with steamy sex scenes between Lady C and her husband's gamekeeper. The trial was a sensation, partly because the defence called in witness many of Britain's most famous literary figures. To insiders, the defining moment was the evidence of the radical writer Richard Hoggart, who was described (by Kenneth Tynan in the *Observer*) as 'a short, dark young Midland teacher of immense scholarship and fierce integrity' while his opinions were characterised as 'the stubborn, uncompromising voice of the radical English moralist'.

But the most famous moment, showing in the crudest possible form the gulf between Life at the Top and as it was lived by the vast majority of the population came from the prosecuting counsel Mervyn Griffith-Jones. As Anthony Powell put it, his phrasing was particularly inappropriate in front of a jury, 'five of whose members were either illiterate or had stumbled over the oath.' 'Would you allow the servants to read it?'[5] Powell claims that in the subsequent debate in the House of Lords one peer declared that 'I should not object to my wife or daughter reading the book but I have the strongest objection to it being read by my gamekeeper.' To be fair to the English legal system, Griffith-Jones was not a typical lawyer. As a judge, he became famous for the number of those appearing before him who were acquitted by the jury. 'His main concern,' wrote Geoffrey Robertson, 'was that counsel should sit up straight and not slouch in their chairs.'[7] But the most important result of the Lady C case was that from then on it became virtually impossible to prosecute any book with even the slightest pretensions to literary worth. These included the eighteenth-century pornographic classic *Fanny Hill* – a fun read even now but scarcely distinguished literature – while even the ban on *Last Exit to Brooklyn* was overturned on appeal.

A year after the Chatterley trial, Hoggart appeared, far less successfully, as a moralist in another sphere, as the guiding light, indeed the author, of the Report of a Committee on Broadcasting, headed by a leading industrialist, Lord Pilkington, which reported in June 1962. The report recommended that the ITA should act as the commissioning authority which would plan the programming and sell the advertising while the companies would compete to provide the programmes. It was a typical instance of the moral authoritarianism shared by the right and the Puritan left. The committee studied 636 memoranda and over 200 other papers yet they made no attempt to undertake any objective research and their findings were so skewed against the independent sector as to be sometimes laughable – in one important instance, the committee chose to ignore a finding by the ITA that serious current affairs programmes shown out of peak hours attracted far larger audiences than comparable BBC programmes shown at peak time.

So the committee lost public sympathy, even though the contractors had brought the reaction upon themselves because of their obscenely large monopoly profits. The public's attitude was well expressed by the television critic of the *Sunday Times*, Maurice Wiggin, who found the report's style 'gobbledegook': 'Reading this Report you would think that there is practically nothing wrong with the BBC and practically nothing right with ITV.' This was not how he saw it and, as he pointed out, he watched far more television than the authors of the report (the same criticism was often, and rightly, made of politicians, who rarely if ever had time to watch, most obviously when Parliament was sitting). 'To make the ITA into another BBC,' Wiggin concluded, was 'the hopeless last resort of men who fundamentally fear the operation of a free society.' In Parliament even the BBC's supporters objected to the report's 'moral authoritarianism' and its attitude, shared with nannies, of 'find out what the boy is doing and tell him to stop'. In the end, Pilkington was ignored but led to a Bill which resulted in a levy on advertising income tailored to protect the smaller contractors – an earlier proposal had threatened to ruin them – a general housecleaning by the ITA and the abolition of such horrors as the shopping programmes – which were on the way out anyway.

By this time authority in any guise was on the ropes, but the final blow came in the 'steamy' (figuratively not literally) summer of 1963, a period of a few months which marks the defining moment at which deference died and was buried in a cloud of ridicule and public hilarity. The stories, and the personalities involved were written up – in the most biased possible fashion – by the most distinguished, normally courageous, idiosyncratic and – in social attitudes old-fashioned – judge in the country, Lord Denning, whose philosophy was summed up in the phrase 'I must do justice whatever the law may be' and who invariably preferred his own ideas on justice rather than confine himself to the narrow letter of the law. His report on the Profumo affair* makes fascinating reading because the learned judge showed just how far society in general had wandered from the straight and narrow moral and sexual path he represented.

But before Profumo came the hotly contested divorce case involving the Duke and Duchess of Argyll, which notoriously featured a photograph of Her Grace providing fellatio to a headless man. Apart from

* It was reissued by The Stationery Office in 1999.

119

the fun provided by guessing the possessor of the male apparatus involved, revealed after his death forty years later as belonging to Douglas Fairbanks Jnr, the case was interesting not in itself but because it was the first time since the war that such goings-on in high society had been revealed to the general public. To those in the know, the lady's behaviour was not that surprising. In the early 1930s the Duchess, then the lovely Margaret Sweeny*, had, or so she later claimed, slept with a different young man during every one of the hundred nights of her season as a debutante. Nevertheless the press were appallingly unfair to her, for the Duke was a nasty piece of work, a drunk who had married Margaret – or so he told a friend – only to get his hands on her money, and he demonstrated no hesitation in showing the photos to his friends. In his summing-up, the judge showed that the underlying lesson of the Chatterley case, that women were just as entitled to have strong sexual feelings as men, had not penetrated the whole judiciary. For he condemned the defendant as 'a highly sexed woman' whose activities were designed 'to satisfy a basic sexual appetite' which, by implication, ladies, above all Duchesses, were not supposed to possess. This was a reflection of a much more serious piece of legal misogyny: that in a divorce case any adulterous wife was automatically deemed the guilty party and generally deprived of the custody of her children, whatever the attenuating circumstances,

The Argyll divorce blended with the description of orgies provided by one of the sauciest persons in the festival of fun that summer, Mandy Rice-Davies, shrewdest of show-girls†, who was one of the witnesses who told the learned judge of 'a group of people who hold parties in private of a perverted nature. At some of these parties the man who serves the dinner is nearly naked except for a small square ace apron round his waist' with a sign reading 'Please whip me if the service fails to please'. Because he wore a mask, he was unrecognisable – which resulted in a hilarious game to guess who he might be. 'He was also a "slave" who is whipped . . . The guests indulge in sexual intercourse one with the other, and indulge in other sexual activities of a vile and revolting nature.' (This is pretty lip-licking stuff from the old Puritan and reminds me of the – possibly mythical – headline in one of Rupert Murdoch's papers after a collection of pornography had been confiscated by the Australian customs authorities: 'Keep this

---

* Under her maiden name, she was mentioned in Cole Porter's song, 'You're the Tops'. She was furious because her name was rhymed with Mussolini, who was also considered the Top by many famous people in the early 1930s.

† She gained immortality with her remark 'He would, wouldn't he?' when Lord Astor denied her claim that they had slept together.

filth out of Australia,' it trumpeted, adding thoughtfully, 'six pages of pictures inside.')

The Argyll case was only peripheral to Denning's inquiries, which were supposedly concerned exclusively with the Profumo affair, the tale of two very different, but both in their ways very brilliant, people, John Profumo, whose political career was ruined, and Stephen Ward, a society osteopath who committed suicide. There was a large and entertaining supporting cast of call girls, peers and leading politicians (white), gangsters (black), policemen (mostly shady), the security services (cynical), judges and prosecutors (vengeful), and of course a classic heavy, in the shape of Yevgeny Ivanov, a Russian diplomat, naval officer and KGB agent. Once the scandal had broken, the public was kept fully informed by editors and journalists (either sensationalist or Doing their Duty, depending on who you listen to). For the press was already furious with the government because it had jailed two journalists for contempt of court for refusing to reveal their sources in an earlier enquiry into a Russian spy, William Vassall, at the Admiralty.

Profumo, the grandson of an aristocratic Italian immigrant, had an impeccable background and enormous charm. Helped by his marriage to a beautiful – and classy – film star, Valerie Hobson, he rose elegantly and without any great apparent effort to reach the post of Secretary of State for War, a post just below Cabinet level, though much later he claimed (to Woodrow Wyatt) that he wanted to leave politics anyway but had been persuaded out of such a step by the Chief Whip. Ward was undoubtedly the most brilliant osteopath of his generation but one who would ask his patients after he had treated them, 'Now that you've had some physical relief can I offer you the emotional equivalent?', introducing some of the pretty girls who graced his establishment. Sexually, it was said that, although he was 'well-endowed', Ward preferred to be a spectator, a voyeur rather than an enthusiastic participant. He also, rather pathetically, had two fantasies: that his artistic gifts were more than his undoubted talent for sketching instant likenesses of his clients and other celebrities; and that he could perform a major role in bringing Britain and Soviet Russia together. It was this latter fantasy that led to a prosecution which amounted to persecution and the subsequent suicide of a butterfly broken upon a wheel, whose only real fault was a love of living on the edge.

Thanks to his many distinguished patients – who in the past had included both Gandhi and Winston Churchill – Ward had become, in his own mind at least, a fully-paid-up member of Society. That was not Lord Denning's view. He described Ward, absurdly, as 'the most evil man I have ever met'. Denning displayed a not inconsiderable prurience: 'Mr Kennedy, can you tell me what fellatio is?' was typical

121

of his questioning. After describing how Ward used to pick up girls and take them to his cottage by the Thames for the delectation of his friends, the judge went on: 'There is evidence he was ready to arrange for whipping and other sadistic performances. He kept collections of pornographic photographs. He attended parties where there were sexual orgies of a revolting nature.' Unsurprisingly, too, Ward's finances were by no means orthodox, and Denning demonstrated a financial Puritanism worthy of an old-fashioned bank manager. Ward, he revealed, 'did not keep a banking account. He got a firm of solicitors to keep a sort of banking account for him, paying in cheques occasionally to them and getting them to pay his rent . . . He had many cash transactions which left no trace.'

Yet the undoubted star of the show was Christine Keeler, universally acknowledged as one of the most beautiful girls in London. Even Denning was forced to admit that 'she had undoubted physical attractions'. Ward, he added, introduced her not only to a great many chaps but also 'to the drug Indian hemp and she became addicted to it. She met coloured men who trafficked in it and she went to live with them.' Hotcha, as we used to say. The setting for the early acts in the tragic farce could not have been more beautiful: a charming, albeit somewhat rundown cottage by the Thames below Cliveden, the family home of the Astors. It was Bill, Lord Astor, a friend and patient, who allowed Ward, and his ever-changing troupe of friends, to use the cottage and it was there that both Ivanov and Profumo met Keeler at relaxed, casually sexy weekends.

That Ward was undoubtedly acting as a link between Britain and Russia was not wholly fantastic – though I disagree with the importance placed on their relations between MI5, Ward and Ivanov by Phillip Knightley and Caroline Kennedy*. It was an MI5 agent who showed the situation in its proper light in a report when he said of Ward that 'I strongly suspect that he is the provider of popsies for rich people'. This was precisely the sort of language used by Len Deighton's down-market fictional secret service agent Harry Palmer, who had first appeared in print the previous year. For 1963 was also the year that the spy-secret agent literary industry got into full swing. Kim Philby had fled to Moscow, John le Carré had added a new dimension to the spy story genre with his classic *The Spy Who Came In from the Cold*, and the first James Bond film had been a huge success. In fact, MI5 was the only organisation that emerges from this sorry story with any credit: it was dismissive of Ward's hopes of becoming an agent – though not as dismissive as Denning made out – but found Ward

* In *An Affair of State* (Jonathan Cape, 1987) – an otherwise convincing account of how Ward was framed.

useful in feeding information to his friend Ivanov and hearing from the Russian in return.

The affair broke in early 1963 when George Wigg, the Labour Party's obsessional, unpleasant expert on security, took advantage of Parliamentary privilege to allude to the goings-on – although the story would have broken in any case at the trial of one of Keeler's West Indian lovers, Johnny Edgecombe, who had shot at her. (Keeler would no doubt have informed the court that Edgecombe was jealous of her affair with Profumo – except that she skipped off to Spain before the trial.) As it was, Profumo lied to his colleagues and then to the House of Commons by denying any carnal contact with Keeler: in fact, he had not only slept with her but had obviously rather fallen for her. But his colleagues believed him – he was One Of Us – and it was only after a great deal of newspaper pressure and a spate of semi-revelations that he confessed all to the House of Commons and resigned, to devote himself, quietly and honourably, to good works in the East End of London. Perhaps the most revealing comment on the affair came in a rather absurd, generally sneery, book about Britain by a French author, Paul-Michel Villa. 'Politically,' he wrote, 'there was nothing in the affair that was either important or sordid' – by French standards anyway – 'elsewhere he would have hung on, his party would have stood by him, people would soon have forgotten. But not in England. A gentleman does not lie; if he commits this mistake he resigns.'[8]

Perhaps inevitably, Ward himself became a scapegoat. Neither the police, nor indeed MI5, had taken the various peccadilloes he and his friends had committed at all seriously, but after Profumo's disgrace the order clearly came down from on high – probably from the Home Secretary, the stodgily reactionary Henry Brooke – to get him. Brooke had already shown his cackhandedness in a number of widely publicised affairs, trying for instance to deport a young Jamaican girl found shoplifting goods to the value of £2. Ward was initially prosecuted on three charges of living on the earnings of prostitution – even though all unbiased witnesses agree that he was the least money-grubbing of men (as witness the financial habits so vividly described by Denning). He simply wanted to *matter*, to be a contender in the Great Game of espionage.

Ward was prosecuted by the seemingly ubiquitous Mervyn Griffith-Jones and appeared before a judge who obviously shared the view of Ward which Denning was to express so vividly later that summer. Poor Ward got no help from his posh friends – notably Astor, who had just married a strait-laced model, Bronwen Pugh, who, not surprisingly, wanted her new husband to forget his sleazier friends. MI5 did not intervene to save someone who, if not one of their agents, had been used by them, even though afterwards they admitted that they really didn't expect the outcome. After some legal jiggery-pokery which prevented some of his witnesses being heard, capped by a brutally one-sided summing up, Ward, who until then had assumed that he would be found innocent, went home a broken man. As George Gale, a solidly conservative journalist put it, when the jury delivered its verdict, 'Ward was half guilty, half innocent, half dead, half alive in the most deeply disturbing trial I have ever had the misfortune to witness.' Ward's distinguished defence lawyers were by no means alone in believing the guilty verdict was a political fix but, inevitably, the Lord Chief Justice ruled that no transcript of the trial should be made available.

Then came a final blow: Ward heard a BBC art critic savaging an exhibition of his sketches, saying that he had merely a 'tiny talent'. That destroyed his last fantasy, of starting a new life as an artist, and that night he 'swallowed enough Nembutal to kill a horse', in Knightley and Kennedy's words – the guilty verdict was pronounced only when he was already half dead. Immediately afterwards, all the sketches of the royal family in the exhibition – including one of his former friend Prince Philip – were bought anonymously and lost to posterity. At his funeral his remaining friends – all from the new world of letters and the theatre, none from society – left a wreath with a card on it which told the whole story:

> To Stephen Ward
> Victim of Hypocrisy.

The entire affair, coming so soon after the Lady Chatterley trial, had greatly helped to loosen the nation's moral corsets. 'My mother, now in her late seventies,' recalled a correspondent in a letter to the *New Statesman*,[9] 'always maintained that the most socially significant consequence of the Christine Keeler affair was that it made talking about sex at dinner parties possible.' If it did nothing else, the Profumo affair put an end to the long years in which sex had been an unmentionable activity.

As for the policemen involved, one was promoted to superintendent, but after his death three years later was found to have £30,000 (around £500,000 in today's money) in his bank account – the same sum offered by one of Ward's most vicious enemies, the disgraced Labour MP John Lewis, for information leading to Ward's conviction. Another left the Met soon afterwards 'under a cloud'. Politically the affair demonstrated very clearly that the sixty-nine-year-old Macmillan, who had panicked the previous July and sacked half his Cabinet, was out of touch, indeed had to admit that 'I do not live among young people

124

fairly widely'. In the long run, although the establishment had won a battle – albeit only against the wretched Ward – it had lost the war. It could no longer be taken seriously.

Nineteen sixty-three was a boom year for the new satire industry. The fashion for satire had been launched two years earlier with the revue *Beyond the Fringe* starring four immensely talented Oxbridge graduates – Peter Cook, Jonathan Miller, Alan Bennett and Dudley Moore – from the generation of the mid-1950s. (Two were from grammar schools, and all four went on to well-deserved fame and fortune.) It was Peter Cook, the most anarchically talented of them all, who started a short-lived night club called, naturally, The Establishment in partnership with a Cambridge friend, Nicholas Luard. They bred a much longer-lasting magazine *Private Eye* which reinforced the point that most of the satirists, like the angry young men, were by no means politically radical. As Emma Tennant, the ex-wife of Christopher Booker, the first editor of *Private Eye*, pointed out, her husband and his friends were really 'schoolboys . . . *Telegraph* readers in disguise'.[10] This was true not only of her husband, who became a regular contributor to the *'Torygraph'*, but also of his long-time successor, Richard Ingrams, who clearly saw himself as the heir to the right-wing anarchical tradition of G. K. Chesterton and J. B. Morton, author of the long-running and often hilarious Beachcomber column in the *Daily Express*.

The Argyll and Profumo affairs were naturally grist *to Private Eye*'s mill: 'Come ye and stare at ye breasts of a duchess . . . Come buy my sweete pornographie, pictures of ye famous lovinge me.' For these satirists were savage rather than revolutionary, showing Macmillan as a decrepit Roman emperor lounging in the midst of dancing girls and prancing homosexuals. What they were depicting, wrote Brian Moynahan, 'was the fall of Rome'.[11] Their impact was vastly widened by two short-lived television series on the BBC – *That Was The Week That Was* and *TW3* – which achieved record audiences. But many of those involved – most notably the compere David Frost – soon settled down to become what can only be described as establishment figures.

Yet the Age of Deference was not dead. That autumn Macmillan was succeeded by Alec Douglas-Home, until the previous year Lord Home. He was the beneficiary of a Bill introduced by a young Labour MP, Tony Wedgwood Benn, when he inherited the title of Viscount Stansgate. Helped by the arrival of life peers in 1958, who had introduced an element of merit into deciding who should sit in the House of Lords, Benn started a successful battle to enable peers to renounce their titles and resume their political careers in the House of Commons. By 1963, two of the candidates, the second Lord Hailsham and that most aristocratic of politicians, the fourteenth Earl of Home, were prepared to divest themselves of their peerages, a clear demonstration of the marginal status possessed by the House of Lords in politicians' minds.

After a coup led from his sickbed by Macmillan, who hated the obvious candidate for the Tory leadership, R.A. Butler*, Lord Home emerged – a not inappropriate term to describe the convolutions involving the Magic Circle at the heart of the Conservative Party – as Prime Minister. Indeed Harold Wilson, the new leader of the Labour Party, was not far off the mark when he presented the affair as the machinations of an aristocratic cabal. Enoch Powell, who refused to serve under Home, stated flatly that 'The Queen was a victim of a violation of the Constitution . . . It is unthinkable that a Prime Minister should say "here is my resignation" and then "here is my advice".' The whole episode was a proclamation that the Queen had in effect abdicated her rights when it came to the choice of a Prime Minister between General Elections. Within a couple of years the Tory party had bounded into the twentieth century by inaugurating a far more democratic system, one which resulted in the choice of four successive leaders from the lower or lower-middle classes, backgrounds far less socially privileged than those of most contemporary Labour leaders.

Royalty apart, deference disappeared from the British scene on January 25 1965 with the death of the ninety-year-old Sir Winston Churchill. No matter that he had been much hated by many people – including the Conservative Party – for much of his life, his death, and above all the funeral the following Saturday, brought forth a genuinely deep and widespread display of emotion towards this unique figure.

The moving splendour of the funeral itself was matched by *The Times*'s description of 'a warrior's funeral in a warrior's church' – St Paul's Cathedral – which was grand and simple at the same time, an occasion that was 'not chilling' because of 'the shared intimacy in personal memories of this great and loveable man . . . The beat of the single drum on the great drum horse, which was to haunt us all day . . . the strains of the Dead March† were borne thinly up Whitehall on the cold morning air to be taken up by band after band'. For it was the drums that set the tone of the occasion – 'the great drum horse with kettle drums swathed in black crepe . . . the insistent throb of drums [which] announced the coming of the procession' – and which most struck *The Times* journalist and indeed any spectator – that and Churchill's journey to his final resting-place, an unassuming country graveyard near the grandiose family home, Blenheim Palace. There was also, of course, the saluting battery on Tower Hill as the coffin was carried to a barge on the Thames, which 'looked like a print of

---

* Probably because Butler had been an arch-appeaser twenty-three years earlier.
† From Handel's oratorio *Saul*, a traditional accompaniment to such funerals.

THE DEATH OF DEFERENCE

some Crimean cannonade', its passage signalled by a 'herd of cranes at Hay's Wharf opposite [which] started dipping their long necks in an eerie, impressive civilian salute' on a primarily military occasion.

But the funeral combined two emotions: that 'we shall not see his like again' and that, as Patrick O'Donovan put it in the *Observer*: 'This was the last time that London would be the capital of the world. This was an act of mourning for the Imperial past. This marked the final act in Britain's greatness.' It really was the end of an epoch.

Notes

1. Asa Briggs *History of Broadcasting in the UK* OUP 1995.
2. *The Anatomy of Britain* Hodder & Stoughton 1962.
3. *Manchester School.*
4. *The Warburgs*, Chatto & Windus, 1993.
5. *The Strangers All Are Gone*, Heinemann 1992.
6. *The Justice Game*, Chatto & Windus 1998.
7. *L'Angleterre un monde a l'envers*, Hachette, 1967.
8. *New Statesman*, September 18 1998.
9. *Girlitude*, Jonathan Cape, 1999.
10. *The British century*, Weidenfeld & Nicolson, 1997.

7

Swinging Yes, Hanging No

'We no longer terrorise homosexuals. We do not force mothers to bring forth unwanted children into the world . . . we do not murder by the rope.'

PAUL JOHNSON

YOUTH, ITS ASPIRATIONS AND new-found confidence fuelled by the disrepute of its elders – and the money it had to play with – was the key to that extraordinary period, the mid-1960s. 'We had a great time,' remembered the author Jenny Diski, 'listened to good music, wore a uniform of our own invention, played like children among the drugs and light-shows, fucked copiously, took to the streets, and seriously frightened the horses in Grosvenor Square, and all the while felt righteous, that we were blowing away the dust of the world.'[1] The difference between her generation and that of her children at the end of the Millennium was that she and her friends knew that 'whatever our form of Sixties activity, it was done in the sure and certain knowledge that when we had finished there would be jobs to go to'. There was, wrote Philip Whitehead, 'a raffish optimism, a feeling that things were on an upswing of talent and opportunity, if only everyone over forty would somehow get out of the way.' The confidence was reinforced by simple demographics: in the years after the war the birth rate shot up, compared not only with wartime levels but also with those of the depression years, and the numbers and the mentality of these baby-boomers have remained a major factor in changing British life ever since the 1960s. In the words of thirty year-old Brian Morris, owner of the ultra-trendy Ad Lib club: 'A kid of twenty-three or twenty-four isn't a kid any more. Twenty years ago he'd have thought himself one. Not today. The young work hard and they make a lot of money. Twenty years ago ambition itself was unfashionable. Now it isn't.'[2]

The end of national service in the late 1950s, combined with the vast increase in student numbers, greatly encouraged the idea of youth as a separate class, no longer afraid of authority – especially that of their elders – and with time and money on their hands. George Melly called it a 'revolt into style' and, as Trevor Royle put it, 'it was almost as if a safety valve had been released . . . the freedom from conscription was one of the reasons for the rapidly mushrooming youth culture.' Colin McInnes felt that he was 'in the presence here of an entirely new phenomenon in human history: that youth is rich'. This represented the end of the traditional picture of the industrious but inevitably impoverished apprentice. Indeed, the demand for immediate and well-paid, if dead-end, jobs spelled the beginning of the end of the valuable institution of apprenticeship. By contrast, an increasing number of children were staying on in school to eighteen rather than leaving at fourteen.

The new image, and reality, of the young combined two phenomena, those of the 'teenager' and the 'generation gap' – a term that first surfaced in 1967. Both descriptions were an admission that there was a legitimate difference between young and old and that the younger generation were not automatically bound to follow in their parents' footsteps, the first sign that differences in age could be as important as the gulf that had previously divided the classes. For there started to be far more social movement than there had been in the early post-war years. Of the children in York studied by the Rowntree Foundation, half of the low-income group had escaped into either 'intermediate' or 'comfortably-off' segments of society between 1950 and the mid-1970s.

Macmillan's admission that he did not frequent the young would not have mattered even five years earlier. In 1963 it did. In the 1962 BBC Reith Lectures (their author and subject a reliable guide to the cultural state of the nation) Professor G. M. Carstairs, a psychologist and future vice-chancellor of the University of York, talked of 'the vicissitudes of adolescence' – itself a subject unthinkable ten years earlier. Worse, they included a discussion of sexual behaviour, which naturally provoked much hysteria in the press – touching the same nerves as were affected a year later when Dr Alex Comfort defined a chivalrous boy as 'one who takes contraceptives with him'.

These youngsters were different from their older brothers and sisters, still more so from their parents, and it was Labour's failure to understand that they were escaping from the rigid pecking order imposed by proletcult that came near to destroying the party twenty years later. In 1959 Mark Abrams, a leading market researcher, wrote *The Teenage Consumer*, thus combining two of the key words in the vocabulary of the 1960s – and introducing the idea, which still dominates much marketing talk, of the young (and assumedly affluent) consumer as a target audience. For although the young represented only 5 per cent

129

of the country's income, their lack of financial responsibilities meant that they bought two out of every five record-players, nearly a third of the cosmetics and toiletries, and over a quarter of all the cinema tickets sold. In response, in a trend that was to prove a permanent feature of the marketing landscape, the whole leisure industry naturally geared up to satisfy the young.

When Abrams pointed out that the new audience were different from the old proles in their attitudes, his ideas, which were prophetic of the 1980s, were pooh-poohed by the ultra politically correct New Leftist Raphael Samuel because they were based on such a small sample, but Abrams proved to be right. For the gap involved an ever-deepening gulf between the young and political parties – though not necessarily political causes. As T. O. Lloyd put it: 'The people who worried about the country's role in the world were serious-minded men and women who wanted the country to be influential in some much more dignified way and the young people who set the new fashions were much less interested in the question.'

The very idea of such emphasis on the young and thus on the new was bound to produce a reaction, that nothing young or new was any good, that both emphases were symptoms of a more general disintegration of society. Most of the doomsters were from the other side of the generation gap but, most surprisingly, they also included Christopher Booker, the first editor of *Private Eye*. In *The Neophiliacs* he quoted (approvingly) what William Hazlitt had written (disapprovingly) about Shelley: 'Whatever was new, untried unheard-of, unauthorised, exerted a kind of fascination on his mind . . . Spurning the world of realities, he rushed into the world of nonentities and contingencies. If a thing was old and established, this was with him a certain proof of its having no solid foundation to rest on: if it was new, it was good and right.'

The new-found confidence of the young was part of a much wider social shift. When Harold Macmillan was attacked for declaring that 'You've never had it so good', his response, in an interview with Jocelyn Stevens, editor of *Queen* magazine, was: 'I've been accused of caring too much for the well-being of the people. I don't think you can care too much about the well-being of the people' – a remark harking back to the poverty he had seen in his constituency of Stockton-on-Tees during the Depression years. Nevertheless Macmillan's words ensured that from then on there would be a revolution of rising expectations. If a year was good, then we were entitled to expect that the next would be even better.

To the Stock Exchange the triumph of hope after thirty long years had been signalled back in 1960 with the emergence of a 'reverse yield gap'. This meant that you got more income from investing in fixed-interest government bonds than in ordinary shares, and was based on the generally correct assumption that in the long run you would make up in capital gains from the shares what you lost in immediate income from gilt-edged. The same optimism applied to every aspect of British life – that every year social relationships, sex, the arts, television, not to mention public services, ought to be on an ever-rising curve. And since 1960 politicians have been increasingly unable to deliver a country in which every day in every way everything improved sufficiently to satisfy an increasingly demanding public. The changes in the national psyche were well caught by the journalist Francis Boyd when he wrote (in the *Guardian*) on the findings of the 1961 census: 'We have become a nation of debtors ... there is a basic discontent with what has become very strongly an era of materialism which expresses itself "in a grasping after unearned wealth" ... we are healthier and wealthier than we were ... we are eating more and spending more time (with more frustration) in commuting ... the picture is essentially of a swelling middle class, migrating when it can into outlying rural or suburban or small town areas around the great cities.'

No institution was left untouched by change and the tensions it created. Perhaps the most remarkable quotation I came across from the 1960s was from a television interview – itself a total novelty – given by Dr Coggan, Archbishop of York, to Adam Faith. 'I am one of those,' declared the Archbishop, 'who feel that sex is a thoroughly good thing, implanted by God. I'm not one of those who belong to the generation who thought it was a sort of smutty thing that you only talked about hush-hush.' The change in the Church's outlook – not just to sex but to Catholicism, previously just as forbidden a subject – had started in 1960 when the elderly Archbishop Fisher visited the Pope, the great, the open-minded John XXIII. This was a total transformation for a churchman who had, as he once said, grown up 'with an inbred opposition to anything that came from Rome ... and I saw no reason for differing from that opinion as the years went by'. Yet, rightly, he saw the visit as 'the final achievement of my arch-episcopate' and his successor recognised that it 'opened a door which will never close' – and indeed was opened still further by his successors.

By the 1960s the Church had become markedly less aristocratic: the Standing Committee of the house of laity did without any Etonians, symbolising a Church which would be, in the canting phrases of the times, 'efficient sophisticated, progressive'. The pedestrian New English Bible replaced the magnificent, albeit less easily comprehensible King James Bible, one of the glories of English literature and source of hundreds of familiar phrases. By contrast, the rebuilding of Coventry Cathedral, destroyed by German bombing, proved an artistic triumph

131

– despite the later sniping about it. For the first time in generations, the Anglican Church had been able to harness the best talents of the time. Basil Spence was the architect, John Piper designed the stained glass and Graham Sutherland an enormous tapestry, while the opening of the cathedral was graced by the premiere of Benjamin Britten's masterpiece, the *War Requiem*.

Fisher's successor, Michael Ramsey, Bishop of Durham, fitted the times. He was seemingly the natural successor to the wartime radical Archbishop William Temple, whom he resembled, wrote the religious historian Adrian Hastings,[4] 'in the breadth of his concerns, the immensity of his commitments, the impression of confident modernity he conveyed, the engaging geniality and optimism of his temperament'. There was a general, and as it turned out unjustified, air of optimism in the Church after the successful decade of the 1950s. This was symbolised by a report by a layman, Leslie Paul, which predicted further progress and thus a need for far more priests. 'There is', wrote Adrian Hastings, 'something rather pathetic, indeed a little ludicrous, about the Church turning for the first time to lay sociology . . . and being quite so grotesquely misled – for the early 1960s represented a high tide which has been receding at different rates ever since, a decline which was particularly sharp in the decade following Paul's prognosis.'

Change was inevitably accompanied by dissension. In the 1950s the best-selling Christian author had been the traditionalist Oxford don, C. S. Lewis. In the 1960s came a bombshell, *Honest to God*, written by Bishop John Robinson during a short stay in hospital with the encouragement of his superior Mervyn Stockwood, Bishop of Southwark*. Robinson was trying to get rid of the idea of God as an old man with a beard 'up above the bright blue sky' and rejecting traditional Christianity as an 'alien norm'. Instead, he thought, belief was more difficult because would-be believers were 'stuck with images of God that misled them' – ideas largely borrowed from theologians such as Dietrich Bonhoeffer and Paul Tillich. This splendid tirade sold nearly a million copies within three years.

The row created by Robinson's 'honesty' was as nothing compared with the problems which the 1960s created for the Roman Catholic Church. It had been the great beneficiary of the 1944 Education Act, which increased the number of Catholic schools and, above all, the quality of teaching in them. The combination provided the church with a growing and increasingly articulate middle-class membership, ensuring that it ceased to be the religion composed largely of Irish

---

* Known affectionately as Merve the Perve, this delightful churchman combined a genuine populism with high church opinions and a love of social life symbolised by his mid-Lent champagne parties.

immigrants and a handful of the 'recusant' families so glamourised in *Brideshead Revisited*. Catholicism was being steadily integrated into British – or, to be more precise, English – life at all levels. By 1961 one in eight marriages were in a Catholic church. The renewal was symbolised by Cardinal John Heenan. As Archbishop of Liverpool, he was a confident, articulate spokesman on television even before he was promoted to Westminster in 1963 to succeed the rigidly unimaginative Archbishop Godfrey. In the next few years, Heenan ensured that the Church received further help in establishing new schools, and symbolically, he attended Winston Churchill's funeral, the first time a Catholic prelate had been present at a state funeral since the 1530s.

But in the 1960s the replacement of the Latin Mass by celebration in the local language split the Catholic Church, and not just in Britain, in a manner foreshadowing the row over women priests in the Church of England thirty years later. A vociferous and influential minority deplored the change, forgetting that as Hastings, himself a Catholic priest, put it, 'in the typical parish the old Latin liturgy had provided neither beauty nor understanding, only a remote, poorly performed rigmarole'. He admits that 'the replacement was at first feebly done' but 'with the passing of Latin the clergy seemed more approachable, and thus less of a caste apart'.

But the Pandora's boxes being opened in the Catholic Church were as nothing compared with the problems created by the royal family in its efforts to edge a little closer to both its subjects and the second half of the twentieth century in a series of belated and dangerous gestures. In 1964 Anthony Sampson, not a man with an exaggerated reverence for the 'mystery' surrounding the institution, had warned that 'once you touch the trappings of monarchy, like opening an Egyptian tomb, the inside is likely to crumble'. The initial sign of the new image was the Queen's visit to Greenwich to knight Francis Chichester after his solo round the world journey in an imitation of Queen Elizabeth I's similar gesture to Sir Francis Drake. This was the first indication of the steady opening up of the Palace and its inhabitants after 1968 when Commander Colville was succeeded as Press Secretary by Sir William Heseltine, who saw the need to sell the royal family actively to the public. He was supported by Prince Philip, who felt that 'we are fighting an election every day of the week'. Typically, the Queen said merely that she would do what was felt to be necessary. The single most innovative step, initiated by Earl Mountbatten, was the BBC film, *Royal Family*, screened in 1968, which was based on a year's access provided to the director, Richard Cawston – over a hundred years earlier Bagehot had described the idea of a '*family* on the throne' (his italics) as 'interesting'.

The film showed the royal family not as icons but as distinct personalities, the Queen relaxed and witty when off-duty, Philip imaginative but a caged bird, Anne confident and matter-of-fact and, perfectly accurately, her elder brother as gawky and uncomfortable. The film was successful, for, as Pimlott puts it, 'the sense of the family as individuals, and as a group, is powerful'. But, once the royals had been marketed as the perfect family, they were trapped, obliged to live up to an image of perfection that became increasingly unreal over the next quarter of a century. As a future Press Secretary, Michael Allison, put it, 'It started the rot, but how long could the curtains be held in place?' For throughout the decade the bets on the stability of the family had been doubling up all the time. When the Queen's fourth child, Prince Edward, was born in 1964, the Archbishop of Canterbury spoke of the royal family as a stable element in socially shifting times, 'setting to all an example of what the words "home and family" most truly meant'.

The process of romanticisation continued the next year with that classic case of 'the invention of tradition', the investiture of Prince Charles as Prince of Wales by his mother. The occasion was so artificial that it did not arouse much popular enthusiasm, even though Lord Snowdon devised an ingenious stage set composed of three slate thrones in the middle of the courtyard of Carnavon Castle. The process of 'popularisation' took another step when the Queen went on 'walka-bouts' during a visit to Australia – the first sovereign since Charles II three centuries earlier to have mingled relatively naturally amongst her subjects.

But by now the family itself was under attack. In the 1967 Reith lectures, Sir Edmund Leach said simply that 'far from being the basis of the good society, the family, with its narrow privacy and tawdry secrets, is the source of all discontents' – a view exaggerated by such fashionable psychiatrists as R. D. Laing. Five years earlier Carstairs had pointed out that 31 per cent of all girls who married in their teens were pregnant. He went on to argue that 'many societies get on well without pre-marital chastity' and in Britain 'sexual experience with precautions like contraception is becoming a sensible preliminary to marriage'. This made it more likely that marriage, 'when it comes [note the when], will be a mutually considerate and mutually satisfying partnership'. Satisfying perhaps, but not necessarily permanent. A Matrimonial Causes Act in 1967 and a Divorce Reform Act two years later made getting a divorce far easier. Astonishingly, after the post-war surge in divorces of casually married wartime couples, the number of divorces had actually gone down between 1950 and 1960, but more than doubled in each of the two following decades to reach 159,000 in 1980.

Surprisingly slowly, the pill, which had become available at the start of the decade, was starting to be used more widely. In 1966 the path had been cleared for women to retain control of their own bodies when the first Brook Clinic was opened and started to dispense the pill with reasonable freedom, although most family doctors would not prescribe it to unmarried women until much later in the decade. A Family Planning Act allowed local authorities to provide contraceptives and 'planning advice'. The change in attitudes towards women's sexual behaviour can be charted through the history of the National Council for the Unmarried Mother and her Child. Already by 1962 its annual report was able to state that 'the implicit, sometimes explicit, criticism of the unmarried mother [has] faded'. Nevertheless, as late as 1965, the council was declaring that 'our society is more compassionate to the unmarried mother than it was a generation ago, but she and her illegitimate child are still seen as a threat to normal family life'. By 1973 its name had changed in line with a changing society, the words 'unmarried mother' being replaced by a term that was to become famous in the following decades, the 'one-parent family'. The state, too, reflected these changes in attitude. In 1966 councils started to provide housing for unmarried mothers. A year later they were granted the same tax allowances as those for divorced or widowed parents. In 1975 illegitimate children were granted the same rights of inheritance as their legitimate siblings. A year later the Seebohm Report led to the creation, for the first time, of local authority social service departments to deal with single mothers.

There was one man who managed to exploit the new mood of social relaxation to the full, Roy Jenkins, Home Secretary for two crucial years between 1965 and 1967. He had outlined his aim, of creating what he termed a 'civilised society', as early as 1959. Writing in the *Spectator,* he declared that 'on a whole range of issues where much progress remains to be made, hanging, Wolfenden, the licensing laws, betting reform, Sunday Observance, divorce, theatre censorship, police control, the abortion laws – there is immensely more to be hoped for from a Labour Home Secretary than from the most liberal Conservative minister'. Jenkins, the son of a miners' leader imprisoned – briefly – for his activities, was the last paladin of what Noel Annan called Our Age of the well-educated who grew up between the wars. His definition included only the more liberal-minded, those whom Sir Maurice Bowra called members of the Immoral Front, so many of whom 'were aware of the advantages they started with in life that they were so hostile to the ethos of their elders'.

Jenkins was younger than Annan and Bowra – he was in his forties – but although there were compromises along the way, the changes he set in motion amounted to a social revolution on a scale never before seen in Britain in so short a time – only Sunday Observance and the licensing laws proved resistant, although the 1961 Licensing Act had allowed a much freer sale of drink through the new-fangled supermarkets and on Sundays, leading to a complaint by a non-conformist minister that 'Swansea has bowed the knee to Bacchus'. Even before Jenkins's arrival at the Home Office, capital punishment had been abolished, the only real opposition coming from a relative handful of die-hards.

Jenkins's technique was to get a pressure group to push for the change, then a backbench Member of Parliament would introduce a bill on a subject that was bound to be contentious. For many of his successes revolved around sex, the act itself (homosexuality), its results (abortion) and its depiction (obscenity). But once the bandwagon was rolling, the minister responsible – Jenkins – would give way as gracefully as only he, most elegant of political operators, knew how.

But he was not just a political operator; he had been prepared to stand up and be counted well before he entered government. In 1958 he had been one of the small group which had founded the Theatre Censorship Reform Committee, this at a time when all plays were vetted by the Lord Chamberlain, with a staff that consisted mostly of ex-Guards officers. Given the political atmosphere, anti-American plays were banned as a matter of course, as were the works of a long and distinguished list of writers, and in this context John Osborne's play, *A Patriot For Me*, based on a famous scandal surrounding a homosexual army officer in the Austro-Hungarian army before 1914, was a deliberate snub to the censors.

The problem was brought to a head by Edward Bond's play *Saved*, which featured a baby stoned to death in its pram. In January 1966 the Royal Court Theatre (which had started the theatrical revolution with *Look Back In Anger*) tried to evade the law by transforming itself into a club for the performance. The theatre was prosecuted and fined fifty guineas. Jenkins, using his habitual indirect approach, got Annan to open a debate in the House of Lords and soon theatrical censorship, which had stultified the development of the London theatre for over 200 years, was no more, rather to the relief of the Lord Chamberlain, Lord Cobbold, of the time. Adventurous producers could then of course have been indirectly censored by lack of access to the funds administered by the Arts Council, but Lord Goodman, its chairman in the late 1960s, did not 'regard it as the function of the Arts Council to judge the quality of every performance in every part of the country . . . there are no rules that can be laid down, no criteria that can be applied, except the criterion of common sense.' Nevertheless the theatre remained strictly a middle-class preserve. The only attempt to unite the workers and art was Centre 42, a doomed attempt by the playwright Arnold Wesker in alliance with the TUC which was to be situated in the Round House, a splendid edifice just north of Camden Town built as an engine house and then transformed into a spirits store.

The battle for legalised abortion, which was already available to richer women, was a much tougher matter. The first Bill was introduced by Renée Short, a left-wing Labour MP, in 1965. Two years later, a new Bill was introduced by the young, newly-elected David Steel, the future Liberal leader, who had been encouraged by Jenkins. There was one limitation: abortion was to be controlled by the doctors and not available on demand. But by the end of the decade thousands of unfortunate young women were flocking to London to have the abortion denied to them at home, particularly in Ireland, providing a symbol of a culture and society far more relaxed and forgiving than could have been foreseen ten years earlier.

Jenkins's toughest fight was over the proposal to remove the ban on homosexual acts between consenting adults even though it, like the abolition of capital punishment, had been the subject of parliamentary debates over the previous decade. Probably the bravest piece of pro-homosexual propaganda was *Victim*, an influential film released in 1961 about a homosexual who is blackmailed. It starred the homosexual Dirk Bogarde, best known as a wholesome screen idol. It was the first time in the British cinema that one man had said to another that he loved him. As Patrick Higgins noted: 'Bogarde himself wrote the scene and insisted that it should be included, declaring, ''There's no point in half measures. We either make a film about queers or we don't. I believe the picture makes a lot of difference to a lot of people's lives.'''

After the Labour MP Leo Abse had launched a ten-minute rule bill to 'test the water' in the House of Commons, the real battle was launched in the House of Lords in early 1965 by a courageous and eccentric peer, the Earl of Arran (universally known as Boofy), who proposed that the age of consent should be twenty-one. After a spell as a lowly employee of the Rothermere empire in charge of arranging car parking space and like tasks, Arran became an eccentric 'provocative columnist' on the London *Evening News*, where he lashed out at a lot of people, including the Swedes and the Swiss. But his maiden speech in the House of Lords after inheriting his title in 1959 was on the first proposals of the Wolfenden report. The idea of legalisation aroused all the forces of homophobia. The Chief Scout, Lord Rowallan, predicted that the country would go the way of Greece and Rome, Field Marshal Viscount Montgomery, by then a very old man, suggested that the age of consent ought to be eighty while the Lord Chief Justice Rayner Goddard warned their Lordships of the existence of buggers clubs (he later told Arran that all the letters he received asked for the address of such clubs). The Bill received careful support from Jenkins after the 1966 election had resulted in a near hundred-seat majority for Labour. Nevertheless the battle, even in the House of Commons, was a hard-fought one and the Bill only passed at 5 am on American Independence Day in 1967.

The argument revealed some interesting cross-party overtones. Richard Crossman (who had voted for reform throughout) noted in his diaries that he found it 'an unpleasant Bill . . . it may well be twenty years ahead of public opinion; certainly working-class people in the north jeer at their Members at the weekend and ask them why they're looking after the buggers at Westminster instead of looking after the unemployed at home.' By contrast the vote also revealed the existence of a group who were to grow into the 'libertarian right', unwilling to interfere in people's private lives – Sir Keith Joseph, Nicholas Ridley and the young Mrs Thatcher. But the strain told on Arran, who received a continuous stream of hate mail and was greeted by graffiti all over London saying ARRAN HOMO, and the poor man took to drink.

The publication of Michael Holroyd's life of Lytton Strachey in 1967 opened the floodgates, not just to an over-exposure of the largely homosexual Bloomsbury group which had enjoyed such a disproportionate influence on the culture of the country but, more broadly, to an examination of the influence of homosexuals and, eventually, to the whole idea of Gay Pride. Unfortunately many of its enthusiasts forgot Arran's parting words: 'This is no occasion for jubilation, certainly not for celebration. Any form of ostentatious behaviour, now or in the future, any form of public flaunting, would be utterly distasteful and would, I believe, make the sponsors of the Bill regret that they have done what they have done.'

For the situation remained muddled. Jeremy Thorpe, the leader of the Liberal Party, never dared confess to his homosexual past. This state of affairs culminated in a farcical trial in the mid-1970s when one of his ex-lovers tried to bring his affairs into the open and it took all the powers of the establishment to stop him. At the same time there was a farcical coda when the magazine *Gay News* was prosecuted for publishing an allegedly blasphemous, but in reality rather laughably kitsch, poem about the crucifixion.

Yet Jenkins had left the Home Office before he had cleared one last hurdle, the decriminalisation of cannabis. Whether he could have eased the path, if not to legalisation, at least to decriminalisation, is one of the major unanswered questions of the 1960s. Drugs, not just cannabis but every other type, were very much a phenomenon of the decade. In 1961 an official committee reported that 'trafficking' was not widespread (and largely confined, so far as the tabloids were concerned, to 'coloured pedlars'). The Dangerous Drugs Act 1965 prohibited hash at the precise moment when it had become a drug of choice for the young, and this despite the appearance in *The Times* of a letter which had set out the arguments against criminalisation and urged research into allowing the smoking of the drug on private premises, a sign of the many such pleas over the following thirty five years. Nevertheless police activity was stepped up after the drug-related death of Harold Macmillan's nephew Joshua in 1966. The Drugs Squad, it said, knew druggies from the fact that they wore what were then called gym shoes and are now known as trainers. Its head, Detective Chief Inspector Vic Kelaher, was in charge of a bunch of cops as bent as even the Met had seen. Kelaher and his colleagues were backed by the sinister, criminal and immensely influential figure of the solicitor Arnold, later Lord, Goodman. Knowing that Jenkins would not be in favour of prosecutions, Goodman went straight to the Director of Public Prosecutions to ensure that John Hopkins, one of the underground's most influential figures, was arrested on drugs charges.

The fact that Goodman felt he had to circumvent Jenkins to prevent the reform of the laws on drugs is not the only reason for suspecting that the Home Secretary wanted to liberalise the laws, as witness that favourite device of his, the appointment of a distinguished committee to make a report. In 1967 such a group was brought together under Lady Barbara Wootton, a well-respected sociologist. Their views were cautious: the report merely pointed the way to further research and to a drop in the penalties for possession. Unfortunately the report arrived in the Commons in January 1969, a year after Jenkins had been replaced as Home Secretary by the archetypal social conservative James Callaghan. He smeared the lady and her colleagues as the 'cannabis lobby' and declared in so many words that any change would be over his dead body. And there the situation rested for thirty years; Wootton's report was not even mentioned in her obituaries, and a major opportunity was lost. Worse was to come: the 1971 Misuse of Drugs Act laid down a prison sentence of up to five years for the mere possession of cannabis and it was not until 2001 that David Blunkett, as Home Secretary virtually decriminalised the drug and then only after considerable pressure from such unlikely groups as the police, who felt that chasing after users was a waste of precious time. The criminalisation of a 'substance' far less dangerous in small doses than tobacco may have alienated a whole generation, or perhaps they were already alienated. As Jonathon Green points out, 'The simple fact of smoking a joint . . . was sufficient to render oneself an outsider, a subversive'.

Jenkins's reforms have long been accepted as part of normal life. By contrast the one phrase that people remember about the 1960s, Swinging London, described an episode, covering only the middle years of the decade and directly affecting only a minority, albeit an influential one, within the metropolis. It was assumed that nothing ever happened in the provinces; they were simply where people came from. But most people, even in London, even those in what was becoming known as 'the media', were outside the magic circle, and many felt it. The famous statement that 'if you can remember the Sixties you weren't there' is profoundly misleading, implying that the whole younger generation was permanently stoned. It wasn't. Michelene Wandor's verse expresses the feelings of what was probably a majority of adolescents, certainly of those outside London:

> The sixties was a time when many people went to pot
> Except for me.
> I did not
> During the sixties
> I yearned
> A lot

But it was because of Swinging London, and the talents that it nurtured, photographers and designers of everything from clothes to furniture, that, for the first time for generations, foreigners started to regard England – or rather London – as a place of opportunity and freedom and not just, as it had been in the 1930s and 1940s, a refuge from oppression. London was slowly taking over from Paris as the European city setting the cultural pace – a process helped by the puritanical side of de Gaulle's regime and the influence of his wife, 'tante Yvonne', a devout Roman Catholic from the depths of provincial France. The newcomers included an important group of cultural refugees from Australia, and a rather different group of South Africans, mostly Jewish, largely lawyers and businessmen escaping the apartheid regime. From the United States came talented writers, and film and theatrical producers and directors, all refugees from McCarthyite persecution, like Carl Foreman and Joe Losey, and from Canada Sidney Newman, who created ABC television's *Armchair Theatre*.

Unusually, the pace was set by a royal couple, probably the first time that a female member of the royal family became the leader of a fashionable set. In doing so, Princess Margaret and her husband, the brilliant photographer Tony Armstrong-Jones, the first artist ever admitted into the royal family, provided a sharp contrast to the generally staid and frumpy image which had been presented by the royal family since the abdication of the Duke of Windsor in 1936. Unfortunately Armstrong-Jones had to accept the Earldom of Snowdon to appease traditionalists who feared that the Queen's nephews and nieces might be simple 'Mrs' and 'Misses'.

The glamorous couple set a seal of classlessness – albeit superficial

– on the London scene. Margaret even bought a Mini, the first classless car – previously there had been subtle gradations: Hillmans were just that bit more respectable than Fords, Morrises and Austins, and so on. But then there was a lot of rather phoney classlessness abroad, symbolised by 'mockney', the false cockney accent affected by public schoolboys. In fact, the gradual disappearance of RP (Received Pronunciation) was a contentious business. 'What does arouse public rage,' Harold Nicolson was assured by a high-up BBC mandarin, was not American accents but 'the upper-class or "U" accent. They even complain that the news announcers all speak "la-di-da". He assures me that, at least as far as the news is concerned, the BBC will stick to its guns.'

It didn't of course, for the 1960s did see a start in the acceptability of non-RP pronunciation. But not all accents were acceptable: it was all right for an accent to be cockney or northern – especially scouse (or, of course, Scottish) – but the distinctive 'Brummie' accent from Birmingham remains naff to this day. But, according to Michael Parkinson, everyone at Granada 'had to have a northern accent and if you didn't you had to leave town' – from the start Bernstein had insisted on basing most of the company's programme-making in Manchester. Moreover the Granada influence spread as producers left for other, often more profitable jobs. Parkinson was exaggerating (Jeremy Isaacs, one of Bernstein's favourite protégés, still retains strong traces of his Glasgow Jewish accent) but certainly 'provincial' accents became de rigueur among the more fashionable sections of the media elites in London just as much as Manchester. On the *Sunday Times* in the early 1970s, I found myself working with colleagues I termed TNPs, Tiresome Northern Persons, because they tended to exaggerate what they claimed were their humble origins.

Nevertheless the process was a slow one. In the 1970s a friend of mine from Derbyshire overheard her then boyfriend and his mother mocking her accent: she then painstakingly removed the agreeable native burr from her voice. Edward Heath's strangulated tones were the clear result of his efforts at linguistic gentrification, while Mrs Thatcher deliberately eliminated the Granthamesque overtones in her speech – though they did emerge on one occasion when she accused Neil Kinnock, the Labour leader, of being 'frit', the splendid local term for being frightened. By contrast, William Hague later consciously retained and even emphasised his Yorkshire accent.

Democratisation was more genuine when it came to clothes and indeed to lifestyle in general. Before the 1960s, as Trevor Lloyd put it, Savile Row was admired but 'one of the features of a gentleman's clothes is that they are never quite up to date'. By the 1960s fashion was not confined to women and, as Julie Burchill, the very epitome of street-cred has pointed out, in contrast to the supposedly more democratic France and the United States: 'Here it is cheap and cheerful working-class youth, from the Teddy Boys to the Spice Girls, who have decreed what that season's Look will be; even the most exclusive and expensive of British couturiers such as John Galliano and Vivienne Westwood attempt to identify themselves with "street" fashion'. But once the Beatles had started wearing Pierre Cardin jackets, if only for the photographers, the rules were clearly on their way out. For clothes were the biggest single visual sign of liberation – though not of girls, however sexually liberated they might be. In their mini-skirts and tight skimpy sweaters they were labelled 'dolly birds', and they remained pure sex objects. But even they were making a deliberate gesture of proclaiming, 'I am young; I am not like my parents' generation; I dare to be different.'

Classless trendy clothes can be traced back to the 1950s when one Bill Green, trading as Vince, had set himself up near the Marshall Street Baths in west Soho, the home for young gays flexing their pecs. He then moved to nearby Carnaby Street, where he was joined by a number of other influential shopkeepers, including John Stephen, who had learnt his trade in the military department of Moss Bros. He opened a boutique, a slightly camp term of French origins, a mile removed from the world of the chain stores. But the epicentre of swinging clothing, as of swinging London as a whole, was Chelsea. There Mary Quant, an ex-pupil of Goldsmith's School of Art, and her husband Alexander Plunket Greene opened Bazaar. This was only one of the names made famous within a few months in the mid-1960s. There was Biba, the shop set up by Barbara Hulanicki and her husband, and, for the truly rich, the clothes created by Ossie Clark and his wife the textile designer Celia Birtwell. Only a few lasted the course, for – apart from Plunket Greene – Swinging London was, to put it mildly, not really imbued with business sense. Indeed its end can be pinpointed with the closure in 1972 of the massive but totally uncommercial Biba store in Kensington High Street, the former Derry & Toms. And twenty years later there was a miserable coda when Clark, the most talented of them all, was murdered by his (male) lover.

Naturally classlessness spread to the models. In the 1950s the model models, as it were, had been led by Fiona Campbell-Walter, the daughter of an admiral and the very image of an upper-class English rose, and Shirley Worthington, who was known as 'The Fair Miss Frigidaire'. But appearances were deceptive. Campbell-Walter for one admitted that her life had not been exactly staid. Moreover she knew and resented the fact that she was modelling dresses not made for her but for older women who formed the then exclusive clientele of couturiers. By the early 1960s she and her like had been replaced by one of the icons of the decade: the extremely pretty, overtly sexy and classless Jean Shrimpton, whose image had been created by another iconic figure, one of the decade's most famous photographers, the Cockney David Bailey. But hers was not the only image: by contrast there was the ultra-slim, boyish, androgynous figure of Twiggy.

Unsurprisingly it was her photograph which adorned the cover of the first issue of the *Sunday Times Magazine*. Its editor, Mark Boxer, a Cambridge friend of Snowdon's, introduced the new wave of artists and photographers to a much wider public through the medium of a paper that until the late 1950s been staid and was to become infinitely more classless as the 1960s progressed. The trendiness had a nasty side, for example, the worship of a handful of fashionable criminals, notably the brutal Kray brothers, who terrorised much of the East End for years before they were finally put on trial in the late 1960s. Ronnie and Reggie Kray also provided rent boys for such as Robert Boothby, the bisexual politician who had been the long-time lover of Harold Macmillan's wife, Lady Dorothy. They were even included in a book of David Bailey's photographs, his *Box of pin-ups*.

But fascination with crime was not confined to readers of the *Sunday Times*. In 1963 the Great Train Robbery had riveted the whole country. More significantly, the robbers (who had after all beaten up the driver so badly that he never worked again) were portrayed as anti-heroes. Pick of the bunch was Ronnie Biggs, who escaped from prison a couple of years later and lived in Brazil for the following thirty-five years amidst much publicity, returning, voluntarily, to Britain only in 2001. It was, wrote Brian Moynahan 'a pop age crime'. Biggs remembered a gang member dancing the twist in excitement whilst another 'was singing the Gerry and the Pacemakers song "I Like It"'.

For it was the media that were the major beneficiaries of the increasingly wide pool from which Oxbridge had been recruiting, albeit exclusively from the public and leading grammar schools, since the early 1950s. If Cambridge supplied more than its fair share of creative talent, particularly in the theatre, this was due to a combination of the intellectual rigour preached by the critic F. R. Leavis and his wife Queenie, and the creative vigour of the theatrical innovations practised by 'Dadie' Rylands. Their – separate – efforts produced a unique blend of theory and practice in the British theatre of the 1960s and 1970s. But Cambridge also produced a whole generation of Tory politicians who were to dominate the scene in the 1980s and 1990s, many of them, like Kenneth Clarke and Norman Fowler, educated at grammar schools. These graduates could easily be absorbed in the newly booming communications industries such as advertising, public relations, journalism and, above all, broadcasting which were far more open to the bright newcomer than older-established sectors.

143

I was lucky enough to be part of this *galère*, first on the *Economist*, and then, in the late 1960s and early 1970s, on the *Sunday Times*, which really was, as its publicity put it, 'One of The World's Great Newspapers'. We were arrogant, though also, I like to think, talented. We were the equivalent of the 1980s City yuppies, the Masters of the Universe. Anything was possible: 'You only went to work on the *Economist*,' remarked the wife of one of my colleagues, 'because you couldn't be bothered to be brain surgeons.' At the start of the decade our efforts, generally employed to debunk anything and everything, had been encouraged by the Public Bodies (Admission of the Press to meetings) Act, introduced by one Margaret Thatcher in her first year as an MP, a Bill which, most importantly, allowed the press into all council meetings. The new journalism was symbolised above all by the Insight team on the *Sunday Times* who, almost every week, published some sensational discovery or another. Many were purely ephemeral but some, such as the campaign against the raw deal suffered by victims of thalidomide, were hugely important. Many of them resulted in books, and it was the combination of the *Sunday Times*, the agent Michael Sissons and the publisher André Deutsch which provided a bridge to enable the many talented journalists from Oxbridge to write serious works of contemporary history.

Inevitably there was opposition to any sign of classlessness. At the inquiry into whether Roy Thomson should be allowed to buy Times Newspapers, Cecil Harmsworth King, the chairman of The Mirror Group, expressed the immortal view that 'Of course you'll have to give them to that uneducated Canadian and his dim son'. The backlash came four years later, when twenty-nine members of the editorial staff of *The Times* – a palace guard known collectively as the Black Friars* – signed a letter complaining that the paper was plunging down-market, had indeed gone so far as to include stories about the Beatles. 'The general effect of what has been done,' they pronounced, 'has been to diminish the authority, independence, accuracy, discrimination and seriousness of *The Times*.' Ironically the editor to whom they were complaining, William Rees-Mogg, was the very model of a mandarin, interested above all in opinion not news. They, like him, mistook lengthy ponderous opinion pieces for journalism.

Even books boomed in the 1960s – sales of Penguins, a mere 12 million at the end of the 1950s, had reached 29 million by 1968. But the increasingly dominant, innovatory medium form in the 1960s was not literature or even the theatre but television, the most important witness to the trends of the age. There were the campaigning producers, most obviously Jeremy Isaacs (backed up by the journalistic flair of

* At the time the paper's offices were at Blackfriars.

the former *Mirror* journalist Desmond Wilcox) with their programmes on abortion and other social problems. It was, for instance, a programme contrasting the victims of road accidents and happy drunks about to drive off after a session in the pub on New Year's Eve that triggered the introduction of the legal ban on drunken driving. The dramatists contributed campaigning programmes of their own, particularly on social evils such as homelessness – *Cathy Come Home, Up the Junction, Poor Cow* and *Edna the Inebriated Woman.*

The ever-increasing number of soap operas featuring an ever more diverse range of experiences, mostly sexual, were to have more permanent and long-term effects. These were not confined to adult viewers. In 1978 the BBC introduced *Grange Hill,* set in a secondary school, which tackled every kind of social issue from drug abuse to sexual problems and was used by official bodies to infiltrate useful information and advice into the young viewers' minds. By the late 1990s even the grandfather of them all, *The Archers,* Radio 4's pride and joy, included spouse-beating, the outing of homosexuals and a woman priest.

From the late 1950s onwards, the BBC had shed its image as 'Auntie' and was demonstrating a nimbleness of response well demonstrated by its response to the pirate radio stations in the North Sea in the early 1960s. Despite strenuous efforts by such as Tony Wedgwood Benn, the minister responsible, to close them down, they – and above all the records they played – represented the newly sacred voice of the young and their DJs – John Peel, Simon Dee and others – became heroes. Inevitably the pirates engendered another dose of cultural sniffiness. If they were to be invited ashore to become legitimate, intoned the *Guardian,* 'then that invitation should be extended only on the understanding that they accept greater responsibilities'. The Reithian-Pilkingtonian rearguard showed its claws in an anonymous editorial which refused to admit that any of the BBC's output could be pure entertainment, and, defying the injunctions of the BBC's founder, Lord Reith, made no attempt to inform, let alone educate its audience. And when Radio 1, the BBC's highly successful answer to the pirates, started in September 1967, Anne Duchène wrote, also in the *Guardian,* that it 'must in fact be a fairly arduous aspect of public service, catering for so much sustained mindlessness'.

Yet, despite all the talk of trendiness and anything going, the public as a whole was still easily shockable. When the word 'flies', as in 'your flies are undone' was first used in 1963, viewers were astounded to hear the term. Moreover, when Kenneth Tynan used the word 'fuck' for the first time on television on November 13 1965 – in a late-night satire programme produced by Ned Sherrin on the BBC and during a discussion on censorship with Mary McCarthy – he was clearly nervous. 'I doubt,' he said, 'if there are very many rational people in this world for whom the word "fuck" is particularly diabolical.' It had been Richard Hoggart who had first expressed the hypocrisy underlying the ban on the f-word. As a witness at the Lady Chatterley trial, he had been asked if the word gained anything by being spelt out f**k as was normal at the time. He replied simply: 'Yes, it gains a dirty suggestiveness.' Nevertheless there was an uproar following what Tynan had said, there were thunderous editorials and the BBC felt obliged to issue a statement of regret. Mind you, a mere decade earlier the comedian Max Miller, the Cheeky Chappie best known for his double entendres, had been banished from the airwaves for two years after ending his act on BBC radio with the couplet:

When roses are red they're ready for plucking
When girls are sixteen they're ready for – good night ladies and
    gentlemen*

But while Oxbridge continued to dominate the print and broadcasting media, another educational force had arrived with the art schools. Ours had always been a predominantly literary culture, but this time the new cultural scene was largely visual. The most obvious influence was the Royal College of Art under Robin Darwin, a member of the most powerful cultural clan in Britain. The importance of the RCA and a handful of other schools such as Goldsmiths in South London was explained by Pearce Marchbank, himself a graduate of the Central School of Art. He told Jonathon Green that this was because 'art students had very open minds – we were interested in everything that was going on', and not only in their subject. For the 1960s were artistically inclusive, a trend encouraged by the growth of the Arts Council. As late as 1962, the government's grant to the Council was barely more than the money it cost to maintain the British Embassy in Washington but this situation was transformed by an unlikely combination, that of the Arts Minister Jennie Lee, the tempestuously beautiful widow of Aneurin Bevan and herself a ruthless operator, and the chairman of the Council, Lord Goodman. In the late 1960s the two of them ensured that the grant was greatly increased.

The Council merely reflected the great explosion in British art. As early as 1957, Richard Hamilton had defined Pop Art as 'Popular (designed for a mass audience), Transient (short-term solution),

* Another favourite of Miller's had been the rhyme:

> Mary Had a little lamb
> She also had a duck
> She put them on a table
> To see if they would . . . fall off

Expendable (easily forgotten), Low-Cost, Mass-Produced, Young (aimed at youth), Witty, Sexy, Gimmicky, Glamourous, Big Business'. At the time the ideas he expressed had enormous influence, partly because they were a deliberate snub to High Art, which was seen as passé and class-ridden. The new artists required new galleries, and none were more trendy than the Indica Gallery, which became a sort of club for the in group, and the RF Gallery opened in Duke Street in Mayfair in 1962 by Robert Fraser, an Old Etonian known as Groovy Bob. His critics called him, rightly, a groupie, but he selected stars such as Andy Warhol, Bridget Riley and Richard Hamilton himself, who painted a famous image of Swinging London starring Mick Jagger.

It was RCA graduates such as David Hockney, Peter Blake, Peter Phillips and Allen Jones who provided the sensation of the Venice Biennale in 1963. Six years later, Bridget Riley, the leading Op artist, was the first British artist to win the top award at that year's Biennale, a success which reinforced the notion that London, if not as important as New York, was usurping Paris's historic position in the world of the visual arts. This trend was confirmed by the way that Sotheby's under Peter Wilson was creating the modern art market and replacing the Paris-based dealers who had previously dominated the market in the more important works of art – a term Wilson enlarged to include hundreds of new categories of 'traded art'. London's new eminence was backed up by the conscious effort, led by the then Sir Anthony Blunt* and reinforced by immigrants such as Niklaus Pevsner and Ernst Gombrich, to transform art history into a respectable academic discipline and not just, as previously, a refuge for debutantes.

But for most people it was pop music which showed the change in British life most obviously. For the key theme tunes of the 1960s were precisely that, tunes, and for most people still form the most enduring and memorable legacy of the era. It was no coincidence that Peter Blake, one of the best and most durable of pop artists, designed the cover for the Beatles' album *Sergeant Pepper's Lonely Hearts Club Band*. The seismic shift in British pop music had started in the late 1950s. But it was divided. After Elvis Presley had hit Britain in 1957 with 'All Shook Up' the worship of Presley and other rock heroes was largely confined to working-class kids in their secondary modern ghettoes; this was music associated with the Teds, the Mods and the Rockers. Classier, in social terms anyway, was 'skiffle', a name derived from the Chicago jug bands of the 1930s and adopted twenty years later by British musicians. The most important group was led by Lonnie

---

* He was stripped of his knighthood when his spying activities were revealed in 1979.

Donegan, who had discovered American music as a national serviceman in Vienna listening to American forces' radio stations. He joined the Chris Barber jazz band – jazz was a largely middle-class phenomenon – which had a skiffle spot. The songs he sang – like *The Rock Island Line** – were major hits, not only in Britain, where Donegan had thirty hits between 1955 and 1962, but also in the United States, where he was awarded the supreme accolade of a cover story in *Time* magazine. Donegan was a transitional figure – his last Number One hit was 'My Old Man's a Dustman'†. But over the next few years the relationship between British and American pop music changed from a colonial dependence to an imperial dominance.

It was my sister-in-law, Sam Arnold-Forster, who had grown up in the musical desert of the 1940s and 1950s, who perfectly expressed the feeling of release and relevance brought in by the new music of the 1960s. 'Too many of the songs of my youth,' she wrote, had the word 'Moonlight' in their title and all of them 'were totally remote from the people who were supposed to consume them and sounded as though they were written by elderly men in shirt sleeves and braces in somewhere called Tin Pan Alley. Sammy Kahn used to boast that he could write a song in five minutes. I can believe him. Oh how easily I can believe him ... But then suddenly people were writing songs about things they cared about. And what songs! "Mr Tambourine Man", "Bridge Over Troubled Water" '[3] – to which I would add Beatles' songs such as 'Eleanor Rigby (All the Lonely People)'. As William Mann, the music critic of *The Times*, put it in a decidedly portentous article, 'They have brought a distinctive and exhilarating flavour into a genre of music that was in danger of ceasing to be music at all ... the songs of Lennon and McCartney are distinctly indigenous in character'.[4]

Nevertheless the shock of the new took some getting used to. In the beginning even Cliff Richard, later to be a mother's dream and naffest of singers, was considered dangerous – for a short time anyway. To George Melly and other jazz fans, rock was no more than a 'contemporary incitement to mindless fucking and arbitrary vandalism ... what we failed to recognise was that the whole point of rock 'n' roll depended on its lack of subtlety. It was music to be used rather than listened to: a banner to be waved in the face of "them" by a group who felt themselves ignored or victimised.' By contrast, an unnamed critic quoted by Sir Michael Tippett wrote of the Beatles that 'their

---

* According to the song, it was 'a mighty fine line' but went bankrupt the year the song dominated the charts.

† Another novelty number which I recall with some, albeit embarrassed, affection was 'Does your Chewing Gum lose its flavour on the bedpost overnight?'

unique quality was to know at which points a scrap of ordinary language needed to be touched in order to make it sing.'[5] Tippett's informant had seized on one important point: that, for the first time, the young musicians wrote their own lyrics and so could express the feelings of a class – usually working-class and often from the provinces – which had never previously been represented. Later in the 1960s, the great pop festivals on the Isle of Wight and elsewhere provided massive proof that youth culture, famously characterised by 'sex, drugs and rock 'n' roll', was here to stay.

The transformation, the new confidence, also affected classical music like Tippett's, which became bolder and more original than ever before. It even affected that most traditional English musical activity, the choir. There was a massive swing from the very English restraint well demonstrated by the choir of King's College Cambridge to the full-throated expression of feeling: the choir of my elder son's school, Wandsworth, created by Russell Burgess, a maverick music master, became a favourite of Benjamin Britten because of the openness of the choir's sound.

The pop musicians were attacking on two fronts. The Beatles, the 'mop-heads' in their neat Cardin jackets, represented, in public anyway, all that was most wholesome about popular music. By contrast there were the Rolling Stones. Their first manager, Andrew Loog Oldham, actively promoted them as a group which 'didn't wash too much . . . and they don't play nice-mannered music', the very epitome of adolescent rebellion. But this was not political: the only truly radical British pop artist was Dusty Springfield, whose protests against apartheid predated the era when such radicalism became commonplace in the British pop world.

While the young were playing, so too were their fathers: many errant husbands were encouraged by the arrival of hundreds of thousands of young foreign girls to act as au pairs, in effect amateur nannies. They were either escaping from overly strict parental backgrounds and so were far more relaxed than their contemporaries who had stayed at home, or came from sexually freer societies than that of pre-1960s Britain. Indeed, it was said that the phrase 'Swedish au pair girl' was the sexiest in the English language for many a married man.

But even the steadily decreasing number of stay-togethers were enjoying the luxury of lives more comfortable than ever before. There was plenty of room for improvement. Until the 1960s the taint of Puritanism hung over the idea of a hedonistic lifestyle, especially amongst the radical classes. It was the ubiquitous Michael Young, author of the 1945 Labour Manifesto, in an essay he called 'The Chipped White Cups of Dover', who broached the idea that we should take our 'life style' seriously enough to try and impose our standards on manufacturers. But the paper was rejected by the Fabian Society on the grounds that consumerism was not merely irrelevant to socialism but actually hostile. In the *New Statesman* John Morgan suggested that it was absurd to suggest that a Surrey stockbroker and a Sheffield steelworker could have the same interests. But Young's paper led to the foundation of the Consumers' Association in 1957. Though increasingly useful, it provided a classic case of the Best and Brightest preferring to be critical onlookers rather than to participate in economic activity.

Inevitably, as housing grew more affordable, there was an increased obsession with the home – always a characteristic of British middle-class life. The concentration on improved home comfort was boosted by the sheer number of dwellings built during the decade. The numbers jumped from just over 300,000 in 1960 to 426,000 eight years later – of which over 200,000 were in the public sector, virtually all built by local councils. However, until the mid 1960s the idea that houses should be warm was ridiculous; central heating was only for foreigners. Then, by a curious, almost osmotic process, the British bourgeoisie was converted to the delights of not freezing at home. This mass conversion began with an advertising campaign for oil-fired central heating, featuring Mrs 1970 – a symbol not only of warmth but also of the (often exaggerated) power of advertising. Now houses were often furnished with more modern furniture, although family pressure stymied at least one innovator, Donald Gomme, who introduced the stylish G-Plan furniture. More permanent was the success – albeit limited to a relatively select section of the urban bourgeoisie – of that perennial trend-setter Terence Conran who had founded his first enterprise, the Soup Kitchen, in the early 1950s and opened his first Habitat shop – naturally in Chelsea – in 1964. Conran and his imitators appealed to the new class of middle-class housewives (and their husbands) who were better educated and thus more confident and independent of their parents' tastes.

Even more socially widespread was the habit of taking holidays abroad. This is generally associated with the 1960s, but was, partially at least, merely a case of taking up pre-war habits again – in 1939 a million and a half people were taking holidays outside Britain. But these were middle-class travellers. The package holiday was, if not classless, then at least available to a far wider social spread. The first package-holiday tour (to Corsica) organised by the refugee Vladimir Reisz had been arranged as early as 1949. But it was the arrival of jet airliners in the early 1960s which democratised a habit previously confined to the professional classes, that and the appeal of 'Sun, sand and sex' as featured in the advertisements for Bacardi rum.

150

Guards officers in mufti – the way we – or some of us anyway – lived as late as 1958.
Source – PA

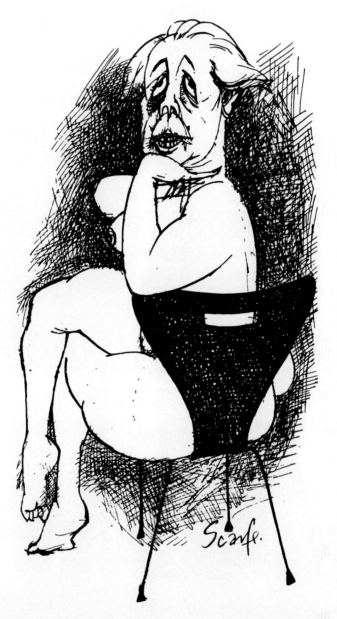

A new ferocity: Gerald Scarfe on Harold Macmillan in a pose reminiscent
of Christine Keeler.

Source – Hulton Archive/Keystory

The contrasts of 1977: the Queen and her loyal subjects v the Sex Pistols, whose fans were even more enthusiastic.

Source – Hulton Archive

Source – Hulton Archive/Keystory

Gay life then and now: in 1954 Michael Pitt-Rivers, Lord Monagu of Bealieu and Peter Wildeblood went to jail; in 2000 Gay Festivals were a routine matter.

Source – PA

Models at – very
different – homes:
Fiona Campbell-
Walter, the belle of
the 1950s and Jean
Shrimpton, sex
symbol of the sixties.
*Source – Hulton Archive –
Kaus Kallmorgen*

*Source – Hulton Archive –
Terry Fincher*

Source – Hulton Getty/Keystory

Respectable marchers en route from Aldermaston to London. From left: three MPs - Sidney Silverman, Emrys Hughes and Michael Foot.

By 1968 riots like these in Grosvenor Square had got decidedly more serious.

Source – Hulton Archive

The end of the tower block: in 1968 Ronan Point in the East End of London collapsed after a gas leak.

Source – Hulton Archive/Evening Standard

Churchill's funeral cortège in Trafalgar Square: truly the end of an epoch.
Source – PA

If holidays to ever more exotic destinations became increasingly democratic, the same cannot really be said of that over-hyped evolution, that of English food, or rather food in Britain. For the working classes exotic food was almost exclusively confined to the ever-increasing hordes of Indian and Chinese restaurants. Most of the only non-ethnic initiatives consisted of fast food chains, most obviously the Wimpy bars, which were awful. As late as 1965, the ineffable Selective Employment Tax was based on the idea that being served food in a restaurant was an economically undesirable activity.

Early attempts to improve cooking through the pages of women's magazines nonetheless involved the use of packet soups and other prepared foods as basic ingredients. 'For a bachelor girl's party – and it all comes out of tins' was the title of one article at a time when, as Stephen Mennell puts it, 'the impact of technological changes in food manufacture and marketing came first'.[6] Yet the idea of taste slowly entered the vocabulary of food, notably with the word 'spicy', 'which was to become a cliché epithet for any dish containing virtually any flavouring beyond salt and pepper'. 'Rationing went on for about thirteen years,' wrote Laura Mason and Catherine Brown, 'enough for a generation to grow up without really knowing anything of their food traditions. Rationing was a terrible expedient with two effects. It created an itch for excitement, for something novel on the food front, be it glittering seduction by the ease and plenty of the United States or the more sophisticated lure of the Mediterranean described by Elizabeth David.'[7] Yet the British tradition was there. Mason and Brown found 400 items from cheese to spreads, from varieties of apples to breeds of sheep.

The first restaurateurs on the scene were the founders of the Aberdeen Angus chain and Frank and Aldo Berni, both exploiting the longing of the British for steak. The Bernis were Italian immigrants who devised a winning formula, a 7s 6d (37.5p) menu which offered a large Argentinian rump steak, chips, peas, bread roll and butter followed by cheese or pudding. This all-conquering formula – as served by successors of the Berni Inns such as the Beefeater and Harvester chains – has proved infinitely more durable than more fashionable notions for these pioneers were fully aware of the general public's gastronomic limitations. Surprisingly, it took two men, both with their roots in the normally puritanical Fabian tradition, to enlarge the culinary horizons of the middle-classes. The first was Raymond Postgate, who in 1951 created the Good Food Club, an organisation which existed solely to produce *The Good Food Guide*. Postgate represented a notable break with the tradition that food expertise was foreign and right-wing (attributes combined in André Simon, who had dominated the gastronomic scene in the pre-war years). A socialist and brother-in-law of the famous socialist political scientist, G. D. H. Cole, Postgate produced a guide that was a simple and effective means of involving the small minority of the public which took food seriously to funnel their ideas through a publication which depended almost entirely on its readers' opinions and thus gradually enlarged their culinary horizons. In 1962 *The Good Food Guide* had been taken under the wing of the Consumers' Association and thus entered the mainstream of consumerism.

The low basic level of culinary expectations was shown by the repeated statements in the *Guide* for at least its first decade that a meal was 'good of its kind'. The *Guide*'s major rival, run by the Hungarian-born Egon Ronay, was showier ('What they do in Wales could be called gastronomic rape except that they don't even seem to derive pleasure from it') but well into the 1960s Ronay's inspectors showed a surprising naivety when describing serious – and above all posh – restaurants. Ronay's impact was to be the greatest at the lowest level of public nourishment, in improving the generally appalling standard of meals served in the increasing number of motorway service areas. Many of these were owned by Charles Forte, who systematically destroyed any idea of decent food in the hundreds of restaurants and hotels he controlled, although previously some of them, the former Trust Houses in provincial and market towns, had at least tried to preserve the English tradition of a decent portion of the traditional 'meat and two veg. Forte's pernicious system of portion control ensured bland standardisation and poor quality throughout his group's hundreds of hotels and restaurants.

The second, and far more important, influence was the appearance of the TV chef in the bearded, avuncular form of Philip Harben, who fully understood the need to encourage viewers to cook with wine and spice but without frightening them. But his Fabian background emerged in his notion that the best means of enlightening the British public lay in community feeding, notably through the continuance of the British Restaurants which had provided nourishing, subsidised meals throughout and immediately after the war. His colleagues Jane Beaton and, above all, Margaret Patten continued the slow educational process in women's magazines. In *A Century of British Cooking*,[12] Patten mentioned as typical, smart 1950s dishes 'cock-a-leekie, calves liver pâté, tournedos Rossini, steak Diane, quiche Lorraine, crêpes suzette, apple strudel and baked Alaska' – many of which involved a strong element of showing off. The 1960s in their turn brought dishes such as avocado with prawns, mushrooms à la grecque, vol au vent, prawn cocktail (commemorated in a book on the period, *The Prawn Cocktail Years*), lemon meringue pie, coronation chicken and so on.

Soon the experts could assume greater ambitions on the part of their audience. 'Sauce-making is not really difficult,' wrote Beaton in 1962. By then, according to Mennell, 'there is a more cosmopolitan feel to the magazines, and the food found in the cookery columns has become strikingly more diverse and adventurous than, say, it was in the 1930s'. An increasing number of housewives, educated members of the middle classes who before the war would have employed cooks and in a later generation would have had jobs rather than stayed at home, provided a ready audience for authors who could guide them in their fundamental revolt against the sad tradition that food meant nourishment, not taste, and that it should not be discussed, even at table. The most dramatic change came in the image of garlic, for generations the purest symbol of the general undesirability of foreigners and their strong-tasting (and even more strongly smelling) foods. By 1964 the thriller writer Len Deighton was able to publish a cook book entitled simply *Où est le garlic*?

But the outstanding star of the movement was Elizabeth David – one of the few writers who was not an actress, for the dramatic element in cookery writing and broadcasting was evident well before the show-biz element became dominant in the 1990s. When she was writing her first books in the late 1940s, Mrs David was expressing a natural longing for exotica and her recipes included ingredients that were totally unobtainable – until the 1960s it was, for instance, virtually impossible to buy olive oil except in Boots the Chemist, where it was sold in tiny bottles and intended primarily for cleaning out your ears. As a result, as Julian Barnes points out, reading her books was 'a sort of gastroporn' because, like an adolescent reading a girlie magazine, you couldn't get the real thing. Ironically, in her later life David produced three books in which she showed an enormous understanding and appreciation of the very English traditions she had unwittingly undermined through her earlier and much more influential works. Yet her first books did not sell in any great numbers until they were issued in paperback in the 1960s, and even then her influence was restricted to a relative minority of middle-class households. Far more influential were the supermarket chains, which steadily widened the choice of food available, though again they concentrated their efforts on middle-class areas. And after 1961, when they gained the right to sell alcoholic drinks, the supermarkets started to sell increasing quantities of wine so that by the end of the Millennium they had become the dominant influence in selling the increasing quantities of ever-improving wines drunk by the British middle classes.

The only truly popular gastro-movement was the Campaign for Real Ale, a result of the increasing standardisation of beers in the 1960s and the introduction of lagers which were, by and large, mostly low-alcohol fizz. But it was the cheese-makers who suffered even more than the makers of the best English ales. Before the war there had been no fewer than 15,000 creameries. Then came the heavy hand of rationing and the industrialisation and standardisation that went with it. This involved the banning of farmhouse cheese-making and the imposition of a standard national cheese, made in a mere 126 establishments. The whole tradition of serious English cheese-making – with the single exception of Stilton, whose makers had prudently registered the name before World War I – had seemingly been lost. The restoration process, which was only partially successful, was almost entirely due to the perseverance of a single grocer, Patrick Rance, who in the 1970s and 1980s started a revival of some of the dozens of native cheeses. Yet the industry had preferred to spend large sums of money on an invented variety, Lymeswold, which marketing gurus unsuccessfully tried to impose on the British public in the 1970s. It was an appalling insult to the many fine cheeses which could have been promoted instead.

Even so, at the end of the century there were only 350 cheese-makers and they laboured increasingly under their heavy-handed treatment by food standards inspectors. The most blatant case was in Lanarkshire, where the very same inspectors who failed to detect the outbreak of an epidemic of e-coli poisoning which killed dozens of people, spent years persecuting Patrick Harrington, maker of the delicious Lanark Blue. He was not the only victim. In early 2001 James Aldridge, one of Britain's finest cheese-makers, died a broken man after being persecuted by the Department of Health, which had imposed a blanket ban (the first ever imposed) on him after a single instance in which one of his cheeses had caused a case of e-coli. Even though the ban extended to cheeses which did not contain e-coli, the persecution continued. Despite this manifest abuse of justice, the Court of Appeal ruled in favour of the Department of Health on the grounds that they had been motivated by a perception, however mistaken, that there was a danger to public health.

For British officialdom has never accepted the desirability of authentic food. The book by Mason and Brown on the traditional foods of Britain was the result of an inquiry conducted under the auspices (and at the expense) of the European Union. It revealed hostility, 'official and personal, to the very idea of the investigation.

Crosscurrents of resentment were provoked by intrusion from outside; then there was the wilful obscurantism of many British people when thinking of food as more than a daily necessity'. The authors received no co-operation from any of the many bodies supposedly trying to promote British native foodstuffs. This, they concluded, 'seems to reflect our national determination to ignore much of real worth'. Too many of their entries end with the phrase 'made by a single producer' or 'baked in only one place'.

The zeitgeist made its influence felt even on that most British, and most traditional, area, sport. And nowhere more obviously than in football – only rugby union was to remain firmly amateur for another twenty years – where, until 1961, the players, however famous, were paid fixed maximum wages. It took the threat of a strike by the players, led by the chairman of the Professional Footballers' Association, Jimmy Hill, later to be the country's most famous football commentator, for their employers' organisation, the Football Association, to see reason. The chairmen of the clubs were typical of the small business class of their time, totally unwilling to lose control over their workers. The psychological breakthrough came when the comedian Tommy Trinder, the chairman of Fulham, announced that the England captain Johnny Haynes, coolest of footballers, was an entertainer, not a mere artisan, and should be paid as such. Nevertheless, while the players had been enfranchised in the 1960s, the ordinary fans continued to be treated as proles. Their situation, and the design of the country's stadia, was only transformed in the 1990s as the result of the Taylor Report after the Hillsborough disaster in which nearly a hundred Liverpool fans were crushed to death. And their new-found strength was to be dramatically confirmed a few years later when the Manchester United fans rose in – successful – revolt against a takeover bid for their club by Rupert Murdoch.

Until the early 1960s professional football was still largely based in the Midlands and North rather than in the South, where London was the exception. Indeed, the 1966 World Cup was the first time that the whole nation – as opposed to the working classes – had rejoiced in an English soccer victory: socially this united the country to an extent which would have been unthinkable even a few years earlier. Since then, the centre of gravity has moved south and a higher proportion of teams in the league are from southern England as the support has become more classless – indeed rather sickeningly trendy so, for today every politician has to support, or at least pretend to support, a team. In the 1950s it was unusual for Top People, or indeed the professional middle-classes as a whole, to watch soccer. The life-long devotion of John Sparrow, the Warden of All Souls', to Wolverhampton Wanderers counted as one of his eccentricities, as did the philosopher Freddie Ayer's devotion to Tottenham Hotspur. But then Ayer's enthusiasm could be explained by the fact that the Spurs team was Jewish, while Arsenal, its great North London rivals, was generally reckoned to be anti-Semitic. This racial-religious division was not unusual, separating Liverpool from its rival Everton, and City fans from United in Manchester. In England these tribalisms have now

155

virtually disappeared – but the same cannot be said in Glasgow, where one of the top teams, Rangers, remains solidly Protestant, while its great rival, Celtic is traditionally Irish-Catholic.

Democratisation even spread to cricket with the abolition of the distinction between amateurs and professionals, and the consequent abolition of the Gentlemen v Players game which followed the death of Sir Henry ('Plum') Warner, who had ruled the game with a rod of Victorian iron until his death in 1963. As Christopher Martin Jenkins, the BBC's cricket commentator, remarked, the abolition of amateur status was 'more a reflection of changing attitudes in society than a radical shift in the character of cricket' – although Wimbledon remained an all-amateur event (theoretically, anyway) until 1968, when professionals were allowed in.

Such changes were best summed up in one word: money, its power and its increasing acceptability symbolised by the introduction of the first sponsored competition, the Gillette Cup. But then a number of games were being revolutionised and globalised, thanks to both the arrival of jet air travel and international television coverage, itself the result of the launching of TV satellites in increasing numbers. Golf was an obvious example. Until the 1960s there had been a distinction between the ordinary club professionals, who were primarily teachers and shopkeepers, and the small band of tournament-oriented professionals loosely attached to clubs which were glad to have such illustrious names as Dai Rees and Henry Cotton associated with them. By the end of the decade, the tournament players representing the brute force of ever-increasing prize money won the right to dominate their trades union, the Professional Golfers Association. By that time 'golf was a global media commodity', as Ray Physick and Richard Holt put it, 'in the 1950s even a good tournament player would have expected to spend some of the winter months at his club, to which he might retire when his competitive days were over. By the 1970s there was a world market for good players who could play all the year round.'[8] By then what we would now call 'corporate sponsorship, above all by the tobacco companies, was beginning to play a major role – as with a golf championship sponsored by Players. In the late 1960s Colin Chapman's all-conquering Formula 1 Lotus team was being backed by the tobacco giants.

But by 1968 London was becoming markedly less swinging, indeed such riots as there were that troubled year were far less significant than those in France or the United States. Nonetheless, the crowds that gathered in Trafalgar Square and the tens of thousands who marched to the American Embassy in Grosvenor Square in March 1968 to protest against the Vietnam war were angrier, more determined and less prepared to co-operate with the police than their predecessors a

156

decade earlier who had supported the Campaign for Nuclear Disarmament.

Sadly, CND was not as significant a phenomenon as it appeared at the time, except in the narrow context of the history of the Labour Party. 'In its moral absolutism,' wrote Bogdanor and Skidelsky, 'CND was in the great dissenting tradition in British foreign policy . . . what was completely novel about CND was its clientele. It represented the first appearance of youth on the political stage.' The Campaign had been sparked off in early 1957 by an article in the *New Statesman* by J. B. Priestley as an appeal to a youth which was cynical but 'waiting for something better than party squabbles and appeals to their narrowest self-interest', a declaration of 'something great and noble in its intentions that would make them feel good again'. (The 1957 Defence White Paper, with its increasing reliance on nuclear weapons, merely emphasised the point). Unfortunately, with the exception of a handful of union leaders, it was an almost entirely middle-class movement. But it was, literally, a dress rehearsal for the 1960s: the demonstrators' long hair, beards and jeans were in deliberate contrast to the prevailing norm.

Ten years later protestors and police alike had hardened in their attitudes. Throughout the decade the police had appeared increasingly unfriendly to the whole middle class, what with speed limits and the drink and drive laws introduced in 1967. But for the middle-class young, the alienation was almost complete. During the 1960s drug-taking, which had been normal in the first war, largely to enable the upper classes to cope with the appalling casualties among the younger generation, was democratised. It led to divides between old and new generations and, more publicly, between the natural inclinations of the young and the law. When a letter was sent to *The Times* to ask for a change in the drug laws, its signatories included only two MPs, the young Brian Walden and the deeply disreputable Tom Driberg, but it did include such media worthies as David Dimbleby and Jonathan Aitken.

The police had always 'fitted-up' working-class suspects and in the 1960s extended the habit to middle-class suspects such as those suspected of using drugs and, more particularly, to middle-class demonstrators. It was routine for the police at West End Central Police Station, headed by Detective Inspector Harry Challoner, to arrest demonstrators, force their fingers round builders' bricks and then have them and the bricks finger-printed. The most notorious case occurred when there was a riot outside Claridge's hotel to protest against Queen Frederica of Greece and thus against the totalitarian military regime in her country. Challoner's efforts were encouraged by such judges as Melford Stevenson, who, when confronted by evidence of such fakery by the police, intoned that 'counsel has no duty to be a loudspeaker to a maladjusted set'. Eventually his superiors discovered that Challoner was not overzealous but a paranoid schizophrenic. Nevertheless, as he told Geoffrey Robertson some years later, he did not regret sending innocent people to prison: 'Of course not. My voices were right. They were all guilty.'

The participants in the drug scene took it less seriously than their opponents, for whom it meant the end of any ordered, hierarchical world. The alternative society and the underground as a whole was, as Jonathon Green put it, 'an educated movement, drawing on the alienated children of the comfortable bourgeoisie'. 'There was no working class in the underground,' Cheryll Park, a young working-class Northerner told Green, 'because nobody did any work.'[16] John Lennon – the only Beatle from a middle-class background – went so far as to sing (in 'Working Class Hero'), 'You think you're all clever and classless and free but you're all fucking peasants as far as I can see,' and, as so often with Lennon, one cannot be sure if he was being ironic.

The authorities' fear of the revolting young was naturally distilled in their attitude to the Rolling Stones. This escalated into a patently ridiculous fear that the group were a conspiracy to engineer the end of British civilisation as we knew it. Away from his music, Jagger himself, with his middle-class upbringing, middle-class love of money* and middle-class prejudices (including an unusually hostile attitude towards drugs), was a totally unsuitable figure as a symbol of revolutionary youth. War broke out in early June 1967 after an interview in the *News of the World* on the subject of 'The Secrets of the Pop Stars' Hideaway' (Keith Richard's country house in rural west Sussex), in which Jagger talked about LSD – which he rarely if ever took and which the interviewer thought was merely another name for hash.

Jagger foolishly sued for libel. A week later, the police raided the house and found Marianne Faithfull lying naked on a rug armed with Benzedrine pills which Mick Jagger, in a rare moment of gallantry, claimed were his. From this incident somehow sprang the story that Jagger was attempting to insert a Mars Bar into her vagina, a myth which summed up the duality of respectable response to the pop stars: 'Aren't they awful?' and 'Oh, what fun' – no thought was given to the degradation which would have been involved for Ms Faithfull. After a trial in front of an unsurprisingly hostile judge, Jagger and the art dealer Robert Fraser, who had also been in the party, were sentenced

* By 1970 the Stones' ever increasing fortunes were being managed by an ultra-respectable banker, Prince Rupert Von Loewenstein, inevitably known to his friends as 'Rupie the Groupie'.

to short jail sentences and photographed handcuffed together, a sight which engendered a wave of sympathy for them. Then they found an unlikely ally, the ultra-respectable William Rees-Mogg, who wrote an editorial in *The Times* with a title taken from Alexander Pope's famous phrase 'Why break a butterfly upon a wheel'.

But it was two trials in 1971 which spelled the end of the old, and in retrospect almost innocent, world, of sex, drugs and rock 'n' roll and the onset of the fear of terrorism which was to dominate the first half of the 1970s. The first was the trial of the editors of *Oz* magazine for obscenity after they had published an edition for children including such delicious items as Rupert the Bear, a favourite character in the *Daily Express* at the time, 'exercising his penis'. The magazine had been founded in Sydney in 1963 and symbolised the radicalism imported by the many Australians – Germaine Greer, Richard Neville, Colin McInnes amongst others – who formed a core group in radical 1960s London. The notion of the '"philosophy of *Oz*"', wrote the leading radical advocate Geoffrey Robertson, 'was a contradiction in terms. It was a coffee-table magazine for a revolution which would never happen – unless someone in authority took it seriously' – which of course they duly did. Following a heavy raid by Chief Inspector Luff, the publisher Richard Neville and the editors, Felix Dennis and an Australian lawyer, Jim Anderson were arraigned before Mr Justice Argyle, the very parody of a reactionary judge – he later told an interviewer that he knew Neville was a 'card-carrying Communist' for reasons that were to remain obscure. After the longest trial for obscenity in British legal history, all three were found guilty*. But the verdict was overturned by the Court of Appeal after one of the judges had sent his clerk out to buy some of the pornographic magazines routinely stocked by newsagents (in Soho at least). This so shocked the innocent Lord Chief Justice, Lord Widgery, that the verdicts were overturned.

The enormous publicity surrounding the case naturally contrasted the prosecution with the failure to pursue the hundreds of publishers of real hard-core pornography. The lame explanations of the head of the 'dirty squad', Chief Inspector George Fenwick, infuriated even the easy-going Home Secretary, Reginald Maudling, and were major factors leading to the appointment of Robert Mark to clean up the Met and the imprisonment of 400 policemen. These were headed by Commander Wallace Virgo, previously in charge of the Obscene Publications and Drugs squads (the cops were so corrupt that one of them

---

* A young journalist, Anna Wintour, later known as Nuclear Wintour for her icy attitudes as editor of American *Vogue*, had offered to marry Neville to prevent him being deported.

even edited a spanking magazine), Chief Superintendent Bill Moody, Fenwick himself and, to crown it all, the head of the flying squad, Commander Kenneth Drury, who had rather stupidly spent a holiday in Cyprus with a leading porn baron. As Mr Justice Mars-Jones put it, they had turned 'the Obscene Publications Squad into a vast protection racket . . . corruption on a scale that beggars imagination.' They all went to jail except for Luff who, as a deeply religious man, had objected to *Oz*'s perversion of youth. He was allowed to go off to do missionary work.

By contrast, the trial of members of the Angry Brigade that same year marked the arrival of the much, as it were, heavier 1970s. The prosecution started when the police had found some of the Brigade's names and addresses in the belongings of a petty thief called Jake Prescott. Even though it became clear that this loose group did hoard arms and that they may well have been responsible for bombings, the judge – Melford Stevenson again – and the papers had a field day. 'These guerrillas,' declared the *Evening Standard*, 'are the violent activists of a revolution comprising workers, students, trade unionists, homosexuals, unemployed and women striving for liberation' – a neat summary of the bogey persons of the day and one totally unrelated to the handful of Brigadiers. The trials were a warning of what was to come when Britain was confronted by a genuine menace from the IRA during the period 1974–76.

The counter-culture left no cultural monuments, no lasting works of art. But it did produce a new breed of entrepreneurs such as Tony Elliott of *Time Out*, Richard Branson of Virgin and, above all, Felix Dennis. Dennis had not been sent to gaol because the judge considered him too stupid to have been an active conspirator. But he took his revenge: by 2000 he had become a multi-millionaire thanks to his magazine publishing business, while the *Daily Express*, the paper he had parodied, has been bought by a pornographic publisher. On a broader level, the underground's attitudes (among them, 'doing one's own thing') and at least some of its institutions have now been absorbed, as Juliet Gardiner puts it, into mainstream British life in the form of 'fringe theatres, art centres, natural food stores'.

In the longer term, even when the baby-boomers' generation was forced to settle down, to accept bourgeois norms, they could not in all conscience attempt to impose on their children the same restrictions, the same standards as had their parents. They had set off a revolution whose effects can be seen to this day, and not just in the continuing popularity of pop festivals, but, more generally, in the enduring sensitivity of young people in general to good causes and the subsequent determination of youth to assert itself. But then in the 1960 the mood of the whole country had changed. In 1970 when Anthony Sampson sat down to revise his book *The Anatomy of Britain* published only eight years earlier, he found that five sixths of the contents had to be re-written.

Notes

1. *London Review of Books*, July 6 2000.
2. John Crosby, *Weekend Telegraph*, April 16 1965.
3. Letter to the *Independent*, February 28 1993.
4. *The Times*, December 23 1963.
5. In *Moving into Aquarius,* Routledge & Kegan Paul, 1959.
6. *All Manners of Food*, Basil Blackwell, 1996.
7. *Traditional Foods of Britain*, Prospect Books, Totnes, 1999.
8. *Journal of Contemporary History*, Summer 2000.
9. Bogdanor and Skidelsky op cit.
10. The Justice Game, Chatto & Windus 1998.

8

Hitting the Buffers

IN OCTOBER 1964, when Harold Wilson became Prime Minister, the American sociologist Edward Shils had greeted his arrival as heralding 'a conception of new possibilities of life'. Wilson himself tried to don the mantle of the recently assassinated President Kennedy with a similar 'hundred-day programme'. He was helped by having a Cabinet of an unsurpassed intellectual – and in some cases political – calibre. Yet within a hundred days he had returned to the same stop-go economic policy followed by his predecessors and was reduced to referring to the 'spirit of Dunkirk' which he had previously mocked as a symbol of the British capacity for covering a defeat with the gloss of success.

At the time the hopes he personified did not seem unreasonable. Wilson, the ultra-bright technocrat, was a total contrast to his apparently languidly aristocratic predecessor, the fourteenth Earl of Home (a greatly underestimated figure who was capable of retorting that his opponent was the fourteenth Mr Wilson), promising to bring 'the white heat of technology' to Britain. Yet, ironically, Wilson's greatest single political success – apart from the balancing act which enabled him to keep the Labour party more or less intact for a dozen turbulent years – was the effect on the Tory party of his person: Wilson was a provincial lower middle-class figure who proved that there was an alternative to the old elite.

By 1970, when Wilson was defeated by Edward Heath, it was clear that he had failed, partly through his own gutlessness – and the inability of the trades unions to join him in the second half of the twentieth century – and partly because of endemic problems within British society. The failure of political will he embodied could not cope with the structure of a society which was still not being modernised with sufficient speed or thoroughness. For the much-vaunted social and cultural upheavals of the 1960s had their limitations. Etonians might have adopted working-class accents but they still assumed they would have a leading role, and although the City and industry attracted an increasing proportion of the ever-growing numbers of graduates –

previously largely confined to journalism and advertising – the Labour Movement and trades unions remained unaffected by the mood of the 1960s. Worse, a number of fundamental reforms went badly astray, partly because they had been imposed from above, without regard to the feelings of the people most involved.

The mood of Wilson and his ministers swung between megalomania and incompetence. 'The impression brilliantly conveyed to the electorate in 1964,' wrote Peter Sinclair, 'was that some undefined negative attitude implicit in "stop-go" and some unspecified kind of governmental amateurism were all that had deprived Britain of rapid growth in the 1950s and early 1960s. Purposeful and dynamic government [i.e. planning] would suddenly restore her rightful rate of growth.'[1] The hope that this would lead to such growth was killed by two decisions by Wilson in the first days of his first administration: not to devalue a currency which had been overvalued for years and increasingly reduced the incentive to expand; and not to take economic power away from the Treasury and hand it over to a department which would be solely concerned with the economy, leaving the Treasury to be the British equivalent of the American Bureau of the Budget.

For Wilson, devaluation was an exceptionally tricky subject: he did not want Labour to be associated with another one since an earlier government had been responsible for the devaluation of 1949. In 1964, however, an immediate devaluation would have been perfectly politically acceptable, indeed a logical step since Wilson had campaigned on the theme of 'thirteen years of Tory misrule', even though he knew that orthodox financial opinion – personified by Lord Cromer, the Governor of the Bank of England, who threatened to resign – was dead against such a step. But devaluation, it was thought, would represent a defeat.

As a result, until 1967, there was a blackout on discussion of the topic. When an earlier crisis, in January 1963 after de Gaulle's veto of our entry into the European Common Market, had caused a run on the pound, the editors of *The Times* and the *Economist* had been hauled up before the Governor, who claimed that their discussion of the subject had cost the reserves the then enormous sum of £300 million. There had been another opportunity to devalue in July 1966. Yet Wilson and his chancellor Jim Callaghan chose instead to impose restrictions which finally cooled the 'white heat' of economic progress. As Alan Watkins put it, they 'destroyed the foundations of socialist literature since 1919 by removing the delusion that socialist government automatically involved relatively seamless economic progress and some of its edifices as well – including Anthony Crosland's Future of Socialism'. Typically, the British Motor Corporation, which had just hired thousands of extra workers in anticipation of increased demand, had to sack them all after the imposition of the restrictive measures which replaced devaluation, a devastating blow to morale amongst managers and shop-floor workers alike. Yet even then, and in marked contrast to their reaction to Mrs Thatcher's 1981 budget when 364 economists protested publicly, not one stood up to object to non-devaluation – a far more damaging policy.

Wilson was finally forced to devalue in November 1967 in what was, technically, an exceptionally smooth operation. Unfortunately he made matters worse by appearing on television to explain that it 'does not mean, of course, that the pound here in Britain, in your pocket or your purse or in your bank, has been devalued'. This remark elicited the reaction that, if Wilson had been the captain of the *Titanic*, he would have explained that the ship had stopped to take on ice. The British public is not easily fooled. It saw through Harold Wilson's declaration that weekend, for devaluation did not remove the sense of crisis, partly because its effects, and those of the restrictive measures which, sensibly, accompanied the decision, resulted in short-term pain.

The aftermath witnessed a meeting of high farce between Cecil Harmsworth King, the megalomaniac press lord and chairman of the Mirror Group, Earl Mountbatten and Sir Solly Zuckerman, the eminent scientist whom Mountbatten had brought along as a witness. Accounts of the meeting vary but it is clear that King launched into a tirade about the sad state of a nation which badly needed A Strong Man and proposed Mountbatten for the role. His choice was a shrewd one, for his candidate possessed a bigger ego and sense of himself as a Man of Destiny than almost any other Englishman in the twentieth century. Zuckerman stormed out of the meeting, calling King's proposal rank treachery, and even Mountbatten was not seriously tempted into accepting the role for which King had cast him. On December 6 1968, a day that became known as Mad Friday, there was a pseudo-crisis when people – the financial markets anyway – came to believe that it was the end, that Wilson had resigned, even that the Queen had abdicated. But this farcical incident was merely a foretaste of the much more important plots and fears during the later years of the 1970s.

More significant was the way that the British electorate neither forgot nor forgave Wilson for the devaluation crisis, any more than they did the humiliation inflicted by the IMF on the Labour government in 1976 and that by George Soros and other market operators on the Major government with the departure from the European Exchange Rate Mechanism in September 1992. But this was a short-term disaster that led to nine years in which, for the first time since 1945, Britain's growth rate exceeded that of our European 'partners.'

Wilson's second failure of nerve came in Whitehall. In theory the only hope for the British economy lay in the foundation of the Department of Economic Affairs as a ministry capable of taking a broader view than the Treasury. In the event Wilson simply used the administrative arrangement to create a state of 'creative tension' between James Callaghan at the Treasury and the brilliant, erratic (and increasingly drunken) George Brown at the DEA. Callaghan's position was strengthened by the natural refusal of the Treasury to play second fiddle and within a few months the DEA was left without any control over the macro-economic management of the country.

Nevertheless the DEA was allowed to develop a National Plan. This was a logical development of the ideas of corporate economic progress which had been encouraged by the Tory government in the early 1960s and had led to the creation of the National Economic Development Council. The plan itself was a spin-off from the realisation that Europe had got it right economically since 1945; now there was a systematic attempt to catch up through indicative economic and industrial planning – an attempt which increasingly aped the model of the French with their five-year plans. Although regional development had been instituted in the 1930s, the post-Suez mood gave the idea a major boost and it continued until it was killed off by Mrs Thatcher twenty-five years later. 'In fact,' as Peter Sinclair noted, the famous National Plan consisted 'of little more than the printed replies to a questionnaire sent to industries about their inputs and outputs on the assumption of 25 per cent growth by 1970'. Twenty years later, its obituary was spoken by Freddy Erroll, who had been President of the Board of Trade when NEDC was created. He looked at a photograph of the founder members and remarked to John Hoskyns after a long pause, 'Ah, John. God! What a waste of time it all was.'

The ideal of state involvement unconnected with nationalisation had its successes, notably the restructuring of much of British industry into larger units in the late 1960s under the auspices of the Industrial Reorganisation Corporation, a bunch of bright young men who subsequently went into industry and the city. They included Sir Alistair Morton, the saviour of the Channel Tunnel scheme, Sir Christopher Hogg, later of Courtaulds and Reuters, and John Gardiner, a future chairman of Tesco. For the IRC's young men showed that some, at least, of the Brightest and Best were prepared to go into business – just as troubled businesses were prepared to accept outsiders. But in the words of the IRC's second managing director, Sir Charles Villiers, they were 'disturbers of the peace'. Previously industrial decisions had been taken on political impulse. There was and remained no idea of planned progress, an idea abhorrent to the mandarins of the Treasury, capable of thinking only in terms of annual budgets unless their political masters cracked the whip. Typically, when modernisation of the railways was undertaken in the mid-1950s, it was a series of leaps, not the continuation of a planned programme. As a result, dozens of different types of diesel engines, many useless, were introduced in British Railways' eagerness to take advantage of what it knew would be a short-lived burst of investment.

Worse, industrial decisions were still being based on political rather than industrial rationale. The British steel industry was permanently crippled by Macmillan's decision in the late 1950s to go ahead with the construction of two medium-sized steel works, one at Ravenscraig in Scotland to appease the Scots, the other at Llanwern near Newport in South Wales, rather than build a single, world-scale plant. The result was that Ravenscraig was closed in the late 1980s and steel-making ended at Llanwern before the end of the millennium. The same pattern was followed with the motor industry, where plants were located on Merseyside and in Wales and Scotland for political reasons.

For it was in the motor industry that the government's policy failed its biggest test. Throughout the 1960s the situation of the British Motor Corporation – Britain's largest producer, whose marques included Austin, Morris and MG – grew steadily worse, through mismanagement and its inevitable corollary, dreadful industrial relations. Even the world-wide fame of the Mini did not help, for the undoubted genius of its designer Alec Issigonis did not extend to the economics of production engineering and consequently the car could never be produced profitably because it was so complex. In 1969 the government faced a choice. The sensible solution – adopted by the Heath administration with Rolls-Royce in 1971 – was to let BMC go bankrupt, then rescue it from the ashes under new management: this at least would have provided an opportunity to introduce a new, and more realistic industrial relations climate within the group. Instead the IRC merged BMC with Leyland, which by this time included not only the buses and heavy trucks on which it had built its fame and fortune but also Rover, famous for the Land Rover. The merger was inevitably a disaster because the business continued to drift and had to be rescued time and again, at great expense to the tax-payer, in the following twenty years.

Indeed, when a new managing director, Michael Edwardes took over in 1977, the management literally did not know the cost of producing a Mini, a model which was, as usual, losing a lot of money – though not as much per car as the Triumph TR7 sports car being produced at a factory at Speke in Merseyside which Edwardes promptly closed down. Typically, the problems were attributed exclusively to the workers, but management should have taken some of the blame. 'Even I know it's a bad product,' one worker told Philip Whitehead. 'If the workforce had any say in the design, that could be a good car [but] a plant of 2,500 men doesn't even have a suggestion box.' The, partly mythical, idea that workers on Merseyside were particularly uncontrollable was finally put to rest only in the late 1990s when Ford rebuilt its Halewood plant, which had been notorious for decades for its dreadful industrial relations record but was transformed into a model of co-operation when it started producing a new Jaguar model. Nevertheless Edwardes's straight talking – and the sacking of the notoriously 'Bolshie' senior shop steward 'Red Robbo' – did greatly improve productivity and reduce stoppages from the annual level of 350 to which they had climbed in the first half of 1978.

For the IRC's efforts were inevitably largely ineffectual, as was indicative planning as a whole, in the absence of a proper infrastructure – not only in terms of physical plant, but also of managerial skills – and of a properly trained and co-operative work force. The IRC had to confront an even more fundamental problem: the lingering amateur tradition in British business. Peter Menzies, the able and civilised deputy chairman of ICI, told a journalist in the late 1960s that it would be wrong for British business to 'take up the American pattern . . . the people of Western Europe want a wider life . . . in a sense we're in something of a quandary – we want to keep our private lives while staying in the first league'. Another industrial leader was quoted as saying, 'Even the most energetic Englishman won't buy this business of total dedication to the company. I feel that in giving myself 75 per cent of the time I'm doing quite enough.' The most extreme case was the Institute of Directors, which represented independent businessmen. It was run as a club whose director was a retired major-general whom it was pointless to try and interview after lunch.

The idea of modern, purposeful, growth-driven management was confined to a handful of – inevitably American-owned – businesses. The most obvious case was Ford, the breeding ground for a disproportionate number of Britain's business leaders in the following decades. At Ford the atmosphere was far removed from the clubbiness to be found in Shell, British Petroleum or ICI. The culture was classless and brutal, summed up in a remark made to a friend of mine on his arrival: 'Why are you here, for money or power – or both?' Such companies were strictly controlled by their (inevitably American) head offices – in Ford's case especially after the parent had bought the minority shares in the British subsidiary in 1961. The managing director of the British subsidiary of Procter and Gamble, another thrusting innovator, especially in marketing Fast Moving Consumer Goods (or FMCGs) such as the newly introduced detergents, was sacked by return cable in the late 1950s when he displayed a rare moment of independence by suggesting moving the company's head office to London from far-away Newcastle.

The limitations imposed by inadequate economic management were most obvious in the case of well-run businesses, none more so than General Electric, the combination organised by the IRC of Britain's three major electrical and electronic manufacturers under the management of Arnold, later Lord, Weinstock. 'The history of GEC', wrote John Plender, was a good example of how 'bad macro-economic management has fostered an extremely defensive managerial culture in industry. Weinstock was the prime example of that culture, and his temperament was very suitable for managing a capital-intensive manufacturing business in a period of poor policy, difficult labour relations and exceptionally high inflation'.[2] Naturally his policy – and the 'cash mountain' it engendered – became far less fashionable in the expansionist 1980s. Weinstock had inherited four computer manufacturers in assembling GEC, but within a few years none of them was competing except in small specialist niche markets because of his failure to invest in the key products of the new electronic revolution (his most destructive step was to close one of the world's most advanced factories making computer chips.)

Weinstock famously never visited any of the literally hundreds of factories in his empire. This highlighted a tendency identified by Hugh Parker of McKinsey: 'Too many managers,' he said, 'don't identify themselves with the interests of the managed. They stay aloof – at arms' length from the workers.' This tendency was fatally enhanced by the arrival of such firms as his, whose brilliant young consultants were employed by any major company trying to prove that it was keeping up with the latest managerial fashion. This was greatly welcomed at the time as proof that Britain was professionalising its companies' management, not only through the employment of firms like McKinsey but also through the creation of business schools, particularly that in London, which has always been a world leader. Unfortunately the thinking of the new 'experts' included a fatal flaw: the assumption that industries were all alike, followed the same rules, required no specialised knowledge but could be perfectly well managed by generalists who would, of course, know better than the poor souls who had been managing the businesses at the time without the benefit of an MBA. In a sense 'managerialism' was the natural successor to Balliolism, the idea that a generalist could master any given subject and was vastly superior to mere specialists.

Balliolism had assumed that the products of the college were prepared to take decisions. But the new mood of the 1960s seemed to discourage still further the whole concept of 'leadership', associated as it was with the Old Ways. The result is that it has, seemingly, been bled out of the English psyche, to be replaced by the 'advisory mentality'. This has led to the refusal to take responsibility on the part of too high a proportion of the educated classes, as witness the disproportionate number of able men and women who have flocked to relatively risk-free professions (the law, accountancy etc) and to the more comfortable service industries rather than riskier ventures.

Curiously, the spread of the advisory mentality was considerably boosted by one of the undeniable economic success stories of the 1960s, the emergence of London as one of the world's three major centres of international finance. By 2000 it had overtaken one of the others, Tokyo, and internationally was as important as the other, New York. The markets were ever-expanding. First, as currency restrictions were eased came the trading in foreign currencies. These expanded into an increasing variety of ever more elaborate financial instruments which originated in the imposition of an Interest Equalisation Tax by the Kennedy administration involving a 15 per cent levy on purchases of American securities by foreigners. Hence the emergence of a truly international market called, rather misleadingly, the Euromarket. The first financial instrument to be floated was the Eurobond. Success invariably has many fathers and there are a number of contenders for the title of Eurobond inventor, but despite fierce competition, the king of the London institutions involved – and certainly one of the pioneers – was naturally SG Warburg. This even though it was said (by Ian Fraser, a loyal ex-employee) that Warburg himself was 'weak as a technician' and 'could not read a modern British or American set of accounts' – but then Warburg always was a one-off.

With its ever-spreading branches, the international financial services industry was to provide increasing numbers of increasingly well-paid jobs over the rest of the century. Despite recurrent waves of panic that it might transfer to Paris or Frankfurt, there has never any real possibility of the markets not being based in London. This fear – itself a typical symptom of British lack of confidence – was never serious, for soon London had developed a unique 'critical mass' of lawyers, accountants and all the other professions required by the bankers and brokers. Moreover the market was always dominated by Americans, who rarely if ever speak anything except English, and many of the inhabitants of Frankfurt and Paris, the two centres most frequently mentioned, have the unfortunate habit of not speaking English very well, if at all. So London soon became and remained what the journalist John Plender once described as 'the Clapham Junction of the world's financial markets.' But, crucially, virtually all the jobs involved were advisory; only the traders in shares, bonds and foreign exchange had to make decisions.

So the 'know-all' advisory mentality affected every nook and cranny of British life. The first, small sign came in 1968 with the fate of the Routemaster bus, the world's finest and perfectly adapted to the particular conditions prevailing in London's generally narrow and increasingly crowded streets. But that year a young transport economist, Christopher Foster, persuaded Barbara Castle, Labour's Minister of Transport, that the managers of London Transport were backward-looking and that the – cheaper – standard buses used in the provinces would do just as well. Of course they didn't. As the operators had predicted, their brakes and transmissions in particular couldn't take the strain. The advisory tendency reached its peak with railway privatisation. A group of 'experts' including, of course, Foster, by now Sir Christopher, turned their backs on the management of British Rail, which had come up with a number of solutions, all based on the realities of the railway industry as a system and all involving dividing the network logically into large units. Inevitably, the experts decided on a theoretical solution – of extreme fragmentation into over a hundred companies – which resulted in both a colossal loss to the tax-payer when they were sold off and the chaos which prevailed for half a decade. Not surprisingly, by the end of the Millennium, accountancy and management consultancy amounted to nearly 2 per cent of British GDP, a jump from 1.4 per cent in the early 1980s*. Management consultancy alone accounted for 0.8 per cent of the total, double the proportion in Germany and four times that in France, home of strong leadership.

However effective the managers had been, they would still have been thwarted by the complex, chaotic structure of the British trades union movement and the 'them and us' mentality firmly embodied in its leaders. As a result, the unions could never deliver the sort of collaboration with employers and the government which had worked such wonders in Germany after the war. This was shown most dramatically in 1969 when, with Wilson's firm backing, Barbara Castle, by then Secretary of State for Employment and Productivity, had proposed a major change in industrial relations legislation to construct a firmer legal framework for the trades unions, aiming to democratise their procedures, and including a twenty-eight-day 'conciliation pause' in any industrial dispute to allow tempers to cool.

It was perfectly possible to criticise Castle and Wilson for their tactical mistakes or to attack some of the individual proposals within the package which Castle called 'In Place of Strife', for they could have involved sending trades unionists to jail. But the White Paper simply encountered a total brick wall, with the unions – encouraged by Jim Callaghan – refusing to consider any changes at all. Outside the trades unions, the proposals were widely popular and generated the first rise in Labour's standing since devaluation eighteen months

* The figures are artificially swollen because so many firms have hived off functions such as accountancy which were formerly included in their basic business activity.

earlier. Yet Wilson felt obliged to abandon the idea in face of the way that, as he put it, Hugh Scanlon, the left-wing leader of the engineering workers, had 'put his tanks on my lawn'. The idea was replaced by a almost completely meaningless 'solemn and binding undertaking' by the unions to co-operate, a phrase which was ridiculed as 'Solomon Binding'.

The unions' attitude of non-co-operation with management found an echo in the vast majority of the brighter students at Britain's best universities. Their outlook was summed up in a much quoted passage in Margaret Drabble's *The Ice Age* about a character called Anthony Keating, who graduated in the 1960s. 'It never once crossed Anthony Keating's mind that he might get a job in industry . . . despite the fact that major companies were at that time appealing urgently for graduates in any field . . . Anthony Keating, child of the professional middle classes, reared in an anachronism as an anachronism, did not even see the offers . . . he thought himself superior to that kind of thing: that kind of advertisement was aimed at bores and sloggers, not at men of vision like Anthony Keating.' At the same time a new mythology of business was being presented in highly successful television series, all with dramatic titles like *The Plane-Makers, The Power Game* and *The Troubleshooters,* which provided a new – and generally unjustified – patina of drama to business life. Unfortunately these series were far too dramatic, far too unreal to have acted as effective recruiting propaganda for the industries involved.

Of course industry, the vulgar business of actually manufacturing things, has never been popular with the brightest Brits. But until the 1980s the distaste extended to the whole capitalist system. Sir John Hoskyns felt that 'businessmen were almost an underclass in the Britain of the 1960s and 1970s'. At the end of the 1960s Hoskyns was told 'very grandly' by Paul Johnson, then the editor of the *New Statesman*, that 'he would never, as a matter of political – perhaps even moral – principle, buy an ordinary share in a business of any kind'. Yet by the end of the millennium his son Luke had made his name as one of the sharpest operators in the country's restaurant and leisure businesses and his father was proud of his lad. Typically, wrote the *Independent* columnist David Aaronovitch of his contemporaries at university in the 1970s, 'The main reason for our distaste for private enterprise was social. It was uncool . . . Our ambitions were to be rock stars, or failing that (less money, same nookie) sociology lecturers . . . The kids who did aspire to join companies and become entrepreneurs [not the same thing!] were creepy pale boys with glasses and repressive parents . . . For many years I was broadly in favour of anything that stopped business from happening at all. Strikes were great, pickets (especially flying ones) were romantic.'

171

In a sense, the managerialists were part of a general trend, of a new meritocratic elite. Many decisions, all disastrous, were the result of half-baked ideas imposed from above by an amorphous new class – town planners and architects, educational theorists and supposedly moderate opinion formers, politicians, academics and journalists who showed themselves as adamantly, ruthlessly, authoritarian in their supposed moderation as they had done over Europe.

This tendency was shown to the full in the sphere of town and country planning. This had two major successes, both introduced in the early post-war period: the new towns designed to take hundreds of thousands from over-crowded cities – above all, London – and rehouse them in New Towns; and the creation of the Green Belt around cities to ensure that urban creep did not extend too far. But in the 1960s and 1970s such planning involved some equally sizeable and equally long-lasting failures. The most obvious were the destruction of town centres, especially those sacrificed to major urban road schemes, and the rehousing of the poor in tower blocks*, both signs of a systematic and fundamentally patronising unwillingness to recognise the concept of neighbourhood and community. It was John Major, who had begun his political career as chairman of the housing committee on Lambeth Council, who best expressed the problems they posed:† 'Many [estates as a whole, not only tower blocks] were built as solutions to inner-city problems; ironically they have now become major contributions to the problem. There they stand – grey, sullen concrete wastelands, set apart from the rest of the community, robbing people of ambition, of self-respect.'

Much of the damage was due to the impact of a single personality: planning and local government was dominated by a single figure, a civil servant, and a female one at that, the extraordinary figure of Dame Evelyn Sharp, simply (and usually fearfully) known throughout Whitehall as the Dame. She was the first woman to rise to the top of the Civil Service and her uniqueness was recognised when she was ennobled as one of the very few civil servants of the time to reach the House of Lords, indeed the only one who had not been head of the Treasury or of the Civil Service. She spent the last twenty years of a career which was prolonged beyond the normal retirement age, first as Deputy Secretary at the Ministry of Town and Country Planning and then for eleven years – far longer than was usual – as Permanent Secretary of the Ministry of Housing and Local Government, retiring only in 1966. Her ministry's dual role was both powerful and unusual,

---

* The ten poorest local authorities accounted for nearly a half of all the country's total of 4,500 tower blocks.

† In a 1995 speech to the Social Market Foundation.

since it represented a deliberate break with the sort of national planning that had been characterised by the 'social engineering' of the Labour government: there was now no external check on the ministry's activities. Her power was all the greater because she was no normal bureaucrat. Unlike most civil servants, wrote her former subordinate James Jones in the *Dictionary of National Biography*, she 'had an extraordinary flair for putting the issues, either in writing or across the table, plainly and summarily. Her manner was short, to the point, and forthright . . . Ministers found this candid directness compelling.'

Only one of the ministers under whom the Dame had nominally served had the arrogance and the intellectual capacity to argue back and to cope with this formidable figure: her last, Richard Crossman. The picture he paints of her in his diaries is both convincing and terrifying as the distillation of most of the women in senior positions before the days when it became possible to combine a career with marriage and children. When he arrived in October 1964, 'she was a year past retirement age and she is only in the Department because she can't bear to leave. She is a biggish woman, about five foot ten inches, with tremendous blue eyes which look right through you, a pale unmade-up face, uncoloured lips. She is dressed as middle- or upper-class professional women do dress, quite expensively but rather uglily. She is really a tremendous and dominating character' – no mean tribute from so bossy a figure as Crossman.

Like the Fabian Beatrice Webb fifty years earlier, she wanted 'improvement and social justice quite passionately and yet [was] a tremendous patrician and utterly contemptuous and arrogant, regarding local authorities as children which she has to examine and rebuke for their failures. She sees the ordinary human being as incapable of making a sensible decision' – a scorn which spread into her attitude for anyone, however well-qualified, who disagreed with her. Politically, as Crossman had spotted, her importance lay in her close relationships with municipal authorities throughout the country. 'She was known up and down the country as a very real person' wrote Jones, 'whose likes and dislikes were pungently expressed whatever the occasion or the company . . . Local authorities had a profound respect and regard for her.' Unfortunately for Britain's post-war reconstruction, she does not seem to have had any aesthetic sense or any interest in architecture or landscaping. Moreover her power was absolute. When Harold Wilson asked why good housing was being pulled down to make way for – almost invariably unsympathetic – modern developments, the Dame pooh-poohed his views. And when Crossman pointed out that 'local authorities are far worse than private developers. They will often destroy buildings and leave a huge open space for years afterwards because they have planned things so badly', her retort was symptomatic

173

of her tunnel vision, her mother-hen attitude towards the country's municipalities – and her megalomania. 'You're attacking my local authorities again,' she said, 'there's nothing in what you say.'

The forces she represented were able to ride roughshod over democracy. At Basingstoke, one of the more successful new towns, under a half of the population came from the London housing list, i.e. the people who were supposed to be re-housed. But any initiative by Crossman met the feeling of the Dame and her chosen officials that they 'were very much her personal creation and she controls policy very closely'. Nevertheless Crossman preferred Basingstoke with its 'lack of snobbery and autocracy and stratospheric good living which certainly exists within the New Town corporations' among the senior – unelected – officials 'who do what they damn well like and don't listen to the local people' – a characteristic they shared with the Dame.

Sometimes the Dame and Crossman agreed, and this was a frightening and paradoxical combination for Crossman (who himself lived in a comfortable old farmhouse in Oxfordshire) shared the contemporary fashion for 'pure' clean modernist architecture as against the very British tradition of cosiness. Typical was Crossman's admiration for Cumbernauld New Town east of Glasgow which he described as being 'on the top of a long, high, bleak ridge . . . a very grey Scottish town which has settled into the ridge with an enormous lot of roads and a fascinating variety of modern houses. Up-and-down houses, vertical houses, horizontal houses, and everything, including the churches, fitting into the style, everything done in a tremendously austere, exhilarating, uncomfortable style. I thought Atticus this morning in the *Sunday Times* was extremely apposite when he pointed out that this was the kind of thing which Dame Evelyn and I are excited about, in contrast to the cosy garden suburb atmosphere of Stevenage or Harlow or Basildon.'

The garden suburb – itself a fine and human development concept and one that was followed, to some extent anyway, in most of the New Towns – was the only real planning concept invented by British town planners but it was later largely ignored. The tragedy in the rebuilding of the country's major towns and cities was not the triumph of any particular dogma, but the ignorance and muddle-headedness of those involved. One major influence was the idea which spread fast during the late 1950s and 1960s that the motor car would always win, hence the importance of sweeping away the jumble of narrow streets characteristic of most historic town and city centres. This doctrine went largely unchallenged at the time simply because there were so few professional town planners, so most of the plans were left to city engineers – the classic case being Birmingham. Thus it was inevitable that, as Crossman pointed out, 'in 2000 Wigan, without a city architect or a town planner, will look just as bad as the old 1880 Wigan looks in the eyes of the 1960s'. In Bradford there was a new housing drive, 'but, alas, the planning is poor, the architecture dull, the city architect obviously not up to it. What can one do about it? Not much'.

When they disagreed, Crossman was helpless against the ferocious will-power of the Dame and her allies. Moreover, they were in a hurry. Typically her ministry rushed forward decisions such as the total redevelopment of the Packington estate in Islington in the face of determined opposition by the locals. If they hadn't rushed out the letter announcing what they were going to do, said the Dame, 'we'd never have got our decision'. Even when he didn't have to contend with the Dame, Crossman could do little. Visiting the waterfront of Plymouth, a city that had been razed to the ground by German bombs, he thought it needed 'complete redevelopment as a mixed commercial/ residential area for middle-class people, artists and lawyers. But no, Plymouth Council, with a solid Labour majority, require it for people on the housing list and are determined to build conventional council houses' – and not all the Minister's dialectical skills could persuade the councillors otherwise.

The legacy which was left to succeeding generations as a result of post-war reconstruction was not all the Dame's doing. It also owed a lot to the architects, some foreign refugees, many others Marxists from the Architectural Association, influenced by the purity of the work of the Bauhaus and, above all, Le Corbusier. The most dogmatic and inhuman of such architects was Erno Goldfinger – the James Bond villain was indeed named after him – who was responsible for the redevelopment of the Elephant and Castle in South London amongst other horrors and who died, bitter and defiant to the end, in 1987. Appropriately, it was James Dunnett from Goldfinger's own office who provided the best obituary: 'One has a feeling that this is Stalin's architecture as it should have been.'

The forces for brutalist redevelopment were led by the developers who could entice the municipal authorities with their grandiose schemes for bringing in new businesses and thus increased income from the rates. It was their impetus which ruled supreme, for in most towns and cities there was little of the civic architectural sense which prevented the heart of many Continental cities from being destroyed (though this applied only to the centre: such cities as Paris and Amsterdam are surrounded with rings of concrete towers – 'barracks for the working classes' – on a scale undreamed of by even the most megalomaniac British developers). The trend was nothing new since, as Peter Mandler says, 'before the war they had horrified early conservationists by remodelling high streets to accommodate the large multiple shops'.[3]

175

The results were disastrous. There were mega-horrors in cities, Birmingham's Bull Ring being perhaps the most notorious, while smaller, more historic, towns were simply vandalised. As Mandler points out, 'in Gloucester 200 listed buildings were demolished in the 1950s and 1960s, dismembering the city core. At Bath the Georgian core was faithfully preserved but defined so narrowly – only a few hundred yards across – that it was soon dwarfed by high buildings on its edge', and even Oxford and Cambridge did not escape unscathed. As the number of projects increased, from fifteen in 1959 to over 500 six years later, so did their ambitiousness: 'They were characterised by gigantism and the technological quick-fix. Huge tracts of inner city were to be cleared and rebuilt with retail and office developments. Urban motorways were to provide ready vehicular access.' In such an atmosphere of rebuilding mania, even the redoubtable Crossman was helpless. He could not even prevent the destruction of the beautiful eighteenth-century Eldon Square in Newcastle to which he was 'passionately opposed'. He was helpless, partly because Dan Smith, the unquestioned boss of Newcastle later jailed for corruption, was a great personal friend of the Dame. In the end, the development never happened, leaving a gaping hole in the middle of the city (a similar disaster occurred in the City of London when the fine nineteenth-century Coal Exchange, which boasted a particularly fine iron-work interior, was demolished to make way for a road scheme that was soon abandoned).

Even a non-sentimentalist such as myself can't but agree with John Humphrys that[4] 'because of the adhoc way most of the [historic high] streets had grown up, you'd have found a whole load of other things: churches, chapels, cafés and pubs; the hotel where the Rotarians met; cinemas, a theatre if you were lucky, and a town hall . . . a Victorian primary school, the public library, the run-down premises of the Sea Scouts . . . solicitors' offices with polished brass plaques, maybe a street market, whose commercial flavour was quite different from the shops because it was about badinage, humour and haggling over prices; perhaps a small park and a war memorial, and even private homes.' And all of it a world away from the pure, antiseptic shopping experience of a retail mall.

The problems created by tower blocks – a fashion that lasted less than a couple of decades, and which was replicated, usually on a larger scale, throughout the world – were exacerbated by the fact that they were often used as dumping grounds for the – invariably deprived – inhabitants of the worst of the slums. Moreover, the authorities played their part in making things worse: the Treasury refused to pay for any shops to go with the pioneering, much praised Alton Towers in Roehampton on the edge of Richmond Park. Some years later, and in

176

spite of pleas from the residents, the Greater London Council declined to install a concierge in the lobby of some of the blocks for which they were responsible on the grounds that they would be 'snoopers . . . vassals of fascism'.

In Rochdale Crossman saw and described the changes in Deeplish, in the centre of the town. Both new and old sound equally unappetising. It was a 'so-called improvement area and its houses have been given thirty more years of life; yet they are little dwellings, each with a tiny courtyard behind, the tin bath hanging on the wall of the courtyard and two steps across it the toilet in a shed. Upstairs in the houses there was a fairly stenchy smell, beds unmade in each house I visited and blankets with no sheets. It's a primitive dismal life in Deeplish; and high above are the five great tower blocks which Wimpey have clamped down in the middle of the town.'

For the tower block was a false solution to a real problem, that of rehousing the urban poor, the masses huddled in the slums. Yet as early as 1957, the architectural historian Ian Nairn had published two prophetic books (*Outrage* and *Counter Attack* [5]) which not only pioneered the idea of civic evolution rather than revolution but also described how Georgian squares achieved high housing density – one of the key aims of the rebuilders – with infinitely greater architectural values. It was only in 1968, after a gas explosion in Ronan Point, a system-built tower block in East London which collapsed when the fasteners came loose, that the fashion faded, leaving behind a legacy of universal disaster.

The tower block's obituary was eloquently pronounced by Rory Campbell, writing when Trellick Tower, the last of London's tower blocks to be built, was to be pulled down[6]. 'The nightmare would start moments after entering the lobby. Stench of urine, beer and stale sweat would seep from shadows, the lights would be smashed again and the corridor vandalised into gloom. Silence did not mean that no one was there. Walk, and the broken bottles and syringes crunched underfoot . . . With luck, one of the tower's three lifts would be working. Fresh graffiti, used condoms and a passed-out vagrant might have been waiting inside when the doors parted.' The lift 'would often stop at the wrong floor, open into darkness and the sound of dripping water . . . The block would be full of memories of suicides, rapes and attacks'. The nostalgia for past cosiness showed itself in 1977 when the former inhabitants of a street in Rugeley held a party to celebrate the Queen's Silver Jubilee in 'their' street even though it had been demolished years earlier. In November 1997 Geoff Nicholson visited the museum – not surprisingly in Blackpool – devoted to *Coronation Street* and, in particular, the earlier members of the cast. Both resort and museum, he wrote, 'celebrate a warmly inauthentic version of working-class life. They're nostalgic for a past that never existed, yet they somehow know this'.[7]

The intolerance, the desire to impose a uniform solution, seen in town planning was just as visible, though less harmful, in education with the general introduction of comprehensive schools, in themselves a superficially democratic and sensible solution to Britain's deep-seated educational problems. Educationally, comprehensives may have been a – qualified – success. Socially they were a disaster, a classic case of two steps forward, at least one back, exacerbated by the effects of continuing stop-go economic policies. When Labour came to power in 1964, it announced that the school leaving age would be raised to sixteen by 1970. But this ideal fell victim to Labour's economic problems and was postponed until 1973. Unfortunately, as David Hargreaves put it, 'Utopian social engineering – defining an ideal, such as comprehensive schooling or market mechanisms, and then sticking fast to a national blueprint to achieve an ideal – will no longer do.'[8] For, in Paul Barker's words, 'The idea of comprehensive schooling was just one possible way to run schools: not bad in the semi-rural Pennine valley I grew up in; in cities an almost total mistake'.[9]

It did not help that education was not organised on a national basis, except in Wales and Scotland where standards were and remained higher, partly because education was seen as a means of advancing your chances in life in societies which were markedly less class-based than in England. But in England itself the very idea of central control was anathema – typically, the fact that in France the minister of education knew exactly what subject children were studying at any given moment in the school day evoked not envy but astonishment, accompanied, more often than not by jeers. To Labour, wrote Alan Watkins, 'it was a subject best left to local authorities, preferably Labour ... the Department of Education was a client ministry'[10] – as dependent on the educational establishment as was the Ministry of Agriculture on the National Farmers' Union. Even examinations were left to a number of local boards which seemed to have no coherent idea of the exact standards they were applying and never seem to have thought of consulting their fellow boards. As a result the Minister was relatively harmless, merely holding the ring – this was one of the reasons why Ted Heath, who needed a token woman in his Cabinet, placed Mrs Thatcher in this department.

Not only was the power over education dispersed; the educational infrastructure was also in a bad way. The schools were short of 20,000 primary school teachers, many classes had over forty children and a substantial proportion of school buildings were aged and decrepit. There had been little school construction during the inter-war years, so most schools dated back to the first surge in popular education in

178

the years between the 1870 Education Act and the First World War. A welcome attempt to use prefabricated school buildings had helped but even these proved rather shoddy. Furthermore, because of the failure to spend enough on primary education, the secondary schools were left with an impossible task.

The continuing prevalence of 'proletcult' had also meant that expectations continued to be lower than in other industrialised countries. Even after the introduction of comprehensive schools, wrote A. H. Halsey, 'the majority remained in blighted ignorance that education had anything seriously constructive to offer to either private or public life ... the essential fact of twentieth century educational history is that egalitarian policies have failed.'[11] I became aware of the limits of educational aspiration general in the public sector in the late 1960s when the headmistress of my elder son's excellent primary school urged us to send him to a selective school at the age of nine because she had done all she could for him. The most obvious reform was the abolition of the grammar schools and their absorption into the comprehensive school system. Indeed it became a mantra, an object in itself, rather than a step towards better schooling for the masses. As one Labour Minister of Education, Anthony Crosland, famously put it, 'If it's the last thing I do, I'm going to abolish the fucking grammar schools.' Yet at the time Labour ministers sent their children to private or grammar schools as a matter of routine and Harold Wilson saw no reason why Roy Jenkins should not become Minister of Education even though his children had been educated privately. As early as 1959, Crosland had been warned by the political journalist Alan Watkins that 'abolishing the grammar schools without simultaneously "doing something" about the public schools would hinder rather than help the cause' – yet Crosland (like many of his fellow ministers a member of the intellectual elite and a product of a major public school) turned his back on the idea, ostensibly because any reform would cost too much.

'In the late 1960s,' wrote Andrew Adonis and Stephen Pollard, 'the state grammar schools and quasi-state direct grants schools were intact and together easily outclassed the independent sector in terms of academic output.'[12] But rather than go comprehensive, most naturally preferred to take the independent route. This had two consequences: it barred the fast track to the academic heights previously enjoyed by a minority of bright working-class children, leaving those from the inner cities to struggle in ill-equipped sink schools, however bright they were, and it forced the public schools to pull up their socks academically. These two developments enormously increased the gulf between the comprehensives and the private sector. In addition, virtually all the best comprehensives were, indeed still are, in the wealthiest middle-class suburbs or in favourable locations (two of my children attended an excellent one in Oxford, full of the children of academics whose parents couldn't afford private education). The pious hope expressed by a Labour resolution in 1965 that the move would 'preserve all that is valuable in grammar school education for those children who now receive it and make it available for more children' proved to be pie in the sky.

In any case, comprehensives were aiming at a fast-moving target because the middle classes had grasped the obvious fact that the road to advancement for their children lay increasingly in what and not whom you knew. This resulted in ever-increasing pressure for standards as measured by examination results and the proportion of pupils who got into Oxbridge. In 1969 only 38 per cent of places in Oxford were awarded to children educated privately, but by the end of the Millennium most of the colleges were – genuinely – struggling to keep the proportion below a half. Before 1939, it had been the boarding public schools that had enjoyed the greatest prestige, for largely social reasons, but in the post-war era the desire for competitiveness ensured that it was the best day schools in the cities that became the most difficult to enter. This tendency was vastly increased by the soaring cost of boarding education (in the case of my own school, Harrow, the fees are now nearly forty times what they were in the late 1940s) and the wish of an increasing number of middle-class parents to keep their children at home. But even the poshest of schools was infected by the competitive environment. Most notably, Eton started to take examination results seriously.

The state sector was further hampered by the increasing job opportunities for educated youngsters – especially women. By the early 1970s, there were so many other jobs available to anyone with the semblance of a proper education that the supply of teachers had failed to keep pace with the demand. One result was that only too often entrants were neither very bright nor properly taught at teacher training colleges, although standards improved in the late 1970s when only graduates could get into teaching. Before then the experience of Ken Livingstone, the future Mayor of London, was probably typical. He says that his three years at the now defunct Philippa Fawcett college of education were a waste of time. 'In 1970 there was a national teacher shortage and they were desperate to get anybody in.' He was supposed to be training to become a science teacher for 'not very academic' secondary school kids. 'You were basically taught to start every lesson with the word sex, for instance by discussing the sex life of the ant. That would get their attention and stop them stabbing each other . . . But sooner or later you exhausted the list of animals with feasible bonking habits to talk about . . . Basically everybody who sat the exams passed unless

180

they had a nervous breakdown or took drugs during them.'[13] Instead of sociology, the special subject he had been studying for three years, he decided, with no preparation, to sit the psychology paper and still passed. It confirmed his 'wretched estimate of the whole process'. He recalled with dread the mandatory teaching practice at Wandsworth. 'We're not starting the lesson until you give me the knife' was one vividly remembered opening line: 'they were ghastly little villains who knew every trick in the book'.

At these colleges the vague notion of 'personal development' proved no substitute for the hard grind of the learning process. It has taken thirty years to start to undo the damage to standards caused by pure child-centredness, allied to the low quality of the teachers and their gurus. Some critics trace the problem back to the Plowden Report whose author, Bridget, Lady Plowden, was herself the wife of a leading public servant turned industrialist. In fact it was a well-balanced report. New teaching methods, it said, should be subject to 'astringent intellectual scrutiny'. It warned against 'trivial ideas and inefficient methods' and, although it advocated treating children with respect – which involved, for instance, the abolition of corporal punishment – and providing more opportunity for learning through personal discovery, yet it acknowledged that 'time does not allow children to find their way by discovery to all that they have to learn'. But Plowden provided an excellent excuse for the sloppy thinking associated with the (generally not overly-intelligent) theorists of the new learning – it should never be true that 'those who can't, teach' but in all too many cases it was certainly true that 'those who can't teach, teach education'. Unfortunately too, inspired teachers who could rely on their personalities to teach in new and unorthodox ways assumed that their techniques could be copied by the great majority of their inevitably less charismatic colleagues.

The sheer sloppiness of the new unlearning was exacerbated by the fact that the teaching unions, particularly the biggest, the National Union of Teachers, were precisely that – unions which had no interest in professional standards and had always been divided. Crossman saw the results in Buckinghamshire. In this, by no means the most advanced local authority, primary schools 'work on an extremely advanced liberal theory which requires that no child ever be strained, and that no effort be made to teach the children intensively'. Many of the horror stories about such education are true. In the early 1970s, a journalist friend then working on the *Guardian* – a paper which was a firm believer in progressive educational methods – went to inspect a possible primary school in London for his young son. The headmistress apologised. 'We believe in good manners,' she explained, 'and teaching the children to read and write. That won't suit you.'

The argument over education came to a head with the behaviour of the teachers at Tyndale School in Islington. Not only were they 'progressive' but, as the headmistress of a neighouring school said at the time, 'absolutely fatally and arrogantly refused to engage in any kind of real dialogue or debate with the parents, or indeed inspectors ... One teacher painted a yellow line across the playground of his school with the legend "No parent beyond this line" '. This attitude was a foretaste of the arrogant and exclusivist attitudes of Labour activists later in the decade.

Standards also suffered because, as Paul Barker pointed out, 'the trauma of reorganisation was a distraction'.[14] Among its advocates, 'there was a reluctance to acknowledge that there were very bad casualties'. As a friend who was deeply involved in the changes told me, 'There was so much emphasis on the problems associated with the massive reorganisation what with the mergers of secondary moderns, comprehensives, grammar schools, that there seemed little time left over actually to improve the standard of education. For there was a period when organisation took priority over educational concerns. The worst effects were felt at the primary level, where the schools were largely ignored, leaving the newly formed comprehensives to cope with a high proportion of eleven-year-olds who were, effectively, illiterate.' And even when Jim Callaghan launched 'A Great Debate' on education in 1976 it had little effect.

A deeply pessimistic, albeit only too convincing, view of the consequences amongst 'the kids at the back of the class' came from David Hargreaves, author of *Social Relations in a Secondary School*, based on his experiences teaching in Salford. The kids 'were in danger of becoming the detritus of society. They'll be in their mid-fifties now. Grandfathers perhaps. Is it all we've done down the years to create a replication of families without skills? Unemployed, on welfare, even involved in crime? The biggest challenge is: after two generations has life changed for kids like these?' Nevertheless there was very considerable progress. The percentage of students with one or more A levels rose from under 8 percent in 1962–63 to over 20 per cent by the late 1980s – while girls did even better. Nevertheless, although the numbers of children from the manual working classes with better exam results had increased, this was only in line with the general increase, but not in proportion to their numbers in the population as a whole. This failure was due not only to the soaring rate of unemployment among the unskilled in the 1980s and 1990s but also to the failure to adopt a report which advocated day-release vocational training. This in turn sprang from a typical obsession with academic respectability, which meant an aping of Oxbridge even by the polytechnics, created in the late 1960s from the former technical colleges.

The great expansion in higher education, of which this was a part, was naturally greeted by the cry 'More will mean worse', a cry most famously uttered by Kingsley Amis in *Encounter*. In fact Amis and his like should really have been attacking the low level in the country's secondary schools, for it was this that resulted in increasingly ignorant students. In the event, most of the expansion in university education occurred in the older red-brick universities. But public attention was concentrated on the seven new universities aimed at breaking the monopoly historically enjoyed by Oxbridge. They never did so, partly because of the social and intellectual snobbery involved, partly because the courses they offered, though less narrow than those of the older establishments, tended to be too vague and waffling. But the new universities and the polytechnics did play a largely unrecognised role, not only by increasing the flow of graduates several times over but also in providing the country with what can only be described as a highly successful 'educational and training industry' in which hundreds of thousands of foreigners come here to study a very wide range of subjects, ranging from simply learning English to such esoteric subjects as museum administration.

But as the historian A. J. P. Taylor, himself a Manchester graduate, pointed out, 'They all assert the doctrine that university education is a way to escape from life, and not a preparation for it.' Only Warwick, near the largely industrial Midlands, tried to establish the sort of links with industry that were normal in Germany – and even this attracted demonstrations in 1970. These were based on the assumption that universities should be exclusively devoted to pure education rather than training, preparation for careers, a noble theory best expressed by the rightly revered Marxist historian Edward Thompson in his book *Warwick University Ltd*. Only one educational novelty was an unqualified success, the Open University, an initiative which Harold Wilson said, only too correctly, would be considered the single most important achievement of his time at 10 Downing Street.

If education was at least a partial success of the 1960s, racial relations were a disaster. In the public mind the decade was associated with the growth of Caribbean and, above all, Asian immigrants. The latter had escaped from Kenya and, above all from Idi Amin's Uganda as a result of racial persecution there as well as from the Indian sub-continent, the source of more purely 'economic' migrants. Everyone was aware of the problems posed by the need to absorb so many newcomers so obviously different from the natives. In 1965, what came to be known as the race relations industry was founded with the establishment of the Race Relations Board, which was given greater scope three years later. The official opposition to any form of racialism was shown by the prompt sacking by Edward Heath of Enoch Powell, a member of his Shadow Cabinet, after a speech in April 1968. In this, perhaps the single most famous speech in the second half of the twentieth century in Britain, Powell prophesied dire consequences if immigration were to continue. His was not a spontaneous outburst but clearly a response to the failure of the Opposition to attack a new Race Relations Bill that had just been introduced by Jim Callaghan, the Home Secretary. This proposed a tightening up on Commonwealth immigration but at the same time to strengthen the laws relating to racial discrimination.

Powell's speech included the phrase (which he originally wanted to leave in the original Latin) about 'the Tiber flowing with much blood'. At the heart of what became infamous as the 'rivers of blood' speech was the assumption that black immigrants, in particular, would not want to integrate; the idea 'was a ludicrous misconception and a dangerous one to boot'. Both the speech itself and the reaction to it revealed a hitherto unsuspected depth of racial prejudice which Colin MacInnes called a 'safe haven' for the prejudiced. Previously all had seemed (relatively) well on the race front: the racialist Notting Hill riots of the late 1950s had been quashed thanks to the firmness of Justice Salmon, the LCC* had had in David Pitt a gentle black chairman and black American leaders, including the firebrand Malcolm X as well as Martin Luther King, had come and gone without trouble.

The black cause had not been helped by the prominence of some seriously wicked figures amongst the black community, often supported by the same sort of trendies who had been attracted to the Kray brothers. The most obvious example was Michael de Freitas (who later called himself Michael X), a chancer who convinced such rightly respected journalists like Jill Tweedie – as well as perfectly sane Caribbean activists like Darcus Howe – that he was not a thug but a genuine political leader. A few years later he was executed for the murder of a British girl groupie who had followed him to Trinidad.

Powell's supporters included skinheads, who represented exaggerated white, British working-class masculinity, sported boots, braces and shaved heads and displayed violent racism. But it was the support for Powell by stalwart members of the working classes, including the London dockers and the porters at the Smithfield meat market, which obviously upset the left's previously heroic image of the working classes. 'We were just completely shocked numb,' wrote the socialist doctor David Widgery. 'It was predictable in so many ways and yet still quite shocking. You suddenly realised how little influence the left really had, how the roots of the political organisations . . . had been

* London County Council, the body governing Central London.

184

rotting in the soil ... It did more to me than the May events and Czechoslovakia rolled into one.'[15]

Stuart Hall, the distinguished Jamaican-born sociologist, had just moved to Birmingham and wrote how 'I will never forget the impact of the ''Rivers of Blood'' speech. I remember the sudden, shared feeling of fear, the sense of hostility, the huddling together against the impending violence, the unspoken aggression in the streets as little groups of black men and women came together to discuss how to respond to the violence it seemed calculated to unleash. There were already reserves of resentment in places like Birmingham, Coventry and the Black Country' – where a racialist Conservative, Peter Griffiths, had won Smethwick in the 1964 election. 'Now the dyke had burst, the taboos were broken: and we felt suddenly adrift in an alien country.'[16] Darcus Howe recalls: 'We were frightened for our lives. I remember the terror, the savagery of that moment. Several families packed up and left the country for Canada and the United States.'[17] C. L. R. James, the Marxist historian and the greatest writer on cricket in the history of the game, was booed when he suggested to the West Indian Standing Conference that the Powellite movement would not go far with the British people. Fortunately, however, within a couple of decades he had been proved right.

But at the time all official attitudes towards blacks were ambiguous, none more so than that of the police. A classic case is that of the Mangrove, the emblematic West Indian restaurant in Notting Hill. By the late 1960s, wrote Darcus Howe[18], it had become 'the black culture capital of the UK and perhaps the headquarters of radical chic.' The local police inspector, says Howe, 'knew black men by their name, their wives, and their offspring. But he was the colonial governor incarnate and if for some reason he did not like the cut of your jib then life was made pretty hard.' One person whose 'jib' he didn't fancy was Frank Critchlow, the owner of the Mangrove, so he kept raiding it for drugs. Critchlow complained, says Howe, 'to every institution known to man' and eventually called a protest meeting. It numbered 150 people 'guarded by police three times our number'. There was shoving and violence, and the Home Secretary, Reginald Maudling, 'described us as black conspirators determined to destroy the British Police'. A solicitor advised Howe to plead guilty of assault claiming that, in doing so, he would get only five years in jail, but he preferred to defend himself. But, as Howe says, 'I learnt that the establishment has its dissenters. The magistrate asked for the evidence that we had incited people to kill police officers. The prosecution quoted ''kill the pigs'', which was chanted by the demonstrators.' To which the magistrate made the devastating response: 'If the demonstrators had shouted ''fuck the pigs'', would you have taken it literally?' Nevertheless the case went to the Old Bailey, but after a trial lasting 55 days a jury of ten whites and two blacks freed most of the accused, and the rest got only suspended sentences.

Although race relations remain a rumbling problem, there has been a great deal of tangible improvement – above all, in London – in relationships between the dozens of races now firmly implanted in Britain. The same cannot be said of the problems in Ulster, where the two communities, Protestant and Catholic, remain as firmly divided as they were thirty years ago, held together only by a fragile peace and an even more fragile power-sharing agreement. Nevertheless this is a great improvement in the situation before the British government intervened in 1968, when the Catholic minority finally erupted after a long period in which English radicals had totally ignored the blatant religious discrimination in the province, at every level, including, and especially, the government itself. At a time when every other regime in the world displaying such blatant discrimination was under attack, there was an almost total silence on the part of radicals concerning the situation in Ulster.

Yet, ever since the province had been separated from the rest of Ireland in 1921 and granted a very wide degree of self-government, the Protestant Unionist majority had applied a policy akin to apartheid towards the substantial Catholic minority. Electoral boundaries were fiddled, and systematic discrimination was a matter of daily life. Not without reason was the province called 'John Bull's political slum'. The neglect was exacerbated by the influence in Ulster of the Catholic Church, which, like its counterpart in Quebec, was perfectly prepared to allow its members to suffer because it made them easier to influence, indeed dominate. As a result, there was little unrest within the minority and thus, and notably unlike Britain's former colonies, no centre of revolt with which English radicals could empathise.

Before 1968 the House of Commons had assumed a hands-off attitude, laying down that all matters involving Ulster were to be left to the devolved government at Stormont*. MPs of Irish Catholic descent such as Kevin Macnamara who tried to ask questions on the subject were ignored by the left as well as by the government. In general, as the historian of Irish broadcasting Rex Cathcart explained: 'Questions were not asked because they were the concern of another place. So the greater British public learnt little of what was going on in its own backyard' – the BBC's controller in Ulster had to meet his colleagues from the mainland in hotel rooms because he suspected that his telephone was bugged by Orangemen† .

* The building outside Belfast which housed the Northern Ireland parliament.
† Members of the Orange Order, which dominated Ulster politics as the Broderbond did those of the Afrikaner regime in South Africa.

The Catholics' first demands were relatively mild including, for instance, the disbanding of the B Specials, who were effectively an armed Protestant militia. The leaders of the rebellion were a new generation, many of whom had benefited from post-war educational reforms imposed by the central government. These, as Anne McHardy pointed out, 'allowed the sort of backstreet kid he [John Hume] was – the son of an unemployed docker and a jobbing shirt stitcher – to go to schools previously reserved for the wealthy. Education fuelled the civil rights movement and precipitated the fall of the Stormont government. In 1964 Hume had criticised the Roman Catholic stand, writing, ''There has been no attempt to be positive, to encourage the Catholic community to develop the resources which they have in plenty, to make a positive contribution in terms of community service.'' '[19]

At first the British troops sent to the province were welcomed by the Catholics as liberators. The soldiers' attitude was summed up by a young officer who told Brian Moynahan, 'We went down in box formation, as though we were putting down a riot in some banana republic ... the whole place was a nightmare.'[20] But within a few months historic divisions had re-emerged. With discreet help from some ministers in the Irish government, the IRA emerged in a new guise when the relatively apolitical 'Provisionals' split from the Marxist Official IRA. For over a decade the Official IRA had been quiescent – in 1959 I worked on a film (*Shake Hands With the Devil*) which was based on the assumption that it was purely an historic phenomenon. The combination of the IRA terrorism and the totally obdurate attitude of the Protestant majority led to thirty years of misery for the province, summed up in an anonymous poem:

> Peace is sleeping.
> Few, few shall live to see the time
> When you my city cease to pine.
> God is weeping[21]

Within a couple of years, and despite the escalating violence for which it was responsible, the IRA had attracted considerable support amongst the Catholic community in Northern Ireland. For, like the Communist Party in British factories, it was the only organised force prepared to fight for the rights of the downtrodden – the difference being that in Ulster, 'the forces of reaction' were violent as well as dominant. The support was greatly increased by the blunders of the British government, caused partly by the fact that no-one in authority in Whitehall (or in Belfast for that matter) knew anything about the Catholic community in Ulster. In 1971, against the advice of the Army commanders on the spot, Reginald Maudling, who as Home Secretary was still in charge, ordered 341 Catholics to be interned. Because the intelligence agencies within the province were so ignorant, many of those interned proved to be totally unconnected with the uprising. The creation of the so-called Diplock Courts, which provided for trial without jury because jurors were so vulnerable to sectarian attack, merely made matters worse. But it was the army that provided the final blow to any hope of reconciliation between the Catholic community and the British government in January 1972 when fourteen Catholic demonstrators were shot down by British paratroopers. The resulting wave of condemnation – which included the burning down of the British embassy in Dublin – led to the end of the old Stormont state and direct rule from London which was to last over a quarter of a century.

This provided a glimmer of hope since the British viceroy (for that is what he was) was William Whitelaw, subtlest of Tory politicians. Miraculously he managed to entice all the parties involved – including the IRA – around the negotiating table and produced the Sunningdale agreement for a power-sharing government. But Heath had to recall him to Whitehall at the critical moment to cope with the miners' strike which was disrupting the economy in late 1973. The Unionists rejected Sunningdale as the first step to a united Ireland ('Dublin is merely a Sunningdale away' was the chant) and deposed their leader, Brian Faulkner. Heath's mistake was typical of the man, a far-sighted idea wrecked by his lack of political antennae and of the ability to communicate on a personal level with anyone, least of all his ministers and advisers (although whether these human qualities had been submerged by the colossal effort Heath had made to transform himself socially is an unanswerable question given his notorious reluctance to reveal any of the depths of his character).

The Sunningdale failure was only one of many. As Kenneth Morgan observed, 'The decline in the authority and legitimacy of the central organs of government, so visible in the Wilson years, was being re-enacted now.' In 1968 the first draft of what became known as Thatcherism – above all, a reliance on individual initiative rather than government intervention – was sketched out by Tory leaders and their advisers at the Selsdon Park Hotel south of London, giving rise to the expression Selsdon Man. It was in this spirit that Heath had started after his unexpected electoral victory in the June 1970 General Election. The dash for freedom was doomed because it was premature. The electorate was simply not prepared to put up with a level of unemployment of over a million, so when a downturn took it above that figure, Heath panicked and reverted to the type of corporate government which in fact suited his temperament better than that of Selsdon Man. Whether he would have stood firm had his first Chancellor of the Exchequer, Ian Macleod, not died only a few weeks after his appointment and been replaced by the lightweight and obedient Tony Barber, is one of the great 'what ifs' of post-war British history. My own guess is that the times were not sufficiently a'changing for Macleod's death to have made much difference, but Heath's aborted laissez-faire revolution, like the 1905 uprising in Russia, proved to be a foretaste of a more successful uprising a few years later.

But, as with Wilson, the biggest obstacle to Heath's plans came from the working classes and the unions. It was the workers, notably those at the Upper Clyde shipyards who, through a successful and well-publicised sit-in, demonstrated, both literally and metaphorically, that they were not prepared to bear the brunt of the results of a laissez-faire industrial policy. And it was the unions who wrecked Heath's industrial relations legislation. His National Industrial Relations Court proved to be powerless: the unions simply threatened to expel any union that registered under the Act. In the words of the Communist Party's trades union organiser, Bert Ramelson, 'We proved that a law doesn't mean anything if everyone is against it. We got solidarity up and running – if they stick together they can't put us all in gaol.' This followed a farcical episode when five dockers in breach of the Act had to be removed from Pentonville Prison through the intervention of a little-known official, the Official Solicitor.

But the biggest blow came from the miners, still relatively underpaid and still attracting public sympathy. When they struck in the winter of 1971–72, even the *Daily Express*, then still an important force of conservatism, demanded 'give them the money', for the public still felt guilty about the human cost of mining coal. An inkling of the much more violent events of the 1980s was provided by the success of flying pickets from other coalfields led by a young radical from Yorkshire, Arthur Scargill. These had long been a feature of disputes and were particularly effective in the 1972 strike. But in this instance, 'Arthur's Private War', flying pickets from Yorkshire prevented lorries from leaving the Saltley Gate coke depot in Birmingham after the police had refused to use enough force against the hundreds of thousands of demonstrators Scargill had mobilised. It was, he told the *Guardian*, 'the greatest day of my life, everything I have always believed in and idolised crystallised'. The demonstration had no real effect, for the strike was already bound to be successful because the power stations were running out of coal. Nevertheless Scargill was not the only one to believe that he alone had delivered the miners, and thus by extension the British working class as a whole, from the tyranny of Heath's industrial legislation.

Heath's doom was sealed, not only by the unions' opposition, but also by the failure of the British capitalist system to take advantage of the way he and Barber eased the restrictions under which banks had previously operated. The only group to take full advantage of the opportunity was a gang of get-rich-quick financial operators, symbolised by Jim Slater of Slater Walker and his acolytes who ran numerous 'satellite' operations that he used to juggle the prices of the shares in which he was involved at the time. The result was short-termism gone mad and a refusal to think in terms longer than the three-week account operated by the London Stock Exchange. Indeed, Slater's downfall can be said to have started after the publication of an article in the *Sunday Times* based on research by Charles Raw showing the number of deals Slater and his associates had indulged in during a single account. The inability to think in longer periods was aptly symbolised by Slater's refusal to invest in the newly discovered oil fields in the North Sea, even though he had the chance. But he knew he was only an operator, telling Nigel Broackes, who built up Trafalgar House, a proper business in property and construction, 'Let's face it, none of us here are interested in management.'

Heath's dreams were finally crushed in the winter of 1973–74 by the economic upheaval following the oil crisis, which ended the post-war economic boom in so devastating a fashion and provided the miners with an excellent reason to demand more money – a demand Heath had eventually to concede after the country had been forced to work a three-day week. He was defeated in an ill-timed General Election in February 1974 – his campaign theme 'Who governs Britain?' was itself a guarantee of defeat given the natural reply was 'Anyone but you'. The collapse of government in general was symbolised by the nervous breakdown suffered by Sir William Armstrong, the Permanent Secretary to the Treasury who had, effectively, been Heath's Deputy Prime Minister during his last months in office. But it was Heath himself who had posed the stark choice facing Britain: 'The alternative to expansion is not, as some occasionally seem to suppose, an England of quiet market towns linked only by trains puffing slowly and peacefully through green meadows. The alternative is slums, dangerous roads, old factories, cramped schools, stunted lives.'

Notes

1. *'The Economy: a study in Failure'*, The Decade of Disillusion: British Politics in the Sixties, ed M McKie and C Cook, Macmillan, 1972
2. *A Stake in the future*, Nicholas Brealy 1997.
3. *New Towns for Old* in *Moments of Modernity*, Rivers Oram Press, London, 1999.

4. *Devil's Advocate*, Hutchinson, 1999.
5. Both *The Architectural Press*, 1955.
6. *Guardian*, March 11 1999.
7. *Guardian*, April 17 1999.
8. *Demos*, 1994.
9. *New Statesman*, November 29 1999.
10. *Independent on Sunday*, June 4 2000.
11. *Educational Priority*, HMSO.
12. *A Class Act*, Hamish Hamilton, 1997.
13. *Guardian*, May 5 1998.
14. *New Statesman*, November 29 1999.
15. *The Left in Britain 1956–68*, Penguin, 1976.
16. *New Statesman*, April 17 1998.
17. *New Statesman*, February 20 1998.
18. *New Statesman*, December 4 1998.
19. Review of John Hume's biography (?) by Paul Routledge, *Financial Times*.
20. Moynahan, op cit. He was reporting for the *Sunday Times* in Ulster at the time.
21. *Love Orange: Love Green, Poems of Living, Loving and Dying in Working-class Ulster*.

9

The Ice Age

'All over the country people blamed other people for the things that were going wrong ... Nobody knew whose fault it really was, but most people managed to complain fairly forcefully about somebody ... a huge icy fist, with large cold fingers, was squeezing and chilling the people of Britain.'

MARGARET DRABBLE, *The Ice Age*

THE LATER YEARS OF THE 1970s were a period of national helplessness, in which no one believed that change was possible, a feeling naturally exacerbated by the failure of Edward Heath's reforms, the first oil crisis of late 1973, the miners' triumph that winter, and the Heath's defeat in the election he called in February 1974. The following five years witnessed the gradual acceptance of Britain's post-war failure. This was taken as absolute rather than relative and naturally engendered a good deal of breast-beating and self-loathing. Already, at the end of the 1960s, James Alt discovered that although people thought that they personally were doing rather well, they thought that the country as a whole was doing badly. And as the 1970s went on, they felt that the government could do less and less to control inflation. In Alt's words they had become 'realists'. His conclusion? That 'in large measure then, the story of the mid-1970s is the story of a politics of declining expectations' – the 'feel bad factor'.[1] The essays on the condition of England written in the 1970s were inevitably far more defeatist, far more resigned to the inevitability of further decline than those written fifteen or twenty years earlier. Many were written by Americans, always glad to reinforce their preconceived notions that Britain is irretrievably decadent, and possessed titles such 'The Future that doesn't work: Social Democracy's Failures in Britain', 'The Politics of Economic Decline' and 'Is Britain Dying?'

In Ulster the situation went from bad to worse. When Harold Wilson returned to power in February 1974, he did not dare to confront the backlash when the Ulster Workers Council ordered a general strike.

192

Firm, early action could have nipped it in the bud. But it was left too late. Fatally, Wilson lacked courage in a crisis. As Lucy Faulkner, the widow of the deposed, moderate Prime Minister Brian Faulkner, put it: 'The British government itself was intimidated before the people of Northern Ireland were intimidated.' The result was the death of power-sharing for nearly twenty years and what can only be termed appeasement of the Unionists by Wilson and, above all, by his successor Jim Callaghan. They allowed the province to elect more MPs and not to enact some of the social legislation of the 1960s, notably homosexual law reform. They both hoped to salvage the situation by pouring more investment money into the province – over £50 million was thrown away by backing the production of an impractical, gull-winged sports car proposed by an American huckster John De Lorean. But De Lorean summed up the situation succinctly when he said: 'The worse the area, the more financing they'd give us.'

It was a poem of Rudyard Kipling's that best summed up the financial crisis of the first eighteen months of the Labour government:

> Then the Gods of the markets trembled, and their smooth-tongued
>   wizards withdrew,
> And the hearts of the meanest were humbled, and begun to
>   believe it was true
> That all is not Gold that Glitters, and Two and Two make four,
> And the Gods of the Copybook headings limped up to explain it
>   once more.

In the City there was a double crisis. The brash 'secondary banks' which had been the stars of the 'Barber boom' collapsed like the proverbial pack of cards. The crisis culminated in the statement by the chairman of the National Westminster Bank one Saturday morning that his bank, which was a major lender to the banks and property companies that were falling all around him, was not bankrupt. The rescue of selected banks was masterminded by the Bank of England through a 'Lifeboat' that found room only for banks whose collapse would have caused a 'systemic' crash, i.e. endangered the whole financial system. The crisis culminated in the curious case of Slater Walker's Singapore subsidiary. Its managing director Richard Tarling went to jail. But Slater himself, the – very active – chairman, remained untouched though he never again became director of a publicly quoted company. (Whether this had something to do with the fact that he had managed Ted Heath's private investments remains a matter for legitimate speculation.)

In the winter of 1974–75 the London stock market tumbled to pre-war levels. By December 1974 the *Financial Times* Index was down to 150 – it had been established at 100 back in 1935 – and the position was not improved with the collapse of Burmah Oil, one of Britain's largest and supposedly most solid companies. By New Year's Eve 1975, the index closed at 161.4, less than half its (already battered) level at the beginning of the year and the lowest level since May 1954. But a group of City institutions, headed by the Prudential Insurance, galloped to the rescue at the sight of such bargains and the index rose by nearly a half by the end of January of 1975.

The crisis of confidence resulting from the turbulence of the previous two years was stemmed only through the Referendum on our membership of the EEC in June 1975. This, it was assumed, would mark the triumph of the 'moderate' political classes, and would heal the divisions within the Labour Party. Harold Wilson had come to power in February 1974 proposing to renegotiate the terms of our entry into the EEC. He, and everyone else, knew that this was a farce, designed to appease the anti-marketeers in his party. With the terms duly 'adjusted' – though no-one noticed much difference – he could play his master stroke, a referendum on our entry, with members of the Cabinet free to work on either side and thus keep the party together. The idea was a total constitutional novelty and was deeply disliked by the pro-Europeans, never ones to allow the people any say.

In the words of Reg Prentice, a Labour minister turned Tory, the campaign united 'the majority of realistic and moderate politicians of all three political parties'. They were aided by the clergy, organised by a future cabinet minister, John Selwyn Gummer. Even the Consumers' Association, supposedly the spokesmen for the lobby most obviously neglected by the producer-oriented Common Agricultural Policy, firmly supported our remaining in the EEC. The pros could outspend the antis by ten to one and the media were hopelessly biased in their favour – indeed Con O'Neill even believed that the antis were not entitled to equal air time. For me the uniqueness of the occasion was marked by the pro-Europe sticker prominently displayed in the front window of my then neighbour, David Dimbleby. Normally the most scrupulously neutral of commentators, he obviously never stopped to think that he was, for once, taking sides over a political issue.

Against the pros were a minority whose leaders could easily, and in many cases justifiably, be labelled as extremists, notably politicians such as Tony Benn and Enoch Powell – who had to be kept strictly apart. A poll of the pro and anti-market figures revealed that all of the pro-market names drew a positive reaction from the general public. By contrast six of the eight anti-marketeers scored negatively for, not surprisingly, we were a weird, marginal bunch. As one of the handful of journalists in the anti-camp, I felt totally isolated, above all from virtually all my friends in the media. The marginality, the craziness, of the antis formed one of the major arguments against withdrawal. In the words of Anthony Crosland, 'To withdraw now would create in this country a mood of poor man's inchoate chauvinism, reviving old dreams of Empire and special relationship that have had such disastrous effects on British policy-making since 1945.'[2]

The pros relied heavily on the public's mood of insecurity. The general feeling of despair was well summed up by Sir Christopher Soames. 'This is no time,' he declared, 'for Britain to consider leaving a Christmas Club, let alone the Common Market.' For it was assumed, wrongly, that if we left the EEC would not have been anxious to conclude a free trade agreement with their biggest market. The theme of our helplessness outside the EEC was relentlessly rubbed home by industrialists and politicians alike: 'A vote to leave the market,' intoned Harold Wilson, 'would have a serious and damaging effect on employment'.

By an accident of timing, one of the antis' most powerful weapons, the cost of the CAP, was blunted by freak conditions in the world's food markets. The referendum period saw the only months in the last forty years when world food prices rose above those prevailing in the EEC and membership actually saved us from a – very temporary – shortage of sugar. On this accident of timing the Europeans built a mountain of theory. 'If we left the market tomorrow,' said Shirley Williams, 'we could not expect any reduction in the overall cost of our food as a result.' Cannily the pros never tackled the question of sovereignty – indeed, the Europeans would never admit even to themselves that they were leading Britain down a federalist path. According to Alistair McAlpine, the improbable treasurer of the European League for Economic Co-operation, 'the subject' – of a Federal Europe – was 'mentioned only on a few occasions and then only to confirm that such an idea was out of the question'.[3] In Hugo Young's words, referring to the implications of the European Court of Justice, claims that our legal system would not be affected 'while not untrue . . . could be said to understate the matter. It certainly conformed, as did the entire Yes campaign, to the old familiar rule, the golden thread of deceptive reassurance that runs through the history of Britain's relationship with the European Union up to the present day'.[4]

Although the pros won easily – losing only the Shetlands – this reassertion of the dominance of the Great and the Good proved strictly temporary as longer-term trends asserted themselves. 'As summer advanced into autumn,' wrote David Butler and Uwe Kitzinger, 'it became very hard to find in the media any allusion to the events that had culminated on June 5.'[4] And by the end of the year Mrs Thatcher was installed as leader of the Tory party and the Labour party was back to its old divisiveness, this time in suicidal mode.

195

For the success of the Great and the Good in the referendum did not entirely subdue the mood of panic, especially as the latent economic crisis rumbled on throughout the next eighteen months. Right-wingers were alarmed at the antics, as they saw them, of Harold Wilson's second administration, especially the radical and ill-conceived policies of Tony Benn, the Trade and Industry Secretary. According to James Lees-Milne, the writer Sacheverell Sitwell passed on the warning of 'influential city friends' that 'we' have only three months to clear out of England. Another friend told him to 'hoard his cartridges, for there would be shooting within that time'. Lees-Milne felt that 'feebleness has been this country's undoing . . . I think it very possible that there may be fighting within four months'. If the extremists (on the left, naturally) pressed their demands, they would 'have to be resisted with force by a super-leader'.[5] This was no exaggeration. David Kynaston quotes a stockbroker, Lord Roger Manners. In early 1974 he expected 'a complete economic collapse any day, when we shall be in the same condition as Germany was in 1923'.

The only real conspiracy which affected Britain at the time was that of the IRA. The bombings it carried out on the mainland in 1974–76 not only contributed to the generally jittery atmosphere; they also led to some appalling miscarriages of justice, including that of the Birmingham Six, who were wrongly convicted of a particularly terrible bombing in the city. But most of the English, rather than the Irish, conspiracies engendered by the panicky atmosphere were pretty farcical and, usually, right-wing, fed by the fear of a communist takeover. Politically – and despite the communists' influence in the unions – these fears were ungrounded. I remember my then accountant, a solid Stalinist, roaring with laughter at the names of his colleagues mentioned in an article in the *Sunday Telegraph* as dangerous conspirators, for he was only too aware that they were incapable even of collecting branch subscriptions. At the other extreme, but indicative of right-wing attitudes at the time, was the way that Lord Lucan's friends refused to co-operate with the police when the peer disappeared after murdering his nanny, having mistaken her for his wife. The group came first, society as a whole a long way behind.

The most glamorous right-wing grouping was headed by a well-known general, Sir William Walker. The most visible was the National Association for Freedom. NAFF brought together a war hero, Lord De L'Isle and Dudley VC, and the members of a whole array of right-wing organisations, There is no doubt that Harold Wilson, though naturally paranoid, was the object of conspiracies organised by extremists within MI5. But there were also more farcical groupings. Mike Molloy, the editor of the *Daily Mirror*, and Bruce Page, the editor of Insight on the *Sunday Times*, were summoned to a dinner given by

Sir Val Duncan, chairman of the mining group Rio Tinto Zinc, for a gathering which included a number of leading businessmen. Duncan explained that the assembled company was preparing to mount a coup and had ample finance and arms to do so. Moreover, they had bought a number of printing presses and asked whether the two distinguished journalists would be prepared to produce a paper to support the coup. Molloy and Page pointed out that they were both Labour supporters (indeed Molloy's paper was the government's staunchest journalistic backer) and left the dinner.

More sinister was the recrudescence of the National Front, which achieved a number of local election successes, thanks in part to what their leader, Martin Webster, called the 'robust young men' – what we might call football hooligans. Although the Front gained seats in local council elections in London's Docklands, an area which had many supporters of Enoch Powell, they were effectively countered by the Anti-Nazi League, one of the rare radical organisations which understood that radicalism had to be fun as well as worthy. The future Labour minister Peter Hain was one of those who recognised the need to launch 'footballers against the nazis, rock against racism' – and to run concerts and carnivals as well as demonstrations.

The apparent awfulness of the present naturally bred a generally inward- and backward-looking mentality, a worship of the past. Writing from the United States – where he had fled to avoid the taxman – Henry Fairlie, the journalist who had coined the term 'establishment' twenty years earlier, observed how Britain had become like a family, cosy and secure but also 'suffocating everyone in his or her place; everyone doing and saying and being what he or she has always done and said and been'. As consolation, the family could 'reach for the family album, pull out the family tree, fall back on the richness of its own history ... from this distance, the interest that the English are today taking in their past seems, not merely eccentric, but lunatic'.

In 1977 Tom Nairn summed up the situation as seen by a stoutly socialist, indeed anti-royalist, socialist writer: ' "Moderate", "orderly", "decent"; "peaceful and tolerant", "constitutional"; "backward-looking", "complacent", "insular", "class-ridden", "inefficient", "imperialist" – a realistic analysis of the British state must admit these two familiar sets of truisms are in fact differing visages of the same social reality. That Arcadian England which appeals so strongly to foreign intellectuals is also the England which has, since the early 1950s, fallen into evermore evident and irredeemable decline – the United Kingdom of permanent economic crisis, falling standards, bankrupt government, slavish dependence on the United States and myopic expedients ... The only useful kind of speculation has assumed a geriatric odour: a motorised wheel-chair and a decent funeral seem to have become the actual horizons of the 1980s, without design or conscious consent.'[6]

As Stephen Collins pointed out, one result of the loss of the old certainties was 'self-definition through loss. At its core is the self-indulgence involved in revelling in the defeat of the stylish and the graceful by the harsh realities of the functional, the effective, the modern ... The result is the psychological or cultural mechanism by which sheer pastness confers a charm, the frisson of irrecoverability, the pleasures of longing'.[7] The cry of heritage in danger had been raised for the first time since 1945 in 1962 because of the threat to the Euston Arch, the squat, unremarkable portico to Euston Station – this only a few years after the Great Hall of the station itself, a far more remarkable structure, had been pulled down without much of a protest. Until the late 1960s preservationists, particularly those who, like John Betjeman, worshipped at the shrine of Victorian architecture, were mocked. But after the arch had been destroyed, it became unthinkable to touch Saint Pancras Station nearby. From then on buildings not in themselves especially beautiful, many considered the height of new, functional vulgarity when they first appeared, have come to seem the quintessence of a more loveable age. They have included nineteenth-century terraced houses, 1930s cinemas and steam railways – the list still grows by the day. For, as Collins wrote, in such an atmosphere, 'culture is regarded as something that happens elsewhere, and in England the elsewhere of choice for many people is the past'. In the 1970s television echoed the nostalgia with the roaring success of series such as *The Forsyte Saga* and *Upstairs Downstairs*.

It was in the mid-1970s, following an exhibition in 1974 at the Victoria & Albert Museum entitled 'The Destruction of the Country House' that the organisation Heritage in Danger was launched, even though the threat was no greater than it had been for nearly a hundred years since the late Victorian agricultural depression first started to put the squeeze on the finances of the landed aristocracy. And when, in the early 1990s, Britain acquired its first Ministry of Culture, it was disguised as a Ministry of National Heritage. For the 1970s were eminently a time for nostalgia, and for preservation. Old-established bodies such as the Council for the Preservation of Rural England became more radical, less consensual, the Ramblers' Association hardened its attitude towards the lack of access to so much of Britain's countryside, the membership of the Royal Society for the Protection of Birds increased sevenfold in the decade and that of the National Trust – which itself became more militant – fivefold, to reach a million before the end of the decade. 'For the first time in the countryside,' wrote Howard Newby, 'we have an articulate population which knows its way round politically and which is prepared to speak out against

198

the practices of the local farmers and landowners'[8] – who, in their quest for ever-increasing production had removed an estimated 15,000 miles of hedgerows. 'Thanks to the farmers,' wrote Marion Shoard apocalyptically, 'the English landscape is under sentence of death'[9] – although again the threat was not new, had in fact been growing since 1939 when farmers were urged to increase food production as much as they could, a tendency naturally increased by the CAP which paid so much for any food, whether it was needed or not .

Even the royal family was not immune from the prevailing querulousness, an attitude most obviously expressed in arguments about the royal finances. These were not a new subject for discussion. 'Although British monarchs in this century have been extremely well-off,' wrote David Cannadine, 'this has never prevented their representatives from pleading poverty on their behalf, and asking for more money or more concessions.'[10] But, increasingly, these representatives had to justify themselves more than they had in the late 1940s over the allowance to the Duke of Edinburgh after his marriage, or over the fate of the £200,000 the King had saved from his civil list during the war. Yet, even then, the debates demonstrated that there was a strong school of Labour members who wanted a 'Scandinavian monarchy'.

In 1971 a select committee examined the Queen's finances. Many, by no means left-wing, Labour members openly criticised the existing situation and it was that extreme moderate Roy Jenkins who first raised the point – one that was to become more newsworthy twenty years later – as to whether the royal family should not earn their own living. But the most important warning signal hoisted during the committee's hearings was the attitude of the *Sun* newspaper, which asked its readers whether the Queen deserved a pay rise. Four out of five decided that she didn't, a point of satisfaction to Rupert Murdoch. He had bought the paper – the short-lived successor to the Labour movement's own daily, the *Daily Herald* – for virtually nothing when it had almost folded in 1969. A brilliant popular newspaperman, he immediately transformed it from a sober broadsheet to a sensational tabloid. Because he was the first proprietor in the history of the British press who was using his British papers largely as a springboard with which to finance his global ambitions, he was totally out of control so far as the British establishment was concerned, especially as he did not crave for a title or to please the royal family. Quite the opposite: he was and remains a ferocious republican with an open contempt for the royal family, an extreme case of his attitude towards the whole British establishment.

In the mid-1970s the veteran anti-monarchist, the Labour MP Willy Hamilton, published a book *My Queen and I*, pouring scorn on the monarchy, the amount it cost and, prophetically, on the 'model family' mythology, an attack which led 89 Labour MPs to vote against a proposed increase in the Queen's civil list allowance. At the same time her constitutional impotence was underlined in 1975 when her Private Secretary, Martin Charteris, accepted that the Governor General of Australia, Sir John Kerr, could dismiss the Prime Minister, Gough Whitlam, without informing Her Majesty.

The 1970s are so generally regarded as indescribably awful we forget that the status, and often the conditions, of half the population improved, sometimes dramatically. Historically, British women had suffered from many of the same disadvantages as their sisters in the rest of the world. However, in many respects – education, careers and job prospects – they were better off than women in Catholic and, above all, Muslim countries or indeed in some secular societies such as Japan, all of which were still unable at the end of the twentieth century to come to terms with the possible equality of women.

In the late 1960s, those infallible indicators of opinion, women's magazines, had signalled the restlessness of a new generation of better-educated women. Those publications whose attitudes were summed up as 'knitting for royalty' suffered sharp falls in circulation. But the most prophetic publication was *Nova*, launched in 1965 by a strong-minded future Labour minister, Alma Birk, and described as 'A new kind of magazine for a new kind of woman'. It tackled a whole range of previously unmentionable issues such as racism, homosexuality, immigration and casual sex. One memorable cover featured a beautiful black child with the caption: 'You may think that I look cute, but would you live next door to my mummy and daddy?' Naturally *Nova* also looked at the problems encountered by supposedly liberated women. A typical article published in 1968 was headed 'I have taken the pill. I have hoisted my skirts to my thighs, dropped them to my ankles ... lived with two men, married one, earned my keep, kept my identity and frankly ... I'm lost.' By 1971 a *Nova* cover featured a virtually nude model sexily touching her vital parts. Its influence spread: *Cosmopolitan* defended the right of women to be sexually active and by 1972 no bras were being worn by presenters on the children's programme *Magpie*. At the same time bisexuality – though only men's – began to appear in the shape of Mark Bolan and David Bowie. Even romantic novels, the staple diet of housebound women, were changing, notably those of Sheila Holland, who wrote under the name of Charlotte Lamb. Even though many of them were published by the ultra-conservative firm of Mills & Boon, Holland was, wrote her obituarist, 'at the forefront of stories that went "beyond the bedroom door"'.[11] Indeed her best novel, *The Long Surrender*, published in 1978, was about a woman who had been sexually abused as a child.

Yet Englishwomen continued to suffer from a unique disadvantage: Englishmen, especially – but by no means exclusively – those who had been to public schools, didn't actually like women; indeed they hid from them in the exclusively male clubs which were a special feature of British social life. There were clubs for every sort of English male, working men's for the proles, golf clubs for the middle sort, in St James's for the posh. They had one thing in common: no women, largely, I believe, because the members were afraid of the opposite sex. And it is this smell of fear which hangs over the whole story of what I would call the second emancipation of women in the 1970s.

Remedies were sorely needed, though they could not eliminate the profoundly condescending attitudes encountered by women, especially when they tried to assert their financial independence – for they were almost invariably less well-paid than men doing an equivalent job, itself a rarity. When Jack Cohen, the founder of Tesco, was reproached for not paying Daisy Hyams, the legendary head buyer who was the foundation of his firm's success, as much as the other directors, he replied simply, 'Oh she's married. She doesn't need the money.' Women were routinely refused mortgages and loans: even if they had substantial incomes in their own right, they required a (male) co-signatory. The result was recalled by Ann Leslie, who explained how, even though she was the highest-paid feature writer on any newspaper, bank managers refused 'pretty young women' like her. She should simply find a husband and stop worrying about such matters. In the end she found a mortgage 'not because I had a right to it, financially or otherwise, but because another condescending man – the chairman of the building society in question – happened to like my work and his suddenly snivelling underling was ordered to grant me the mortgage after all "as a favour to this clever girl" '.[12]

High-achieving women like Leslie faced not only male chauvinism but also a more insidious, less publicised problem: jealousy on the part of other women. In an unusually frank admission Mary (later Lady) Warnock reflected on how 'there has long been a certain excitement about being, not so much the first woman to do this or that, as the only woman'.[13] As a 'token woman . . . a woman did not always feel unmixed pleasure at being joined by another woman' who might be 'cleverer, more attractive, better dressed, more articulate, more successful in combining femininity with power than she herself'. When Warnock started examining at Oxford she 'had to be extremely careful not to be unfair to any woman who looked likely to get a First'. And this from a woman who had been the renowned headmistress of a single-sex school (Oxford High) for high-achieving girls.

Inevitably, in the supposedly liberated 1960s, even, indeed especially, women who were both bright and beautiful suffered from a condescension which could degenerate into persecution. And none suffered more than Caroline Coon, a pre-Raphaelite beauty who was one of the icons of the decade and who founded Release, the drugs advice service. As she pointed out, 'Those optimistic, loving images of naked young men and women dancing with flowers in their hair at Woodstock were eliding into pictures of women being tied up and beaten . . . the only way to be desirable as a woman was if you were a "dolly bird"* – a terrible phrase because "doll" means childish and disposable, while "bird" isn't human.'[14] There was no escape – 'If you had a miniskirt on you provoked rape; if you didn't, you were told only ugly girls get raped. If you said no, you were a frigid bitch; if you said yes you were a loose slut.' To make matters worse, such women were under pressure from their mothers, who had often been deprived of a life of their own and so were jealous, insisting that their offspring should copy their example, marry and breed.

As in the United States, one of the major spurs towards feminism was the appallingly macho behaviour of the male revolutionaries of the 1960s. The really defining moments came when women discovered that such men did not extend their revolutionary attitudes to relations with the opposite sex. Typically, Sheila Rowbotham, the well-known feminist, found that her lover, the economist Bob Rowthorn, was not interested in her opinions. 'Political revolution,' wrote Jenny Diski, 'was a boys' game. Women were lovers, secretaries, tea-makers, but co-revolutionaries only when they behaved like the boys.'[15] When Rowbotham tried to give her views at meetings of the *New Left Review*, the editor, Perry Anderson, started to refer to her as 'that girl'. For even the left was simply not aware of women's rights. Geoffrey Robertson and his fellow Rhodes scholars were quick to protest at the lack of black scholars from South Africa or Rhodesia but, he wrote, 'it had not occurred to any of us in 1970 that women had never been eligible for selection, or that such discrimination against them might be in any way objectionable'.

In early 1969, however, another, more libertarian, less orthodox socialist magazine, *Black Dwarf*, edited by the showman-intellectual – and future TV producer – Tariq Ali allowed Sheila Rowbotham to edit an issue in which she declared that 'Men! You have nothing to lose but your chains', tackling a central issue of feminism throughout the ages, men's fear of the potential strength of – and thus their dominance by – women. But it was only the following year that History Workshop, established in 1967 by the brilliant left-historical impresario and intellectual Raphael Samuel to help everyone write their own

* Nomenclature was always important. For older – pre-1960s – men they were 'the ladies' and then 'gels' or 'chicks'. Only in the 1970s, and with much effort, did they become women and even then, if they made a fuss, they were mocked as 'wimmin'.

history, got round to discussing women – and even then the women were roundly booed. From this sprang a host of discussion groups, a generally increased awareness among women – mainly but not exclusively of the left – of the problems they had in common and even, albeit indirectly, demonstrations such as the famous irruption of feminists at the 1970 Miss World competition in the Royal Albert Hall.

But the crucial contribution was made by Germaine Greer, one of the band of Australian immigrants who had filled so important a role in radical movements of the late 1960s, with the publication of her bestseller *The Female Eunuch** – which was dedicated to Coon, whom she described as 'loud, virile and beautiful'. As her fellow feminist Rosie Boycott said, Greer had 'wit and style and intelligence and beauty and guts [which] made her impossible to ignore: she could not be attacked, as so many feminists were, as ugly lesbians who protested basically because they couldn't attract chaps'. For she was obviously, outrageously sexy, prepared to expose her sexual organs in a magazine to help promote the cause of liberation. But perhaps Greer's biggest contribution, even if an indirect one, was to give women the courage to talk about all the horrors, rape, domestic violence, child abuse that had previously been unmentionable. She was not a joiner and therefore sometimes resented by mainstream feminists such as Rowbotham. It was her disciple Boycott – full of the determination and confidence derived from an education at Cheltenham Ladies' College – and Marsha Rowe, another Australian, who founded *Spare Rib*, the national magazine for the women's movement, while yet another Australian, Carmen Callil, was one of the trio responsible for launching the feminist, and extremely successful, Virago publishing business, dedicated to reissuing out-of-print and often forgotten books by women writers.

Greer's influence, however, did not stretch to working women (nor, in fact, did that of the more orthodox left-wing feminists). Here the battle was left to less glamorous but more practically effective women. The first intimation of women's militancy had come in the summer of 1968 with a strike by sewing machinists at Ford's massive plant at Dagenham in East London – always a hotbed of male militancy (and of systematic racism). The machinists pointed out that they had to pass tests on three different types of sewing machines and therefore should have been classed as skilled. They lost their case but gained a substantial pay increase. The key figure in the struggle was the late Audrey Wise, first from her base working in USDAW (the Union of Shop, Distributive and Allied Workers) and then as a Member of Parliament. As she pointed out, many women's wages were only just over half

---

* The book was so successful that Greer had had to go into exile for a year to avoid the then ruinous tax payable.

those of men. And even though the overwhelming majority of canteen workers were women, as were three fifths of office and clerical staff and nearly half of the workers on the production line, only a handful were skilled workers.

Wise would flatly contradict trades union leaders when they found excuses such as 'women are hard to organise and they won't join the unions'. In fact, they formed over a quarter of trades union membership but only 2 per cent of officials – and many of their husbands wouldn't let them go to a meeting every week (Aubrey Wise was lucky: her husband John, a former engineer blackballed for his political activities who had become an optician, was immensely supportive). Women were deprived of training 'in case they marry', so they had a kind of permanent 'temporary' status, while widows were to be given a small handout and expected to keep quiet. When Wise was serving as President of USDAW she confronted Vic Feather, the formidable General Secretary of the TUC, with the old Russian proverb: 'I thought I saw two people, but it was only a man and his wife.' The attack was not unjustified. When the TUC under Feather defeated Barbara Castle's In Place of Strife proposals, it was clear that one of the elements in the mix was anti-feminism. In conversation with another official, Jack Kemp, Feather agreed that the unions might have been wrong but 'we taught that bitch Barbara Castle a thing or two.'*

For there were few union leaders who were both democratic and genuinely respectful of women's rights. At a private dinner in 1972, my wife tackled Jack Jones over the lack of buses serving our elder son's school, at a time when his members were not allowing women to drive buses – a major grievance when conductresses were conducting a campaign to improve their lot. Jones explained that he was calling weekly meetings of the relevant branch in an – eventually successful – effort to lift the ban.

Nevertheless, during that dismal decade, and thanks to both their own efforts and the legislation passed by the generally reviled Labour government of 1974–1979, the conditions of women of all classes had greatly improved, legally anyway, as had that of immigrants – the 1976 Race Relations Act outlawed discrimination and made it an offence to stir up racial hatred. The first Equal Pay Act had been passed in 1970 – although unfortunately it was based on the idea of comparability and therefore did not help the very many women working in all-female work environments. These included nests of low pay such as sweat shops, canteens and the like. Some of the results could be quantified. In the decade women's pay grew from under two thirds of men's to nearly three quarters – while membership of trades unions grew, though

---

* Feather told the story to Alistair McAlpine.

even in 1975 women accounted for little more than a quarter of the total numbers, partly because the trades in which women worked were, by no coincidence, less unionised than all-male industries such as mining. Despite union opposition, the government's legislative record was impressive. A Sex Discrimination Act was passed and an Equal Opportunities Commission was created, then attacked for being too timid, itself a healthy sign of many women's increased awareness of their rights. A Matrimonial Property Act recognised woman's contribution to the family income through their work in the home.

Even more fundamental was the willingness, for the first time, to accept the idea of male brutality to women in the home. It was only when Erin Pizzey set up a Women's Refuge in Chiswick in West London in 1972 that the horrors of domestic violence came into the open – and their cause was greatly helped when the left-wing MP Jo Richardson piloted the Matrimonial Violence Act through Parliament in 1976 and with the foundation of the Rape Crisis Centre, even though only too often judges were still apt to say that the victim was 'asking for it' when confronted by a rape case. Yet women remained hesitant. As late as the mid-1970s Anna Raeburn, the 27-year-old who ran the advisory service for *Forum*, a magazine designed to take the guilt out of sex, confessed that 'I thought if you even talked about sex you had to be a whore, a doctor or a lesbian'. By the end of the 1970s, the feminist writer Beatrix Campbell could tell Philip Whitehead that 'the Seventies were a women's decade and there have been mighty changes in women's lives . . . There have been real changes in women's expectation at work, in their personal lives, that can't really be recorded and measured statistically.'

But male radicals fared worse than the women. In an atmosphere foetid with fear and suspicion it was perhaps inevitable that the power of the secret services would be enhanced. A Labour attorney general was persuaded (for fear of being thought a commie?) into an ill-advised prosecution. This became known as the ABC case, named after the three defendants: Crispin Aubrey, a reporter from *Time Out,* John Berry, an ex-soldier, and Duncan Campbell, a scientific prodigy, all of whom were accused of divulging secrets (over a bottle of Chianti, in private). When it was revealed in detail at their trial that the 'secrets' they were accused of revealing – all concerned with Sigint, the state's elaborate system of communications intelligence – included sites already on Ordnance Survey maps and many others which had been issued to every airline (including Russia's Aeroflot), the judge, 'Bill' Mars-Jones, told the Attorney General, who had authorised the prosecution, to unauthorise it. But this was a lone failure. The prevailing atmosphere within the Home Office was becoming decidedly less tolerant, especially after the removal of Alex Lyon, a left-leaning minister, when the authorities' attitude towards immigration became much less sympathetic.

While the Labour government was on what would now be termed a 'law and order kick', at constituency level the party was being taken over by a new brand of leftists, the type Keynes described as 'the left enthusiasts who turn against anything if there seems a chance it could possibly happen' and whom I would term 'Futilitarians'. This is no exaggeration, as can be seen from their almost universally dismal record while they controlled a number of boroughs, especially in London, in the 1980s (and when they tried to start a newspaper, the *News on Sunday*, the result was a farcical episode that cost their predominantly trades union backers £6.5 million).

The 'polys' were, in the words of Ralf Dahrendorf (who as head of the LSE had come across many of them), 'the educational class . . . who have never left the world of schools and colleges and universities. They combine radical politics with petit bourgeois life styles . . . they like to glorify the working class, though not without making sure that their distance from it is never forgotten. They live in communities of equals. They have even begun to create their own political party, by pushing working people to the outskirts of the Labour Party'. Indeed, they formed an exclusivist sect, unwilling to allow outsiders into the local parties they controlled.

As a result, during the 1970s the Labour party was organising itself – or rather disorganising itself – to ensure that after its defeat in 1979 it fell apart. But the party had been crumbling long before. In 1960, after the party's crushing defeat at the 1959 election, Anthony Crosland had already warned in *Encounter* that the members were saying the defeat was the fault of the voters 'who were not good enough for us' and that they would await the crisis of capitalism which they thought imminent. This, he wrote, 'betrayed a priggish self-satisfaction, a contempt for the judgement of ordinary people and an indifference to their interests, which is wholly alien to the party's tradition and, in itself, enough to condemn it to opposition and sterility'. Crosland's prediction was only half true then, but it was nonetheless fully borne out over the next twenty years. The slippage grew apace in the latter half of the 1960s with the – quite reasonable – feeling amongst many party members that Harold Wilson's government had failed to live up to its promises, while the political breakdown of the Communist Party and CND released strong forces into the bloodstream of the Labour Party, which virtually collapsed under the strain.

Then came a fatal, if little remarked step – the opening of Labour party membership to extreme leftists in 1971. This provided a point of entry for many former communists – as well as for younger lefties who would probably have joined the Party twenty years earlier. But

206

they differed in two crucial respects from the older generation of communists: they were not disciplined and they had no respect for learning or intellectual abilities. When Mick Costello, the Communist Party's last industrial organiser, joined the party in the 1950s, 'it could produce working-class intellectuals as no one else could do. People were taught to respect culture. In a gathering of communists one can talk on a more intellectual level than among people with much more formal education'. By the 1970s the whole left – communists and Trotskyists alike – were politically splintered beyond recognition, with the official Communist Party itself split between reformers (later described as 'Euro-communists') and the 'Tankies' – hard-liners who had approved of the Russian use of force against the liberal Dubcek regime in Czechoslovakia in 1968.

But the majority of the individuals involved were indeed the 'Polyocracy' which emerged from the creation of the polytechnics in the late 1960s. They formed a new class in British society, albeit one familiar elsewhere, a new, and generally second-rate pseudo-intellectual group, only too aware that they were considered second-rate because of the very fact they taught in polys and not in universities. They were also affected by the transformation of Marxism. In the past, Marxist students had obeyed Lenin's dictum that a good Marxist student is a good student. But the triumph of a sort of bastard Trotskyism in the 1960s liberated them from the need to work at their studies (or to think clearly, if at all). Moreover, old-style communism had had a vision of the future, even if it was fatally flawed, whereas the new lefties were faithful to the sentiment expressed in Groucho Marx's famous song: 'Whatever it is I'm against it.'

They formed a large number of usually tiny groups, what the French would call *groupuscules*. By far the most important was Militant, which had been founded in the 1950s in Liverpool, always a centre of militancy, as the Revolutionary Socialist League. It developed the policy of 'entryism', infiltrating the local Labour Party, and in the 1980s captured the local council under the leadership of a real Jack the Lad called Derek Hatton*. In the 1980s, wrote Francis Beckett, 'Militant was to play a leading part in ensuring the survival of the Conservative government'.[16] Only members of Militant and rival groupings had the time and the energy to argue interminably, until, as one friend of mine put it, 'the old ladies at the back of the room would get cold and tired and slip away', allowing the militants to take control. The result was what Tony Benn called 'the democracy of the committed' – i.e. the untiring and unrepresentative minority of futilitarians.

* Hatton was known locally as Digsy. In the late 1980s, after he had been removed from office, he turned his talent to a combination of commentating and public relations.

This New Left – not to be confused with the distinguished group of intellectuals of the same name who had left the Communist Party after 1956 – concentrated on forcing MPs to toe their version of the party line, notably by mandatory reselection under which even (indeed, especially) the most senior and respected MPs would be forced to be reselected by their local party before each election. The policy was masterminded by the Campaign for Labour Party Democracy, run by Vladimir Dere, one of the few effective revolutionary figures in post-war British political life. The increased radicalism of many of Labour's constituency parties was first demonstrated in Lincoln in 1973 after the local MP, Dick Taverne, had voted in favour of entry into the Common Market. He resigned and stood at the subsequent by-election as Democratic Labour. He won, but his natural supporters such as Roy Jenkins obviously felt that it was premature to break away from the party, and Taverne went on to lose his seat in the General Election in October 1974.

The Communist Party's increasing disarray did not greatly affect communist influence in the unions. Indeed, it probably increased during the decade. In 1972 the TUC lifted a twenty-two-year ban on communists attending meetings of trades councils, and gradually communists came out of the closet, as it were, and into the mainstream of union activity. Furthermore, the party's headquarters in King Street was more likely to take its orders from union leaders than to give them, thus virtually eliminating the influence of the Soviet Union that had done so much to hamper the party's efforts in the past. When Bert Ramelson, the party's industrial organiser, claimed that he had only to 'float an idea early in the year and it will be official Labour Party policy by the autumn', he was exaggerating, but not by much. Ramelson and his colleagues changed tactics: 'The left,' wrote Beckett, 'found a better tactic than railing against union influence' – which had previously been generally right-wing – 'and that was to work through the unions themselves.' The party was characteristically disciplined: rather than try and impose communist general secretaries throughout the Labour Movement, they allowed its members in each union to apply their own tactics and support such staunchly left-wing but non-communist officials as Jack Jones of the biggest single union, the Transport and General Workers, and Hugh Scanlon of the Engineering Workers, another demonic figure for the right.

But by the 1970s the workers were no longer prepared to follow their union bosses automatically, hence the idea that salvation was to be found in listening to them, or rather their self-appointed leaders, the shop stewards. This ideal's spokesman was the noble and ultimately tragic figure of Jack Jones, who sincerely believed in shop-floor democracy. His attempts, backed by Tony Benn, to form workers' cooperatives helped compound the chaos which resulted in Thatcherism. The sheer unreality of such dreams was shown by three experiments in worker control: a newspaper, the *Scottish Daily News*, a multi-purpose factory at Kirby in Liverpool, and the attempt to resurrect the Triumph motor-cycle factory at Meriden. They were all doomed from the start and not only because the concerns involved were inevitably on their last legs when they were rescued. The unreality of the experiment was shown by Jones's remark that 'You don't need research and development for motorbikes'. Not that the factory was necessarily doomed – fifteen years later it was resurrected by a local entrepreneur and by the end of the century had become a source of super-bikes so competitive that four out of every five was exported.

In 1976 Britain's precarious economic situation, based on the inflationary consequences of the oil crisis of 1973 and the feeling in international financial circles that things were out of hand, led to a credibility crisis. A more respected government could have raised money from the markets but, as Dennis Healey, the Chancellor, put it, 'You've got to persuade people that it's worth lending to you, and that they'll get their money back.' So the IMF had to be called in to bail us out, forcing Healey to turn back at Heathrow on his way to an international financial conference to deal with the crisis. It was triggered by the way that the preliminary figures for Britain's balance of trade had shown an uncomfortable deficit. But this could have been ridden without dramatic action had Britain not been perceived as so weak – especially as the preliminary estimates were always unduly pessimistic, and even more so in this instance.

In the end the IMF's terms were not that severe – largely thanks to the negotiating tactics of 'that foxy peasant', as Treasury officials admiringly termed Jim Callaghan, who had replaced Harold Wilson as Prime Minister earlier that year. Nevertheless they introduced the idea of 'monetarism', economic discipline based on the supply of money and not on the budget balance, which was to dominate official British economic thinking for the rest of the century. The whole crisis was a sign that to the rest of the world Britain was just another basket case, a banana monarchy as it were. It was the final nail in Labour's coffin but, typically, it was a largely unfounded crisis. The agreement which resolved it naturally involved a guaranteed reduction in the public sector deficit – which of course involved sacrifices by the workers in the public sector, many of whom could ill-afford the discipline imposed by an incomes policy.

The IMF crisis was important not only because it emphasised the gulf between the Labour Party and the government – Healey was heckled and booed when he tried to defend the terms at the party's conference a month later. It was also deeply humiliating and encouraged the feeling that such crises were inevitable every few years. Britain's image had descended very low – when the British ambassador to Germany asked for help from Chancellor Helmut Schmidt, he was simply given a lecture on how the British had messed up their economy before Schmidt went on to make slighting parallels between Britain and East Germany. 'Nothing,' echoed Brian Walden, then a Labour MP, 'could ever be done properly, nothing bold could ever be tried' – especially not by a Labour government. Thenceforward, wrote the historian Brian Brivati, all the leadership could do was to 'preach the positive virtues of surrender to the market' and accept that 'unemployment was a price to be paid for control of inflation and increased productivity'.[17]

The next year proved a turning-point in perceptions of Britain's true situation. The unreality of the public face of the establishment and people's underlying feeling was shown by the immense popularity of the Silver Jubilee celebrations in 1977 when the Queen basked in the obvious delight of the crowds at seeing her. 'Betty* rules OK' ran at least one graffiti. This was to be the high point of her reign; from then on it was downhill all the way. That year also marked the retirement of Martin Charteris, a Private Secretary who combined a genuine love for the Queen with a shrewd sense of realism and a willingness to express his feelings. By setting themselves up as a model family, the royals were asking for trouble, especially as the Queen boasted on how 'we have been fortunate in our children' – the previous year her daughter Princess Anne had been the first member of the royal family to represent Britain at the Olympic Games.

But within a few months came a foretaste of the problem that was to do so much damage to the monarchy over the following quarter of a century, the divorce of Princess Margaret and Lord Snowdon. It was not the first divorce in the family. In 1967 the Queen's cousin, Lord Harewood, a distinguished musical and opera impresario, had divorced his wife – herself a foreigner – to marry Patricia Tuckwell, three years after they had had a child. But, in the public mind, Harewood was not closely connected with the royal family. Margaret obviously was. Her marriage had been a very open one. Although clearly in love at the outset, both sides had lovers and by all accounts it sounds like the sort of dysfunctional marriage most of us have come across at one time or another, full of flaming rows and one of the couple stalking out of social occasions – and therefore a marriage totally different from that of any previous royal couple.

But the worship of the Queen was largely confined to the older

---

* Although by now this rather homely diminutive seemed decidedly old-fashioned and had already been replaced by the grittier, cooler Liz.

generation. In a brilliant essay Jason Cowley explained how as a lad growing up in the 'nowhere zone of the Essex-Hertfordshire borderlands' he found that 'Britain . . . was an extraordinarily drab place in which to be young: closed, parochial, complacent, tired.'[18] Cowley examined the many books and films which explored that crucial year of 1977, including a novel – *Human Punk* by John King – about 'a young punk's existential journey through a suburban Slough' and other explorations of urban life in the North of England in the year when the Yorkshire Ripper started to murder women who were not prostitutes. All these were examples of the crumbling of British urban society, a disaster generally attributed to the effects of Thatcherism.

For Cowley, as for so many others, the refuge was music and the then powerful musical press, virtually the only outlet for the feelings of the frustrated young, featuring bands which 'delighted with flirting with Fascist imagery and, like the Thatcherites, were set on breaking violently with the past'. Above all, was punk which was 'essentially a movement of working-class disaffection'. In 1977, the Sex Pistols and their mentor Malcolm McLaren provided the last, most typical and most powerful expression of the idea born far back in the mid-1950s of rock as the legitimate expression of dissent against the prevailing social consensus. McLaren himself was a veteran of the upheavals of 1968 and, typically, embittered by what he perceived as a sell-out by the Labour Party. The Pistols had it all: punk involved spit, bondage and swastikas, and its drugs of choice were not soft, but hard – glue and amphetamines. Seeing the Pistols, said one teenager, was like standing on a land mine, while Maclaren called himself the barbarian at the gates of Buckingham Palace. It was all summed up in a single song by the Pistols, combining 'God Save the Queen' with such phrases as 'A Fascist regime' and 'She ain't no human being'. This, unbelievably, was the number one hit single in Jubilee week, though it was not listed as such in the charts and, of course, never played on the BBC.

The despair so effectively exploited by the Pistols affected even relatively well-balanced kids such as Norman Cook, later to become famous as Fatboy Slim. 'Like many other boys in the mid-Seventies with too many rebellious feelings and no good vehicle through which to express them, he briefly embraced heavy metal. Like the liveliest of his generation, he was rescued [!] by punk. In September 1976 his brother brought home the first Damned album. Cook was captivated. "It was someone else who screams like I want to scream." ' Yet 'my sister said I was the most endearing, cuddly punk she'd ever seen'. But Cook 'was angry. Underneath I was seething with rebellion waiting to happen'.[19] (Over twenty years later, he remains staunchly anti-monarchist in line with the deliberately provocative rhetoric of another group, the Housemartins.)

In a sense Maclaren and the Sex Pistols were doing a necessary job since, as Sir Alfred Sherman put it, 'someone had to question the unquestioned, think the unthinkable, set our problems within a broader historical context'. For politically, wrote Cowley, it was 'the year in which the Butskellite* consensus finally began to unravel', a year in which successive crises led the small group of maverick advisers and thinkers orbiting around Margaret Thatcher and Keith Joseph to believe that history was moving in their direction, one summed up by the political philosopher John Gray as 'radical discontinuity with the past'. That year, they started publishing pamphlets attacking nationalised industries and trades unions and lauding the virtues of an 'enterprise economy'.

What became known as Thatcherism goes back to 1968, a year generally thought of as belonging to the revolutionary left. Yet it was also the year that reaction reared its head – and not only in the shape of Enoch Powell – the year that the term New Right was first used. It was also the year a brilliant young ex-Treasury official, Peter Jay, started to write in *The Times* about the new idea of monetarism and Roy Jenkins was forced to adopt monetary targets, albeit not the full doctrine of monetarism. That same year, 1968, the Institute of Economic Affairs, the cradle of Thatcherism, which had been treated as a joke since its foundation thirteen years earlier, started to publish pamphlets on trades union reform, and that before the failure of In Place of Strife. In a Fabian Society pamphlet, David Collard warned that the new generation of economic liberals were not just tired old Manchester-school liberals but must be 'respected for the quality, consistency and rigour of [their] approach to the treatment of private industry'. Keith Joseph formulated for the first time since 1945 the neo-Victorian contrast between the 'worthy poor' and the 'feckless poor' that was to become such a major strand in Thatcherite theology. To cap it all, at the party conference in October the youthful Mrs Thatcher delivered what is considered the first Thatcherite speech on 'what's wrong with politics'.

The drift in the Tory Party, the revolt of many ordinary party members which led to the election of Mrs Thatcher as Tory Party leader in 1975, had been in evidence since 1973. At the Tory conference that year, held in the middle of the turmoil caused by the oil crisis, a delegate from Yorkshire advocated what would later be thought of as a purely Thatcherite economic policy involving the abandonment of economic interference by the state. Yet in the event Thatcherism was defined not by the grass roots but by a small and unlikely band of conspirators, the only ones in that turbulent decade to have thought

* After Rab Butler and Hugh Gaitskell.

through their ideas and rendered them palatable to the political mind. The band included three people – a politician, Keith Joseph, a Unilever executive, Norman Strauss, and an ex-communist propagandist, Alfred Sherman – who could best be described as mad Jewish professors, a nuclear physicist, Terry Price, and a solid solder turned businessman, John Hoskyns, whose basic aim was to remove what he saw as the stranglehold the unions possessed on the British economy.

They knew that they were fighting on a number of fronts. For a start, continuing decline was assumed to be inevitable. For thirty-five years, wrote Hoskyns, 'academics, journalists and civil servants had been rationalising the country's decline in almost genetic terms. The thesis had been developed and polished to the point where it was impossible to think thought that did not fit easily into it' – words written in 1980, when the Thatcher government was trying to introduce cash limits to government expenditure at a time, when as Hoskyns says, 'inflation was presented [in a paper from the Treasury] as it if were an Act of God – like, say, a bad harvest'.

Even more fundamentally, they were theorising in an environment which discouraged such activities. As Ben Pimlott noted, 'British political culture looked down on theory, treating it as foreign and totalitarian. The Tories sneered at Labour for allegedly adhering to Continental doctrines, and Labour, embarrassed, sneered at its own intellectuals, calling them "desiccated calculating machines"'.[20] Attlee regarded theory as 'stuff and nonsense' while the only British Prime Minister since 1945 to have read *Das Kapital* was the improbable figure of Sir Alec Douglas-Home, who had had plenty of time to do so while he was on his back with tuberculosis during the war. Harold Wilson boasted of only having got to page two, an admission inconceivable in a left-of-centre politician in any other Western European country, but did so because of the imperative need to prove his credentials as a common man.

The key intermediary between the conspirators and the 'real' world of politics was Sir Keith Joseph. He came from a rich Jewish family but had a strong sense of public duty and understood the limits of free markets especially as largely inapplicable to welfare. He was not a pure Thatcherite by any means, indeed had founded a housing association in Paddington to help find proper housing for poor tenants of criminal landlords. Termed, not unreasonably, the Mad Monk, he combined a brilliant mind* with a very Jewish tendency to agonise over every

---

* A Fellow of All Souls, Joseph was the most important of its alumni, although not the only one, to have provided intellectual fuel for the Thatcherite revolution. Others included two future cabinet ministers, William Waldegrave and John Redwood, as well as Robert Jackson, briefly an education minister.

change of attitude, every decision. Nevertheless, even Mrs Thatcher (at first anyway) invariably hailed him as the most important guru and prophet of Thatcherism. Yet he was a one-off, 'a major politician', as Peter Clarke put it, 'whose driving ambition was not focused simply on his own advancement'.[21]

In a series of speeches, Joseph sketched out the underlying problems facing Britain and provided solutions, many of which formed both the theoretical basis of pre-triumphalist Thatcherism and the subsequent thread of continuity with Tony Blair. He had been in politics for nearly twenty years but, he wrote, 'It was only in 1974 that I was converted to Conservatism'. That spring he had helped to found a home for like-minded thinkers, the Centre for Policy Studies, which was immensely influential in the early 1980s because it provided an intellectual framework for a future Tory government that involved thinking the unthinkable about monetary controls and, above all, controlling the unions.

Yet as early as 1972 Joseph was making forward-looking speeches which could have been delivered by Tony Blair. Rights, he declared, must be accompanied by responsibilities, notably to look for work, and he went on to address the problem created by the 'dependency culture': 'We spend more on welfare without achieving well-being while creating dangerous levels of dependency.' But at the time, as he said, 'we were motivated by the desire to maintain stability at all costs. But stability can be won only by riding the waves, not by drifting with them. Stability entails controlling events, not surrendering to them. By sacrificing our ideas, our instincts, our better judgements to the quest for stability, we end up sacrificing stability to convenience.' He also tackled the problem of the 'cycle of deprivation', of the creation of an urban underclass, generally attributed to Thatcherism. For, just as sex was popularly supposed to have begun only after 1963, so the horrors of mass unemployment and social deprivation were thought only to have begun after 1979. Both suppositions were wrong.

But it was in 1974, the year Ted Heath was twice defeated by Harold Wilson, that Joseph emerged both as a prophet and as a possible successor. In one of several important speeches, he identified inflation as 'the most important issue before the country' – an issue that was 'largely a self-inflicted wound'. He called for an end to the fear of unemployment engendered in his generation 'by memories or images of the 1930s' and pointed out that 'we are moving into the make-believe economy where we make motor cars that no one wants and put three men on a train . . . when only one is needed. This is going through the motions, keeping up appearances, window-dressing a fraudulent façade . . . Monetary control is a pre-essential for everything else we need and want to do; an opportunity to tackle the real problems:

labour shortage in one place, unemployed in another; exaggerated expectations, inefficiencies, frictions and distortions.'

But he was always a man of passionate – if ever-changing – beliefs rather than a politician able to conceal his true feelings, and he destroyed his chances of leading the Tory Party in a speech in October. This contained an unfortunate reference to the idea that the lower orders ought to be encouraged to have fewer children through better birth control. 'The balance of our population,' he said, 'our human stock, is threatened.' The furore the speech aroused was, writes Whitehead, 'agony for a sensitive man whose tormented self-questioning now took in his own fitness for leadership. His marriage was rocky, his family edgy; he flinched from the exposure of which this was a foretaste.' He thus left the field open for Mrs Thatcher. In June 1974 she had told an interviewer that she 'did not expect to see a woman Prime Minister in her time'. But Joseph's withdrawal from the race forced her to stand, or at least that is how she put it. 'If you're not going to stand,' she told him, 'I will, because someone who represents our viewpoint *has* to stand.'

But the result of the conspirators' work was that the Tory Party – or at least its leadership – was far better prepared intellectually for power than any other in British history. As Paul Hirst puts it, 'The first Thatcher government was unique in modern British history: a party led by a clique of intellectuals with a strong commitment to a radical ideology'[22] – the only comparable government, Labour's of 1945, appears vague, wishy-washy and far less radical. Nevertheless this was not how the conspirators saw the situation. Before the winter of 1978–79, even Hoskyns felt that the party was 'all set to go into office only marginally less unprepared, amateurish and confused than previous Labour and Conservative governments had been'. Callaghan's own policy provided a foretaste of Tony Blair's ideas twenty years later. He had already arranged a pact with the Liberals which provided him with the support needed for Labour's otherwise virtually non-existent majority. As the Liberal leader David Steel put it, Callaghan wanted 'to play the next election as the leader of a left-wing party heading towards the centre while she (Thatcher) is the leader of a right-wing party heading towards the right.'

But even the conspirators felt afraid to start a serious public debate on the unions' power. This was far more anarchic, far less controlled by anyone (including the Communist Party) than was assumed by its opponents. In the words of Sir Denis Barnes, who had been Permanent Secretary of the Department of Employment throughout the turbulent later 1970s, the union movement 'has no institution for self-regulation of [its] activities. It has so far resisted attempts by governments to regulate its main activities by law. For these reasons it presents governments with a unique problem. The difficulties this causes for governments and the country may be too serious for the status quo to be maintained'.

The unions' dominance at the time over the Labour Party – particularly over Michael Foot, the Secretary of State for Employment, who felt that his only role was to carry out their wishes – cannot be exaggerated. I vividly remember a meeting of the Labour Party's Home Policy Committee which had to decide whether unions were to be the only bodies though which the workers' opinions could be channelled following the report of the Bullock Committee on workers' rights. At that point, David Lea, a senior official of the TUC, got up and virtually forbade any further discussion. Unions ruled, whether OK or not. Their influence was strong enough to ensure that the 1959 film *I'm All Right, Jack*, with its relatively sympathetic portrayal by Peter Sellers of a union activist, was not allowed onto the nation's television screens during the 1979 election. Yet at a local level the unions – indeed the left as a whole – could be vulnerable against a truly stubborn employer. The battles of the 1980s were foreshadowed by a strike in 1977 at the Grunwick film-processing plant in north-west London which employed mostly Asian women when pickets (including a number of moderate Labour ministers like Shirley Williams) were defeated with the help of the notorious Special Patrol Group of the Metropolitan Police.

Jack Jones and Hugh Scanlon, the dominant union leaders, were haunted by the spectre of unrestrained hyper-inflation and had delivered three years of relative wage restraint, but by 1978 even they could not restrain the restless masses below them, although they found James Callaghan more to their taste than his predecessor. 'Behind the scenes he was a fixer and a bit of a bully,' wrote Francis Beckett, 'to the average trade union official he was almost as good as one of their own.' But, continues Beckett, 'At his (Jones's) last TGWU national conference the shop stewards, who owed their power to his leadership, used it to tear him apart.' This despite his far-seeing plea for 'a shorter working week, for example, to ease the unemployment problem rather than just a total free-for-all in wages.'

In the event, the status quo was permanently upset and the Tory conspirators saved by the collapse of Labour's policy of pay restraint, which had been stretched beyond endurance. Any relaxation was naturally greeted by the cry, 'If there is a free for all, we want to be part of the all'. 'Saved by the Unions' is the appropriate chapter heading in Hoskyns's book. The Winter of Discontent – a cold one, which made matters worse – was almost as bad as Tory historians have subsequently made out. Of course, if Callaghan had called an election in September 1978, as had been expected, he could have avoided the disaster that awaited him the following May. But he didn't have the courage, waiting until virtually the last possible moment to go to the country.

During the winter the public sector unions were in the van, especially workers in the NHS, who in many cases did abandon their responsibilities, as was claimed by the Tories and denied by their supporters. Bernard Donoughue, the head of Callaghan's policy unit put it simply: 'A million and a half public sector workers went on strike, closing hospitals, schools and local authority services throughout the country. The railways came to a halt.' Union officials 'publicly and without apology or sign of compassion announced that they would not allow the sick into hospital: and an official stood before the television cameras and stated that "If people died, so be it."' [23]

The NHS, Britain's proudest post-war achievement, provides a classic case of the decay. In the 1970s, and not only in Britain, wrote Charles Webster, 'the period became characterised by the dilemma of "doing better and feeling worse"'. The proportion of national income devoted to the NHS had risen substantially, from 4.1 per cent in 1964 to 5.3 per cent fifteen years later, and staff had doubled since 1948. During the same period, the system's efficiency had rocketed, with patients staying for far shorter a time in hospital after operations, and the figures for every indication of the nation's health showed a steady improvement. Nevertheless, although Britain remained at the bottom of the health expenditure league, as she had throughout the post-war period, we continued to depend on immigrant doctors – a fifth of the total in 1979 and a quarter in the 1990s. And the historic differences in mortality rates between different classes – and regions – showed no sign of narrowing.

Yet the later 1970s showed substantial and unprecedented signs of restlessness. The first disruption in hospitals caused by medical staff since the foundation of the NHS came in 1975, when junior doctors grew angry at their combination of overwork and lousy pay. This was followed by another row, this time with the whole medical profession, when the government tried, unsuccessfully, to phase out paybeds in hospitals. Not surprisingly, as Webster says, in the last years of the decade 'the already tenuous advances enjoyed by the health service came to a sudden end and the system relapsed into a state of siege. In the last phase of the Labour government, the combined effects of cuts in public expenditure, bitter industrial relations, the tide of resentment from vulnerable groups about failure to improve their services, and the evident bankruptcy of leadership on the part of health ministers precipitated the NHS into a state of crisis and demoralisation worse than ever before or since.'

The problems of the NHS were only part of a wider crisis. But the workers involved had a case. What was never made clear, certainly not in the tabloids, was that these strikes were revolutionary gestures of total despair at the hopelessness of their lot, the knowledge that those involved could not escape from their wretched situation of low pay and poor conditions. As one activist told Philip Whitehead, 'We were beginning to frighten society. There was the small person actually beginning to climb out of the mire and say, "Hold up, I'm part of society and I've got rights." ' Such pleas were ignored for the following twenty years.

Worse, terminal indeed, was the reaction at the heart of government. Initially Callaghan had underestimated the depth of the problem, and laughed it off on his return from a EEC summit in sunny Guadeloupe (though he did not use the deadly phrase 'Crisis, what crisis?' attributed to him by the tabloid press*). 'There was a deathly calm in Number Ten, a sort of quiet despair,' wrote Donoughue. Callaghan himself was 'depressed and almost paralysed into inactivity, and he became very tired. I think his basic problem was that, having grown up as a politician working with the trade unions, he didn't know what you did when you were fighting the trade unions, and he was very reluctant to take [them] on.' As Peter Shore told Philip Whitehead, 'We were engaging [in] what I called occupational tribal warfare, as though every separate group in the country had no feeling and no sense of being part of a community but was simply out to get for itself what it could, and I thought that was terribly damaging to the Labour Movement and the whole long tradition of solidarity, of socialist commitment.'

If ever there was a pre-revolutionary situation, this was it. Yet to this day large numbers of highly intelligent people still refuse to admit that the crisis was so serious as to result, if not immediately, then in the forseeable future, in complete social and economic breakdown. Even twenty years later, the assumption that we could have continued to 'muddle through', the failure to admit that fundamental changes were required, pervades the attitudes of the majority of the chattering classes when they are faced with the contention that, without Mrs Thatcher, there would have been no future for this country at all.

Earlier in the decade there had been one observer who had perceived Britain's problems but saw that the situation was by no means as hopeless as the many cries of despair made out. The exception was the late Bernard Nossiter, the London correspondent of the *New York Times*. Nossiter wrote a shrewd, totally heterodox book called, provocatively, *Britain: A Future that works*.[24] His argument was simple: 'Far from being sick, the place is healthy, democratic, productive, as

* What he actually said was 'I don't think other people in the world would share the view that there is mounting chaos.' Which was almost equally untrue.

stable a society as any of its size in Europe. It is transforming the heritage of the industrial revolution, shedding its plants, the mills and some of the values that made them work. It is slowly becoming a post-industrial society where a decreasing number of men and women are concerned with the production of goods, and an increasing number with things of the mind and spirit – services in the economists' accounting' – albeit while it retained industries 'near the frontier of knowledge'. Nevertheless, 'more and more Britain will earn its way by trading its skill with words, music, banking, education and leisure for the products of more traditional societies.' He was not the first observer to have come to this later over-hyped but not totally unrealistic conclusion. As early as 1965, the novelist Colin MacInnes had written in the introduction to *England half English* about how 'Our industry and commerce are, by all accounts, increasingly inefficient, whereas our artists of all descriptions (including those who design male and female dresses) are not only altering our whole style of living but earning vast sums for us in foreign currency abroad. I do hope that before long some sociologist-economist will publish figures showing what sums are earned overseas by artists – beginning with the Beatles.'

But Nossiter was being rather premature and his views, so close to those of New Labour twenty years later, were so anathema to the prevailing American view of a Britain in inexorable decline that on his return to New York he was allocated a job reminiscent of a 'graveyard shift', that of correspondent to the United Nations. All that was needed, though, to start the transformation was will power – that and the belief in the future which had become increasingly rare during the previous twenty years. Unfortunately, the only person with the necessary qualities was Mrs Thatcher.

Notes

1. *The Politics of Industrial Decline.*
2. Quoted in Susan Crosland, *Anthony Crosland* Jonathan Cape 1982.
3. *Once a Jolly Bagman*, Weidenfeld and Nicolson, 1997.
4. *The 1975 Referendum*, Macmillan 1976.
5. *Ancient as the Hills*, Diaries 1973–74, John Murray 1997
6. *The Break-Up of Britain*, New Left Books, London, 1977.
7. *Guardian*, November 4 2000.
8. *Green and Pleasant Land*, Hutchinson 1979
9. *Theft of the Countryside,* Temple Smith 1980
10. *History in Our Time*, Yale University Press, 1998.
11. *Guardian*, October 222000.
12. *New Statesman*, January 23 1998.
13. *A memoir, People and Places*, Duckworth, 2000.

14. *Guardian*, August 9 1999.
15. London Review of Books, July 6 2000.
16. *The Enemy within – the Rise and Fall of the British Communist Party*, John Murray, 1995.
17. *New Statesman*, February 28, 2000
18. *New Statesman*, October 30 2000.
19. *Observer Magazine*, April 18, 1999.
20. *London Review of Books*, September 3, 1998.
21. *London Review of Books*, July 19 2001.
22. *From Blitz to Blair*, Weidenfeld & Nicolson 1997.
23. *Prime Ministers: the conduct of policy under Harold Wilson & James Callaghan*, Jonathan Cape 1987.
24. *Britain: A Future that works* Deutsch 1978.

10

The Handbag Revolution

'England's a very difficult country to move'
                          BENJAMIN DISRAELI, on his death-bed

DURING THE WEEK AFTER SHE left 10 Downing Street in November 1990 Mrs Thatcher received over 35,000 letters of support. One of the most unexpected came from the left-wing Labour MP Denis Skinner who wrote that, although he hated almost everything she had done, he none the less admired her for the fact that she, and she alone, had believed that change was possible. Skinner was right. She had refused to allow her administration to play the same role as that of her predecessors, defined by William Armstrong as 'managers of Britain's decline'. For her success was that of a triumph of the will and it is perhaps a sign of the English mentality that this phrase is automatically associated with Hitler's Nuremberg rallies, as recorded by Leni Riefenstahl. Thatcherism was not fascist, despite its enemies' claims, but can best be likened to a severe operation involving a great many side-effects and scars, some of which still refuse to heal even twenty years later. The real question is whether the operation was necessary. My own belief is that yes, there was a cancer of despair which needed eliminating, and that Mrs Thatcher's cure, for better or worse, was the only one on offer.

The key element in her success was her conviction that change was possible, rejecting the 'feeling of helplessness . . . I don't accept that. I believe we not only can, we must [change]'. Her first election manifesto made it clear she was not alone in believing that the Labour party had 'reached a dead end. The very nature of the party now prevents them from governing successfully in a free society and mixed economy'. But, she added, 'Our country's decline is not inevitable. We in the Conservative Party think we can reverse it, *not* because we think we have all the answers but because we think we have the one answer that matters most. We want to work *with the grain* of human nature helping people to help themselves – and others' – the 'and

221

others' sounds like an afterthought, while it is easy to imagine the emphasis she would have put on the words which were in italics in the original. Perhaps the most fundamental change she wrought was to replace the worship of the gallant loser – like Captain Scott, for example, or a whole succession of British post-war heavyweight boxers – which had characterised our attitudes throughout the twentieth century, with the worship of success, although both attitudes assume a zero-sum game in which life consists exclusively of winners and losers, a debatable viewpoint to say the least. Sooner or later, most witnesses realised the fundamental nature of her aims. As Phillip Whitehead wrote: 'She set off to change the whole political agenda.' 'She is,' as the Queen Mother told Woodrow Wyatt approvingly, 'a revolutionary or she is nothing.'

To achieve her simple but seemingly impossible objectives, she knew that she had to get rid of the notion that Britain was held together by a series of vague concepts such as those of fairness, decency, compromise, consensus, liberties, having one's say, tradition and community. The hitherto sacred term 'consensus' was a particular fetish. Even before she came to power, when Sir Anthony Parsons, then the Ambassador to Iran, said mildly that 'Most people in the country, including me, believe in consensus politics,' her reply was passionate and brutal. 'I regard them as Quislings, as traitors,' she said, adding, 'I mean it.' Indeed her (largely self-promoted) image, that of the housewife, wielding her broom against the institutionalised sloppiness that she – and many other people, not naturally Thatcherite themselves – felt had gripped so many aspects of British life, was not entirely inaccurate.

Her original prospectus soon proved to be fraudulent – the famous advertisement created by the Saatchis which proclaimed that 'Labour isn't working'* was followed by a decade during which unemployment tripled. To make matters worse, the fact that she quoted from Saint Francis – 'Where there is discord, may we bring harmony' etc – on her arrival in Number Ten did not prevent her being the most divisive Prime Minister in British history. Indeed, she aroused stronger emotions amongst supporters (devotees, one should really call them) and opponents alike than any other ruler, prince, king, let alone Prime Minister, in British history since Oliver Cromwell.

She was not the first outsider to lead the party. As the daughter of what the French would call a *notable de province* – a provincial

---

* According to Chris Powell (*How the Left Learned to Love Advertising* published by his advertising agency BMP DDB) – Mrs Thatcher herself was opposed to the advertisement, allegedly arguing that it would be seen as an advertisement for Labour because it had Labour in the headline.

luminary – she was of decidedly superior social origins when compared to Edward Heath, the son of a jobbing builder from the back streets of Broadstairs, although both had succeeded, by character and perseverance as much as intellectual superiority, in getting to Oxford at a time when the university admitted only a handful of pupils from outside the public and major grammar schools.

It soon became apparent that she was even bossier than she was decisive – qualities often confused in male descriptions of strong-minded women. But decisions mattered: as a result, the elaborate machinery of courts of inquiry and Royal Commissions much in favour with previous post-war administrations was treated as merely a device for delaying or preventing decisions – which, of course, is what it was. Above all, she was serious in what she did. Her mind was an irony-free zone (as is that of her spiritual successor, Tony Blair). 'One has to remember,' Willie Whitelaw once famously remarked*, 'that she has little sense of humour, and therefore if you have a sense of humour you are always slightly suspect with her.' Her seriousness inevitably led her to a deep disgust for the – to her frivolous – 1960s. 'We are reaping what was sown in the 1960s,' she told the *Observer* in 1982. 'The fashionable theories and permissive claptrap set the scene for a society in which the old virtues of discipline and self-restraint were denigrated.' She had a point. Between 1962 and 1980, the number of divorces had soared from 23,000 to 150,000 annually. One result was that by 1976 there were 750,000 one-parent families and by 1980 140,000 abortions a year – the highest rate in Europe and a sad testimony to the lack of sexual education.

Perhaps inevitably, she was a total philistine. This first found public expression in the early 1960s, when as chairman of the Art Society in her Finchley constituency she ordered the removal of a picture, a white board with a white splash on it painted by a CND and left stalwart, Jeff Nuttall. Why? To her the 'splash' was clearly an ejaculation. To the pure, as they say, all is impure. As Minister of Education, she had imposed museum charges for the first time. Yet, for all her apparently reactionary views – Stuart Hall called her regime a case of 'regressive modernisation' – she was liberal about people's personal lives. Several of her cabinet ministers, including Douglas Hurd and Nigel Lawson, divorced (Lawson to marry his already pregnant secretary), and this was an aspect of her character that she had first shown when she voted for homosexual reform soon after her arrival in Parliament.

To her faithful supporter and party treasurer, Alistair McAlpine, she was 'a great diva, difficult off the stage but pure magic when she

---

* This remark, like many quoted others in this chapter, comes from Hugo Young's *One of Us*, Macmillan, 1989.

came to grips with a great aria'. John Hoskyns, a notably sane and dispassionate witness, was surely not the only one to feel that his relationship with her was 'a mixture of affection, loyalty, frequent misunderstandings, exasperation and occasional disappointment' – closer, above all more personal and emotional, than that normally felt by associates for a Prime Minister. Typically, at one discussion she was 'as ever, passionate, at full throttle on every tiny issue – and big ones too'. She was, said Hoskyns, 'providing political leadership to the country but not management leadership to the Government. She herself broke every rule of good leadership: bullying the weaker colleagues, criticising them in front of each other and in front of their officials' – a habit which got worse over time.

Comparing her with a diva was shrewd, for she remained acutely feminine. She had, for instance, the habit of blaming other people for decisions which she disliked. These included the Anglo-Irish agreement (which she attributed to American influence*) and our entry into the European Exchange Rate Mechanism (due, she explained, to pressure from her Cabinet). When Woodrow Wyatt discussed with Douglas Hurd how he had changed her mind over German reunification, they agreed that this attitude applied to many another argument. 'She recognises that you were right,' said Wyatt. 'She never recognises that,' said Hurd, 'she just does it and behaves as though it was her idea all the time' – a trait of leaders through the ages.

All her qualities – and faults – were displayed in her attitude toward the EEC. Her re-negotiation of our contribution to the EEC budget in the early 1980s in response to a projected deficit of over £1,000 million – 'our money' as she said so often and so correctly – was a brilliant tactical victory, albeit one which displayed her usual hectoring style. As Robert Armstrong† put it, 'She was more skilful than anyone I've ever met in combining rhetoric which was faithful to her principles with policies that were totally pragmatic.' The result, as the EEC's legendary secretary-general Emile Noel told Hugo Young, was that she 'obtained much more than was reasonable'. Her style infuriated not only her European partners, especially Schmidt and Giscard d'Estaing, but also British Europeans such as Hugo Young who found her demands 'rapacious'.

In power she was by no means the true Eurosceptic she subsequently became. Rather, she was pragmatic, for instance promoting the Channel

---

* Another explanation is that it was fuelled by the kindness shown to her by Gareth Fitzgerald, then the Taoseach, when she was a newly elected and very fragile leader of the Opposition.

† Like his predecessor William Armstrong he was ennobled after being Secretary to the Cabinet.

Tunnel, albeit as a private venture, and, more significantly, accepting the single European Act, which further dug us into the EEC, and even our ill-fated entry into the European Exchange Rate Mechanism, the precursor of the single currency. But by that time even the Labour Party had come round to accepting Europe. A speech by Jacques Delors at the 1988 TUC conference converted trades unionists to the idea of Europe, so much more sympathetic and less capitalist-in-tooth-and-claw than the Thatcherite regime. The conversion ensured that the opposition to Europe was increasingly in the hands of xenophobic right-wing conservatives, who could so easily be dismissed as extremists. But by then, as Hoskyns put it, 'The European Project was already turning out to be essentially political but undemocratic, riddled with protectionism, fraud, empty rhetoric, appalling incompetence and political double-talk. In our view it was creating divisions and mistrust in Europe, rather than removing them.'

No description of Mrs Thatcher's style would be complete without stating the obvious fact that she was considered exceedingly sexy by many men: a beguiling dominatrix with long, elegant legs and flashing eyes. What's more, she knew it – and thus the use to which her charms could be put. When Jim Prior told her she sounded very sexy because she had a cold, she replied tellingly, 'I don't need a cold to be sexy, Jim.' Like many first-generation female successes, she was by no means feminist, doing less than nothing to encourage women in her government. Yet many women admired her for her gutsy success in a political world which was, then as now, overwhelmingly chauvinist – under Blair, old-fashioned condescension has merely been replaced by laddism. Not surprisingly – according to Alistair McAlpine anyway – her admirers included Marcia Lady Falkender*, who 'was very taken with the idea of having a woman prime minister in Britain' – a feeling enhanced by her own sufferings from the anti-feminist atmosphere in the Labour Party.

A natural correlation of her own sexiness was her preference for men who were smooth and persuasive, flashy rather than solid (with one exception, her husband Denis, the archetype of the devoted and dependable rock relied on by many female stars in every walk of life). As the businessman Chips Keswick told Woodrow Wyatt, 'she has a weakness for raffish characters who make or seem to have made a lot of money' – or who were simply plausible and attractive. The most obvious and extreme example was her only son Mark, of whom no one else seems to have a good word to say. As Woodrow Wyatt noted: 'A different note comes into her voice when she speaks about Mark. She obviously dotes on him. I think he is a pretty good washout. He

---

* As Marcia Williams, she had been Harold Wilson's closest political adviser.

gives a lot of trouble to his mother. She puts up with him as mothers do with their favourite son or child.' During the six days when he was lost in the Sahara on a car rally in 1981, she was caught in tears more than once. Others who received more than their fair share of favours included ministers such as Cecil Parkinson, Humphrey Atkins, David (Lord) Young (of whom she remarked, 'Other people bring me problems, he brings me solutions), Alan Clark and Kenneth Baker. According to Wyatt, 'she quite likes him [Baker] buttering her up and she says "Oh Ken" and then she lets him change something.' But getting too near could be dangerous: the attractive John Moore was over-promoted, returned to work too soon after catching pneumonia and disappeared into outer darkness (the House of Lords) soon afterwards. She also befriended non-ministerial charmers such as Woodrow Wyatt and Jeffrey Archer – though she drew the line at that successful seducer, Jonathan Aitken, to whom she never gave any kind of ministerial appointment, allegedly 'because he made Carol' – Mark's twin sister with whom he had an affair – 'cry'.

She was also traditionally feminine in enjoying a good chat to explore and validate her own feelings. On Sunday mornings, she would talk at length with a succession of courtiers, at first Alfred Sherman and, toward the end of the 1980s, Woodrow Wyatt. They would be among those invited at Christmas to Chequers, where there was a distinct order of precedence. The nearer you were to the beating heart of Thatcherism, the nearer Christmas Day you were invited. At the Christmas lunch itself the regulars included Tim Bell and his wife, the Alistair McAlpines and often Gordon Reece, her personal image maker, as well as, according to McAlpine, 'other people who were down on their luck or lived nearby'.

In western democracies great – or at any rate successful – political leaders rarely if ever come to power with a coherent political philosophy. According to his faithful amanuensis Alain Peyrefitte, even de Gaulle 'was the opposite of a doctrinaire: a pragmatist who ran a mile from abstract ideas, theory and, above all, ideology'. In cabinet he would always ask, 'So what about practicalities? What should we do?'[1] As for Mrs Thatcher, like most successful democratic politicians, she operated through a mix of gut instinct, individual prejudice, opportunism and the assumption that effective action was possible.

Despite her genuflections in the direction of such gurus as Frederich Hayek and Sir Keith Joseph, her basic policy was to pick and choose from the philosophical menus on offer. In the words of Ben Pimlott, 'Pragmatic to the core, she took up philosophers she agreed with and allowed her instincts to be dignified as an ideology'.[2] She did not necessarily take all the items on offer entirely seriously. Early in their discussions Terry Price and John Hoskyns had devised an impossibly complex diagram to describe Britain's troubles and the solution to them. When they presented it to Mrs Thatcher, she giggled and said that it resembled a piece of chemical engineering. Her basic attitude was expressed at an early meeting of her private think-tank when she declared, 'The other side have got an ideology they can test their politics against' – they didn't, but she assumed that they were all inspired by Marxist notions – 'we must have one as well.' Yet she was clever enough to use theory for her own purposes, to an extent perhaps never before employed by a British Prime Minister.

As a result, wrote Mary Warnock, Thatcherism was born of a 'hotch-potch of ideas: it was not a philosophy so much as a set of policies, not all consistent with each other but all founded on passionate conviction'. Yet the mixture of attitudes added up to a coherent view of the world: she simply wanted to be in charge of a country which was free from union dominance and provided opportunities for all. Her use of theory (and organised groups of theorists) was copied by the Labour Party, which had previously relied almost exclusively on the Fabian Society but which within a decade enjoyed the advice of a number of newly formed think-tanks.

The lack of a moral dimension in her way of thinking shocked both sides of the political divide. As the historian Peter Clarke put it, 'after the Tories had failed to find a messiah with Ted Heath Mrs Thatcher proved to be 'a more plausibly messianic figure' who 'erratically fulfilled some of the relevant prophecies by driving everyone except the money changers out of the temple'.[3] She had certainly abolished British guilt about material advance by letting the money changers into the temple and, in doing so, had forced those with more traditional British values to defend them. Many of the more arrogant members of her intellectual opponents seemed to have resented or denied the necessity of defending their values or were unable to express their opposition to 'Thatcherism' at all convincingly, usually fighting her on her ground of instinctual reactions rather than intellectual refutation.

From the right, Peter Hitchens was equally disgusted. 'In search of a guiding ideology,' he wrote, 'the Tories could come up with nothing better than the brute force of the market, whose inhuman logic of course ignores patriotism, morality, tradition and beauty.' This finds an echo in what David Marquand defined as 'economism' – 'a mixture of vulgar Marxism and bastard Cobdenism, an assumption that the economy is, in some mysterious sense, prior to society, that economic considerations should trump other considerations, that society should be tailored to fit the economy, instead of the other way round.'[4]

But to her it was the individual and, to a lesser extent, the family which counted. Her famous remark 'There is no such thing as society' was made in an interview with *Woman's Own* in 1987 and became the catch-phrase summing up the later, openly uncaring Thatcher. But family mattered, and it included those who worked for her. If you were 'one of us', she cared and clucked (and bossed) like the legendary Jewish mother. When she cried on leaving Downing Street, wrote Alistair McAlpine, he knew that it 'was for the friends she left behind at Chequers and at Number Ten'. But her social nihilism led inexorably to the destruction of any loyalty to any group, company or organisation, or to any ideal. With her famous question 'Is he [rarely she] One of Us?', she invented her own establishment .

Yet Mrs Thatcher's anarchism – or, if you prefer, her nihilism – was enormously helpful to groups who should, in theory, have been amongst her most vehement opponents, like other women, gays and members of ethnic minorities. It was particularly ironic that she, the most exclusivist of leaders should have broken down so many of the social obstacles in the way of the formerly excluded and opened their way to fame and/or fortune. Above all, she allowed the idea of opportunity for all. One statistic largely ignored by Mrs Thatcher's opponents is that during her reign the number of people – usually well-qualified and ambitious – who left Britain for Canada and Australia, the traditional havens for the adventurous, plummeted, from 42,300 in 1980 to 2,800 a decade later. She did much to replace a pecking order based largely on the accident of birth with one founded on achievement – although for her this meant exclusively monetary success.

Her idea of 'usness' certainly did not include the majority of her earlier Cabinets or the more traditional elements in the party which she led and from which she so conspicuously dissociated herself. 'I am the rebel head of an establishment government,' she once declared. In Woodrow Wyatt's words – they were about Lord Derby but could have applied to any other lordly figure – she 'requires of ancient aristocrats that they should be outstandingly good before they overcome the stigma of being aristocrats'. For she declared open war on the 'so-called grandees', the upper-class amateurs. Hers was the first ruling elite in the history of the Tory Party in which talent carried the day over birth. Twenty years on, it is easy to forget the hatred she inspired in traditional Tories (in 1940 Churchill had faced a similar hostility, before he, like Mrs Thatcher, became an iconic figure for his party). According to Alistair McAlpine, they hated her 'hair, hated her voice, hated her accent, and indeed many of them hated the whole idea of her. Along with the feminists, they disliked her because she had achieved the leadership of the Tory Party whilst asking for no concessions as a female'.

So it is not surprising that in practice she was just as exclusivist as the most snobbish of her predecessors. Her exclusion zone included most of the members of the Cabinet she was saddled with after the 1979 election as well as anyone who, like Sir Ian Gilmour, represented the compassionate, civilised, pre-Thatcherite, One Nation Toryism. She transformed the Tory party. Similar to the entryism of Labour's militants was that of the *garagistes*, the second-hand car salesmen and their like, who had backed her and whom she represented so well. The term was coined by the witty and ultra-wet MP Julian Critchley who said, quite correctly, that her rise to power was the result of what he called a 'peasants' revolt' – a phrase which accurately summed up the attitude of the Tory hierarchy to their party members. But, confronted by a leader to whom you had to stand up and argue back, Critchley and his kind were helpless: 'We've always been brought up to believe that it's extremely rude to shout back at women.' Inevitably, those who could cope with her best had been brought up by their mothers and not by that fearsome breed, the old-fashioned nanny.

But she didn't care. She felt instinctively that she incarnated a General Will which she alone, rather than any organisation, represented without reference to the bodies to which she was nominally responsible. As late as 1988, when all internal opposition to her rule had long been crushed, Woodrow Wyatt could say, 'It's funny that she remains the only real opposition to her own government. She sometimes looks on them as though they were an entirely different group.' As a result, although both major political parties suffered from her revolution, she merely ensured the transformation of the Labour Party, while she effectively destroyed her own party through turning it into an instrument of her increasingly dictatorial rule.

'Class,' she told *Newsweek* with characteristically sweeping inaccuracy, 'is an invention of the communists.' If so, it had proved very useful for previous Tory leaders. In the 1950s it had been the deferential working classes, and above all their wives, who had voted Tory. Under Mrs Thatcher, the situation was precisely the opposite. Even before 1979, the British working class, formerly solidly proletarian and with no such thing as success, financial let alone social, on their horizons, had been evolving. A survey of social changes which the Macmillan government had commissioned in 1962 pointed out that 'the only certainty to be drawn from the 1950s seems to be that Britain could not lapse back into working-class poverty, as during the 1930s. The average man now has much more to lose, and has made too great an investment in his own future as a middle-class citizen and householder'. Later, another study found that nearly a quarter of the working classes had moved up in the decade after 1972. They had first been identified by the market researcher Mark Abrams as early as 1961. He pointed out that the Labour Party was losing 'ambitious people, middle-class people, young people, office workers and scientists', so out of date was its image even then. For there had been numerous shifts in Britain's class system, even before 1979. In 1964 the working class was nearly three times the size of middle-class groups; by 1983 the two groups were of nearly the same size.

Instinctively, Mrs Thatcher took advantage of the aspirations of the 'average man' of the survey and in doing so enormously widened the fundamental divide within a class which the Labour Party at least imagined to be still solidly proletarian. On the one side was a new and appalling mass of victims, true proles without jobs or prospects, living in conditions not really superior to the stews of Victorian London, without hopes – albeit with television sets, which merely rubbed in the existence of an increasingly comfortable majority. On the other side came the mass of the more ambitious natural Thatcherite supporters, unprecedented working-class success stories often summed up as 'Essex people'. The term came to stand for a class hated equally by both sides of the political divide: they were newly independent, did not stand on rank or privilege, saw no limits to the money they could earn or spend. 'Essex girls' attracted particular attention and jokes, none of them particularly tasteful*. They were also supposed to be badly educated – an error easily refuted by the fact that girls' schools within the county regularly figure as enjoying the best results of any in the country. They naturally attracted the hatred of Labour traditionalists because they had escaped from the working-class ghettos of the East End of London. And for obvious, snobbish reasons they also engendered a colossal condescension from high Tories such as the commentator Simon Heffer, who had however to acknowledge that Essex Man's trading skills made him eminently employable as 'the direct descendant of Adam Smith'.

Their rise is generally symbolised by the menacing figure of Norman, later Lord, Tebbit and included entrepreneurs such as Alan Sugar, who exploited his 'trading skills' to tame the personal computer and introduce it into millions of households. More fundamental symbols were the songwriter Ian Dury and the writer Julie Burchill. Dury, an intelligent and gutsy star, never allowed his severe polio to interfere with a singing career which included hymning such heroes as 'Billericay Dickie'. Burchill, who worshipped her father, an unrepentant communist, also appreciated Thatcherism as a liberating force. It was based, she wrote, on 'clever working- and lower middle-class children who were bullied simply for being bright by their clod-hopping con-

* Typical was the nickname given to the tunnelling machine used in digging the Jubilee Line under the Thames to the Millennium Dome. It was called Tracy, one of the Christian names (like Sharon) associated with Essex girls. Why the name? 'She comes from Essex and she goes all the way.'

temporaries. Scratch a Thatcherite and find an outsider ... it leaves one with very little fellow-feeling or loyalty to the lower classes, believe you me'. And it was the mother of another future journalist, Suzanne Moore, who remarked, 'Suzanne's reading, she's a bit depressed.' Significantly it was Essex which showed the way the political wind was blowing. Under Mrs Thatcher all fifteen seats in Essex went Conservative. Later, once Labour had lost Basildon in 1992, I knew they were doomed. By contrast, in 1997 fifteen of the seventeen* went Labour.

It was that distinguished immigrant, Ralf Dahrendorf, who perceived the change most clearly, lamenting that 'the beautiful balance which held the country together has been upset. Social rabies, at least, has invaded Britain's shores'. This he attributed to the 'decline of the acquiescent middle class of old, or rather the rise of more aggressive middle-class groups which demand their place in the sun and espouse unfamiliar values'. The Thatcherite middle class was 'located socially right on the boundary between blue-collar and white-collar groups. What it wants is economic progress ... In a sense this somewhat undefined class – or is it an assemblage of unrelated individuals? Indeed, is it all of us to some extent? – is the modern version of the Victorian middle class. It is dissatisfied, therefore striving for new horizons'. I do not know of a better definition of Thatcherites, Thatcher and indeed Thatcherism.

It was the 1987 election that best showed the size, location and nature of her support. Throughout the south of England, manual workers voted more heavily in favour of her than the electorate as a whole. Labour, which had enjoyed much the same support eight years earlier, was now trailing more than a dozen points adrift. She received the same level of support amongst the first-time buyers of shares who had lapped up profitable offerings in such companies as British Telecom. The Thatcherite working class, and not only those in Essex, spent the money they earned, assuming that they could always go out and earn more; there was none of the traditional English feeling that 'they don't make money any more', that money was a zero-sum game. This attitude was shared by immigrants, and it is one of the major paradoxes of Thatcherism that it was she, the most narrowly British (or rather English) of prime ministers, who most openly welcomed foreigners, provided only that they were 'one of us'.

In early 1978 she had spoken of people's fears that 'the country might be rather swamped by people with a different culture'. Afterwards she told a shocked friend, 'It was what people thought, so why

---

* The country's ever-increasing population meant that the county had gained two more parliamentary seats in the meantime.

not say it?' Her understanding of the underlying mood stopped dead the rise of the British National Party in the late 1970s. But there was one major exception – her extremely positive attitude towards Jews. This can be traced back to her childhood. Her sister Edith had as a pen friend a Jewish girl in Vienna who passed through Grantham on her way to the United States on a scheme run by Rotary International. In her memoirs Mrs Thatcher does not mention Edith but does say that she knew that Adolf was up to no good when he suppressed Rotary Clubs. Nevertheless this did give her the opportunity, denied to all but a handful of English children, to learn about the results of Hitler's policies at first hand. Moreover, her doctrine of self-help struck a chord with Jews, which was just as well since one in five of her constituents was Jewish. This gave rise to her only recorded unscripted joke when she was being shown round Tel Aviv by the British Ambassador, the late Sir John Barnes, who explained that there were a great many poor Jews. 'Not in my constituency, Sir John, not in my constituency' was the instant riposte, though, on reflection, she may not have meant it as a joke.

From the start, many of her advisers – not only the conspirators but also the Saatchi brothers who directed the party's advertising – had been Jewish, but the earliest beneficiary of her approval was the Chief Rabbi, whom she raised to the peerage as Lord Jacobovits. He believed profoundly in self-help, in duty, not rights. He was also obviously grateful that Mrs Thatcher had eliminated, albeit by deeds rather than words, the lingering taint of anti-semitism that had hung over the Tory Party for a century or more. Before Mrs Thatcher's arrival Jewish Tory MPs such as Sir Gerald Nabarro and Robert Adley (né Adler) had had to conceal their Jewishness. Nevertheless even Jacobovits was not a pure Thatcherite. In his first speech to the House of Lords he had called for tolerance towards asylum-seekers: 'Remember that we are all, each one of us, temporary residents on this planet where we have to learn the art of living in harmony before our visa expires [surely a parallel which could only have occurred to a representative of an insecure deracinated race] and we are called on to migrate to another world.'

But as her rule became more personal, so did her reliance on what might be termed 'court Jews' – mostly courtiers glad to be of use, though there were exceptions: Nigel Lawson went his own way as Chancellor of the Exchequer. But one of Mrs Thatcher's later cabinets was sneered at by a necessarily anonymous but not untypical Tory toff as composed of 'more Estonians than Etonians'. This remark exposed perhaps the most fundamental change in British society over the past twenty years – the absorption into British society, and the increasing importance, especially economic, of immigrants, either of the second generation, like the Jewish members of Mrs Thatcher's cabinets, or the first generation of Asian newcomers. This phenomenon represented not only a triumph for Britain's (relative) capacity to absorb newcomers, even if they were not white; it also provided a long-term boost to the stock of native entrepreneurs.

Harold Wilson's 'kitchen cabinet' of intimate advisers had been largely composed of court Jews who depended totally on him for their access to the corridors of power – and some, like Lord Kagan and Sir Eric Miller, were crooks. One of Mrs Thatcher's later cabinets included Malcolm Rifkind, Leon Brittan and David Young as well as Lawson. Things had changed so far that when another Jewish minister, Michael Howard, was attacked, it was not because he was of Jewish descent but because he was so creepy (remember the accusation by his erstwhile colleague Ann Widdecombe that there was 'something of the night' about him).

Despite – or, perversely perhaps because of – her intellectual crudeness, Mrs Thatcher attracted a surprising number of writers and intellectuals, including some erstwhile Labour supporters, such as Hugh Thomas, whom she ennobled, and Kingsley Amis, who loved her for her iconoclasm. More typical of even the most open-minded, established intellectuals was Mary Warnock, philosopher, former head mistress, charter member of the Great and the Good. Warnock had begun by admiring her for her ability to handle interviewers ('such as the snaky and clever Brian Walden'), her 'determined out-facing of the unions', and even her down-to-earth attitude to the British economy.

But soon Warnock's own attitude, like that of the majority of outsiders who came into contact with Mrs Thatcher, turned into exasperation and then into downright loathing. This change in attitude was largely thanks to her habit of hectoring her audiences at great length, permitting no interruption. Universities were a particular target, with Warnock finding herself on the receiving end of a rant about 'their arrogance, elitism, remoteness from The People, their indifference to the economy, their insistence on wasting time and public money on such subjects as history, philosophy and classics'. As a result, 'Thatcherism in education meant a philistine subordination of scholarship to the immediate demands of vocational training'. Equally legitimately, Warnock and her husband, himself a distinguished philosopher, agreed in denouncing her 'appalling rudeness' and 'deep philistinism, amounting not just to a failure to understand but a deep hatred of culture, learning and civilisation'. Mrs Thatcher not only did not like or encourage other women; she behaved in a decidedly unladylike way, as witness the way she systematically monopolised any discussion. Yet Warnock's attitude also reflected the Puritanism still inherent in the British intellectual – she admitted that she had never 'felt entirely at

233

ease with women who use a lot of make-up'. So she inevitably hated Mrs Thatcher's 'gaudy clothes and her now rampant hairdressing. New suit, electric blue with fitted jacket, metal buttons and big lapels . . . this suit expressed directly, like a language one had always known, the crudity, philistinism and aggression that made Margaret Thatcher's character'.

The snobbery, the exclusivity, implicit in Warnock was explicit in Noel Annan, who expressed perfectly the old way of thinking in his attack on John Carey's book *The intellectuals and the masses*, which, he alleges, was responsible for 'politicians like Margaret Thatcher and Tebbit who were to enjoy clipping the dons' wings': 'Men and women can rise to their own merits; but, if they are honest and reflect, how many will admit that someone – a friend of the family, a teacher skilled in writing testimonials or an employer or senior colleague who took a shine to them [sic] – gave them their chance.' In other words, don't work, network.

Such criticisms were as nothing compared with the gut reactions of the vast majority of the literate, academic and creative, who came to be called the chattering classes, a typically reductive term. They felt that the country was occupied by an alien force, an attitude which echoed that of Evelyn Waugh and his like at the triumph of prescriptive Puritanism under the post-war Labour government. In the 1980s intellectual snobs attacked Mrs Thatcher because she was so obviously Not Like Us, and such opposition was not confined to the cabinet or London's more exclusive clubs. It was encouraged by Mrs Thatcher's intellectual crudity, which was totally alien to intellectuals who characteristically love ambiguity, uncertainty. This hostility emanated from the British equivalents of the French 'intellos' who, with far less justification, had almost universally rejected General de Gaulle twenty years earlier. In 1988 a group of intellectuals headed by the rightly respected historian and biographer Ben Pimlott went so far as to found a magazine called *Samizdhat*, as if Mrs T's government was the equivalent of those in communist countries which imprisoned, tortured and killed dissidents.

Some critics went even further. Famously, Jonathan Miller found the Prime Minister 'loathsome, repulsive in almost every way', singling out her 'odious suburban gentility and sentimental, saccharine patriotism, catering to the worst elements of commuter idiocy . . . Why hate her? It's the same as why the bulk of the human race is hostile to typhoid'. To Alan Bennett, she was a typical opera-goer, 'a genre that absolves you from thinking', while the playwright Peter Nichols claimed, not unjustly, that she spoke for taxi-driver Tories. In 1985 she received the ultimate insult, an unprecedented refusal by her alma mater, Oxford University, to grant her an honorary doctorate – significantly, the scientists rejected her even more emphatically than dons from the humanities. There were many elements in the opposition, especially hatred of her insistence that universities existed solely to help business – a Green Paper had called openly for higher education to serve the national economy 'more effectively'. It was fuelled by her meanness to the universities (although this did not, of course, affect Oxford, with its enormous capital resources, too greatly).

But a good deal of the opposition had a strong element of hypocrisy in it. Lord Goodman stated that he was 'violently opposed to greed, and [I] consider it objectionable that certain people are able to make fortunes without any form of control'. This was rich coming from a man who had a band of Friends of Arnold whom he tapped regularly for substantial contributions to whatever causes he happened to be pursuing at the time and who had generally made their fortunes through greed.

Mrs Thatcher's many and varied opponents had one important element in common: none of them ever came forward with a convincing analysis of how and to what extent things had gone wrong and proposed any other policies – she was right when she talked of TINA: There Is No Alternative. Moreover, Mrs Thatcher enjoyed nothing more than a battle – as Douglas Hurd observed, she 'was happiest when she was up against the wall'. As she remarked to that faithful Yorkshire bulldog, her Press Secretary Sir Bernard Ingham, after one particularly bruising battle: 'The thing about you and me, Bernard, is that neither of us is [sic] smooth people.'

Her first and most important battle, which ended with the 1981 budget, was to convince everyone – especially her own party and the cabinet – that she was serious, that she would not be deterred from her chosen course by rising unemployment and deep unpopularity. But she had to move slowly, if only because she started her reign with a classic old-line Tory Cabinet which included seven Etonians, all of whom were wets, supporters of Macmillan and Heath. As a result, wrote the journalist Hugh Stephenson after her first year in power, 'Her rhetoric is radical, even reckless. But from the start her deeds have shown a politician's instinctive caution' – most obviously in the acceptance of a settlement in Rhodesia crafted by that ultimately snobby grandee, Sir Christopher Soames, a deal which handed over power to a Marxist revolutionary, Robert Mugabe. For, as Phillip Whitehead put it: 'The years 1979–81 are now only seen as an epilogue for the Seventies and the old tradition of Tory paternalism.'

Economically, her first two years were disastrous. The 1979 budget, presented by her first Chancellor, Geoffrey Howe, a mere month after the election, continued the strict monetary squeeze first applied by the Callaghan government after the IMF's intervention in 1976. The major

235

difference was that it was now housed within a theoretical framework, that control of the money supply was all that mattered. The problem, as Charles Goodhart of the Bank of England had pointed out, was that once you judge the results by one measure of that elusive commodity 'money', the stuff escapes into another category. At the same time personal tax rates were dramatically reduced, with the top rate dropping from 83 to 60 per cent, a step which Hugo Young, a typically 'wet' commentator describes, as 'the first of many massive gifts to the rich which remain one of the enduring deposits of the Thatcher years'. In reality it was a sensible move, since the previous top rates were both punitive and ineffective, ensuring that anyone with a high income spent most of his time thinking of ever more ingenious ways of avoiding tax. More revolutionary was the doubling of the main indirect tax, Value Added Tax, to an unheard-of 15 per cent, a regressive step which did far more towards tipping the balance of taxation against the poor than reducing the top rate of income tax.

Economically, the budget proved a disaster and merely exacerbated the problems created throughout the industrialised world by the second oil crisis. It caused interest rates to leap, and with them the value of sterling, a double whammy that crushed much of British industry, which was frail at the best of times. In her first two fraught years monetary growth was nearly double the target rates, GNP actually fell by 2.5 per cent whereas in the rest of Europe it rose 5.3 per cent, while unemployment shot up from 5.6 per cent in 1976 to 9.8 in 1981 and 11.2 per cent at its peak in 1986. Nor did she and Howe do any better with their proclaimed aim, to reduce the tax burden on Britain's tax-payers: between 1979 and 1983, the government's tax take rose from 34 to 40 per cent of GNP. They were burdened by the acceptance of a report by Sir Hugh Clegg which set out to compare pay in the private and public sectors and resulted in a rise of £1.25 billion in public sector wages. 'We had,' wrote John Hoskyns with typical moderation, 'started out our long journey towards financial stability with a spot of unintended destabilisation.'

The helplessness of a government sworn not to prop up the many lame ducks of British industry was dramatically demonstrated by none other than Sir Keith Joseph, who was Minister for Trade and Industry. After much agonising, some of it at the Cabinet table, he was forced to provide more money for nationalised industries than any of his predecessors. His budget at the Department of Trade and Industry actually increased to the unprecedented figure of £3.3 billion in two years. Some of the money – like that on steel – was spent sensibly, and some, as he himself was the first to admit, foolishly, notably that on British Leyland. Yet the first two years of the government saw an unprecedented reduction in the number of jobs in manufacturing industry thanks to a fatal combination of the oil crisis, the overvaluation of the pound, high interest rates, the underlying lack of competitivity which plagued so much of British industry, and the new-found ability of management, above all in nationalised industries, to shed workers. But Mrs Thatcher remained undeterred by the open hostility of much of her Cabinet and by a depth of unpopularity among the voters not plumbed by a British Prime Minister since Neville Chamberlain in 1939. The 1980 Tory conference saw her defiant cry of 'You turn if you like, the lady's not for turning'* and the following spring she and Howe doubled her financial bets.

In 1981 she followed her instincts. Taking the advice of outsiders rather than the Treasury, Howe brought out a strict, deflationary budget designed to reduce the burgeoning budget deficit by £3,500 million, through increases that included a higher tax on cigarettes as well as 20p on a gallon of petrol. 'By increasing taxes at the bottom of the recession,' wrote Whitehead, 'the Chancellor served notice that . . . Keynesian reflation was dead.' 'The budget,' wrote Jock Bruce-Gardyne a notably 'dry' commentator, 'formally abandoned the pretence that full employment and economic growth were in the gift of government.' Indeed it amounted to a programme of re-education that unemployment was not the be all and end all of economic policy, as it had been since 1945. Mrs Thatcher knew perfectly well what a risk she was running, for the increase in indirect taxes tightened the squeeze. But when she met her new-found economic guru Sir Alan Walters, she said simply, 'You know, Alan, they may get rid of us for this,' but she added, 'at least I shall have gone knowing I did the right thing.' The budget was naturally greeted with almost unanimous opposition. No fewer than 364 economists wrote a letter to *The Times* prophesying the end of the economic universe at such a flagrant disregard of the orthodoxy that had prevailed since 1945, while the Director-General of the CBI, Sir Terence Beckett, talked of a 'bare-knuckle fight' with the government.

They were wrong: in the following two years (helped, it has to be said, by the reaction to the overvaluation of sterling as a petro-currency after the oil shock of 1979) the value of the pound dropped by over a quarter and interest rates subsided. The economy – and with it Mrs Thatcher's ratings – did start to improve, though not quite as sharply as was claimed (our rate of unemployment continued to rise faster than in any other major industrialised country, although by 1986 France had the same percentage of unemployed as Britain). In fact, by then the country was in the middle of seven years of uninterrupted growth,

---

* A phrase obviously chosen by one of her speechwriters, the playwright Sir Ronald Millar, echoing the title of a play by Christopher Fry, *The Lady's not for Burning.*

albeit starting from a very low point, for as late as 1987 industrial production had barely returned to its 1979 level. Yet, even after the relative success of the 1981 budget and Mrs Thatcher's triumphal re-election in 1983, as Hoskyns says, officials could not believe that the policies of the first term, in which considerations of financial stability overrode that of unemployment, would be continued into her second term. They were, unashamedly and without a second thought. By the time she was thrown out in November 1990, it was clear that though there had been nothing like a Thatcherite economic miracle, she had cleared many of the obstacles for sustained economic advance in the future – though not Britain's educational backwardness.

All the time the government was battling against a stark demographic fact: that the numbers entering employment had risen by 1.5 million in the last half of the 1970s at a time when the number of workers in employment had barely changed. In 1980 the economist Douglas Hague pointed out that 'to hold unemployment down to 1.5 million by 1990, Britain would need two million more jobs in the next decade. Yet the number of jobs today is less than in 1966'.

Like all successful leaders, Mrs Thatcher was lucky, never more so than in 1982 when the Falklands War erupted and she decided to fight a sea battle eight thousand miles away for a handful of forgotten islands. If the 1981 budget was the equivalent of the first battle of El Alamein, which in the summer of 1942 stopped the advance of German forces in North Africa, then the Falklands War was the equivalent of the second battle a few months later, which provided Montgomery with his famous victory and provided convincing proof of the offensive capacity of the British army. For Mrs Thatcher, the Falklands War was the opening of a golden age. Her Argentine opponents may have been an incompetent bunch of thugs led by General Galtieri and their Exocet missiles may have proved unreliable, but Mrs Thatcher was gutsy as well as lucky. And her courage was rewarded with soaring ratings in the polls. We are apt to forget that, despite the recovery after the 1981 Budget, had it not been for the invincible aura which surrounded her after the Falklands War and the suicidal feebleness of the Labour Party, she and the Tories might have gone down to defeat as a result of the devastation wrought by the second oil crisis of 1979 – as did Chancellor Schmidt in Germany and two Presidents, America's Jimmy Carter and France's Giscard d'Estaing. Indeed, the Democrats did not regain the White House for twelve years, while in Germany Schmidt's successor Helmut Kohl lasted for sixteen and in France Francois Mitterrand for fourteen, although the right recaptured the premiership in 1986. But only in Britain did the crises result in any fundamental upheavals in society and the economy, proof that the system was already much less firmly founded than that of other countries.

The golden age of Thatcherism lasted a mere four years, between the Falklands War, which established her authority, and the Westland affair four years later which left Mrs Thatcher with a (not entirely unjustified) feeling that she was untouchable. The saga of privatisation shows clearly the limited ambitions of the newly elected Thatcher government in 1979 and how slow was the introduction of that most Thatcherite of policies. Even in 1980, wrote Hoskyns, 'I tended to under-estimate the significance and potential of privatisation.' The first privatisation, of a small scientific company, Amersham International, was very tentative, but the second, that of the National Freight Corporation, was more ambitious. Furthermore, it was the only one which involved a genuine element of worker participation – many workers were deterred from investing by their union's opposition, which rebounded when the shares rose (unfortunately the experiment did not last more than a decade). But privatisation did not really get into its stride until 1984, with the privatisation of British Telecom, which raised £4 billion.

Unfortunately, the privatisation process was conducted by a hermetically sealed unit within the Treasury, its only contact with the City being Sir Michael Richardson of Rothschild's, who was naturally anxious to ensure that the issues got off to a good start even if the shares were priced ludicrously low, thus providing investors with substantial guaranteed profits at the tax-payer's expense. But Richardson was only reflecting City opinion. At one dinner party, Nigel Lawson, who had replaced Howe as Chancellor, was struck by the way that bankers and industrialists alike 'roundly declared that privatisation was impossible: the capital market simply was not large enough to absorb it'.[5] Hence the low prices, hence also the enormous sums of money poured into the advertising campaigns for the BT and subsequent issues. To make matters worse, the strategy involved selling off the entire capital too quickly, whereas later and cannier privatisers such as the Japanese Ministry of Finance issued their shares in smaller lumps, thus taking advantage of rising prices. But the whole process was a dramatic demonstration of the transformation in Tory attitudes.

Macmillan's famous remark that the policy smacked of 'selling the family silver' was very revealing – and not only because of Mrs Thatcher's reaction, that 'unlike the Macmillans, she didn't have any family silver to sell'. It also implied that the nationalised industries were passive assets, not commercial and industrial activities, capable of generating profits.

The Falklands War, and above all Mrs Thatcher's post-war triumphalism, did bring into the open the most important, most principled and indeed most effective opposition to her rule, that of the Church of England and, above all, its Primate, Robert Runcie. The clash was

239

inevitable: any Christianity worthy of the name involves institutional-ised selflessness, whereas at the heart of Thatcherism lay institutional-ised selfishness and hers was the first and only exclusively materialist government Britain had ever known. Runcie's attitude was echoed by the unusual ecumenical partnership in the devastated city of Liverpool between the Anglican David Shepherd and the Catholic Derek Warlock – although the church's hostility found its most extreme form in the attitude of the Bishop of Durham, David Jenkins, a theological radical and sturdy supporter of the miners' strike.

The church's radical stance was in sharp contrast to its previous relative quiescence. To be sure, Canon John Collins of St Paul's and his wife Diana had been at the centre of a group of social and political radicals such as Archbishop Trevor Huddleston and Michael Scott (both Anglo-Catholics), but their influence over opposition to apartheid and the work of such organisations as Oxfam, Christian Aid and Chris-tian Action lay primarily abroad – it was assumed that the welfare state could take care of the problems of poverty in Britain. Nevertheless the Samaritans were founded by a priest, Chad Varah, and individual priests were active in organisations such as Shelter. But although these move-ments were tolerated by the church, they were never integrated into the fibre, let alone the administrative structure, of the Church of England 'as by law established'. Typically, Nicholas Stacey, the radical Rector of Woolwich, resigned as a priest in 1965 to work full time for Oxfam.

The next year Eric James, a leading radical, had to admit that 'little broad support existed within the church for a radical movement' – the premature death of Archbishop William Temple in 1944 had blighted the dreams of those who had hoped that the church could be associated with liberal social causes. Stacey's action found an echo when Father Charles Davis left the Catholic priesthood in 1968 because of *Humanum Vitae*, the Papal bull which condemned birth control. But the tragedy of the pill went wider, wrote the Catholic historian Adrian Hastings, himself a Roman Catholic. It 'was a tragedy of a whole generation of able priests – perhaps the ablest the Catholic Church in England ever had – who went down leaderless between Rome and their people, but it was the personal tragedy too of John Cardinal Heenan' – who could simply not comprehend the despair and ended his archi-episcopate an embittered man. Heenan's successor at West-minster, Basil Hume, appointed in 1975, was the first Catholic Arch-bishop to be a paid-up member of the British establishment. He had been educated at Ampleforth, the poshest (and best) of Catholic schools, and at Oxford, his brother-in-law was the secretary to the Cabinet and he himself was able to bring the church closer to the British people – and not just their leaders – than any of his predecessors, through his humility and plain speaking.

The first warning shot fired by the churches came in 1980 when that unlikely forum, the House of Lords, defeated a proposal to introduce charges on school transport. Opposition from such figures as Lord Soper, a socialist Methodist, was only to be expected, but opponents also included the Duke of Norfolk the hereditary leader of the Catholic community, and Lord Butler, the architect of the 1944 Education Act. Hostilities broke into the open at the Thanksgiving Service in St Paul's following the Falklands War. Before the service Mrs Thatcher had let it be known that she was firmly opposed to mentioning, let alone remembering the Argentine dead. But Runcie spoke out. 'In our prayers,' he intoned, 'we shall quite rightly remember those who are bereaved in our own country and the relations of the young Argentinian soldiers who were killed . . . Ironically it has sometimes been those spectators who remained at home . . . who continue to be most violent in their attitudes.'[6] This was a clear rebuke to jingoistic attitudes like that of the *Sun* which had distinguished itself with headlines such as 'Gotcha' when the *General Belgrano*, an Argentinian warship, had been sunk outside the exclusion zone which, in theory anyway, limited the battlefield. Next day the *Sun* wrote of 'Maggie's Fury: insult to the heroes' and right-wing MPs lashed out at 'pacifists and cringing clergy'.

Runcie, though, couldn't remotely be described as a wimp since he had earned a Military Cross while serving in the Guards, where he had been known as 'Killer Runcie'. But he attracted wide support: 'Compare,' wrote Adrian Hastings,[7] 'what church leaders had to say about the First World War and what they aid about the Falklands War; it would be hard not to prefer the latter.' Moreover, letters to Runcie ran seven to one in favour of his sentiments and included one from the Queen's Private Secretary thanking him 'most warmly for the sermon' and expressing her admiration for the way in which he met the formidable challenge.

In the eyes of the Thatcherites, Runcie became a Thomas à Becket figure. But there was one notable exception: William Whitelaw, her only link with the toffs and normally the most loyal of supporters. He had been a tank commander in the same regiment as Runcie, their friendship consummated in the fighting in Normandy. It is legitimate to speculate as to whether Runcie was also speaking for Whitelaw. Hostilities intensified further following the very different reactions by church and state to the urban riots that were a natural consequence of the turmoil of the early years of Mrs Thatcher's reign. The riots started in the largely Indian West London suburb of Southall in 1979, spread to the St Paul's quarter of Bristol the next year and to Liverpool and Manchester (Toxteth and Moss Side respectively) in 1981. Among the worst were those in the black London suburb of Brixton, where there

241

was a massive demonstration of the alienation felt by London's black community enraged by the SUS laws which enabled the police to stop and search anyone – and their choice fell overwhelmingly on blacks. Brixton exploded after a police operation called Operation Swamp, which was largely racially driven. In the subsequent riots even fire engines and ambulances were attacked and 279 out of 2,500 police were injured.

The Minister for the Environment, Michael Heseltine, followed the older, more compassionate Tory tradition by visiting the afflicted areas and starting 'inner-city initiatives'. He was the least 'usish' of all Mrs Thatcher's Cabinet ministers: he was a natural Thatcherite because he had been so successful a businessman, but at the same time he was a traditionalist in that he believed you had to make serious money before you could venture into serious politics. By contrast, in her party politi- cal broadcast after the riots in Toxteth, Mrs Thatcher appeared in a carefully tended beehive hairdo with a bowl of flowers to her side, not deigning to mention the problems. This was a classic case of her total lack of interest in the problems of 'them' and their violent reac- tions to her policies. In addition, when she was questioned in Parlia- ment, she refused to admit any connection between unemployment, social deprivation. and any of the riots.

The riots resulted in a report 'Faith in the City', commissioned by Runcie on the damage done to inner cities. The report was a product of the 'liberal' establishment – it had been triggered by a House of Lords debate on a report on the 1981 riots written by a senior judge, the liberal Lord Scarman. It was the work of a distinguished Archbishop's commission consisting mostly of laymen, academics, theologians, social workers, a headmaster, a senior trades union official, clergy laity and a 'significant black presence', and was written by the distinguished, mildly radical Professor A. H. Halsey. 'It is our considered view,' the commission reported, 'that the nation is confronted by a grave and fundamental injustice in the Urban Priority Areas.' Above all, it found 'a profound sense of alienation, experienced by so many residents, not least the young . . . the underlying factors are the same everywhere – unemployment, decaying housing, sub-standard educational and medi- cal provision, and social disintegration'. But, the document concluded, 'We have found Faith in the City'.

The Thatcherite reaction came even before the report had been published – a classic case of the old Welsh rugby tactic of getting your retaliation in first. Mrs Thatcher's own reaction was to compare the Church of England unfavourably with 'the later report of the Jewish community on *their* approach'. 'The Church of England seems now to be run by a load of communist clerics,' thundered John Carlisle, an MP best known for his sterling support of the South African apartheid regime. The *Daily Telegraph* denounced its alleged 'intellectual inadequacy' while, wrote Adrian Hastings, 'The popular press in general denounced it as the work of a group of misguided clerics led by the archbishop'[7] – though Lord Scarman, who had triggered the investigation, declared flatly that it was 'the finest face-to-face analysis and description of the problems of the inner city . . . that we have ever seen'. As a result of the report, the Archbishop set up a church Urban Fund which raised £18 million to be spent in the most deprived areas. Later in the decade, the church's opposition to the poll tax led to more recriminations. 'Oh, the bishops,' Mrs Thatcher told Woodrow Wyatt 'with a long-drawn out sigh', 'I think it would be better if they were disestablished.' The Queen, that well-known Marxist sympathiser, was happy to become the Urban Fund's patron. She was also clearly at odds with Mrs Thatcher – and Tory commentators like Peregrine Worsthorne – in being influenced by her Commonwealth friends in favour of sanctions against South Africa, so much so that Robert Harris could remark in the *Observer* that 'the Sovereign and her heirs are old-fashioned "wets" who would find no place in the present Cabinet'.

But Runcie was the exception to the rule that most of Mrs Thatcher enemies were ineffective, partly because they were so self-deluding in believing that no fundamental changes were required. None were more so than the Labour Party, whose Long March through the desert of political impotence lasted eighteen years, a period lengthened by the unique ability of prime ministers to call an election at any time of their choosing, but above all by the near-suicidal behaviour of the party in the immediate aftermath of the 1979 election – a period during which membership of the party plummeted from 666,000 to 277,000 and had barely risen above that mark a decade later. These figures were emphasised by the slump in voting intentions: in January 1981, 46 per cent of the electorate was pro-Labour, a figure that had halved by the end of the year, a decline unprecedented in British political history and one which, more remarkably, occurred before the Falklands War. By the 1983 election the figure was a mere 27.6 per cent – yet, even in 1959, when Macmillan achieved a parliamentary majority of over a hundred, the Labour vote was nearly 44 per cent of the total.

The Labour Party's near-suicide was the direct result of the upheavals in the membership discussed in the previous chapter. Four leading moderate Labour politicians, headed by Roy Jenkins, left the party in 1980 and formed the Social Democratic Party with the explicit aim of 'Breaking the Mould of British Politics' – a clear impossibility given Britain's first-past-the-post electoral system. The combination of their defection, on top of the 1979 election defeat, was, as the ex-minister Peter Shore told Whitehead, that the Labour Party was 'tearing itself in the frantic search for scapegoats . . . [it was] as though

243

there was a kind of organised system of betrayal built into the Labour Party's parliamentary representation'. The resultant neo-Stalinist purification process extended to include even such distinguished figures as Sir William Gray, who had been Lord Provost of Glasgow from 1972 to 1975. Gray had been one of the first civic leaders to insist that housing estates should have proper facilities such as shops and clinics, and had been an early champion of the rights of Glasgow's Pakistani and other immigrant communities. None of this counted when he became involved with an independent hospital. He was duly expelled from the party.

Inevitably, the moderate Campaign for Labour Victory was outgunned by the Rank & File Mobilising Committee which brought together all the numerous left-wing groups generally termed as 'Bennites', named after the charismatic but hopelessly unrealistic figure of Tony Benn – once, as Anthony Wedgwood Benn, a politician so moderate that he had even supported advertising on the BBC. A new, cockeyed election system devised in 1980 ensured the election as leader of Michael Foot, the most hollow and pathetic figure ever to have headed a major British political party. Though, like Benn, a brilliant parliamentary orator, he had opposed a number of attempts to increase the real powers of Parliament. These included reform of the House of Lords in the late 1960s, Bills of Rights and, more recently, the creation under the aegis of Norman St John Stevas – Mrs Thatcher's first leader of the House of Commons and the first member of her Cabinet to be sacked – of a proper group of parliamentary select committees, each shadowing an individual department.

The divisions within the left were shown when Foot appointed as the party's general secretary Jim Mortimer, a trades union official and former communist, who had run the Advisory Conciliation and Arbitration Service when Foot was Minister of Labour. Mortimer attacked Militant because they were neo-Trotskyists whereas he represented an older Marxist tradition. The Bennites even shocked the unions, seeming to want only their block votes, behaving like the most retrograde Labour leaders of the 1940s and 1950s. 'For the Communist Party,' wrote Francis Beckett, 'a decade of carefully edging the unions leftwards had been thrown away by people who thought the revolution was going to come if only they could force through a few bureaucratic changes in Labour Party procedure.'

The only ray of light was that Denis Healey had defeated Tony Benn, albeit by a tiny margin, in the vote for deputy leader. 'Labour,' said Healey, 'has remained a party and has not dwindled into a mere sect.' But it did not seem like that in 1983, when Labour received only 670,000 more votes than the Liberal-Social Democratic alliance – though, as always, the first-past-the-post election system ensured that Labour retained over 200 seats while the new alliance won only a measly twenty-three. As John O'Farrell put it, 'There are various ways that can lose a party votes in elections. You might have a leader who does not look like prime ministerial material, you might have a manifesto that alienates many of the electorate' – Labour's in 1983 was described as 'the longest suicide note in history' – 'you might have a hostile media, you might appear hopelessly divided as a political party, or your campaign might be poorly organised and unfocused. Or, like Labour in 1983, you might manage all of the above.'[8] To make matters even worse, Foot had fought a campaign, in Paul Hirst's words, 'well suited to the 1880s speaking to the faithful in Labour clubs throughout the country'. He ignored television and subsequently wrote a book putting the blame for Labour's defeat on the media* . He would not allow research of any description, relying on the ecstatic reception he received at rallies of the faithful. Indeed, it was not until 1985 in the aftermath of the miners' strike that the new leader, Neil Kinnock, was able to start reconstructing the party, but even he was not electable, even in 1992.

In fact, it took Mrs Thatcher's deep hostility to the Greater London Council to start the conversion of the left to the power of professional political persuasion. The GLC's far-sighted leader, Ken Livingstone, hired an advertising agency which produced effective posters in a campaign which made Mrs Thatcher seem silly and leaden-footed and which greatly enhanced his reputation. For he was the one Labour politician who understood the shape of the future. He was openly inclusivist, bringing gays in particular into the open political arena for the first time. (Earlier in the decade there had been a disastrous civil war at a by-election in Bermondsey in South London when the retiring MP, a tough, indeed thuggish trades unionist, Bob Mellish†, had campaigned actively against the Labour candidate, the gay liberationist Peter Tatchell, and thus ensured the party lost what had been a safe seat.) Livingstone's flair, his populism – for example, his transport campaign Fare's Fair – made him the only Labour politician whom Mrs Thatcher feared, since he was such a brilliant spokesman for Them. As a result, she ensured that the GLC would be abolished, leaving London for over a decade as the only major city in the world without a city government – and when some authority was restored in the late 1990s, Tony Blair and his court used every dirty trick in

---

* The left remained relatively unsophisticated about the relative importance of different elements of the media – the late John Smith took a great deal of persuading that the upmarket *Newsnight* was not the most watched programme on British television.

† Mellish once described his local party as 'a nice lily-white party'.

the political book in a farcically unsuccessful campaign to prevent 'Red Ken' from regaining his legitimate throne.

The Labour Party's sheer out of touchness with many of its former supporters was demonstrated most dramatically by its opposition to what was probably the single most popular and certainly the most genuinely redistributive of Mrs Thatcher's policies: the right-to-buy policy of selling council houses to their tenants, 1.6 million of them in the fifteen years after 1979, 200,000 in 1982 alone. By 1991, nearly 15 million people, two-thirds of all households, owned their own homes, compared with four million, a mere quarter, at the end of the war and just over half when she came to power. In contrast, by the end of her reign, the proportion of those living in council housing, which had reached nearly a third of the population in 1979, was down to 18 per cent, the same as in 1951. But there was a difference: forty years later the occupants, by and large, were the most deprived members of the population, living mainly 'sink' or 'dump' estates. As Paul Harrison put it: 'If the inner city is like a chemistry lab full of dangerous social reagents, the dump estate is the test tube where they are most corrosively combined.'[9] In fact, the path towards a third way between private ownership and council housing had been shown in the 1970s, when the improbable figure of Lord Goodman chaired the Housing Corporation, which was designed to provide funds for the individual Housing Associations that were largely to replace council house-building in the last twenty years of the century, often in conjunction with private developers.

More predictable, and just as damaging, was the Labour Party's refusal to support any measure bringing democracy to the trade union movement. It is difficult to exaggerate the universal fear of the unions prior to Thatcher's reforms. Before 1979, Ian Gilmour, that most thoughtful and wettest of the wets, had asked whether 'we even need to change union behaviour at all'. In fact, their strength was concentrated in what might be called 'interconnected' or 'time-dependent' industries such as motor vehicles, the ports, the press and television, where either a product was assembled from components from a great many factories or it was valueless if not marketed on time (in the motor industry the problem was accentuated because British manufacturers tended to go in for 'single-sourcing' – getting a component from a single supplier – whereas their Continental competitors would spread their requirements amongst a number of them). But the problem was not as great in industries in which manufacturing plants were separate units as they were in GEC where Arnold Weinstock could pursue a 'divide and rule' policy with considerable success. But the problem loomed large in the eyes of the media because the press and television were so badly affected by what were known as 'Spanish practices', which amounted to massive feather-bedding and ridiculously strict demarcation of jobs. The battle was fought on two fronts, legislative and on the ground. As it was, the much-heralded anti-union legislation was at first slow and tentative, largely because Jim Prior, the minister responsible, was a true wet: the first of Mrs Thatcher's Employment Acts, that of 1982, was mild enough, merely providing public funds to compensate workers sacked as a result of closed-shop agreements.*

Then a ruthless ultra-Thatcherite, the skull-like Norman Tebbit, took over from Prior. Tebbit had left school at sixteen and had subsequently headed the British Airline Pilots' Association, indeed was the only union leader ever to have been Employment Secretary in a Tory government. In 1984 came the crucial Trade Union Act, which provided legal immunity for strikes only after a ballot had been called. The Act was followed later in the decade by three more pieces of legislation preventing unions from stopping members from crossing picket lines and strengthening the barriers against closed shops. As Prior said in an interview on Channel 4, 'Tebbit actually got his legislation through, again a good deal more quietly than I would have expected.' For the change in the country's mood in the six years after 1979 appeared 'almost inconceivable . . . The union leaders had vastly exceeded their authority in the eyes not only of the public generally, but also of their own members'. But these measures were lumped in with others that were far more socially harmful and removed legal protection from low-paid workers and the under-eighteens. It was a clear demonstration of the 'institutionalised meanness' which was one of the most striking features of Thatcherism. After all, the first inkling of her mind-set had come during her stint as Minister of Education, chiefly remembered for her abolition of free school milk and the cry of 'Margaret Thatcher milk snatcher'.

Tebbit himself claimed that all he had done was to return control of the unions to their members through the compulsory democratisation of their structure. This was true, for in themselves his changes were not unreasonable, merely brought the unions within the country's legal structure and were soon accepted. But the acceptance was grudging and owed more to increasing unemployment, and Mrs Thatcher's total indifference to its level, than to the contents of the legislation itself. Most of the unions lacked the will to fight. In a significant decision, in December 1983 the TUC made it clear that its members would not support the print unions in their vicious fight against the attempt by Eddie Shah to print his papers in Warrington without the National Graphical Association, the hitherto all-powerful grouping of the most skilled print workers. By the end of 1984, the majority of members

* These ensured that non-union members could not be employed.

247

of the Amalgamated Engineering Union were demanding the money made available for them to call ballots before strike action.

But there was one union which was never going to take the new laws lying down. The central battle of the 1980s, and the one which put the final seal on Mrs Thatcher's success, was the miners' strike, which dominated the news in 1984 and 1985. For Mrs Thatcher (and many other people) Arthur Scargill, the president of the National Union of Mineworkers, was the embodiment of the 'enemy within' which she found 'more difficult to fight and more dangerous to liberty' than external foes. The battle was intensely personal: when the Queen visited *The Times* during the strike, she observed to Paul Routledge that she thought it 'very sad' and after a pause added, 'It's all about one man, isn't it?' HM never spoke a truer word.

The depth of the feelings involved and the power of Scargill's personality ensured that the battle was far longer, far more bitter and far more suicidal than could have been imagined even a few years earlier. Apart from ruining the industry, it killed off 'proletcult' and finally established 'management's right to manage', which was the central tenet of Thatcherism so far as business was concerned. Even more significantly, it eliminated one of the fixtures in British political life, the power of the miners and the sympathy with which they were generally regarded. It was a class conflict not only between the miners and the authorities. Thanks to Scargill, the war – there really is no other word for it – was far more ferocious than any other labour dispute in British history, including the upheavals involving the triple alliance of miners, dockers and railwaymen just after the First World War and the 1926 General Strike. The battle degenerated into a battle between miner and miner, sometimes from the same pit, in which violence, and not just on the picket lines, became a daily event. The battle spread over much of the country, for the police stretched their rights to include systematic stop-and-search policies on motorways touching the strike-affected areas. Even MI5 was involved and probably had a double agent at the very heart of the union.

It was above all a fight on principle. Scargill's central aim was to safeguard the jobs of miners and their children, while Mrs Thatcher wanted not only management control as well as vastly reduced subsidies, even though the government's contribution, £4 a ton, was less than a third the amount paid by the French and German governments (but because our coal industry was far larger, the total cost was greater). Scargill was fighting against industrial history: over the years after nationalisation the dearest wish of the miners, it was said, 'was that their children should not have to follow them underground'. Indeed, the number of miners had already fallen by over two-thirds from the figure of 700,000 just after the war. It had been Alf Robens, a former

Labour minister, who had closed most pits in the 1960s. Unlike his predecessors he had shut down some because they were not economic, and not simply because they had exhausted their reserves of coal. This was a policy – one which was continued by his successors in the 1970s – that inevitably radicalised the miners and provided Scargill and the left with a continuous stream of opportunities to protest against pit closures.

At first, Scargill had the support of the majority of the miners, who felt that these closures were a rundown too far. Even more important, most of the left rallied to the cause. This was not surprising: after the 1983 election, Labour's lowest point since 1931, Scargill appeared to represent the only meaningful opposition to the Thatcher regime. The coal strike, and the support it received, can be explained only in the context of the desolation of the time. Scargill's charisma and his oratory, combined with the despair felt by so many people on the left, helped radicalise the creative classes.

But there was a flaw within Scargill. As Adeney and Lloyd point out, 'fatally for the miners' Scargillism was based on its founder's unlimited admiration for Arthur (A. J.) Cook, the very similar personality who had led the miners to a crushing defeat in 1926. Both men had been in the Communist Party and both were passionate, spellbinding public speakers. But Scargill could rely on the loyalty of his deputy, Mick McGahey, a communist who had been manoeuvred out of the presidency by Joe Gormley, Scargill's predecessor. McGahey was the archetypal communist-realist who had tried to make nationalisation work. Like any other sane union leader, he would have contrived to negotiate an organised retreat in the face of Thatcher's pressure. He would thus have kept the NUM and the industry in being and able to take advantage of such new techniques as fluidised bed combustion (this greatly increased the efficiency of coal-fired power stations and enabled them to use poorer and thus cheaper coal than had previously been possible). But Scargill's agenda was overtly revolutionary – to wrest power from the state, the NCB and anyone else so that the industry could be run by the union he incarnated. As Adeney and Lloyd observed, unlike any previous union leader, he 'did not keep his Marxism separate from his union practice'.

But Scargill was no ordinary Marxist: unlike other Marxist union leaders, he was not well versed in Marx or Marxist literature. And although he was for a time a member of the Communist Party (and was notably unaffected by events in Hungary in 1956), he left the party under mysterious circumstances – basically because he would never accept discipline (another consequence, and one of which he was fully aware, was that he could never have been an MP). In short, he would leave any organisation he could not dominate, be it the

Communist Party or the TUC. For throughout his life Scargill was a loner – refusing to compete, refusing even to take the 11 plus examination. He had no friends, only disciples, worshippers even, and he demanded total loyalty, total control.

He was utterly ruthless, even with employees at the NUM, whom he treated abominably by ignoring them when he moved the union's offices from London to Sheffield. He carried his solitary ways into his public life. Unlike his predecessors, he never negotiated, he threatened. 'In the privacy of the committee room,' wrote Paul Routledge, 'he could be petulant and overbearing, demanding his own way like a spoilt child.'[10] Yet 'behind the bluster and the mask of self-belief', Routledge continued, 'one feels, lies the little boy who was bullied in the school playground, the sensitive lad who doted on his mother, and was smothered with affection in return.' He was not a sociable being but a workaholic Puritan in an industry where both sides had been fond of endless cigarettes and beers and whisky late into the night. By contrast, he drank red wine, lager or even a small sherry on the rare occasions on which he joined 'the lads'. His solitary superiority was also demonstrated – greatly to the NUM's disadvantage – in his refusal to co-operate with the TUC, an organisation which he assumed would follow him blindly. When the TUC refused to help the print workers who were fighting Eddie Shah, he called it 'the biggest act of betrayal in the history of our movement'.

Scargill's actual experience as a miner was limited to three adolescent years, but he soon started to think of himself as a man of destiny. His first practical step towards domination was when he was placed in charge of delivering coal to miners. He soon became a highly effective 'compensation agent' acting in miners' claims, starting his first battles against right-wing union leadership at pit level and being elected to his first committee post at the early age of twenty two. He soon learnt to exploit the media – especially television, providing a sort of showbiz excitement in a world dominated by heavy-set grey men in suits. In the early 1970s, when unrest in the industry culminated in the battle for Saltley Gate, Scargill was the fluent voice of Yorkshire militancy, and the Thatcher government fully understood the step-change represented by his election to the leadership of the NUM.

He was first faced by Sir Norman Siddall, a well-respected coal industry veteran who had to take early retirement because of a by-pass operation that had gone wrong. Siddall made the obvious case that pits accounting for 12 per cent of output lost £250 million a year – 70 collieries were losing £10 or more for every ton of coal they produced. In his first year as President, Scargill lost a ballot over the closure of a Welsh pit as increased redundancy pay lured many miners out of the industry – 8,100 redundancies grew to 18,000 in 1983–84 as twenty pits closed, and twenty-one more were to follow with the loss of a further 21,000 jobs. Siddall relied on a policy which had served the NCB well since 1945. This involved a gradualist, piecemeal approach based on the tacit assumption that closures were inevitable, and it operated on a local level. But Scargill elevated everything to the status of a national argument, one that inevitably risked the fate of the entire industry.

The argument soon became a war with the deliberately provocative appointment of Ian MacGregor, previously head of British Steel, as chairman of the Coal Board in 1983. MacGregor was regarded, not unreasonably, as Mrs T's hatchet man brought in to close as many pits as possible. Born in Scotland, he had made a brilliant career in the United States, mostly in mining and especially coal. When he took charge of British Steel Corporation in 1980, it was a classic case of an industry that badly needed rescuing. In the 1960s and 1970s its capacity had been built up at a time when – largely because of inferior quality – it had only a half of a home market which was itself shrinking, as indeed was that in much of the rest of the world. By 1977, it was losing £450 million a year. MacGregor presided over British Steel for three years, during which jobs had been cut from 150,000 to 85,000. These swingeing cuts were only made possible because of the workers' exhaustion after a long and eventually pointless strike in early 1980, and because they were backed by a coherent and highly effective management team led by 'Black Bob' Scholey and other executives who had worked for United Steel, one of the best-run companies in British business.

But the miners should have noted one crucial point about Macgregor: that he was not merely a butcher. Within a few days of his appointment at British Steel, he had established a line in the sand, of an annual production of 14 million tons, a level which was far higher than the government had expected, even though it involved continuing losses. At the end of the 1970s, it had required 250,000 steel-workers to produce 20 million tons of steel, in 1980 166,000 to produce 14 million. By 1988, when BSC was privatised – a success story unimaginable eight years earlier – 51,000 workers were producing 14.7 million tons, and by 2000 a mere 33,000 were producing 13 million. The most startling contrast was in Sheffield, famous for its special and stainless steels and as the setting for *The Full Monty*, that cinematic hymn to the destruction wrought by Thatcherism. By the end of the century the metal-working industries in this stricken city employed only a sixth of the numbers who had worked in them in the 1970s, yet production had fallen by only a sixth.

But so far as Scargill was concerned, it was only the sackings Macgregor supervised that mattered. Hostilities started in October 1983 with an overtime ban against a pay offer and plans to close 70 pits. The timing of the strike could not have been worse. After 1973, in face of the quadrupling of the price of oil, there had been a drive for production at all costs. But demand dropped sharply in the early 1980s as the Thatcher slump, which affected above all heavy industries such as steel which were by far the biggest users of coal, drastically reduced demand for electricity.

Scargill had been defeated over a strike against pit closures, and an overtime ban had proved ineffective. Nevertheless his oratory had ensured the loyalty of a cadre of militant shop stewards. Scargill, aching for a strike, insisted that no national ballot was required, that under Rule 41 of the union's constitution individual regions could call their men out with or without a ballot as their rules dictated. In using this pretext Scargill virtually guaranteed civil war within the union and the defection of less militant areas – most notably, the more than 25,000 miners who remained at work in the Nottingham coal field – which was to provide the key to the strike's eventual defeat. Divide and lose: he and his supporters had failed to grasp the fact that miners had changed, that they were now relatively young and well-paid, with cars, houses and mortgages. Inevitably, it was difficult to move men with such bourgeois habits.

The strike started in a rather muddled fashion through a dispute in South Yorkshire and the proposed shutdown of the Cortonwood pit. From the start the Yorkshiremen – notoriously militant and with records of low productivity unjustified by the state of their pits – fought against any miners who continued to work. And 'fought' is the right word. Many previously sympathetic onlookers were horrified by the regular television news pictures of miners intimidating everyone in sight, not just working miners, and not only at the mines or mining villages but also – until the police instituted regular road blocks – along the roads leading to the striking areas. This so disgusted the great mass of the British public that they condoned the violence shown by the police in return for the bricks, stones and other missiles hurled at them. Indeed, the battles were so fierce that it was a miracle that only three people were killed. The atmosphere was not helped by press hysteria led by the *Sun*, which published a picture of Scargill saluting his supporters from an angle which made it look as if he were giving the Nazi salute.

The divisions were not confined to the coal fields: union was pitched against union, and a substantial proportion of the Labour Party – as well as many sincere radicals – backed the strikers to the bitter end. Furthermore, many workers in other industries would have agreed with one miner when he said that this was perceived as the decisive battle for the whole of British manufacturing industry. 'If the pits go,' the miner said, 'the steelworks go . . . the car industry goes . . . you're not talking about 70,000 jobs' – hence that powerful emotive slogan, 'Coal not Dole', which implied, by no means inaccurately, that in the prevailing employment climate, there would be precious few jobs for any workers, and not only the miners, to go to.

But, for all the activity, there was little planning and communications on the NUM side were chaotic, largely a by-product of Scargill's control freakery. Hence the failure to picket the all-important coal-fired power stations, an oversight which was based on the assumption that blocking railway access to pits and power stations would be enough. It wasn't, though, since it ignored the number of unemployed lorry drivers available to the NCB to carry British coal from working pits and foreign coal from the ports. Both lines of supply continued largely unhindered. Moreover, the government machine was well prepared for a strike, for Scargill had drawn an entirely misleading lesson from Saltley Gate. Whitehall – and not only the Thatcher government – had taken the opportunity to devise a new organisation to deal with civil emergencies. As early as 1978, Nicholas Ridley, that most realistic of Thatcherites*, had drawn up a plan for the battle the Shadow Cabinet knew it would probably have to fight. At the power stations supplies were built up, not only of coal but also of chemicals such as chlorine and hydrogen whose absence had crippled the supply of electricity in 1972. At the same time the Central Electricity Generating Board greatly increased the ability of its power stations to use oil instead of coal. The NUM simply ignored these clear preparations for a long struggle because the government had had to give way to the miners in 1981, a defeat which merely made it the more determined to prepare properly for what it knew would be the decisive battle against union power.

Not only was the government well organised but it also had in Peter Walker, the Minister for Energy, an ideal leader. He was a brilliant manipulator of public opinion and a notorious 'wet'– which helped to avoid the impression that this was a purely 'Thatcherite' operation – who had remained in the Cabinet after the 1983 election only after being offered the Energy portfolio. He, like Thatcher, had been deeply scarred by the defeats of the early 1970s when they had served together in the Heath administration. Walker refused to be seen to intervene in the strike or to allow the NCB to exploit the new labour laws – he was all too aware of how Scargill could be transformed into a martyr – but instead relied on the common law, combined with detailed daily tactical meetings providing the latest information on every detail, down to the holiday rotas of the railwaymen manning a vital signal box in the Derbyshire coalfield.

* He warned her, for instance, not to privatise the railways.

253

To borrow a phrase, Walker played a defensive blinder. His calm was needed as MacGregor showed himself wobbly and his negotiating tactics were by no means impeccable. He was also surprisingly moody, prone to both occasional bouts of uncertainty and far more frequent gaffes springing from his total inability to deal with the media and his conviction that hard facts would always be triumphant in any argument. At a late stage in the strike, MacGregor was however stiffened by the arrival of a most improbable figure, David Hart, a fanatically libertarian property dealer who set up residence in Claridge's hotel and, or so it seemed, directed the NCB's policy and tactics from that convenient command post.

Scargill's decisive defeat occurred at the Orgreave coking plant on the outskirts of Sheffield on June 18 1984, by a weird coincidence the 169th anniversary of the battle of Waterloo. He had assumed that Org-reave was as vulnerable as Saltley Gate had been twelve years earlier. It wasn't. Where Saltley was a constricted site, Orgreave sprawled, and where the police in 1972 were not prepared for battle, those in 1984 decidedly were, and had brought riot shields, snatch squads and horses along to ensure victory.

Violence continued to rumble throughout the summer and autumn and reached a peak on November 12 when, not coincidentally, 2,000 men returned to work in North Derbyshire, in marked contrast to what the area manager described as a 'long lonely summer'. The flow greatly increased with the promise of substantial bonuses for those working at Christmas. Early in the New Year, the CEGB was comfortably able to cope with the largest demand for electricity ever seen in Britain. By that time, too, Scargill had fallen foul of the law. As Mr Justice Nicholls remarked, officials of the NUM persisted in 'regarding the laws of this country as applicable to others and not to itself' in refusing to allow that NUM members had individual rights against the union. Scargill got into further trouble when he tried to whisk the NUM's funds abroad to save them from sequestration (as Lord Briginshaw had tried to do with the funds of NATSOPA in the 1970s). Nevertheless support, in kind as well as money, came from a wide and often touching variety of sources, demonstrating just how far the 'Coal not Dole' theme had touched the consciousness of the country.

By March 1985, even Scargill had to admit defeat and the miners returned to work, marching defiantly behind their bands. It was the end of mass, militant unionism in Britain. As one NUM leader put it, 'I don't think you will ever see the like of it again. There isn't another industry which could do it.' The return to work was traumatic. Rout-ledge describes how 'the upswelling of hatred and despair in Yorkshire ... beggared description. Mass pickets ranging from a few hundred to 6,000 gathered to halt the drift back – which was now more of a surge. More than 850 police offices were injured and hundreds of pickets were hurt.' Scargill had conducted 'a strike that would put all others in the shade, costing some £6 billion, lasting almost one year, leading to 10,000 arrests of miners, 1,000 injuries, three dead, a hundred pits closed and 100,000 jobs lost, the splitting of the once mighty NUM, and deep social unease.' It is by no coincidence that the sub-title of Lloyd and Adeney's book on the strike is 'Loss without Limit'. The dispute effectively destroyed the British coal industry. It also badly hurt both the railways, by showing how effectively lorries could move even the heaviest of loads, and the steel industry, by reduced home production and allowing in ever-increasing imports.

In the year after the strike, 40,000 miners left the industry. In the short-term the board managed to increase productivity – by 24 per cent over the pre-strike level – and thus averted a total meltdown in the face of a sharp fall in the price of oil. The industry was finally killed by the fact that, as the chairman of the Electricity Council pointed out in 1986, the price his industry was paying for coal was fifty-five times what it had been before the war, while the price of electricity had risen only nine-fold. The pressure from the electricity industry, by far the coal's biggest customer, inevitably increased when it was privatised later in the decade.

But Scargill remained seemingly unaffected by the misery he had caused his members. In 1987 he moved into a much grander house costing the then immense sum (especially in stricken Yorkshire) of £100,000 at a time when, wrote Routledge 'all around the country his strike-shattered members were being put out on the street by the building societies'. Worse was to come in 1990, when the *Daily Mirror* revealed the foreign origin of much of the miners' funds and how much he had spent without reference to anyone else. For he had received money not only from the Soviet Union – that was only to be expected – but also from Colonel Gaddafi, and this less than a year after the murder of PC Yvonne Fletcher by Libyan 'diplomats' had shocked all Britain.

All this was revealed by the sequestrator who had taken charge of the union's assets, which included nine bank accounts of which the biggest held £1.8 million. Yet Scargill continued to refuse to recognise that he had done anything wrong in unilaterally seizing control of the union's assets. There remained a few loyalists: Paul Foot, a well-respected investigative journalist and a leading light in the Trotskyist Socialist Workers Party, castigated the *Mirror* for the 'worst case of chequebook journalism' he had ever known. As late as May 1991 Ken Loach, the well-known film director, accused the *Daily Mirror* and the TV programme *The Cook Report* of a 'deliberate and uncorroborated smear campaign' against Scargill, claiming that the accusations

255

they contained were in line with the new face of the Labour Party being formulated under Neil Kinnock.

There was a last spark of the old sympathy towards the miners in 1992, when Michael Heseltine tried to shut a further thirty-one mines with the loss of 30,000 jobs. Popular support from Middle England – showing the depth of sympathy so recklessly squandered by Scargill – and the threat of another strike ensured that the decision was rescinded. But this was only a reprieve, even though Members of Parliament proposed a sensible package that included the reduction of imports of French electricity and of heavy, ultra-polluting emulsion from Venezuelan coal as well as a cut-back in open-cast mining. By the end of the millennium there were a mere 13,000 miners employed in the British coal industry, down from 287,000 sixteen years earlier, and even their jobs were not secure. Yet Scargill boasted of the disaster as a self-fulfilling prophecy. 'His long march,' wrote Paul Routledge, 'has left a small army of disillusioned, and sometimes embittered, supporters by the wayside.' Routledge was one of them, for the strike, or rather Scargill, deradicalised much of lefty Britain – Dr Kim Howell, the brains behind the South Wales miners, was perhaps typical: he later became a 'moderate' Blairite minister. The defeat also got the Labour leader Neil Kinnock off the hook because he was no longer obliged to back union militancy. By the 2001 General Election Scargill was leading his own party, the Socialist Labour League, while virtually all his erstwhile left supporters, including Paul Foot, were united in a more serious grouping, the Socialist Alliance.

When Rupert Murdoch moved his papers to Wapping to break the power of the print workers, Routledge, like many other journalists, felt that the miners' struggle was 'also the struggle' of those who refused to move. The battle of Wapping followed much the same course as the miners' strike, but without any of the public sympathy for the workers (though there were hundreds of forgotten, and totally innocent, employees such as the librarians and the secretaries who suffered alongside the print workers). But Wapping did have a major positive result. Many of the 'refuseniks', the journalists who refused to move, went off to provide crucial support for the City Editor of the *Daily Telegraph*, Andreas Whittam-Smith, as he founded the *Independent,* the first serious new daily paper for a century and a half. These two victories were over very different situations: the miners were defeated by the unreality of their leader, the print unions by the grotesque feather-bedding they had enjoyed for half a century or more. Neither situation was typical of management-union relations in British industry, but the battles did ensure that no other group of workers would challenge the power of management – or the government.

The year Scargill admitted defeat was an *annus mirabilis* for Mrs

256

Thatcher, though it did not seem like it at the time, for the pound fell to near $1 and was only saved by massive deposits from the ultra-rich Sultan of Brunei. But the most remarkable and most untypical event of the year – and indeed of the whole Thatcher reign – was the Anglo-Irish agreement, in which, for the first time, a British government admitted the government of the Republic of Ireland into a partnership to try and solve the problems of Ulster. The agreement was the more remarkable because in 1979 one of Mrs Thatcher's earliest supporters, Airey Neave, had been blown up by Irish republican terrorist – the same year that Lord Mountbatten had suffered the same fate. Indeed, she had declared that she would never deal with terrorists – whose number included hostage-takers in the Lebanon and even, in her view, Nelson Mandela. And then, in October 1984, she had had the narrowest of escapes from a bomb planted by the IRA in the Grand Hotel Brighton during the Tory Conference which killed one of her ministers and permanently paralysed Norman Tebbit's wife.

Four years earlier, she had refused to respond to the IRA's demand that its prisoners should be treated as political prisoners. This led to hunger strikes, and she would not give in even when these ended in ten deaths which provided the Irish republican movement with some useful martyrs. The victims included Bobby Sands, who had been elected as a Westminster MP while in gaol. Because the hunger strikers – who were compared to the revolutionaries who had seized the Dublin Post Office at Easter 1916 – had caught the imagination of previously hostile Catholics on both sides of the border 'the republican leadership', as Professor Paul Arthur told Hugh Carnegy, 'had to start moving from being a conspiratorial organisation to a democratic organisation of some sort. It was a huge shift in attitudes. There would have been no cease-fire, no Good Friday agreement, no ministers ready for government, without it.'[11] For the IRA and Sinn Fein adopted a new slogan of 'a ballot box in one hand and an Armalite in the other', a move which was to lead, over fifteen agonising and deadly years later, to a peace agreement when Sinn Fein agreed to participate in the government of Ulster, thus recognising British rule over the province, a denial of its basic beliefs. All of which leaves a major question unanswered. Had a less intransigent British prime minister given in to the hunger strikers, would the change have happened or would the IRA have continued merely as merely an armed group and not the formidable political force into which it developed in the following fifteen years?

There was one more, improbable, trauma to come – the row that blazed up over the future of Britain's only helicopter company, Westland. Mrs Thatcher wanted it to go into partnership with the Americans, while her Minister of Trade and Industry, Michael Heseltine, a confirmed European, wanted to join with the French and the Italians. In early 1986 the row blazed up, Heseltine stormed out of cabinet, shouting 'I hate you', and for a few weeks it seemed that Mrs Thatcher could be toppled. Neil Kinnock, however, was too nice a man to put in the knife and she survived. By then all her enemies had been conquered – Galtieri, the 'wets', the unions, the Labour Party. Perhaps inevitably, her revolution, like many before it, became corrupted by laziness, success, greed, dishonesty and, above all, its leader's megalomania.

By the mid-1980s, wrote John Hoskyns, 'it must have been almost impossible for any of her advisers or colleagues to play the role of candid friend' – the last straw was the departure of Willie Whitelaw in late 1986 after he had suffered a stroke. For her last battle, which she inevitably lost, was against her own instincts. The first external sign came at the 1987 election – which she won despite Kinnock's success in stabilising the Labour Party – when she referred contemptuously to the 'sentimental slop' being talked about the unemployed. Even loyalists were disgusted: Peter Cropper, a highly valued former adviser to both Howe and Lawson at the Treasury, wrote to Howe about this 'loathsome administration'. By April 1988, even the ultra-loyal Woodrow Wyatt 'got a hint that she seemed to think nothing she does is wrong or open to doubt'. Her loyal treasurer Alistair McAlpine had retired, partly because of ill health but also because he felt that Central Office had been corrupted with 'senior officials in Tory Central Office who were in the pay of businessmen and promoting their interests'.

Outsiders realised she was decidedly barking when she announced 'We are a grandmother' at the birth of Mark's first child, for she was clearly losing any touch with reality. As she told the party conference, 'In 1979 we knew that we were starting a British revolution; in fact we were the pioneers of a world revolution.' Then, at the bi-centenary of the French Revolution, she announced to the startled French public that the first real revolution had been British, the Glorious Revolution of 1688.

Her biggest, most arrogant blunder was the poll tax, levied on individuals and designed to replace the rates levied on dwellings. This was the fulfilment of a long-cherished dream. In 1974, as a shadow Treasury spokesman, she had announced that she would abolish domestic rates. Idiotically she tried out the new tax in Scotland, an unpromising test area since by 1987 the Conservatives had lost half their seats and only held one in seven of the country's constituencies. Only the most loyal Thatcherites ever talked of the community charge rather than the poll tax, for it was a tax on people replacing a tax on property and so offended all the instincts of a population who expected taxes to be fair. It also delivered a further blow to her own class, the small

258

business people whose taxes were due to rise. She had indeed lost touch with her roots. Even Nigel Lawson saw clearly what a disaster the tax would be. He instituted inquiries within the Inland Revenue and these showed that the tax would be largely uncollectable. Armed with this – as it proved, accurate – advice, he withdrew from the fray, though did not dare oppose Mrs Thatcher openly.

By the time of her departure, she had sacked her much-praised Chancellor rather than the adviser who disagreed with his policies, and the final blow was struck by none other than Geoffrey Howe after he had been sidelined as Deputy Prime Minister. In a resignation speech, he delivered an indictment, all the more devastating because of his general mildness, of the monster she had become. In the end, her very narrow defeat in November 1990 was largely caused by the incompetence and lack of drive, to put it mildly, of Peter Morrison, whose job, as her Parliamentary Private Secretary, was to rally the parliamentary troops to support her. Morrison was no *garagiste*: his family was one of the richest and most politically influential in Scotland with a large estate on Islay, where they were loathed, and where Mrs Thatcher had stayed on holiday. It was curious, to say the least, that in her last, most decisive battle, she should have chosen so obvious a representative from the historic Tory party.

After her defeat, she made sure that the revolution would continue. As she told Woodrow Wyatt, she didn't want Douglas Hurd to win: 'I don't want old-style old Etonian Tories of the old school to succeed me and go back to the old, complacent, consensus ways.' By contrast, John Major, who had left school at sixteen, was a perfect representative of the Thatcherite working class. Indeed, she need not have worried. Her revolution had been complete, and by now inverted snobbishness had taken over the Tory party to such an extent that Hurd even tried to persuade MPs that he wasn't a real Etonian, only a poor scholarship boy. Her successor, however, inherited one major blessing from the disaster of the poll tax: virtually all the million or more poll-tax dodgers who had disenfranchised themselves would almost certainly have voted Labour in 1992.

Notes

1. *C'etait de Gaulle*, Fayard, 1994.
2. *London Review of Books*, September 3 1998.
3. *London Review of Books*, March 5 1998.
4. *New Statesman*, February 26 1999.
5. Quoted by David Kynaston op cit.
6. Humphrey Carpenter, *Robert Runcie*, Hodder & Stoughton, 1996.

7. *Robert Runcie*, Mowbray, 1991.
8. *Things Can Only Get Better*, Black Swan, 1999. (And merely because it's an extremely funny book doesn't mean that it's not – often painfully – true.)
9. *Inside the Inner City*, Pelican, 1985.
10. *Scargill, The Unauthorised Biography*, HarperCollins, 1993.
11. *Financial Times*, April 28 2001.

11

The Legacy

'The new mood might be philistine, and it might ignore the desire
to help the weak at the expense of the strong, but it could not
be dismissed or consigned to a backwater. It was better suited to
clearing things away than for building them up, but the British
had for some time been trying to build things up without clearing
away what was useless. Rebuilding after the clearance might be
a task for someone else: the removal of rubbish in the early 1980s
was a good preparation for a fresh start.'

T. O. LLOYD – *Empire, Welfare State, Europe*

MRS THATCHER'S REIGN IS BEST SEEN as a gigantic questioning
of received values, for she tested every element in British life, some
of them to destruction. With the single exception of the royal family,
all the country's institutions, even the most long-established, had to
justify themselves. Many broke and most transformed themselves
under the strain. In many instances, of course, as with the shift away
from manufacturing and the division between northern and southern
Britain, she merely intensified existing trends. But her opponents preferred to blame her for every conceivable unpleasant development. If
she had ever thought it necessary to defend herself, she could have
echoed the words of the Italian politician Giulio Andreotti at his trial
when he observed that he was being blamed for every disaster in
Italian history except the Punic Wars between Rome and Hannibal
more than 2,000 years earlier.

Above all, she inflicted the final blows to the cosy, tolerant, smug,
often lazy but infinitely charming England described by George Orwell,
and when John Major quoted a famous passage from Orwell – about
spinsters cycling to evensong et cetera – he merely sounded ridiculous.
For Mrs Thatcher was never entirely suited to the English temperament.
In all the three elections she fought she received between 42 and 43
per cent of the vote, less than the near 50 per cent recorded by both
major parties in the early post-war period. Indeed, more people – over

14 million – voted for the emollient John Major in 1992 than for her. But, possibly thanks to her authoritarian nature and the feebleness of the Labour Party, votes for parties other than the big two, which had dwindled to under 10 per cent in some post-war elections, started to rise, thanks to the Liberals and the nationalists in both Wales and Scotland.

The results of the way she churned the social, economic and cultural soil of Britain so deeply were so varied that it is impossible to chart them in any logical order. The consequences of her whirlwind were often paradoxical: indeed, one of the most dramatic effects was the destruction of many of the historic bases of her own party. This was not only because so many of the 'them' she so despised were natural Tories but because she deprived the party of that invaluable arm, loyalty, described by Lord Kilmuir thirty years earlier as 'the Tories' secret weapon'. But Mrs Thatcher was loyal only to her own ideas and to 'us'. One of the classes she most affected was her own, the small shopkeepers, ruined by the onward march of the supermarkets she did much to encourage. Obviously, it's sad that specialist shops such as butchers and fishmongers should disappear, but we should also remember that Mrs Thatcher's father, Alderman Roberts, himself that most typical of small shopkeepers, used to chase out of his shop any children who came in purely for a ha'pth of sweets.

Furthermore, as A. H. Halsey pointed out, through many of her policies, including the failure to fund adequate community care and above all the way 'the economic individual was exalted and the social community desecrated ... Mrs Thatcher may well be seen by dispassionate future historians as a major political architect of the demolition of the traditional family' – the only social unit of which she approved. Yet, as we have seen in her treatment of adulterous ministers, and in spite of her theoretical Puritanism, her underlying social libertarianism encouraged, or at least did not prevent, social trends such as the openness of gay partnerships, the decreasing need for heterosexual couples to marry, even when they had children – all phenomena totally alien to Tory tradition.

More undesirable was the fundamental change of attitude she inspired. As Ralf Dahrendorf put it: 'Solidarity, neighbourliness, friendliness, gentleness are all virtues which it is easy to extend within a familiar environment, but if the environment changes, those virtues can rapidly begin to evaporate.' Julian Barnes gave one striking example of the 'evaporation': 'At the time she came to power ... carol singers would, as they always had, stand outside your house, sing a carol or two, then ring the bell and, if you answered, sing some more. Halfway through the rule of Thatch, I began noticing that they wouldn't bother to start singing until they had first rung the bell and checked that you were there to listen and pay up. After she had been in power for about ten years, I opened the door one Christmas and peered out. There were two small boys some distance from the house already, unwilling to waste their time if they got a negative response. "Carols?" one of them asked, spreading his hands in a businesslike gesture, as if he had just acquired a job lot of tunes off the back of a lorry and could perhaps be persuaded to cut me in.'

Barnes was exaggerating, but her reign did ensure that future generations would always be aware of the financial element in any decision they made, and that even the most rebellious, the most economically radical, would accept that the rules of the game allowed for making money, for an entrepreneurial spirit and, perhaps most fundamentally, for an acceptance that jobs were rarely if ever for the whole of a working life. Yet in many respects she did not change British attitudes. A poll by MORI after the 1987 election showed that the public was opposed to any further privatisation and on every count – including health and education – preferred the social rather than the market solution (although, as the electorate showed in 1992, they were not prepared to pay increased taxes to bolster the country's public services). And the country's fundamentally charitable spirit remained unharmed, as witness the Live Aid concert organised by Bob Geldof and its successors.

The innate decency of the best of the former ruling class remained intact. When Michael Howard, as Home Secretary, appointed General Sir David Ramsbotham as Chief Inspector of Prisons to replace a notable liberal, Judge Stephen Tumim, he obviously expected a change of attitude. He was in for a shock. The general, accustomed to taking care of his men (and, in this case, women), immediately refused to inspect Holloway, the most important women's prison in the country, because the conditions were so appalling, and continued in the same vein with subsequent inspections. The same attitude was displayed by one of the most socially distinguished of judges, Sir William Macpherson of Cluny, in a report into the death of the black teenager Stephen Lawrence in which he accused the Metropolitan Police of 'institutionalised racialism'.

In the professions the transformation was far more profound. As an in-house man of letters, variously described as copywriter or journalist, D. J. Taylor was in constant contact with the all powerful partners in the leading firm of accountants where he worked. When he arrived 'most of the profession lay sunk in a pre-war routine of gentlemanly torpor and chilly protocols'[1] . On his arrival at Coopers and Lybrand, he was shown 'a page-long memorandum addressed by a partner to one of his senior managers on the correct use of the comma'. For 'the accountancy profession in the late 1980s was still a relatively civilised place in which to work'. Then the atmosphere changed, and not only in accountants' office – a friend of mine retired early from a leading City solicitors where he was a senior partner when he was transformed into a 'profit centre'.

Taylor himself had been taken on by a 'literary-minded interviewer . . . impressed that I had written a novel . . . Come the early '90s, though, commercial hard-headedness had begun to take over. The nice chaps interested in Korean poetry who dashed back on the train to Brighton to act in their local rep were being dislodged by sturdy young philistine number-crunchers. An ex-boss of mine told me that he first began to think of resigning when he had to escort the firm's newly-appointed marketing partner round the Royal Academy. "And this is where they stage the Summer Exhibition, Bob," he remarked at one point. "Oh yes," Bob innocently replied, "What's that?"' With the new men came a new vocabulary, involving terms like 'synergy', 'interface' and 'pro-active' which are now a part of business-speak. There also came a dedication to hard work, for one of Mrs Thatcher's biggest legacies had been to lead the middle classes to assume that work was serious and a necessary element in their professional activities. But it was not sufficient. For the first time since 1945, managers could easily be sacked because they were no longer required and not just because they were perpetually drunk or otherwise hopelessly inadequate. Nevertheless, one shouldn't exaggerate their woes: the survey of Social Attitudes in 1996, after four years of falling unemployment, showed that nearly one in three unskilled and semi-skilled workers had been unemployed in the course of the previous five years, more than double the proportion amongst executives.

The middle classes were also forced into being competitive. In the late 1960s, the IRC had uncovered what Anthony Sampson calls 'a fundamental worry, that the reasons why British growth-rate is so low may be that neither British managers nor the workers want it to grow faster and that no mere tinkering with structures can put right this basic unambition'. Not till Mrs Thatcher changed the rules of the game. Moreover, and thanks largely to the unions' behaviour in the 1970s, the younger generation and the Labour Party were losing their distaste for capitalism and all its works. The alternatives, never very promising, began to look worse. Labour leaders, starting with Neil Kinnock, discovered that, as David Aaronovitch put it, 'the other side of industry was a damn sight more flexible and dynamic than the trade union side'.[2]

Nevertheless, despite the propaganda, Mrs Thatcher – the daughter of an un-entrepreneurial grocer – neither represented nor encouraged entrepreneurial capitalism (although the thousands of managers who found themselves redundant were forced to stand on their own feet for the first time in their lives). But they were cushioned, enabled to avoid real risks, by the enormous benefits enjoyed by members of the middle classes born between 1920 and 1945. They enjoyed inflation-proofed pensions and were the primary beneficiaries from the £100 billion or so given away with privatisation (the difference between the prices at which the industries were sold and their market value today) and the far greater, unearned, risk- and tax-free capital gains enjoyed by the vast majority, those who had bought their houses in the thirty-five years after the war. As a result, the older generation had absolutely no incentive to risk their easily gotten gains, and this risk aversion has been reflected in the habits of City institutions (even those of the misleadingly named 'venture capitalists' who invest most of their capital in the generally under-priced subsidiaries no longer wanted by major groups).

The two stages of Thatcherism are shown quite clearly in the story of London's Docklands. These had been increasingly abandoned in the 1960s and 1970s, partly because the docks could not handle very large ships, and partly because of the appalling industrial relations in them. London was therefore presented with a unique opportunity to redevelop thousands of acres of derelict urban land. Before 1979 the only practical contribution made by the hordes of planners at the Greater London Council was the filling in of most of the Surrey Docks, itself a scandalous piece of environmental philistinism. The only development, at St Catherine's Dock next to the Tower of London, was greatly deplored at the time as an act of vandalism and as bringing 'the wrong sort of development' – in fact, all it amounted to was the construction of a hotel, some flats and a marina, perfectly sensible use of the land. More typical was the demolition of the London Stacks, warehouses which Simon Jenkins described as the noblest of all the early nineteenth-century industrial buildings in Docklands. The destruction – one of the last acts authorised by Peter Shore, then Secretary for the Environment and MP for the constituency involved – provided an obvious example of the mind-set of the times. The – purest Labour – council was interested only in a development which would attract the sort of unskilled jobs suitable for their voters, mostly former dockers. The new building erected in place of the stacks was indeed occupied in 1986, but by Rupert Murdoch, scourge of Labour and the unions, using a totally unorganised workforce recruited almost entirely from outside the area. The same obsession with the continuation of past trends led to the stubborn refusal of Southwark Council to allow the construction of the replica of Shakespeare's Globe Theatre, the long-term vision of the American actor, Sam Wanamaker. The reason? It wouldn't provide unskilled jobs.

The first years of Docklands redevelopment, guided by Michael

Heseltine, were characterised by low-rise, sympathetic indigenous buildings. But then came that most obvious symbol of the later years of Thatcherism, Canary Wharf. It all started when a dynamic banker, Michael Van Clemm, visited the Isle of Dogs to look for a site for a packaging plant for the Roux brothers' restaurant chain in which he had an interest. He found instead an urban wasteland surrounded by water a mere five miles from the City. He called in an American developer, G. Ware Travelstead, who was prepared to follow Clemm's idea that the wasteland could be developed to house, not only the 'back office' clerical functions for the booming City of London, but the bankers themselves. Travelstead, not a world-scale operator, soon disappeared from the scene and was replaced by the Reichmann brothers. They had prospered by redeveloping the heart of Toronto and their grandiose plans for Canary Wharf – not to mention the persuasive personality of Paul Reichmann – matched Mrs Thatcher's dreams of the future. With the help of tax breaks and the proposed construction, almost entirely at the public expense, of an extension to the Jubilee Line from central London, Reichmann built a handsome tower which was soon surrounded by some totally hideous office blocks. The project nearly went belly-up during the recession of the early 1990s but by the end of the century had proved a phenomenal success, financially anyway, becoming a major competitor to the City of London as a location for the capital's financial services community.

Nevertheless Mrs Thatcher was only partially successful in imposing her ideas. Typically, she failed in one of her most fundamental aims, to reduce the size and cost of government. The actual percentage of national income taken by the state did not go down, for the obvious reason that any economies she made in administration were more than swallowed up by the increased bill for social security due to the rise in unemployment. And although she succeeded in reducing the number of central government officials by 15 per cent, this amounted to fewer than 100,000, while the numbers employed in local government went down by a mere 80,000 to just under 2.3 million. Moreover, employment in the health sector soared by 600,000 to 1.7 million and there were 150,000 more employed in education, both figures totally contrary to the impression left by Mrs Thatcher's opponents. But the biggest result of the huffing and puffing, the numerous reports and the introduction of an elaborate 'internal market' within the NHS was the ever-increasing cost of administering the service. Until the 1980s, this amounted to a mere 5 per cent of its total cost. By 1997, in another triumph for 'managerialism', the figure had risen to 12 per cent.

Even bigger exceptions were the economic policies pursued in Wales and, to a lesser extent, in Northern Ireland. His starring role in the miners' strike ensured that she could not easily sack that arch-'wet'

Peter Walker. Following the 1987 election – at his request – he was appointed Secretary of State for Wales after (or so he told Woodrow Wyatt) he had done a deal with Mrs Thatcher and the Treasury 'with regional aid and all that kind of thing'. There he conducted a highly successful neo-Keynesian economic policy, complete with organised government encouragement for new investors, mostly from the Far East. In Northern Ireland, Richard Needham also pursued what Paul Routledge calls 'a sort of latter-day Keynesianism throughout the Thatcher years in a forgotten corner of the British economy'.[3] Unexpectedly, her hatred of the public sector did not prevent a resurgence of investment in Britain's railway system. As Minister of Transport her faithful follower Nicholas Ridley did a deal with British Rail. They could use the considerable sums accruing from the redevelopment of railway stations to invest in improvements to the system.

Even more paradoxically, her policies also gave the other races in the British Isles, most obviously the Scots and to a lesser extent the Welsh, an increasing sense of their own identity which was largely a reaction to Thatcherism as the epitome of Englishness: 'If that's what being English means . . . I want none of it'. When the pound coin was introduced, it became known in Scotland as a Maggie – 'hard, brassy and thinks it's a sovereign' or 'hard brassy and nobody wants them'.

For years a relative handful of voices – notably the brilliant Scottish Marxist intellectual Tom Nairn – had been preaching the doctrine that Britain was a multinational, and thus multicultural, state whose rigid unitary structure was both outdated and the result of an incomplete revolution in 1688 which had transferred authority (some would say absolute authority) from the Crown to parliament. Mrs Thatcher's ruthlessly centralising policies were a striking proof of Nairn's ideas – though it was surprising that Scotland had not been nationalistic before the 1970s, when 'It's our oil' gave the Scottish National Party a rallying cry. The decline in traditional industries, Mrs Thatcher's scorn for the professional classes who had been unionists and, above all, the introduction of the poll tax in Scotland before England, were major arguments in favour of greater independence in a society which remained more egalitarian, more democratic, more concerned with social issues than England. In 1988 the Scottish Labour and Liberal Democrat members of Parliament were among the multitude who signed a Claim of Right which declared that sovereignty in Scotland proceeded from the people and not from the constitutionally correct Crown in Parliament.

Mrs Thatcher's narrow Englishness destroyed the Tory Party in Scotland which as late as 1955 had been the biggest party in the country – although part of its support, particularly in and around Glasgow, was based on anti-Irish Catholic prejudice. But by 1997 there was not a single Tory MP in the country (it took Blair's control freakery to arouse the same feelings in the Welsh after he had tried to impose an alien first minister on them). The Celts had a sense of identity to fall back on but she left the English bereft, searching for their identity, and she did permanent damage to the very idea of Englishness by associating it with the narrowest kind of nationalist philistinism.

The institutionalised meanness of spirit which had so alienated the Scots also ensured that the level of state pensions was tied to the rate of inflation and not, as was previously the case, to average earnings, a policy which had enabled pensioners to share in any increase in national prosperity. In the twenty years after 1980, the state pension for a single person went up two and a half times, average earnings over three and a half times. 'Between 1979 and 1991,' wrote Jonathan Bradshaw, 'average living standards increased by over 30 per cent. However inequalities widened dramatically, families with children drifted down the income distribution [ladder] and many more families found themselves dependent on income support and relatively worse off. This need not have happened. It was the result of the government's tax, benefit and employment policies. If we aim to begin to improve the living standards of children and avoid separating the very large number of them on income support from normal patterns of life in Britain, then the child scale rates of income support must be increased now.'[4] For one of the most significant results of Mrs Thatcher's reign was the increase in the numbers of the social underclass identified so clearly by Sir Keith Joseph in the 1970s. The underclass had always been there, and had only emerged as an identifiable element in society with the general increase in prosperity for the rest of British society.

Unfortunately for the Tory party, many of its new MPs in the 1970s and 1980s were not well off, did not have a professional income on which they could rely and were thus highly susceptible to bribery. Of course, corruption had never been entirely absent from the British political scene. Far from it. In the 1930s Lord Beaverbrook, proprietor of the *Daily Express*, paid a minister the then enormous sum of £2,000 a year to reveal discussions in Cabinet. But in Mrs Thatcher's case, a dubious character and dubious dealings were there in her family, in the person of her son Mark, who was involved in a number of business deals in which his only asset was his name. Time and again senior civil servants would warn his mother of his activities, but she, like many another doting mother, would not listen. The need for money amongst increasingly professional politicians trying to live on their by no mean enormous pay as MPs, combined with the example being set from Number Ten, encouraged a degree of systematic corruption on a scale not seen since the years immediately after the First World War. Under Thatcher and her successor, 'cash for (Parliamentary) questions' replaced the 'cash for honours' characteristic of the earlier period of systematic corruption.

It was in the later years of Thatcher's reign and the early years of her successor that the greedy had their opportunity. Throughout the late 1980s and early 1990s, the British public was greatly entertained by the consequences of the war waged between two foreign-born, totally disreputable tycoons, 'Tiny' Rowland of Lonrho and Mohammed Fayed. The war broke out when Fayed outwitted Rowland for control of Harrods, the retail symbol of British snobbery. Both tycoons needed a group of tame MPs to ask questions and to lobby on their behalf. This was easier for Rowland, for the chairman of Lonrho was Edward du Cann, formerly a highly influential figure in the Tory Party – indeed a major factor in the election of Margaret Thatcher to lead the party back in 1975. His chairman's fees of £400,000 were justifiable only by his political rather than his commercial value. Fayed's man was a lobbyist, Ian Greer, tiny, immaculate, his elegant office boasting a butler, who was the centre of what Geoffrey Robertson describes as 'a spider's web of influence-peddling in Whitehall'. Greer had assured Fayed that 'You need to rent an MP like you need to rent a London taxi' but such behaviour was obviously not likely to maintain, let alone increase, voters' respect for Parliament.

Greer's most important ally in the cash for questions affair was Sir Michael Grylls, who died in early 2001 and did not suffer greatly from his misdeeds. He was the perfect exemplar, not of the *garagiste* tendency but of the moral rot within the respectable upper middle class. The son of a brigadier and himself a former Royal Marine officer, Grylls started his business career importing Spanish wine and was duly convicted of evading exchange controls. He then tried to pass off Spanish sparkling wine as champagne, leading to a famous court case – which he lost. But his great days came in the Thatcher years. As a senior MP (he was elected for a safe seat in Surrey in 1970), chairman of the Tory backbench Trade and Industry Committee and, after 1992, a knight, he was in a powerful position. He did a deal with Greer to receive a 10 per cent commission on all the contracts he obtained for Greer, which in one year amounted to £3 million. This was not surprising since, as Andrew Roth noted, 'whenever businessmen approached Grylls for help . . . he made it a condition that they hire Greer's firm to lobby for them'.[5] The truth started to emerge in 1994 but Grylls prudently retired at the 1997 election before the Parliamentary Commissioner for standards, Sir Gordon Downey, had spelled out the truth.

As Robertson puts it, 'The war was waged . . . under the regimental colours of the Tory backbench Trade and Industry Committee, which included members like Tim Smith, Sir Andrew Bowden and Neil Hamilton . . . The captain, Sir Michael Grylls – encouraging them from behind the scenes. The general – Sir Peter Hordern [the only one to declare his interest as a paid lobbyist for Fayed*] – parading these troops as a show of force to the DTI and its ministers'. These 'Members for Harrods' succeeded in staving off the publication of the exceptionally damaging DTI report on Fayed for several years. Once the *Guardian* began to reveal the extent of the payments – largely thanks to Fayed's fury at not getting any results from his largesse – 'the arteries to the heart of the body politic', wrote Robertson with a characteristic flourish, 'were clogged with grease and it was time for open-heart surgery'.

Neil Hamilton was the most flamboyant character involved, and at one point he was being touted as a candidate for high office. He had been emboldened by his success in suing the BBC, which had accused him of gestures which included giving a Nazi salute on a visit to Berlin, and therefore felt safe in suing the *Guardian*, promising to prove the paper guilty of 'telling sensationalist lies'. Jonathan Aitken, a flamboyant journalist, MP and minister who pursued his own career acting for Arab interests quite separately from the Greer gang, was to sue the same paper with the eventual result that he ended up in jail for perjury.

In Hamilton's case, the revelations which emerged included the way that he – and another right-wing MP, Michael Brown – had not registered their role as paid lobbyists for another of Greer's clients, US Tobacco, in its attempts to sell to children Skoal Bandits, a nicotine chewing-gum which causes cancer of the mouth. Worse (from a parliamentary point of view anyway), Hamilton had lied to Michael Heseltine, his boss at the Department of Trade and Industry where he was a junior minister, giving him an absolute assurance that he had no financial relationship with Greer. Eventually the plaintiffs withdrew their case against the *Guardian* after falling out amongst themselves. Greer was especially furious that Hamilton had lied to Heseltine.

If Mrs Thatcher helped corrupt and disembowel her own party, she forced the Labour Party to transform itself – and not only the party but also the intellectual climate of the left. When James Klugmann, grand old man of the Communist Party (and the individual who had guided several generations of undergraduates into helping the party and/or the Soviet Union), retired as editor of *Marxism Today*, his place was taken by a young intellectual entrepreneur, Martin Jacques, who in the course of the 1980s was to guide leftist thought away from all its preconceptions.

But the Labour Party survived and eventually triumphed. More permanent were the harmful effects of Mrs Thatcher's autocratic poli-

* Though not the amounts, a then-generous £24,000 a year

cies on the independence – and the finances – of local government –
and not only because she abolished the Greater London Council. Other
local authorities were crippled by the policy of 'rate-capping', thus
ensuring that they could raise only strictly limited amounts in tax. By
the end of the century, only a fifth of local government revenue came
from local sources while the councils' power was further reduced
by massive 'outsourcing' – the delegation of their duties to outside
contractors. Above all, they lost their previously overwhelming role
in providing housing for the less well-off. As late as 1970, the public
sector was building 170,000 flats and houses a year. By 1980, this had
dropped to only just over 100,000 and was down to a third of that
number by the late 1980s – and most of this was through Housing
Associations. Indeed, during the Thatcher years the number of dwellings owned by councils dropped by over a million as over 1.3 million
council tenants bought their flats or houses, almost invariably at very
considerable discounts. At a guess, these amounted to at least £20,000
per house, a sum which provided the better-off tenants with a tax-free
gift of over £30 billion, which went to 'us', the more financially secure
members of the working classes who were thus able to aspire to
middle-class status, as exemplified by ownership of their own accommodation.

The power of local authorities was also greatly reduced so far as
education was concerned. Schools were allowed to opt out of local
authority control, getting their money from the central government.
But in Mrs Thatcher's view, 'us' would have their children educated
privately, so standards in the state sector were of no great concern to
her. It was only in 1988 that the government tackled educational standards with the introduction of the national curriculum – a step which
itself owed something to the desire to attack the teaching unions.
Meanwhile further education was transferred to a central body. The
steady increase of numbers going into higher education faltered for a
time after the spending cuts in the 1981 budget, but soon rose again
to the levels seen in the 1960s and 1970s. Nevertheless the quality
of education suffered because staff-student ratios, which had been
decreasing, started to go up – and have never recovered since, making
it cheap and easy for successive governments to increase student
numbers, albeit at the expense of educational standards. Moreover such
so-called inessentials as musical education were dramatically pruned
while school playing fields were sold off to provide funds.

The ruthlessness of Mrs Thatcher's policies also did considerable
damage to the country's previously excellent system of education for
artists and musicians. But she forced change in every cultural institution, often for the worse – as at the Victoria and Albert Museum,
where a typically 'bossy' director, Elizabeth Estève-Coll, swept aside

271

the talents of the curators in charge of individual departments. Never-theless Mrs Thatcher's policies, and above all her meanness to edu-cation and culture, also forced universities and museums alike into taking some positive steps – as well as spending too much of their time scraping around for increased funding. In the course of time, many of them transformed themselves into international centres of training, for education for education's sake had become an increasingly unsustainable concept.

The most obvious fact about Mrs Thatcher was that she was a woman, albeit one who headed a party which was, and has remained, astonishingly chauvinist. Though no feminist, she gave an example which was, more or less consciously, followed by many thousands of her sex and thus marked the end of what Emma Tennant described as 'girlitude ... the dependence, the longed-for protection and the self-reproach of a species which can now only be alluded to self-consciously and with scorn.'[6] 'Thatcherism individualised women's quest for change and gave it shoulder pads and selfishness,' wrote Melissa Benn[7] , but it was nevertheless effective as an instrument of liberation when coping with male chauvinist colleagues and bosses.

Mrs Thatcher legitimised bossiness – though while men are called decisive, women behaving in the same way are still often called bossy – and there were many examples of such behaviour apart from Ms Estève-Coll. Baroness O'Cathain at the Barbican Centre in the City of London was typical, a Thatcherite whose views and policies made her disliked by the staff. The only time they sympathised was when she brought her crippled husband to the Centre for a concert, a move she had previously avoided, because his state somehow showed some sort of weakness, and that was inadmissible in Thatcherite terms. But most women in most contexts remained an underclass. For D. J. Taylor, working in an accountancy firm, ' ''office life'' meant harassed women worrying about their sick children, a tax manager whose husband was suffering from cancer being told ''not to being your domestic problems to work'' and pregnant women having their lives made hell by female superiors'[8] – a classic description of Thatcherism at work. No wonder Taylor still avoids walking anywhere near his former places of work: 'They are too closely associated ... with whey-faced women drudging for fear of the sack.'

As so often, Mrs Thatcher's example led to the destruction of one of the elements that had made the Tory party so powerful: the loyalty of so many women, not only as voters but as almost invariably subordi-nate party workers. The cost was spelt out in the 1997 election when the Tory share of the vote fell more steeply amongst women than men: whereas Labour had a lead of only 7 per cent among male voters, it was 13 per cent amongst women – rising to an amazing 22 points amongst women aged between eighteen and thirty-five. This must have been due partly at least to a – perfectly reasonable – perception that despite Mrs Thatcher, the Tories were perceived as the party of the woman in the home. Indeed, this was recognised in late 1999 in a report by that most Thatcherite of think-tanks, the Centre for Policy Studies, which declared bluntly that the party appeared to hanker for 'the days of the subservient family woman'. The lesson of the Conservative Party's increasing remoteness from the modern English woman had clearly not been learned. In 1997, only one fifth of new candidates were women, and these were mostly fighting unwinnable seats. The problem is simple: female Tory Party activists, traditionalists to a woman, have always resented and hated uppity women who, by trying to become MPs, threaten their perception of themselves. By contrast, Labour had reacted positively, superficially at least, to the challenge. Although its system of 'all-women' short lists was found to be illegal and many people laughed at the 'Blair babes', they do represent a welcome change in Labour thinking.

Mrs Thatcher's total philistinism and her dictatorial nature combined in her assault on the world of culture and the media. Lady Warnock recalls that in the course of a harangue to the board of the Independent Broadcasting Authority she declared, 'People were not interested in freedom of the press but only in having Choice' – which 'meant having available a variety of channels, all of which were truthful and encouraging'. As so often, the results of her instinctive decisions were contradictory. Her hatred of the hitherto all-powerful duopoly of the BBC and ITV led her to introduce Channel 4 as an alternative, but the result, under its first Director, the iconoclastic socialist Jeremy Isaacs, was to provide an exciting new outlet for creative – and almost invariably anti-Thatcherite – talents. By contrast, she greatly lowered the standards of ITV itself by introducing the system of blind bids for individual franchises – a system considered and rejected thirty-five years earlier by the then ITA. The result was chaos, with some winners getting away with minimal payments, while others were landed with cripplingly large annual payments – a combination which led to a permanent decline in the production of programmes which were not necessarily going to attract the highest audiences.

The dumbing-down of commercial television was matched by that of popular newspapers. In 1979 the radical Australian journalist John Pilger had been allowed eleven pages in the *Daily Mirror* to expose the massacres resulting from Year Zero in Cambodia. Even five years later this would have been unthinkable for the *Mirror* was forced to ape the *Sun*. The *Sun* had started down the slippery slope to tasteless journalism under its first editor Larry Lamb, who had urged readers to vote Tory in May 1979 and had been knighted a year later.

Characteristically, three months after the election, the paper published a photograph alleged to be of octuplets but in fact of four babies printed twice. But the *Sun* went further, far further after 1981 under Lamb's successor Kelvin Mackenzie, an editor whose enormous flair was matched by equal doses of ruthlessness and unscrupulousness,. Mackenzie took full advantage of the fact that his boss was a confirmed republican. 'Give me a splash on the royals,' Mackenzie would say to his staff, 'don't worry if it's not true.' In 1982 the *Sun* was reprimanded for publishing photos of Princess Diana five months pregnant in a bikini*. Early the following year, the Palace took legal action when the paper slanted the memoirs of a footman to describe the sex life of Prince Andrew and the American actress Koo Stark as 'Queen Koo's Romps at the Palace'. Unabashed, Mackenzie boasted that the 'Queen gags the *Sun* . . . the first time the Queen has ever taken legal action against a newspaper'.

Whatever sneaking sympathy one might have had with the paper's royal revelations, many of the paper's other indiscretions were simply disgusting. And they were legion. The Falklands War saw the infamous headline 'GOTCHA' celebrating the drowning of hundreds of young Argentine conscripts in the *General Belgrano*. The *Sun* ran fictitious interviews galore: with Princess Stephanie of Monaco when she was under sedation after the death of her mother; with Marcia McKay, the widow of a soldier who had won a posthumous VC in the Falklands; and with another, gravely wounded, Falklands war hero, Simon Weston. There was much racism too: after the arrest of 286 social security cheats in Oxford, the *Sun* published a cartoon suggesting that the majority were black when in fact only four were. In 1988, fifteen complaints against the paper were upheld by the Press Council in a single year. In 1989 the *Sun* surpassed itself when it accused the Liverpool supporters, ninety-five of whom had died in the Hillsborough tragedy, of being thugs and drunks who urinated on the rescue crews.

The *Sun*, still less the *News of the World*, had never pretended to the higher journalism, but *The Times* and the *Sunday Times*, which Murdoch was allowed to buy up in 1981, were quite another matter. In his diaries Woodrow Wyatt claims that Murdoch asked him to ensure that the purchase of *The Times* and the *Sunday Times* was not referred to the Monopolies Commission as it ought to have been because 'the *Sunday Times* was not really losing money and the pair were not'. As it was, because it could be argued that, at the time, in the depths of a recession when even ICI had suspended its dividend, both were losing money, the deal was exempted from examination.

* Four years later the *Current Bun*, as Mackenzie called it, published a photograph of the actor David Niven on his deathbed.

Nor did the journalists on the *Sunday Times* object. Only a dozen out of over a hundred were prepared to defy Murdoch and support an alternative scheme, proposed by Robert Ducas the New York manager of Times Newspapers, which had backing from the City of London.

Here I must declare an interest. As someone who worked for the pre-Murdoch *Sunday Times* for some years, I used to regard him as the Devil incarnate, a man had destroyed what was proclaimed, with some justification, as one of the world's greatest newspapers. Indeed, Andrew Neil, his first editor at the *Sunday Times*, did sack a great number of excellent journalists, often because they were perceived as being far too radical. Furthermore, Neil did much to undermine the primacy of printed newspapers over television by refusing to invest in long-term investigative journalism. But time matures opinions: I now accept that the paper had started to decay even before he took over. In addition, the printing unions were totally out of control – as witness the abortive year-long shutdown at the end of the 1970s which failed to get them to the negotiating table. As Peter Preston, as former editor of the *Guardian* one of Murdoch's stoutest opponents, wrote, 'Many of Rupert's dragons were ripe for the slaying.'[9] It was unlikely, for instance, that Kenneth Thomson, the previous owner, would have held on to *The Times* and *Sunday Times*. And yes, Murdoch did have the guts to bet the farm again and again, notably on Sky TV, which within a decade became a worthwhile alternative to terrestrial television – even in news. Above all, he was a newspaperman who had always been prepared to invest long-term funds in papers (he subsidised the *Australian*, the country's first and only serious national paper, for over a decade). Compared with his successors, such as the financier Lord Hollick or the pornographer Richard Desmond, he appears a positively saintly supporter of journalism and journalists.

The newspaper business – as opposed to individual workers in what was always called 'the print' – was one of the few manufacturing industries which did not suffer from Thatcherism. Elsewhere in the sector, the effects can be seen from the figures. The British industrial proletariat suffered what might best be described as ethnic cleansing. Unemployment, which had not risen above a million since 1941*, leapt by over 1.25 to 2.7 million within two years to reach a peak of 3.2 million in 1986 – and at a time when the economy had supposedly been doing rather well. The losses were, of course, concentrated in manufacturing industry. Almost a third of all the workers employed in manufacturing no longer had their jobs by 1990. Inevitably, the effect on mining was much more severe, although the losses were

---

* There was one exception, 1947, when fuel shortages had badly hampered industrial production.

'only' 250,000 jobs, showing that even at the start of the decade coal was no longer the king of employers – losses in the metals and mechanical engineering sector alone had totalled over two million. Part of the explanation lay with vastly increased productivity – as was illustrated by Macgregor's efforts at British Steel.

Union membership slumped from a high of 13,300,000 in 1980 to just over 10 million a decade later (the numbers continued to decline, albeit at a much slower rate, for some years afterwards). The engineering workers' union lost 750,000 members, half the 1979 total, and the Transport & General 800,000, though it remained the only union with over a million members*, while the once almighty NUM was down to a mere 44,000 members by 1991, under a fifth of its pre-Thatcher total – and a mere fifteenth of its post-war peak in the 1940s. Yet the proportion of the workforce in unions in the late 1980s, at just under 40 per cent, was roughly the same as it had been at the end of the war. For Mrs Thatcher's policies had so alienated even senior employees in the public sector that losses amongst the working classes were largely made up by increasing numbers of professionals. Membership of the Royal College of Nursing rose by 38 per cent in the first seven years of the decade, and the First Division union of senior civil servants actually affiliated to the TUC in a move which showed clearly that even senior mandarins now considered themselves vulnerable employees.

This attitude reflected Mrs Thatcher's contempt for anyone working in the public sector ('If you were any good,' she once told members of the board of British Rail, 'you'd be working in the private industry'). Crucially, the pay gap between the public and private sectors widened, a relationship that has not greatly changed since her departure. By 1995 a permanent secretary, who in 1981 earned nearly half the salary of the chairman of a major company, was down to below a fifth of this level. This had consequences right through the public sector, leading, for instance, to the reluctance of an increasing number of barristers to become judges.

The philosophy of 'us and them' divided the whole country. Worst off were the working classes, divided into the deserving and undeserving poor. The deserving were the entrepreneurial and those prepared to go anywhere for work and take any job they found (to get 'on your bike', as Tebbit put it). But this was less practical than in the 1930s, when Tebbit's father had famously taken this initiative. Then, the majority of the unemployed rented their accommodation. By the 1980s virtually all the working-class unemployed were in council housing. The lumpenproletariat who lost the jobs they assumed would last their

---

* Within a few years it was overtaken by Unison, the biggest union representing public sector workers.

working lifetimes were without hope of finding other employment, helplessly and usually permanently unemployed because they were in the wrong place and almost invariably lacked the educational qualifications to find different jobs. Since 1945 it had been safe to assume that work would come to their community. A deservedly famous TV series, *The Boys from the Black Stuff*, which was set in Liverpool (although it could have been in any other major Northern city), showed a bitterly comic vision of young men going round everywhere asking, 'Gi' us a job', thus demonstrating the bleak despair which prevailed after Mrs Thatcher had turned her back on these devastated towns and cities. A single statistic tells a lot of the story. Between 1977 and 1981 the number of pubs in the North of England, the 'boozers', fell by over a quarter.

The Thatcherites have a point when they say that the bloodbath of 1979–81 was largely the result of a continuation of the monetary policies pursued by the Labour government after 1976, combined with the effects of the second oil crisis and the fragility and over-manning of British industry in general and the nationalised industries in particular. And although the share of manufacturing in Britain's GDP did fall from 31 per cent in 1970 to just under a fifth twenty-five years later, the fall was even steeper in Japan and Germany, albeit from a much higher base, with Britain near the European average. Moreover, there were some success stories: car production rose from its 1982 low of under 900,000 vehicles to reach 1.3 million by 1990 and over 1.6 million a decade later, an increasing proportion of which were 'premium' vehicles such as Jaguars. This was largely due to the most startling industrial success story of the 1980s: the arrival of Nissan, the first of three Japanese motor companies to invest in Britain, which in 1986 opened a major factory in Sunderland, an area devastated by job losses in mines and manufacturing industry. Nissan's attitude was a reproach to British managers: all the staff were treated alike, all were salaried, all wore the same clothes, all ate in the same canteen. For their part, the unions agreed that the workers would be represented by a single union, an arrangement that became the norm in most of the many new plants established throughout the United Kingdom once the miners had been defeated. (One of the few exceptions came in 1990 in Dundee, where the unions refused a single-union deal, an attitude which stopped Ford from establishing a factory in an area of perpetually high unemployment.)

The lumpenproletariat were not consoled by the fact that over a million new jobs had been found in 'banking, insurance and finance'. The beneficiaries included the Yuppies, the highly paid and even more highly visible City kids who offended everyone – traditionalists because they formed the City side of the Essex phenomenon, confident that they could spend and spend since they felt sure of even higher salaries – and bonuses – in the future, and the rest of the country simply because they were noisy and overpaid. But they were in the minority: more typical were the thousands employed in clerical sweat-shops all over the country – as well as the wage slaves recruited in the hundreds of thousands in the 1990s to man call centres.

The contrast between manufacturing and service industries bred one of the major fallacies of Thatcherism, the assumption that manufacturing industry would somehow become totally irrelevant. In particular, Nigel Lawson, the Chancellor of the Exchequer during Mrs Thatcher's heyday, argued, with some justification, that every industrialised country had seen a decline in the share of manufacturing in their national economies. But when he proclaimed this to a committee of the House of Lords, their Lordships replied that only in Britain had there been an absolute decline in manufacturing production. It was Lord Weinstock who posed the fundamental question. Given that by the mid-1980s the so-called 'service industries' accounted for 77 per cent of British employment and GNP, what were they servicing? 'The insurance companies, the banks, the stockbrokers, the pension funds, are providing services to industry. At the base of all this great service industry activity in which we place so much hope for the future lies manufacturing industry. I fear that if manufacturing industry fails, unless we become merely a country entertaining tourists, the service industries, or a large part of them, will go with it.' The Lords committee's report stated unambiguously that 'unless the climate is changed so that the manufacturing base is enlarged and steps are taken to ensure that import penetration is combated and that manufacturing exports are stimulated, as the oil revenues diminish the country will experience adverse effects which will worsen with time'.

Ironically, the strains on the financial sector were so severe as to expose a total institutional – and personal – incapacity to cope with the modern world. The Thatcherite attitude to the City was curiously ambivalent. Yes, it was full of allies and was thought (wrongly) to be the dynamic heart of the British economy. At the same time it was obviously riddled with restrictive practices. Moreover, the Old City had largely ignored – or at least did not play a leading role in – the developments in personal finance over the previous thirty years such as property development, life assurance, mortgages and unit trusts. Most of the bankers and brokers remained content with their traditional businesses – even Siegmund Warburg was never interested in fund management. Hence the contradictions. As early as October 1979, the Stock Exchange rule book was referred to the Restrictive Practices Court in accordance with a characteristic threat from Norman Tebbit: 'We cleaned up the trades union movement and we'll clean up the City too.' And even Nigel Lawson was not always impressed by cries for help – most obviously, when the sale of the government's remaining shares in BP coincided with the stock market slump of October 1987, he ignored pleas from the underwriters who stood to lose up to £1 billion.

Nevertheless Lawson had always been deeply and, for someone so intelligent, surprisingly naively committed to the City. As financial editor of the *Sunday Telegraph*, he had allowed the young Jim Slater to write a column in which he regularly plugged shares in which he had an interest. And as Chancellor of the Exchequer he had so much faith in the insurance companies which dominated the private pensions industry that he allowed them to replace the pensions schemes paid to hundreds of thousands of workers in the public sector – an act which led to the biggest financial scandal in British history when the poor clients were cheated out of tens of billions of pounds by virtually every insurance company through the replacement of their schemes by far less favourable ones.

For it is impossible to exaggerate the indifference to private customers, to private shareholders or to elementary rules of decency displayed by the financial world. At D. J. Taylor's eminent firm of chartered accountants, young and old, otherwise very different, both had a total lack of what might be described as professional integrity. The 'constantly uttered platitudes about "service" and "integrity"' stood 'side by side with the most flagrant bits of sharp practice and dubious client work'. Taylor's firm audited the accounts of many of Robert Maxwell's companies, even though 'everyone below the rank of partner knew there was something shady about the way in which the Maxwell audits were carried out'. At a later date, even the ultra-respectable building societies were found to be paying relatively high interest rates to attract new investors while reducing the rates on longer-established forms of deposits that were inevitably held by older and more vulnerable savers. Worse was to come. In 2000 a row between policy-holders and the management of the Equitable, the oldest and supposedly best-run of all insurance companies, revealed an appalling state of affairs. Its management assumed that it could renege on the promised return on annuities offered in the past, when high inflation and even higher interest rates were the norm. But the Society had never dreamed that the opposite conditions – which reduced the return from fixed-interest investments – could ever prevail for more than a few months. And in the late 1990s they emphatically did. The result? Ruin for the Equitable and losses for hundreds of thousands of policy-holders, many of them journalists like the author, who had thought of themselves as sophisticated investors.

In the mid-1980s the Guinness affair – when insiders provided support for the successful bidder for the Distillers Company, producers

279

of most Scotch whiskies – had showed just how normal it was for bidders to manipulate the market through 'friends' prepared to stump up in the certainty of a short-term profit. Indeed, the Guinness affair was unusual only in the size of the operation and the fact that four of the supporters went to jail. For not only was the City riddled with dishonesty; it was also ill-equipped to cope with an unregulated environment, let alone face the onslaught of well-financed foreign banks, most of the biggest being American, which had invaded London since the mid-1960s. The free-for-all was symbolised by the much anticipated, much feared Big Bang, the outcome of years of negotiations. This contained two main elements: the abolition of minimum commissions and, more important, the end of the jobbing system by which the jobbers made the market in bonds and shares and brokers formed the link with the investors. Evidently, once commissions were negotiable, the old system, that of 'single-capacity' operators, was effectively out of the question. As the economist Tim Congdon pointed out, despite all the publicity attached to the event, this was nothing compared with the Bigger Bang, the explosion in the international financial markets benefiting almost exclusively non-British financial institutions but, increasingly, based in London.

The scramble for the brokers and jobbers immediately after Big Bang was chaotic. 'Some of the purchases were calmly calculated,' wrote John Littlewood, a highly respected analyst quoted by David Kynaston, 'some derived from instinctive opportunism, but many were little more than a panic move to avoid being left out.' A total of £1,150 million was paid out to the partners* and the total cost to the buyers, what with the need to re-equip them and the losses they suffered in the 1987 crash, amounted to an estimated £4 billion.

None of the four mighty clearing banks, famous for their financial brawn rather than the brains historically confined, in theory at least, to the merchant banks, proved capable of competing in a modern international marketplace. Worst-placed was the Midland, which had made a hideous mistake in the mid-1970s by taking over the ailing Crocker Bank in California. By 1986, thanks to Crocker's losses, it was the smallest of the Big Four, little more than half a century after it had gloried in being the world's largest bank. It was then humiliated by a bid from, of all people, the Saatchi brothers, a defining moment in the 'anything goes' atmosphere of the mid-1980s. Within a few years, it had disappeared into the maw of the far better-run Hong Kong and Shanghai Bank, which had profited enormously from the

* A disproportionate amount probably went to the older partners, since the younger ones thought they could make better use of their capital than investing it in their own firm.

consistently fast growth of Hong Kong's economy. Lloyds, the smallest of the four, opted out of the international race at an early stage and remained prudently profitable throughout the hysteria. Barclays made expensive attempts to compete by setting up an integrated merchant bank, but the two cultures, of clearing and merchant bankers, simply did not blend and its choice of senior executives was, to say the least, doubtful. David Dand, an early head of the investment banking side, was a drunk. Worse, Aubrey Buxton became chairman of the whole group in the 1990s because he was the scion of one of the bank's founding families – and despite his, albeit indirect, involvement in the appalling losses suffered by Barclays in the fall of Imry, a property company to which the bank had lent over £200 million. Natwest followed the same path as Barclays even more cack-handedly. In the late 1990s it was taken over by the much smaller Royal Bank of Scotland, a move which restored the bank's fortunes – in the domestic market, anyway – with a speed which showed just how badly it had been run before the take-over.

The supposedly more alert merchant banks were not much better-placed. By the end of the 1970s the *Economist* could say that 'they have become the genteel poor of the international banking community', above all lacking a capital base big enough to compete American investment banks. 'Their ultimate vanity,' wrote David Kynaston, 'more forgivable in the case of Warburgs than most, [was] that the natives could take on the American [and Continental] invaders and somehow punch above their weight' – an echo of the delusion of British politicians throughout the post-war era, and a vanity which was justifiable when they were competing only with the British clearing banks but totally inadequate when they were fighting foreigners with both brains and financial brawn. And after the abolition of exchange controls in 1979, one of the boldest acts of the new government, they did not even have the same grip over domestic investment institutions, which were now looking increasingly outside Britain and thus needed advisers with advice on markets the world over.

The American newcomers had a total contempt for their British equivalents and the atmosphere within their banks was completely different from that in any British institution. When Peter Spira, once one of Warburg's bright young men, moved to an American bank, he found a strange combination of 'dynamically ruthless but bright Americans, a mixture of extremely clever Englishmen and other Europeans and a number of barrow boys who, with their cockney accents and flash suits, were making fortunes as traders ... it was no bar to success that a young trader, when entertaining a client to lunch, might stick his half-masticated chewing gum under the dining-room table'.

The inadequacies of the rest of the City paled before the revelations which followed the financial problems faced by Lloyds, the proudest single pillar of the Old City. Its members, operating within an arrogant and secretive environment, were exposed as an unscrupulous group of insiders who exploited the greed, naivety and social snobbery of newcomers anxious to establish themselves in society, to get something for nothing and, not coincidentally, to avoid taxes – all of which offered ample proof that the cult of 'greed is good' was alive and flourishing amongst the British upper classes well before the arrival of Mrs Thatcher. In the 1970s and 1980s, an increasing numbers of relatively well-heeled Brits had been lured into membership. In the 1970s the salesmen could point, legitimately, to the tax advantages enjoyed by members at a time when the level of tax on unearned incomes could be as high as 98 per cent. In the 1980s greed for – largely tax-free – profit loomed larger, as did the element of snobbery which had always been an attraction and was now obviously even more appealing to Thatcherite nouveaux riches.

In becoming members, applicants also became liable not only for all their possessions but allowed their representatives, the agents, to engage in business two and a half times the level of the assets pledged by the member. By the 1980s the stringency of the rules were being relaxed – for while new members could not include their house amongst their assets, they could furnish a bank guarantee, itself based on its value (an arrangement which provided the bank involved with a fee of 3 per cent on the value of the house). The result was a rapid acceleration in the membership. In the twenty years up till 1975, it doubled to 7,700, then virtually doubled again in the next three years and by 1989 was up to over 34,000 – four times the level a mere fourteen years earlier.

Unfortunately the relationship of the members' agents, the underwriters who took on the risks and the brokers who financed them was not transparent, indeed was often incestuous, and the actual management was left to the mix of upper-class dilettantes and sharp working-class traders usual in the pre-1980s City. Both classes figured prominently amongst the guilty parties of the scams of the 1970s and 1980s. The most obvious scam involved 'baby syndicates', a veritable system of insider trading, in which insiders created special syndicates which were allocated the best risks while the dross was allocated to the mass of outsiders.

But until the 1980s conditions were so favourable that, as one chairman of Lloyd's put it, 'you could be quite thick and be a Lloyd's underwriter and make money'.[10] The problems were greatly exacerbated by the way Lloyd's was run. In an obituary of one former chairman, Sir Peter Green, Godfrey Hodgson wrote that the 'fall from grace' of this 'genial and essentially well-intentioned man ... was

evidence that few, if any, of the insiders in the Lloyd's market succeeded in escaping the cosy insider deals and double standards bred
by an atmosphere of privilege and secrecy'.[11] The result, wrote the
financial journalist Chrisopher Hirst, was that Lloyd's 'resembled a
garden in which the rabbits were in charge of the lettuce' – a situation
not remedied when it managed to get itself excluded from external
regulation in the 1982 Insurance Act. In the following four years Ian
Hay Davison, Lloyds' first outside chief executive, failed, in the words
of another journalist, 'to change Lloyd's belief in its own rectitude'.

In this atmosphere, even the best were infected. Robert Hiscox, a
former deputy chairman, was an example of the more honourable type
of Lloyd's man. He had discouraged potential members with what he
perceived as inadequate assets from joining 'so,' he told Julian Barnes,
'they ran out of this door and into Gooda Walker' – probably the
worst-hit syndicate of all. 'They trusted a 305-year-old institution, part
of Britain and the Empire, and didn't go into it with great depth.'
Unfortunately Hiscox's morals rather slipped when he remarked of the
newcomers, 'If God had not meant them to be sheared, He would
not have made them sheep.' Looking back over the disaster, Hickox
observed, quite reasonably, that 'England can only perish but by Englishmen' – and, only too often, by well-bred ones at that.

Newcomers should have been warned by a spate of scandals which
hit Lloyd's in the 1970s and early 1980s. The worst was the PCW case,
in which an underwriter, Peter Cameron-Webb, and his colleagues had
set up a tangled net of companies which received nearly £40 million
in reinsurance premiums paid by unsuspecting members. Typically,
the case was investigated exceedingly sloppily by Sir Peter Green, the
chairman. Moreover, none of the fraudsters involved in this or any of
Lloyd's many other scams ever went to jail, and some simply went
abroad to live in luxury in Florida or the South of France.

The 'Old Lloyd's' was destroyed in the early 1990s when three
years' losses of over £5 billion far outweighed the £3 billion in profits
accumulated since 1955. The losses resulted from what was called
'long-tail' business. Because claims take such a long time to be settled,
Lloyd's accounts are finalised two years in arrears. But this is far too
short a time for the settlement of claims as complicated as those
involved in civil actions relating to asbestosis. The first mention of
asbestos as a problem I have come across was the report of a conversation on the golf course in 1973 when one insider, Ralph Rokeby-
Johnson, told another that 'asbestos . . . will bankrupt Lloyds of London
and there is nothing we can do to stop it'. Except of course to spread
the loss to thousands of new, innocent names. Seven years later, a
court in California found that one insurance company alone faced
claims of up to $20 billion from asbestosis. The problem is so long-term

that back in 1984 one authority declared simply that 'we really ought
to look forward to 2003 to see how 1979 to 1983 will develop'. No-one
seems to have warned potential members of the problem. Equally.
no-one has managed to find a 'smoking gun', a case in which
'recruiters' deliberately misled potential members.

The recruiters had been well rewarded for their efforts in attracting
potential names, who were contacted at dinner or on the golf course
– there was one club in West Sussex whose members were particularly
susceptible to the siren sounds. Many of these became what were
termed 'deficit millionaires'* and included the usual run of lords, ladies
and country gentlefolk. There were only a handful of victims who
were not guilty of snobbery, greed or eagerness to avoid taxes – notably
the secretaries who were given membership on their retirement. The
unlucky ones were hauled before the – rightly dreaded – Hardship
Committee headed by the icy figure of Lady Archer to be stripped of
their assets and doomed to rely on a relatively tiny allowance. The
final tally of losses was said to be over £20 billion, though this was
greatly reduced by tax allowances. What is perhaps most remarkable
is that all the forced sales – of wine, houses and estates – represented
only a tiny blip in the wealth of the better-heeled. Once the rules and
regulations had been clarified to reduce the insiders' influence and a
series of chief executives had finally cleaned the Augean stables,
Lloyds re-emerged at the end of the 1990s a changed beast, with
corporate capital largely replacing that from individual names, still a
force in the world insurance industry, but no longer unique, just another
financial institution.

Lloyd's survived, individual banks and brokers were sold, often at
exorbitant prices, but Barings went spectacularly broke. Yet it was the
grandest of banking families, the only one to have accumulated five
peerages. Barings had collapsed once before, in 1890, brought down
by lending too much to Argentina, and had to be rescued because it
was so important that otherwise the credibility of the City of London
itself would have been at risk. But in 1995 the Bank of England could
let the bank go under, so great had been the decline in its financial,
though not its symbolic, importance. After 1890, wrote Stephen Fay,
'as bankers they had lost their nerve. But their collapse in 1995 was
a most significant event showing the depth of arrogance-cum-
ignorance-cum-incompetence still possible in the post-Big Bang City
provided, of course, that your name was Baring'.[12]

Institutionally, the downfall proved the impossibility of grafting a
trading operation with a high-earning, high-spending, red braces and

---

* In other words, their debts were more than a million pounds more than their
assets.

284

outsize cigar mentality onto one of the most staid of all London's traditional banks. As so often, disaster sprang out of success, in this case that of an operation run from Hong Kong by one Christopher Heath with Japanese warrants. These enabled buyers of bonds issued by Japanese companies to buy some of their shares at attractive prices. Heath had an unrivalled knowledge of the issuers' prospects and so knew more accurately than any other foreigner the profit to be made on a particular issue. Unfortunately Heath – and thus Baring Securities – suffered so badly from the collapse of the Japanese stock market in the early 1990s that by 1993 the losses were threatening the bank's stability. The supervisors at the Bank of England were worried and Heath was sacked by Andrew Tuckey, the bank's managing director. But the adventure had left the bank eager, too eager, to find a similar golden egg in the Far East.

The bank was brought down by an over-promoted clerk who exploited London's greed, naivety and ignorance of the more sophisticated sectors of the international financial world. The guilty party, Nick Leeson*, wanted to play in the big league, to impress his fellows in other banks, even though he was inexperienced and astonishingly young, a mere twenty-eight when he was finally found out. In their desperate search to replace the profits made by Heath, Barings made the most elementary mistake in trading practice: allowing the same person to supervise the 'back office' which dealt with the paperwork, as well as the trading, so that there was no-one to check on his performance. Moreover, as Leeson told Sir David Frost, the people in London 'wanted to believe in the profits being reported, and therefore they weren't willing to question' them. To make matters worse, they allowed Leeson to be a 'proprietary trader', i.e. to 'invest' the bank's own funds as well as those of its clients. He was, it goes without saying, trading in a type of market which no-one in authority in London knew anything about.

Leeson's activities were further helped, as Fay puts it, by 'the permissive style of management that was cultivated at Barings bank: business first, control second'. The bank was highly political, with Leeson's adventures protected from any detailed enquiries from London by his boss in Singapore. As for the Bank of England, the supervisor responsible, Christopher Thompson, later admitted that he did not understand the activities of Baring Securities, including the gambles Leeson was taking in the level of the Tokyo Stock market – punts which put at risk far more than the 25 per cent of a bank's capital which normally provides a warning sign to the regulators.

* In a typical example of City humour, he was described as a 'man with lots of balls but no Barings'.

In 1992 Leeson had started on a run of massive gambles – using a special secret account, numbered 88888 to conform with the Chinese belief that eight was a lucky number. By the end of 1994, his gambles were already piling up losses but his final undoing sprang from the uncertainty which followed the severe earthquake that hit the Japanese city of Kobe on January 17 1995. The sheer complexity of his activities – which involved a number of forgeries to cover his tracks – eventually gave him a nervous breakdown and he fled with his wife to Kuala Lumpur – though, even a fortnight after the earthquake, his losses would merely have damaged, not destroyed, Barings. For the bank collapsed only after his last desperate efforts to win back his losses by betting ever more frantically on a recovery in the Tokyo market.

Once the truth started to come out, the Bank of England gathered together all the major British-owned banks in London, rather ignoring the importance of foreign-owned institutions, to face Barings' losses, which added up to £650 million. The Bank immediately made clear that no public money would be forthcoming, a sure sign of Barings' diminished importance. The merchant bankers felt that 'there but for the grace of God go we'. By contrast the clearing bankers were less sympathetic, none less so than Peter Birch from the building society-turned-bank, Abbey National. Birch had tried to mount a joint venture with Barings but had found them, in Fay's words, 'pompous, arrogant and ferociously political'. All the bankers were horrified by the continuing arrogance of Barings' top brass and their assumption that their bonuses, which amounted to £105 million, would be paid – a seemingly ridiculous request which had to be taken seriously to keep the team together and to ensure that Barings could be sold off.

Unfortunately, because the bankers hadn't grasped the nature of the business involved, they couldn't put together over a weekend the logical solution, which was to take responsibility for Barings' contracts and unload them over time, a step which would have brought the contracts down to manageable amounts. As it was, Barings was sold for the proverbial £1 to a Dutch bank. 'Credit was lost, honour was lost,' wrote Chritopher Fildes, that wittiest and most perceptive of City journalists, 'Leeson, the agent of this downfall, was greedy, ignorant and panicky by turns, and crooked too. But his panic, ignorance and greed were no more than a symptom of Barings' own. The house had been betrayed by what was false within.' Financially, the charities which had relied on the dividends earned by the Baring foundation, which actually owned the bank's shares, lost their grants. Worse off were the holders of the £100 million of 9.25 per cent perpetual bonds issued in 1993, a classic choice for 'widows and orphans' looking for a safe investment. They lost everything.

The Barings retreated to their country estates, after having removed the valuable family portraits from the bank's walls. The *Daily Telegraph*, normally a loyal supporter of the City, editorialised that 'if Mr Leeson goes to prison while the former board of Barings continues to go to Glyndebourne, this sorry saga will leave the bitterest of tastes'. He did, for four years in a gaol in Singapore. The former chairman, Sir Peter Baring, declared that the episode showed the family's mistake in 'giving too much responsibility to a clerk' and told journalists that his family's bank had been the victim of a plot amongst some unidentified foreign traders. He remained on the board of Glyndebourne for two more years, the same period Tuckey stayed on at Covent Garden, though he failed in his ambition to be chairman.

In fact the take-over of S. G. Warburg by the Swiss two years earlier had marked the end of any hope that any British financial institution – even one so foreign in its origins as SGW – could remain independent. But by then they had become arrogantly British, and not for nothing were they nicknamed Warberrys. As one American put it, they had become 'English and City Establishment through and through'. But after Barings' collapse the sell-out of the other major family-owned merchant banks in the City such as Schroders, Flemings and Kleinwort Benson was only a matter of – a very short – time. The City of London had finally become a foreign colony, with London having a 'branch plant' mentality – though, unlike say the foreign-owned electronic factories in Scotland, it remained the key element in the activities of the firms that controlled its activities.

And the Bank of England? Well, the Barings' disaster wasn't the first it had failed to prevent. The early 1980s had witnessed the expensive collapse in 1983 of the bank owned by Johnson Matthey, the bullion dealers. The Bank had intervened because it was persuaded of the danger of a 'systemic' collapse of the London gold market. Eight years later, its reputation suffered another bad blow with the infinitely bigger crash of BCCI, with losses between $5 and $20 billion incurred by an institution universally known in the City as the Bank of Crooks and Cocaine International. Unsurprisingly, within a couple of years the Bank had lost its power to supervise the British banking system. Yet in 1997 the first act of Gordon Brown, the new Chancellor of the Exchequer, was to delegate control over interest rates to a Monetary Policy Committee organised by the Bank. It has always proved a great survivor.

Notes

1. *New Statesman*, November 8 1999.
2. *Independent*,
3. *New Statesman*, January 22 1999.

4. Quoted in A. H. Halsey op cit.
5. *Guardian*, February 24 2001 (Obituary of Grylls).
6. *Girlitude: A memoir of the fifties and sixties*, Jonathan Cape, 1999.
7. *Guardian*, July 22 2000.
8. *New Statesman*, November 8 1999.
9. *Observer*, March 4 2001.
10. Quoted by Julian Barnes, *Letters from London, 1990–1995*, Picador, 1995.
11. *Independent*, July 31 1996.
12. *The Collapse of Barings*, Richard Cohen Books, 1996.

12

Snapshots from a New Millennium

THE TRANSFORMATION IN BRITISH LIFE continued after the Tories' departure from office in 1997. Constitutionally, Mrs Thatcher made her own contribution with her systematic reduction of the role, importance, financial independence and, by abolishing the Greater London Council, the very existence of local government. As Anthony King points out, its replacement, the Greater London Authority, created in 1999, gives the mayor and the assembly 'a good deal of political leverage but very little in the way of actual political power'.

But it is the Blair government that has made a bigger contribution to constitutional change than anything except our entry into Europe. For the first time in 800 years, hereditary peers no longer have any say in the governance of the land – except for a token ninety-two, less than an eighth of the total, and then only until the government works out the final shape, size, powers and membership of a new second chamber. And, as we've seen, within days of his coming to power, Gordon Brown, the Chancellor of the Exchequer, effectively gave the Bank of England the power to determine interest rates, a key element in economic policy.

Just as fundamentally, Blair has devolved most of the functions of government to a Scottish assembly and rather more restricted powers to a similar body in Wales. From a historic point of view, the new executive in Northern Ireland is even more innovative since the mere fact of power-sharing* (especially between members as historically hostile as they are in Ulster) goes against the grain of British tradition, based as it is on the simple assumption that the winner takes all. By contrast, the Ulster assembly is designed to ensure that the majority – i.e. the Unionists – can never have complete control. Moreover, these new bodies outside England are being elected by a variety of new-fangled electoral systems, none by the first-past-the-post variety previously enshrined in all British elections.

* Members of the executive come from all the major parties.

289

The devolution of power to the Celtic fringe has naturally led to pressure from some of the English regions for more power, and this pressure is itself justified and increased by the resurgence of many of the cities which had been doubly devastated – by Mrs Thatcher's centralising policies and by the consequences of the decline in manufacturing industry. It was, curiously, the expansion of universities which first started to give life to a number of city centres like those of Leeds and Newcastle-upon-Tyne but, above all, of Manchester, which houses more students than any other city in Britain outside London. The gaiety the students brought was ephemeral, the money limited, but they did provide a glimpse of liveliness – and, in Manchester's case, a pop and club scene which became famous the world over.

More important was a revival in civic pride – the first example being the choice of Glasgow as European City of Culture in 1990. Despite the jeers, the city's slogan 'Glasgow's miles better' proved justified. The councils in English cities had problems adjusting to the need to work with private developers for obvious financial reasons. The best example is Leeds, where a Labour council only accepted with some reluctance the idea of a Development Corporation. Together they helped transform the city into the biggest centre for professional services throughout the North of England. Other cities – even Liverpool, for so long the epitome of urban decay – have followed suit, but all such developments leave a ring of poverty and decay around the centre, its salvation impeded because of a lack of education and the virtual collapse of society.

The problems faced by towns and cities outside the South have been exacerbated by the high proportion of immigrants they contain. Unfortunately, in the minds of many people, all of the arrivals since the war have been lumped together. Some, like many of the Bangladeshis in former mill towns, have always been at the bottom of the social and economic heap, while others, most obviously the Asians expelled from East Africa in the late 1960s and early 1970s, have emerged as the natural successors to earlier generations of Jewish immigrants. The first generations worked all the hours God sent to provide their children, 'my son the doctor', with a proper education. As Philip Whitehead put it: 'The corner shop open at all hours, the nurse on the night shift, the kebab house and Chinese takeaway: all added something to the land of the permanently closed tea shop'. They allowed Britain, in Arthur Marwick's phrase, 'to acquire a new cosmopolitanism without shedding its old xenophobia'.

For outsiders to succeed in challenging the existing order required a degree of self-confidence inevitably lacking in the first generation of immigrants, especially those who have succeeded, partly at least by accepting the rules of the existing socio-cultural game. The generation of Jewish refugees from Central Europe did much for Britain in the forty years after the war. But in doing so they helped buttress the idea of English exceptionalism and superiority because of their gratitude to the country that afforded them refuge. The most obvious case was Isaiah Berlin, whose family were refugees from the Russian Revolution. He was one of those who, in the words of Perry Anderson, had done most to serve up to the English a self-congratulatory picture of their own supposedly liberal virtues. His absorption was so complete that at his memorial service William Waldegrave could say quite truthfully, 'If you had asked me to show you what I meant by the ideal of Englishness, I would have taken you to see a Latvian, Jewish, German, Italian mixture of all the cultures of Europe, I would have taken you to see Isaiah Berlin.'

Other staunch Britons, like the journalist Peregrine Worsthorne, the son of a Belgian father, or Norman St John Stevas expressed their gratitude, their obeisance to the Gods of the English, in an exaggerated respect for all the old traditional English values and institutions. By contrast, the new generation was ungrateful, felt, often quite rightly, that it had been discriminated against and that its positive contributions had not been adequately appreciated. This led to a wave of separatism, to demands that each group should be recognised as an independent entity. But this was never as serious a problem as was made out. The acceptance of the minorities that absorption was inevitable and indeed desirable was shown most dramatically in a by-election in 1989 in the Vauxhall constituency of South London, which include the troubled Caribbean stronghold of Brixton. The Labour Party nominated a (white) woman outsider in Kate Hoey, yet the three non-white candidates polled miserably badly. For the British culture did change and with it the attitude of ethnic minorities. A study by the Policy Studies Institute in 1984 found that blacks and Asians invariably fared worse than whites. Fourteen years later a similar study found that there had been a considerable convergence towards the experience of the community as a whole. Some communities of immigrants were doing better than their white equivalents while others were falling further behind.

Even the hardest problem of all, the inevitable and continuing tension between the police and immigrant communities, was tackled, if belatedly. The inadequate response of the Metropolitan Police to the murder of the black teenager Stephen Lawrence provoked the Macpherson Report, which in turn led to a rethink by the Met in response to its accusations of 'institutionalised racism'. Whatever the problems, not just in London, or indeed in Britain as a whole, the situation is far less ugly than in France or, most obviously, in American cities where it is the police who tend to commit the murders and assaults and not racist local gangs.

291

Of course the path to a genuinely 'multicultural' Britain has been paved with obstacles, as witness the history of Europe's biggest and second oldest* carnival, that held at the end of August in Notting Hill. Over the past twenty-five years it has been the scene of riots, repeated clashes between revellers and the police, all surrounded by a mist of ganja. Yet by the end of the millennium it had become a traditional event in which the police had learnt not to intervene – albeit at the cost of some injuries and the occasional death amongst the revellers. Nevertheless, and despite the continuing cultural problems, only Britain could produce a television series such as *Goodness Gracious Me,* with its all-Asian cast mocking the English, let alone *East is East*, a film which, through a mix of tears and laughter, tackled the single thorniest problem faced by Asian immigrants, the painful change from a patriarchal society in which the father decides the marital fate of his children.

Two other signs of absorption have particularly struck me. One is the names of some of the recent contestants in the *University Challenge* quiz which brings together the brightest and best amongst 'British' students. They include Dalyn, Krasun, Vlante, Saha, Gripairos, Gasper, Khawaja, Kreps, Hedgecock, Bjortomt, Mannix. Haverty-Stacke, Midwinter and Underdown. The other is the story of Victor Obugu, capped for Britain as a front row forward in what was previously the most snobby of sports, rugby union, and an entrepreneur with shares in a chain of sports bars called Shoeless Joe's. He lives well, carries two mobile phones and when playing for England carted the whole team off to what he described as 'the best bar in town in Buenos Aires'. This, or so the story goes, turned out to be the best brothel in town, for Obugu felt he could be as much of a card as he wanted, with no need to display the respectability formerly expected of any non-white British sportsman. To him it was not the twenty-six England caps that he treasured most in his playing career but his years with Bath: 'I've played with the same players for over a decade,' he said, 'and there's a closeness which you can't compare with playing for England. It's been a unique experience.'

But the problems remain. Until the riots in many northern towns of the summer of 2001, the inevitable tensions were concealed behind a façade of increasing multiculturalism, itself undermined by the unwillingness of Asians, especially the Muslims, to even try to allow the female members of their families to adopt English ways – or in many cases the English language, a problem highlighted in the film *East Is East*. Moreover, the legacy of the years of systematic discrimination remains alive in 'reverse racism', the desire of well-meaning white

* The oldest is held in Chapeltown and Harehills in Leeds.

liberals to favour ethnic minorities and to insist on the gulf between the races. This is shown most obviously in the determination of social workers to pursue an adoption policy in which race was the determining factor. This denied our common humanity and accepted the American-influenced idea that roots were all that mattered. The prevailing attitude was that expressed by Felicity Collier, director of the British Agencies for Adoption and Fostering, that 'for a child it can be terribly important that the person who brings you up, takes you to school and walks down the street with you actually looks like you'.[1] To which the only real answer is that what matters most is the love parents bring to the child's life. The practice continues, despite repeated government attempts dating back to 1990 to ensure that local authorities considered each case on its merits – significantly, it was a minister of Caribbean origin, Paul Boateng, who went furthest in trying to ensure that local authorities changed their criteria.

On the 'ethnic' side, there remained lingering elements of the old chippy attitude, exemplified by a Report from the Runnymede Trust in 2000. This contained numerous complaints which were, happily, becoming increasingly unjustified, notably that the national culture was still defined by a person's colour and that 'assimilation . . . really meant the absorption by the so-called majority – people were expected to give up everything to belong'. To which Jack Straw, then Home Secretary, replied very justly that 'the concept of Britishness has become an inclusive plural one – with people happily defining them-selves as "Black British" or "Chinese-British" '. This was a rebuke to Norman Tebbit, who defined a true Brit as one who supported the English cricket team whoever they were playing, even if the spectators were of Pakistani origin. Unfortunately, statements like Tebbit's do nothing to mitigate the underlying depth of racial antagonism between whites and coloured people. Such antagonism was dramatically shown in the riots in miserable Lancashire towns such as Oldham and Burnley in the summer of 2001, and illustrated most vividly by the re-emergence of the British National Party at that year's general election, with a vote far exceeding those registered by the National Front during the depths of the 1970s.

There are all too many signs of a more damaging rift, that between Asians and blacks. In the summer of 2000 there were two murders, one of an Asian kid by a gang of blacks, another of a black boy by a gang of Asian youths. These were only the tip of a seething mountain of race hatred, with the Asians despising the blacks and being hated in return as weedy and money-grubbing – unhappy echoes of past white attitudes towards Jews. But the contrast was not new. When she was seventeen, the journalist Yasmin Alibhai-Brown played Juliet with a brilliant black youth as Romeo. Her father never talked to her again.

The new confidence has one extraordinary result: the growth of networking, a practice particularly evident in the career of the Labour MP Keith Vaz and which resembles the old-fashioned British version, except that the monetary connection is so much more blatant. More acceptable to British tastes are the foods the Indian immigrants have created for the delectation of their British customers. These include Bombay mix, a delicious combination of nibbles and spicy nuts, chicken tikka masala, hymned by Robin Cook as England's most typical food, and the whole gastronomic universe known as Balti cooking (allegedly invented in the small Warwickshire town of Leamington Spa). As Gulam Kaderbhoy Noon, one of the best producers of Indian foods, told the *Financial Times*: 'Outside of restaurants, Indian food just twelve years ago was insipid, badly packaged, a million miles from being authentic, full of curry powder and badly cooked.' By the end of the millennium, the market for Indian food was £2.8 billion and an Academy of Asian Culinary Arts had been set up at Thames Valley University in West London (conveniently located near Southall).

If attitudes to different races have changed irregularly and sometimes only superficially, others have been altered surprisingly little by the shocks of the last years of the twentieth century. Over the past thirty years, MORI has conducted regular polls on people's attitudes, and some of the results are highly revealing of trends in social perceptions. Despite fusses about doctors and teachers no longer being as trusted as they were, their scores have actually risen since 1983, as have those of television newsreaders, now considered almost as trustworthy as the judges. By contrast, their fellow journalists are still considered the most unreliable of all. More intriguing is the revulsion against Thatcherite attitudes to business. While back in 1976 over three-quarters of respondents believed that nationalised industries were less efficient than those in private ownership, the proportion has now fallen to two in five. Equally, only one in ten now consider profits as the most important criterion when judging companies – less than half the proportion in the Thatcherite heyday of the mid-1980s, while a general cynicism ensures that the statement that profits 'make things better for everyone' now finds only half as many adherents as it did back in the 1970s – indeed, the proportion in favour of the statement continued to decline throughout Thatcher's reign.

Mrs Thatcher had provided the confidence that things could be changed. She thus psychologically empowered her natural successor, Tony Blair, in his efforts to transform the Labour Party. Mrs Thatcher despised the working classes, while Tony Blair finds them – and above all their representatives in the trades union movement – inconvenient, an obstacle to his vision of The Third Way. Unfortunately, however, this vision is so fuzzy that compilers of dictionaries had some trouble defining both it and Blairism. One early draft of the new Penguin Dictionary referred to 'the absence of a fundamental underlying ideology ... close attention to prevailing public opinion'. The final words of the entry were blander, and further from the truth: 'especially regarded as a modified form of traditional socialism'. David Marquand has produced perhaps the best summary of the two doctrines espoused by Blair and Thatcher. Blairism, he wrote, 'espouses a vision of the entrepreneurial ideal of the early nineteenth century ... It disdains traditional elites and glorifies self-made meritocrats ... Like its predecessor, the new regime is for individual achievement, not collective action ... It is for widening opportunity, not for redistributing reward ... Thatcherism was exclusionary; New Labour is inclusionary. Margaret Thatcher was a warrior, Tony Blair is a healer. Where she divided, he unites ... In place of the Thatcherite cold shower it offers a warm bath ... This may have nothing to do with social democracy, but it is the nearest thing to Christian Democracy that modern British politics have known.'

Christianity is the most obvious leitmotiv in the Blairite philosophy, which is socially profoundly old-fashioned, marking a return to middle-class family values, doing the best for your children, and emphasising respect for the law with phrases such as 'tough on crime, tough on the causes of crime'. But this attitude ensures that Blair is totally unable to come to grips with the elementary fact that the vast majority of his generation, and their successors, smoked cannabis and a substantial minority at least experimented with many other, more dangerous, drugs. So he cannot ride with the new attitudes towards drugs which are less harmful than tobacco, most obviously cannabis. As late as 1998, Norman Tebbit had asserted that everyone involved in the drug trade should be executed. Yet there was a remarkable reaction to a demand in 2000 by Ann Widdecombe then Shadow Home Secretary for the imposition of an automatic £100 fine for possession of even the smallest quantity of cannabis. This produced a frank admission by a number of members of the Shadow Cabinet that they too had toyed with cannabis in their youth – though the New Labour Cabinet, apart from the incorrigible Mo Mowlam, had refused to talk about the subject. But by the end of 2001 cannabis had, effectively been de-criminalised.

Blair also finds it difficult to cope with the whole idea of class, hoping against hope that we are becoming a classless society, his mission being 'to allow more people to become middle-class'. As Andrew Adonis and Stephen Pollard point out, it is 'as though governments distributed rights of passage'. Of course, the numbers of those who consider themselves 'middle-class' have been rising throughout the post-war period – I vividly remember Lord David Cecil remarking in the course of a lecture forty-five years ago that 'since the middle classes have been rising for so long it is surprising that they have not gone further'. But there has been an amazing retreat from the historic fascination with proletcult. This emerged most dramatically when John Prescott, the only serious representative of Old 'Prolelabour' in the Cabinet, told an interviewer that 'by the nature of being an MP and the salary I earn I'm middle-class. My roots, my background and the way I act is working-class, but it would be hypocritical to say that I'm anything but middle-class now'. It was left to Peter Mandelson to blurt out the underlying attitude of New Labour with his reaction to the idea that there should be more working-class MPs, retorting that they were 'northern, horny-handed, dirty-overalled'.

But there is still a substantial underclass which lives without a wage-earning adult in the household and suffers from poor housing, poor health and all the other symptoms of deprivation. 'Two late 1990s figures tell it all,' write Adonis and Pollard, 'a quarter of all children are growing up in families with no working adult, more than twice the proportion in the late 1970s; and a third of school drop-outs – those who leave school with no, or virtually no, qualifications – are unemployed, up from 6 per cent in 1970.' Unsurprisingly, the unemployed are significantly sicker than the employed.

This underclass will not even have easy access to decent food because it's simply unprofitable for supermarkets to open in the areas where they live and local shops invariably go downhill and shut after being vandalised once too often. Even the inevitably limited pleasures enjoyed by the new poor cost more than they ought. They gamble more than average on the lottery, they smoke more than the better-off. Indeed, according to Adonis and Pollard, 'half the single parents and three-quarters of couples on income support typically spend a fifth of their disposable income support on cigarettes. Thus a very large share of social security benefits given to families with low incomes is given straight back to the Treasury through excise tax'. Nevertheless critics of the situation sometimes forget that the parameters of poverty have changed: you are considered poor if you share a bedroom after the age of eleven or don't have holidays away from home. But beneath the statistics is the simple fact that society is not as flexible as New Labour likes to make out: Adonis and Pollard conclude that 'where you are born largely determines where you end up'.

The situation of women often echoes that of the poor: still unequal but still making progress, albeit unevenly. On the credit side there is the vast increase in the numbers of women in higher education, less than a third of the total in 1950, half of a far greater number forty-five years later. But in some respects progress, or rather greater openness, can make the situation seem worse, not better. One of the biggest elements in the increase in crime has been the inclusion of violent assaults in the home against women and children which were common-place, and virtually unreported, even thirty years ago. For, as Caroline Coon put it, 'one of the greatest battles won over the past thirty years has been the ability to talk about child abuse, domestic violence, rape'.

Anecdotal evidence shows the – very varied – state of the gender game. In 1999 an absurd case revealed the extent to which some institutions were behind the times when a female employee sued the Professional Golfers' Association which had tried to sack her for wear-ing trousers to work. Similarly clubs, whether catering to the establish-ment in St James's or for manual workers, remain deeply resistant to women members. Furthermore, there was an enormous fuss when a City fund manager, Nicola Horlick, moved from one bank to another. To many people the idea that a mother of five, of humble origins, could be earning £1 million a year seemed difficult to accept.

Inevitably, too, there is always a step back being taken. Penelope Leach, the leading adviser on how to bring up children, has the unfortu-nate ability to make women feel guilty if they do not devote all their waking hours to their offspring and has thus provided the reason for innumerable traumas (my wife and I were lucky: we brought up our four children under the far more relaxed rule of Dr Spock). Then there is laddism, the addiction to unrestrained male behaviour characteristic of a whole class and one unfortunately matched by the growing phenomenon of the hard-drinking laddette, fearful of being thought a prude or prig. The attitude goes with a male refusal to accept responsi-bility for children. The Child Support Agency, founded in 1993, was not only attacked because it was inefficient and in trying to be fair merely made its rules maddeningly complicated but was also resented because it was trying to ensure that absent fathers helped to pay for their children's upbringing.

The resultant confusion, especially among the increasing number of insecure, unattached thirty-somethings, caused the totally unexpected success of *Bridget Jones' Diary* written by a clever young journalist Helen Fielding. As Alex Clark pointed out, she 'couldn't get a man, couldn't hold a job ... [was] an obsessional neurotic, whose daily record of alcohol units, calories, negative thoughts and 1471* calls is less of an attempt to attain clarity than a continuing counsel of despair. Bridget Jones's real problems, as any psychotherapist would suss out pretty quickly, are low self-esteem, substance addiction, an inability to form intimate relationships with members of the opposite sex and an insufficiently resolved bond with her mother' – clearly a mix which

---

* The code dialled to find out who has phoned.

297

found echoes with a whole generation both in Britain and abroad since the book sold three million copies in thirty countries.

This same pattern of irregular progress can be observed in education. Yes, more children are going into higher education, but the worse-off are still at a severe disadvantage compared to their social superiors. As Adonis and Pollard state baldly, the school system in England, 'more than any other in the Western world, is founded on a division between state and private'. A recent study by the Institute for Education reported that the average gap between classes and backgrounds has not narrowed with the years, and the average education attainments, particularly of lower-class children, is still well below that of our Continental neighbours. Other reports confirm that the level of 'functional illiteracy' is around double that in Germany. The problem remains largely the same as it has always been: the way that working-class parents see no value in promoting their children's education, even though today, as never before, their hopes of a decent livelihood depend on their educational achievements. The result, as a teacher at a low-achieving comprehensive put it, is that 'I'm afraid that Darren, Dean, Damian, Liam and Nathan can't do it, never will do it, and frankly would not give a damn if they don't do it [get decent exam results] at all'. Meanwhile the pressure on private schools to achieve ever better academic results is still growing – so much so that it is more difficult to get into Eton (unless you're a member of the royal family) than into Winchester, the traditional intellectual leader. And in 1996, after the headmaster of Cheltenham College had tried to broaden the intake and increase the scope of the education he was providing, he was sacked for not coming up with examination results as high as those of comparable schools.

Fortunately (for the department he ran so well, if not for him) the Secretary for Education in the 1997 Labour government, David Blunkett, has been blind since birth and thus experienced at first hand the assumption that handicapped children could only aspire to the most menial of clerical jobs. For several years he and his deputy and successor, Estelle Morris, who had left school at fifteen, were able to utilise the brutal but effective Chris Woodhead, whom they inherited as Chief Inspector of Schools and who had taken it upon himself to clear up what he perceived as a terrible educational mess. In doing so, they greatly improved standards at every age level despite the protestations of the 'progressives' of the 1960s who now seem rather passé. But now the changes are going further. As the highly respected David Hargreaves, Professor of Education at Cambridge, says, 'Comprehensives have turned out to be a very transient stage in British education. And not one that has inspired much love, except among activists and specialists. There have seldom been examples of parents

298

parading with placards saying "save our comprehensive".' Alistair Campbell, Tony Blair's ever-blunt Press Secretary, put the situation more crudely when he referred to 'bog-standard' comprehensives. The new willingness to provide a wide range of different types of schools at secondary level could well be the only practical way to reduce the effect of the current educational apartheid, where children in independent schools and in a minority of comprehensives possess an enormous advantage – up to four years in some cases – over children generally from less well-off backgrounds in lesser establishments (though even these will benefit from the extra money belatedly provided at the end of Blair's first term for investment in schools and teachers).

Unfortunately, the institutions of higher education are in a mess. This reflects a continuing strain of social snobbery in the sense that manual labour, however skilled, was judged infra dig, well below the most superficial book learning. Hence the present situation of a society with tens of thousands of graduates in media studies and not enough technicians or engineers, an imbalance compounded with the received idea that research is more prestigious than teaching – a notion challenged by Ms Morris after she had succeeded David Blunkett. Hence the absurd way in which universities are judged not as schools are by the 'added value' they provide to their students but, almost exclusively, by the quality of the research they produce. But there is one major light in the darkness. Despite the collapse of so many dot.com and other internet-related companies, the enthusiasm for computer-based ventures seems unabated. This represents something of a revolution. For the first time for 150 years it is no longer infra dig to be an engineer, since computers are perceived as a clean, socially acceptable form of engineering and thus attract many thousands of able youngsters who would never have dreamt of going in for civil, electrical or mechanical engineering.

Yet it was the long-term shortage of engineers, combined with the results of the 'advisory mentality', which was responsible for one of the major disaster areas of Britain at the turn of the Millennium, the state of Britain's railways and the apparent inability of the company responsible, Railtrack, to get its act together. The shortage of engineers was exacerbated by the appalling mess made of privatisation. Those involved proceeded on the arrogant and wholly unjustified assumption that the people actually running the railway system were stupid and ignorant and so brushed aside their views, notably that railways were indeed a system and should not be fragmented. They were ignored, the system was smashed into over a hundred pieces, and many experienced engineers were encouraged to take early retirement.

The so-called advisers who created the disaster were part of a tribe which includes lawyers, accountants, management consultants, merchant bankers, analysts and the like. They seem omnipotent – and, what is more, vastly overpaid relative to those they are advising, except for a handful of overpaid chief executives whose pay, golden hand-shakes and pensions are seemingly totally unrelated to the profits they earn for the shareholders. 'Fat cats' they were termed after the example set by the first of them, the hapless Cedric Brown, the chairman of British Gas, by no means the greediest of executives.

These often parasitical advisory activities absorb the energies of an ever-increasing proportion of the country's best minds – although the recession of 2001 may well mark the peak of their success. In a survey by the *Economist* written in the late 1970s but which could apply at any time in the last forty years of the twentieth century, John Plender wrote how 'a large number of talented people are duplicating each other's efforts in research and investment management to pick short-term winners in the stock market'. Yet the flow continues. A frightening analysis of Oxford graduates showed that in 1994 nearly a third went into accountancy, the law or 'commerce' – which generally meant the City – against only little more than a tenth back in 1971. Inevitably, the biggest losers were the public sector – and 'industry'.

The results of this migration were an unhappy mix of short-termism and refusal to look at the content of businesses. When Nicholas Berry, one of that rare breed, a real venture capitalist investing his own money, was trying to induce a major Swiss company to move forward into the twentieth century, 'a world-famous institution sent along an investment manager. The man they chose, who represented a holding worth £40 million, was a skinhead. [He] did not consider it was worth knowing much about the business, or any business for that matter. What interested him, as a screen watcher, was the possibility of discovering a minor statistical anomaly between the company's valuation and that of its peer group'. The attitude was only too typical, and this sort of atmosphere was, and is, by no means conducive to long-term investment.

The result is 'heroes' such as Sir Clive Thompson, chairman of Rentokil, so applauded by his fellow businessmen that he rose to be president of the CBI. This was his reward for twenty years in which had propelled his company, in the words of the *Economist,* 'from a tiny royal rat-catcher into a sprawling services giant with 130,000 employees and a peak stock market value of nearly £14 billion.'[3] By promising, and for a time achieving, earnings growth of 20 per cent a year, he was lionised by the British investment community, yet provided a perfect illustration both of its credulity – since no firm, however well-managed, can sustain such a rate of growth for ever – and of the very narrow limits of modern British corporate ambition. Rentokil is the very opposite of the sort of high-tech, cutting-edge enterprise which Britain badly needs and which businessmen surely ought to admire. It always was, and remains, a collection of low-tech, low-wage businesses, providing a jumble of services ranging from pest control to the provision and care of tropical plants for offices. Thompson's attitude to long-term investment was brutally simple and fitted in perfectly with the prejudices of the investment analysts and pension fund managers who were his real audience. 'Often the long-term never comes,' he said, and he naturally devised a pay structure that explicitly rewarded short-term performance and followed it through with a military style of management combined with a 'divide and rule' attitude towards his senior employees. No wonder one analyst commented that 'Rentokil has forgotten to remember that this is a people business'. And as with so many other British business heroes – including, most notably, Sir Richard Greenbury of Marks & Spencers (once voted the businessmen's favourite businessman) the disappointment felt by the City at Thompson's fall from grace was as disproportionate as the earlier plaudits for his success.

The lack of stock market enthusiasm for companies pursuing long-term investment policies has ensured that many famous British brand names – from the *Daily Telegraph* to Sotheby's, from Land Rover to Harvey Nichols – have fallen into the hands of foreigners better able to exploit the long-term potential of the very real assets they represented. The openness of the British economy – and the relative cheapness and docility of British workers – has also encouraged a flow of industrial investment into Britain from all over the world by firms willing to take a longer view. This trend was not confined to manufacturing industry. By the end of 1997, there was not a single British-owned financial institution operating on a global scale. The stock of investment by foreign companies is now worth a full half of Britain's total GDP – up from a fifth only a few years ago. Half of British exports are generated by non-British firms and their superior dynamism ensures that the trend will continue. The acceptance of what is known as the 'branch plant mentality' – symbolised by the welcome accorded to Bill Gates by Tony Blair* – implies that Britain's industrial policy, such as it is, will, increasingly be dictated from abroad, representing a severe and possibly irreversible loss of economic independence.

Those companies which have remained in British hands are increasingly run by foreigners, especially if they were in a bad way when the newcomer took over, thus providing him or her with the opportunity to make fundamental changes. To take a random sample: an Italian has revived Selfridges, an Australian has rescued British Airways,

---

* The reaction to Gates's investment by one distinguished academic, John Sutherland, was simple: 'He liked Cambridge University so much he bought it.'

Marjorie Scardino, an American (and a woman at that), has provided a new impetus for Pearson, owner of the *Financial Times* and Penguin, a Dutchman is trying to salvage Marks & Spencer and, finally, a Dutchwoman, Clara Furse, has given new life to the London Stock Exchange. Even Sir John Browne, who, as chairman of BP, is probably the most successful 'English' businessman of the late 1990s, one so respectable that he was invited to deliver the BBC Reith Lectures, has a Hungarian mother. In sport it's the same story: there's a Swede in charge of the English football team and a Zimbabwean in charge of the England cricket team – which itself is captained by a man called Nasser Hussain – while a New Zealander coached Britain's gold medal-winning rowing eight at the Sydney Olympics.

Britain seems to have lacked the ability to breed confidently decisive chief executives, a field in which Richard Branson is virtually the only well-known name, though a handful of businessmen have managed to combine social vision with entrepreneurial flair like Sir Ernest Hall who transformed the enormous mill complex at Saltaire in West Yorkshire into a highly successful commercial community, while the late Nicholas Saunders of Neal's Yard, retailers of superb and genuine English foods, was both a businessman and a visionary who eventually went off to proclaim virtues of the drug Ecstasy.

But we may be seeing the emergence of a new, post-Thatcher generation of more orthodox business leaders, personified by such confident, unshowy and undeniably effective executives as Terry Leahy of Tesco and Chris Gent of Vodaphone. Older managers were brought up in the atmosphere of defensiveness which was probably a necessary element in industrial strategy during the years until our departure from the European Monetary System in September 1992. This financial earthquake, although a disaster in the short term, marked the beginning of a decade of the steady, non-inflationary economic progress the country had not witnessed since the war.

Inevitably, it has taken some time for confidence in the future to become embedded in the country's business ethic. But there are already signs of the shape of entrepreneurialism to come. Among her other victims, Mrs Thatcher had done severe damage to the idea of the traditional English boozer, particularly those where the industrial proletariat had gone to slake their considerable thirsts with vast quantities of beer. Hence the growth of every type of new-fangled pub, usually owned by individual entrepreneurs such as Tim Wetherspoon. 'If you go back to 1975,' says Hugh Osmond, 'there were pubs, fish and chip shops and Chinese takeaways. Before there was nothing for young people.' Osmond started running bars at university, was inspired by the success of Pizza Express and found further inspiration from a visit to the United States. Helped by changes in licensing laws to allow all-day drinking – which was first introduced in Scotland in the late 1970s amid dire and totally unsubstantiated warnings of unbridled depravity – he and his partner Roger Myers set up their own chains such as the Pelican and the Dome, which he describes as 'a café bar where you could see into the interior: the absolute opposite of a pub where the key is nooks, corners, hidey-holes, browniness'. In 1999, in a coup unimaginable even a few years earlier, their company, Punch Taverns, took over Allied Domecq's 5,500 pubs in the teeth of a bid from the old-established and far larger Whitbread group which had already been accepted by the Allied board.

Over the past couple of decades, workers in the City have usually felt sorry for those in industry, but by the late 1990s an increasing number of well-qualified young people were rebelling against the advisory world, more particularly against the appallingly long hours they were forced to work, mostly spent staring at screens. Anecdotal evidence is backed by the findings of a survey by the French bank Crédit Agricole of European youngsters in early 2000. This revealed that a far higher a proportion of young Brits (35 per cent as against maximum of 26 per cent elsewhere in Europe) thought that the best way to get rich was to start up your own business rather than invest in property (which would surely have been the answer of a similar group ten years earlier). The Brits were more convinced that hard work, rather than luck, was the key to success – but they were notably less enthusiastic about the role played by honesty.

The businesses where Britain should, in theory, still rule are in the media, since so high a proportion of young talent has poured into the sector over the past forty years. Yet here again we have not been able to get our business act together. For all the plethora of talent from actors to producers, writers and designers, most work for the Americans on films which are labelled British but whose profits almost invariably cross the Atlantic. Worse, in many fields we seem to have lost the golden creative touch we possessed in the 1960s. The problem has merely been compounded by government initiatives. Few people can now remember, and none without cringing, such as Panel 2000, a 'task force' of 'cultural achievers' headed by Robin Cook to lead 'a full frontal attack on the myth of a tired Britain'. As Andy Beckett noted, 'Nearly everyone on the panel was over forty.' But culturally, the early years of the first Labour government were dominated by two disasters – the Millennium Dome and the whole idea of 'Cool Britannia'.

The term 'Cool Britannia' was originally coined by that typically 1960s phenomenon The Bonzo Dog Doo Dah Band in a twist version of 'Rule Britannia'. Twenty years later it was resurrected by Sarah Moynihan Williams, an American-born solicitor living in London who won the contest to find a name for a new flavour of ice cream being promoted by Ben and Jerry. By 1997, wrote Andy Beckett, it meant 'rock bands and restaurants, football managers and fashion designers, Union Jacks on everything; by the beginning of this year [1998] it was shorthand for the government's entire arts policy; this spring it has virtually become shorthand for the government itself'.[4] A year later the phrase, and the phenomenon, had vanished, virtually without trace.

Cool Britannia was never more than a silly fad. By contrast, the Dome was a disaster, not just financially but because it demonstrated only too well the hollowness of the cultural pretensions of the Blair government. Dreamed up by Michael Heseltine as the centre-piece of his efforts to reclaim the Thames Gateway, the derelict miles of river-bank east of London, it was seized on by Peter Mandelson, who dreamt of repeating the enormous success enjoyed by his grandfather's project, the Festival of Britain, in 1951. But although the Dome itself was a magnificent structure, Mandelson frightened off the creative team first employed to fill it, and it ended up as a mish-mash, ideal as a day out for parents and their children but in no way representing the Best of Britain, unlike its predecessors in 1851 and 1951.

The final cost of the fiasco was well over £800 million and is the biggest blemish on the largest cultural fund ever made available in Britain. For, just as Harold Wilson's most lasting legacy had been the Open University, so John Major left behind the National Lottery, which has proved an immensely powerful force for good in reviving British cultural (and sporting) life. Results range from the vast increase in British medals at the 2000 Sydney Olympics to the rebuilding, often imaginatively, of most of Britain's cultural monuments, such as Kew Gardens, and the creation of some new and imaginative ventures, most obviously the Tate Modern Gallery and the Eden Project, which has recreated the world's forests in a disused china clay pit in Cornwall.

Characteristically the British looked this unprecedentedly golden gift horse in the mouth and found plenty to criticise. Attention concentrated on the few failures – most obviously, the Dome – and on the fact that so much of the funds in the first few years of the lottery went on a handful of London projects such as the Royal Opera House, which received the biggest single grant, of £78 million. But this was inevitable because these were the showcases for British cultural efforts and there is still plenty of time and money for smaller schemes over the years. More pertinent was the criticism when the chairman of the Lottery Fund paid £12 million for some of Winston Churchill's papers to his greedy grandson Winston.

Even more legitimate was the fear that too much was being spent on buildings and not on the cost of the museums and theatrical productions they housed. For these remained under-financed even after a tough businessman, Gerry Robinson of Granada, had taken over the Arts Council, had acquired increased funds from the government and had spent them sensibly. But still, as the journalist Richard Fairman commented (he was writing about the financial problems of London orchestras but his words could be applied to most British cultural institutions): 'One day economists may look back on this little local problem as an experiment in what happens when free-market principles try to operate in an environment dominated by foreign subsidised competitors.'[5] His point is reinforced by the increasing plight of museums and theatres outside London.

Nevertheless, the country was becoming steadily less philistine. In the 1970s and 1980s Labour-led councils had been in the forefront of philistinism – the most obvious case, as we saw, being the resistance of Southwark Council to the construction of a replica of the Globe Theatre. By contrast, in the late 1990s Labour boroughs came up with a number prize-winning cultural initiatives. These included an imaginative library in the South London borough of Peckham, a new art gallery in Walsall, the gallery in Salford devoted to the works of L. S. Lowry and, a local initiative without any help from the Lottery, the sculptor Anthony Gormley's giant Angel of the North erected by the Great North Road by Gateshead Council.

But Britain could not even reconquer the world of pop music in which it had so excelled for so long. British pop became, very largely, dominated by such as Oasis and the Spice Girls. John Harris isolated the problem after a year in which, for the first time since the early 1960s, not a single British group had been in the US Top Twenty: 'Whereas ''Anarchy in the UK'' was a musical emetic, designed to seize on underlying disaffection and bring it speeding to the surface, the most successful modern rock songs are balmy hymns to the notion that everything's going to be alright . . . there are no Neurotic Outsiders any more.'[6] Among other factors Harris mentioned were the increased absorption of the young in the educational process and the continuing economic boom and the fact that 'the corporate world is now fluent in youth-speak – they have all but killed the idea that to be young is somehow to be cheated'.

Of course, there's a lot of evidence to support the idea that television, in particular, has lowered its aims, has dumbed down. As Alison Pearson pointed out in the *Daily Telegraph*, while the best documentaries can aspire 'to tell us something about the human condition, the docusoap tells us only about the condition of human beings who know they're on television'. And when, at the end of the 1990s, the BBC re-introduced the Brains Trust, it was not for the mass audience it had enjoyed fifty-five years earlier. Inevitably, hordes of graduates with first-class degrees compete to work for every type of programme, however low-grade. But dumbing down is a much exaggerated phenomenon, for the level of British terrestrial television is still far higher, far more experimental, far broader in its approach than anywhere else in the world. Nevertheless, the combination of the commercial pressures imposed by the Television Act of 1990 and the end of the monopoly enjoyed by the BBC and ITV through the increasing proliferation of satellite-based channels means that the enormous audiences, sometimes amounting to the majority of the population, which were possible in the 1980s are now a thing of the past.

Mark you, the idea that watching the same television programmes created some form of social glue was always a trifle suspect – after all, the Queen watched television like the rest of us but the world it showed doesn't seem to have percolated through to HM's consciousness. Moreover, the obsession with the trivia of the lives of television celebrities, mostly well-endowed blondes, is not so different from the pre-war obsession with the lives of society beauties, with the one vital difference that working-class girls can aspire to a degree of fame of which they could never have dreamed before the war.

Nonetheless, there is a general feeling abroad that the cultural best and brightest are having to fight ever harder to justify their ideas and even to return to pre-Thatcher levels of cultural support. For instance, the first instinct of Chris Woodhead was to say 'We're not inspecting music', even though music teaching had been stopped in a quarter of Britain's primary schools. But after an outcry £180 million was found to restart the music programme. Even brass bands have survived against pressures which, as Chris Arnot put it, included 'local authority cuts in school music lessons; against the peer pressures of youth culture which decrees that there are many instruments cooler than a tuba; against the decimation of the mines and mills which spawned so many top bands.'[7]

But it seems legitimate to be depressed at a country in which the term 'life-style' is so important and in which the best-seller lists are dominated by cook books from celebrity chefs, their recipes rarely followed except by deep-dyed self-confessed foodies. 'My wife, who is French,' wrote Theodore Dalrymple, 'experienced a sense of liberation in reverse when she came to this country: at last, a nation in which people didn't much care for appearances, in which even rich people were content to be uncomfortable and ill-dressed. No-one was offended by bad food, was genuinely shocked by it or thought any the worse of anyone for serving it. She found a strange integrity in the indifference to luxury that she found among people who were by no means poor: it seemed to indicate a depth of character, a sense of proportion and the cultivation of more important virtues than those of her native land ... There is nothing whatsoever to be said in favour of the new northern hedonism, which combines the vice of superficiality with that of grossness. As Britain was once said by Dean Acheson to have lost an Empire and found no role, so in adopting hedonism we have lost our virtues and gained new vices.'[8]

Although the BBC has more than its fair share of foodie programmes, it was the only British cultural institution which managed to survive Thatcherism intact (partly thanks to a supposedly Thatcherite chairman, the accountant Stuart Young, who went native). More seriously, it survived the ultra-managerial rule of John Birt, its director general for twelve long years. His brutal style did at least ensure that the BBC would become a major force on the internet, and he opened up the corporation to allow a great many more programmes to be bought from independent producers. But during his later years he lost any contact with the idea that the Corporation existed as more than just a giant managerial toy. Typical Birtite policies included turfing news programmes out of Broadcasting House in Central London, convenient for politicians, leading businessmen and other important interviewees, and banishing them to the White City, five long miles away, to make room for increasing hordes of managers By the end of his reign these accounted for a full quarter of the Corporation's budget. Nevertheless, his ambitions will ensure that the BBC will remain a global player in a future in which the internet and digital and satellite television will play an enormous role. After he left, he was elevated to the peerage and wrote books on management which he (and his publishers) expected to be best-sellers. They weren't – though this did not prevent Tony Blair from giving him an, albeit ill-defined, advisory job in Whitehall.

Nevertheless Birt's reorganisation provided a useful inheritance for his successor, Greg Dyke. He was an archetype of the new breed of television tycoons. In 1984 he had rescued Tvam, the station which provided the early morning programmes for the commercial system. The original team, all famous TV personalities and thus naturally called the Fab Four, had proved to be a total disaster. They, and above all their chief executive, Peter Jay, had tried to impose their own up-market vision, in line with the doctrine Jay had previously expounded with his friend John Birt, that television as a whole had 'a bias against understanding' which gave the pair the right to a 'mission to explain'. But not, obviously, at breakfast. Dyke totally revolutionised the station's output, most (in)famously by introducing a character called Roland Rat, who became the symbol of what was, indeed, an early exercise in dumbing down. But, like so many non-Oxbridge TV executives*, he was fully aware of the need to provide a balanced output,

---

* By contrast David Elstein, the academically brilliant first head of the new Channel 5, introduced a schedule unmatched in the history of British broadcasting for its relentless sleaziness.

as he showed at London Weekend Television before the station was bought – at considerable profit to Dyke and his colleagues – by Granada. As an instinctive operator, he was just what the BBC needed after the Birt regime.

Even before Dyke's arrival, and as so often before, the BBC had shown a capacity to reinvent itself. Typically, Jenny Abramsky, head of BBC Radio, invented the highly successful news-cum-sport station Radio 5 Live. This is infinitely more relaxed and more approachable than Radio 4, which with its rather nannying attitudes remains perhaps the most obvious example of the *de haut en bas* attitudes enshrined in the term Reithianism. But Radio 4 remains a monument. Its, usually older, listeners launch vociferous objections when there is the slightest change in programming or the times of favourite regulars are changed – especially if, like *Woman's Hour, Saturday Night Theatre* and, above all, *The Archers*, they date back more than forty years. In the meantime, the Daily Service has been ministering regardless to listeners' spiritual needs since the late 1920s.

Mrs Thatcher had concentrated her assault on the trades unions representing the working classes and had left virtually untouched the much more powerful associations representing the professional classes, the solicitors, barristers, doctors (particularly the consultants) and even the teachers. All too often, these associations were what was termed 'producer-led': inward-looking, and concerned more with their own interests rather than those of the people they were supposed to be serving. The term became at once a cliché and a useful – and not entirely unjustified – weapon against the professions involved.

Until the late 1980s, the relationship between the doctors and the increasingly under-funded National Health Service had remained the same since the NHS had been established forty years earlier. Waves of administrative changes were then introduced to loosen up the system. But these resulted merely in ever-increasing administrative complexity, especially for the general practitioners. Their increasingly vocal and entirely understandable objections to the way they were being messed around were matched by an equally justified and ever-increasing public concern over the lasting consequences of the independence of the consultants, itself a legacy of Aneurin Bevan's tactics in dividing the profession when he set up the NHS.

Over the decades, the General Medical Council had systematically refused to examine many allegations of misconduct against doctors. In one case, a judge rebuked the GMC for 'serious and disturbing failures' in investigating allegations against an Oxford-based GP. These failures were symptomatic of a general lenience on the part of the GMC in allowing doctors who had been struck off back into medical practice. Throughout the 1990s, there was a series of appalling cases involving negligent doctors left to practise though an over-respect for the status of consultants. The worst single case* was probably that of a consultant gynaecologist, Richard Neale, who had been struck off the register in Canada but was nevertheless allowed to practise in Britain for over a decade. But worse still was the club-like atmosphere in so many hospitals, the systematic hushing up of institutionalised incompetence. In the cardiological department of a famous hospital, the Bristol Royal Infirmary, this resulted in the deaths of an alarming number of children over a long period.

Yet even after the scandals of the last years of the century, doctors could rely on continuing public support. The same could obviously not be said for the country's lawyers. They were attacked on two grounds: because they were self-regulating, and because of the division between solicitors and barristers. Over the years the solicitors' professional organisation, the Law Society, had been racked with internal strife – including accusations of racial discrimination made by a former vice-chairman, a particularly aggressive Indian lady. Unsurprisingly, it proved incapable of dealing with the number of complaints against its members which increased steadily as the public's previous respect for lawyers laregely evaporated. Indeed, by the end of the 1990s, self-regulation appeared to be doomed. At the same time, the profession became increasingly divided between the minority of extraordinarily well-paid – albeit ludicrously hard-working – partners in a handful of large, increasingly international firms based in the City, and the majority of solicitors, above all those in small towns, many of whom struggle to earn a living now that the regular income they used to be able to rely on from conveyancing has been greatly reduced.

All this put the solicitors in a poor position to ask for further recognition in their long-running battle to be able to plead in the country's higher courts. Official efforts on their behalf date back forty years when an otherwise deeply conservative Lord Chancellor, Lord Dilhorne†, made the first attempt to break the barristers' monopoly. Yet until the late 1990s the bar remained probably the single best and most long-lasting example of the pure, unreconstructed pre-1960s establishment, if only because it had avoided reform for so much longer. For even the most distinguished and most radical advocates such as Jeremy Hutchinson (who refused to become a judge) were

* The case of Harold Shipman, a Manchester GP guilty of the serial killing of literally hundreds of his patients over a twenty year period, was not, however, the GMC's fault but that of the police – and the community in which he practised.

† Formerly Sir Reginald Manningham-Buller, labelled, not inaccurately, by Bernard Levin as 'Bullying Manner'. He was always supposed to be the original for Widmerpool, the anti-hero in Anthony Powell's *Music of Time* series of novels.

implacable opponents of change in the system. The bar was also reactionary in every possible sense of the term – which is one of the reasons why the judges, recruited from their ranks, were and still often appear so out of touch*. A survey in 1999 carried out by Mark Solon, whose firm Bond Solon trains expert witnesses, found that too many judges are still sexist – one who had been trying rape cases for twenty years did not know about post-traumatic stress disorder.

Barristers, dodging the famous cab-rank rule that they should take the next case presented to them, used to fight shy of cases involving terrorists or racial equality. When Lord Gifford set up chambers in Covent Garden and instituted an equal pay policy, the world of the law was outraged. Worse, the distinguished legal journalist Marcel Berlins 'used to hear vile, unprintable almost hysterical remarks made about leftie lawyers; I have seen judges in court barely able to speak civilly to radical barristers like Michael Mansfield, such was their hatred of him and the threat they thought he represented to the good order of the law.'[9] No wonder 'it was their badge of honour to be criticised intemperately by others in the legal system'. Nevertheless the judges are now far more liberal; senior judges now include a former communist, Stephen Sedley, and two Law Lords, Hoffman and Steyn, who, as Jewish refugees from South Africa, had witnessed the institutionalised injustice of the apartheid regime. In addition, the Bar Council has proved far more effective than the Law Society in imposing a sort of social discipline on its members, insisting, not before time, on quotas for women and ethnic minorities in the chambers, the small groups in which barristers work. To a small extent, too, solicitors have broken the barristers' monopoly of pleading in court.

But the worst that can happen to doctors and lawyers is that the state will regulate them more effectively. The same cannot be said for the Church of England. Of all British institutions, having ceased so obviously to be the Tory Party at prayer, it has lost the most ground over the past fifty years and at the Millennium its very survival, above all as the Established Church, looked increasingly doubtful. There remains a general, if vague, feeling of religiosity but everywhere there are signs of de-christianisation, with the major church festivals associated more with shopping and holidays than with worship. 'Between 1960 and 1985,' wrote Adrian Hastings, 'the Church of England as a going concern was reduced to not much more than half its previous size'– and other Christian sects, including the Catholics, had not fared much better.

For religion had become fragmented – Hastings lists 'Krishna Con-

* Another reason is the considerable increase over the past thirty years in the number of judges, who all had to be recruited from a relatively small pool of barristers.

sciousness, Scientology, Transcendental Meditation, the Divine Light Mission, the Children of God and the Unification Church' as part of what he calls the 'privatisation of religion' – including the growth of the Orthodox Churches as well as of Hinduism. The Faith Zone in the Millennium Dome was sponsored by the Hinduja brothers, and by far the most impressive religious building constructed since the cathedrals at Liverpool and Coventry forty years earlier was a Hindu temple in Neasden in North-West London. Islam, the most important of all, is a special case, especially after the events of September 11th 2001 – and the American reaction to them – radicalised and alienated previously apparently well-integrated Muslims.

Within the Anglican Church itself these fissiparous tendencies ensured a state of disorganisation bordering on chaos. 'By the early 1990s,' wrote Peter Hitchens, 'the Anglican Church no longer had any recognised or familiar forms of service. Anything was possible . . . Bibles, prayers, hymns, styles of music, arrangement of the building, the clothes worn by the worshippers would all have been entirely unpredictable.'[10] In the Nine O'clock Service in Sheffield, there were 'druidic white-robed figures around an altar resembling a crescent moon . . . hundreds of black-clad figures peer out of the darkness swaying to swirling, strangely ethereal breaths of ambient techno.' Nevertheless, George Carey, Runcie's successor as Archbishop of Canterbury, can point out, not unreasonably, that because of this 'the Church of England is more authentically itself today, and more itself, than perhaps it was a hundred years ago . . . Nowadays you hear people say "I am a Christian" – there's no of course, it's a positive statement.' As Monica Furlong says, 'There is now an almost total absence of those who go to church because convention demands it.' But this makes life more difficult, for 'those who remain are not content with easy answers of what the faith is, or how it is to be lived out'.

Ever since his appointment as Archbishop of Canterbury, Carey has been under attack from all sides, above all as a happy clappy prelate of no great intellectual distinction. Like John Major, Carey left school early and reached the top through luck and determination rather than any special intellectual gifts – proof, perhaps, that in modern Britain success was possible to those from disadvantaged backgrounds even though they were by no means geniuses. But his intellectual inadequacies are important because, as Adrian Hastings points out, the Church of England 'is particularly vulnerable to collapse due to intellectual bankruptcy just because – far more than most – it has long been a thinking church, finding its very heart in major universities'. Long gone are the days when nearly two in five ordinands came from Oxbridge; even longer past are the times when the vicar was a gentleman living in a rectory. Most of these generally splendid residences have now been sold, for the church could no longer afford the upkeep and anyway the incumbent was usually no longer a gentleman.

Large-scale initiatives to turn the tide – such as the Call to the Nation mission declared by Archbishop Coggan in the 1970s and the Decade of Evangelism decided on by the bishops of the Lambeth Conference* in 1988 – were both failures. The key to any recovery seems to lie in smaller, more unorthodox initiatives. In his television series 'Sea of Faith', Don Cupitt seemed to deny almost all the elements of traditional Christianity, yet to Monica Furlong he was 'much the most interesting theologian around, not least because he tries to talk in everyday language'.

Unsurprisingly, the only dynamic forces within Anglicanism combined individual churches and an unintellectual approach. Alpha, the most famous of recent initiatives, is centred at Holy Trinity Church Brompton. Alpha started in 1979 but only really got going in 1991 with the arrival of Reverend Nicky Gumbel. He has an extraordinary knack of combining informality with a pretence of not forcing his congregation into conversion, for his all-embracing welcome bears an uncanny resemblance to Tony Blair's idea of the Big Tent. Alpha now has 1.5 million adherents in 116 countries attending a course seemingly designed for leaders – even in prisons, for today the majority of British prisons run Alpha courses in groups of up to a dozen agnostics. The key to Alpha is the Toronto Blessing† – the calling down of the spirit, laying on of hands, 'long-term healing' taking place 'within the fellowship of the church'.

Alpha, and more particularly Gumbel himself, has an undeniable capacity to touch our inmost fears and thoughts. On the course he attended, the journalist Jon Ronson thought about his own life, how he and his wife had been told that they could not have a baby and 'then we did have a baby and thought that our son, Joel, was a gift from God.' At the obligatory weekend induction course, even Ronson, agnostic and born Jewish, did not find the much-dreaded 'speaking in tongues' which follows the blessing as gimmicky and unreal as he had feared. Ronson thought it 'would be cacophonous, but it turns out to be haunting, tuneful, like some experimental opera'.[11] Monica Furlong had a similar reaction at an Alpha service in South London. For her the best moment came when 'a young woman suddenly began to sing in a very beautiful voice. I could not understand the words', and then

---

* An meeting held every ten years which brings together all the bishops of the Anglican Communion world-wide.

† Named after an incident when four fifths of a congregation in a concrete church near Toronto airport suddenly fell to the floor and began writhing around, convulsing violently and 'singing in tongues'.

Furlong realised that she was indeed 'singing in tongues ... I was transfixed by the purity of it an extraordinarily poetic moment'. Even more significantly, she was also struck by the 'enormous amount of social energy around the church'. But critics such as Hastings point out that 'HTB's* divorce from the real world, together with a simplistic and communal response to all problems, a strong leader and a money-conscious hierarchy, are trade-marks of a cult'.

But if the Anglican Church is to prosper in the twenty-first century, it will have to prove itself capable of absorbing the many devout and able women who form its best hope for the future. They have already come a long way. The Campaign for the Ordination of Women gathered pace after the declaration by General Synod in 1975 that 'there was no fundamental objection to the Ordination of Women', resulting in a Movement set up in 1979 with the backing of a sprinkling of the Great and the Good. The Movement attracted more than its fair share of hysterical attacks from bishops and senior clergy trying to prove that women could never be ordained for a variety of generally rather fanciful reasons. They were supported by the right-wing press – whose descriptions of would-be women priests included such appetising morsels as 'butch women in boiler-suits' and 'Nazi fellow-travellers in T-shirts'.

In 1987, despairing of progress – a situation emphasised by the refusal of Synod to allow women priests from outside Britain to celebrate communion – the Movement invited these priests to say Communion in a small college chapel in East London, a celebration forbidden by the Bishop of London, Graham Leonard. But that same year Synod voted to allow women to become deacons and five years later they gained the right to be ordained as priests. The reformers had a high hurdle – or rather three of them – to jump, since the measure had to receive separate two-thirds majorities within the Synod from lay members, priests and bishops. The result was greeted by the immortal headline – naturally in the *Sun*: 'VICARS IN KNICKERS'.

Despite this overwhelming endorsement, the Church promptly went into a tailspin, thanks to the hysterical forecast that up to 3,000 priests might leave the Anglican Communion. To calm the atmosphere, it appointed 'flying bishops' to officiate in parishes which did not want women priests, giving equal standing to both sides. This piece of cowardice was particularly sad as George Carey is deeply respected by women as being an archbishop who not only supported their ordination but is at ease in treating them as equals. Yet an anti-women movement, the backward-looking Forward in Faith, remains a powerful lobby, even though only 400 clergy left, most – including Bishop

* The normal acronym for Holy Trinity Brompton.

Leonard – going over to Rome while some retired and forty-five have returned to the Church.

There remains a vicious undercurrent of anti-feminism in the Church, and its depth was demonstrated in a television series about Lucy Winkett, the first woman appointed to be a canon at St Paul's. Winkett is clearly intelligent, balanced, articulate and, it has to be admitted, demurely attractive. At one point she was shown in tears after no one who had served mass for her had been prepared to receive communion from her.

To be fair, most of the opponents to the ordination of women probably have problems with their sexuality. But they were gays forced to stay in the closet because the Church cannot accept the fact that a high proportion of its clergy throughout history have been gay – although there are cases of individual parishes which are perfectly happy for their vicars to live openly with a male partner. But the upheaval has greatly damaged the Catholic element in the supposedly broad Anglican Church, a far cry from the 1950s and 1960s when such Anglo-Catholics as Trevor Huddleston – though he also was a closet gay – and Michael Scott could flourish. It is an even worse blow to the body's historical perception of itself as a bridge between Catholics and Protestants. For at the end of the 1990s the Church as a whole seemed to be in bad shape because of lack of leadership. As Furlong puts it, 'Expediency too often is all', and she calls for the church not to give in to blackmail, as it has done in its backsliding over women priests and in its inability to accept homosexual priests, and 'to decide what is right and stick to the decision'.

Nevertheless the Anglican Church remains 'the Church of England as by law established'. But its curious position is increasingly under threat. In 1984 that sternest of logicians, Enoch Powell, set out the church's dilemma when he told Parliament that 'It is possible to have an internally self-governed church in this country, but it will not be the national church, it will not be the Church of England. The Church is the Church of England because of Royal Supremacy, because there is royal – that is to say lay – supremacy.' Disestablishment, in other words, removes the church's right to speak for 'England'.

Indeed the Queen is still Supreme Governor of the Church, but it is now legitimate to ask whether this will last another 450 years. The Queen's position should have been impregnable. The monarchy was the one institution, and she the single person, whom Mrs Thatcher could not affect – the more so because, to begin with anyway, she was mortally afraid of the Queen and was never at ease with her. Yet a suicidal combination of stupidity, arrogance and insensitivity ensured that in the last twenty years of the century the royal family dug what would have been its grave had it not been so firmly anchored in the affections of a majority of the British people.

The Queen was not helped by having as Private Secretary for the crucial years Sir Robert Fellowes, a courtier plain and simple, a creature, who was far less willing to provide positive advice than some of his predecessors, above all Sir Martin Charteris. To make matters worse, the Queen was now older than her advisers and could no longer think of them as helpful uncles or elder brothers. She continued to be reactive, her supporters perpetually hamstrung by her lifelong refusal to take any initiative. But even the best and most appreciated advisers would have been helpless because her problems centred on the family. As an anonymous friend told royal biographer Sarah Bradford, 'The Queen has shown firmness in every area of her life except with her children.' 'If the Queen had spent as much time over the mating of her children as she does with her horses,' a courtier told Bradford, 'all this might not have happened'. But it was not just a question of neglect. It was also one of appalling judgement and a bland assumption that even the most unsuitable consorts for her sons would automatically be transformed upon their marriage.

Only one of her children, Princess Anne, showed how it was possible to do the unthinkable – i.e. divorce and remarry – without fuss or scandal (apart from the discovery of some compromising letters written to her husband-to-be before she had ditched husband number one). But otherwise her divorce from a dim, handsome army officer and remarriage to a much more intelligent but equally handsome naval officer a little younger than herself passed without any publicity*. Anne had been active, indeed tireless in charity work, most obviously her involvement with the Save the Children Fund, which included venturing into refugee camps in some rather nasty, indeed dangerous spots around the world. Unfortunately her brusque, often downright rude manner on other occasions, a trait inherited from her loving father, greatly reduced the impact of her efforts.

Anne knew how to play the royal game, whereas Charles's bride Diana Spencer and Andrew's, Sarah Ferguson, manifestly didn't. And even if they had, they were incapable of fulfilling the role of demure, supportive, unquestioning consort which the royal family assumed they would. Yet first appearances – especially Charles and Diana's fairy-tale wedding – were deceptive. 'No feeling,' wrote Walter Bagehot of the marriage of the future Edward VII to Princess Alexandra in 1863, 'could seem more childish than the enthusiasm of the English' at such an event. As Anthea Hall wrote in the *Daily Telegraph*, the marriages

---

* Like his father-in-law Philip, Anne's second husband, Commander Tim Lawrence, ditched a glittering future in the Navy by marrying into the royal family.

315

provided the prospect of a 'closer-knit and more British monarchy, with two modern-minded young wives as new recruits, whose fresh approach will clear away the last, dour Germanic remains of the Hanoverian regime'. But the Hanoverian monarchy had always had problems with Princes of Wales, and none more so than with the indecisive Charles. He had been advised by Lord Mountbatten, a major influence on his life, to 'choose a suitable and sweet-charactered girl before she meets anyone else she might fall for' – and Mountbatten also apparently laid down that Charles's bride should be a virgin, which eliminated most of the suitable candidates and provided a clear illustration of the growing gulf between the lifestyle and assumptions of the Queen (and her mother) and the social realities of their age. But all the suitable prospects either – like the television producer Lady Jane Wellesley – couldn't face the prospect or – like Camilla Parker-Bowles – had despaired of his indecision. (Diana was not the only victim of the idea of the girl as a sacrificial object to be offered up to some suitable and suitably titled husband. Other examples include the wife of Lord Spencer and the wretched wife of the Marquess of Blandford, the heir to the Duke of Marlborough who just happened to be a criminal druggie.)

Poor Diana, 'as thick as a plank' as she herself admitted and obviously deeply insecure and unstable, was both unbelievably innocent and innocently manipulative. At school she slept in a bed which had over it a photograph of Charles at his investiture as Prince of Wales and she remained a virgin 'because I knew I had to keep myself tidy for what lay ahead'. She even imagined that she could reform the royal family from within. Diana was always going to be a time-bomb waiting to go off or, more accurately, a series of bombs which went off like so many fireworks until the final almighty final explosion in the week following her death.

Diana was indeed a victim of the royal family's ruthlessness. She had been chosen, not by Charles himself, but by his grandmother and her closest friend, Ruth Lady Fermoy, Diana's step-grandmother. What came out, most notably in the 'authorised' biography by Andrew Morton and in the famous *Panorama* interview, was the treatment she received since there were of course three people in the marriage, Charles seeing no reason to give up his long-term mistress, Camilla Parker-Bowles. Within a few years, she and her husband were communicating mainly through written memoranda. Yet 'when Charles duly betrayed her best friend's granddaughter', wrote Anthony Holden, 'continuing his affair with a fellow officer's wife before, during and after their marriage, the Queen Mother betrayed all her apparent principles by condoning her grandson's adultery and taking his side against the girl she had trapped into marrying him'.

When Peter York and Ann Barr* tried to define Princess Diana, they found that underneath her obvious attributes were 'the Old Guard instincts; the tenets of Noblesse Oblige; virginity, marriage – and the wedding list; love of the country, animals; lack of formal education – in short everything that Really Matters'. How, wrote York nearly twenty years later, 'could we have known she'd become the biggest Sloane-killer going; that "the mouse that roared", [as] Tina Brown called her, would become a global Essex Girl, therapy junkie and Versace Groupie?'[12] But Diana was more than that: she was not just the leader, she was the creator, the very embodiment of the idea that London could be the smartest city in the world. At the same time she built up a thoroughly deserved reputation as the only member of the royal family ever to have the common touch, to care openly about the sick, not to be afraid of empathising openly with their problems.

The Queen had probably thought of Diana only as marriage fodder. But her attitude to the prospective brides of her favourite son, the brave, stupid Andrew, was more positive. She found Koo Stark, the American actress – who never discussed her relationship with Andrew – 'nice and gentle', which was fair enough. But quite different was her attitude to Fergie, unquestionably – Diana apart – the most unsuitable consort ever selected by a member of the royal family. 'She was very fond of Fergie,' a friend told Ben Pimlott, 'she liked the way she used to sit with her legs apart, making jokes.' Yet Fergie was obviously the very model of a great, galumphing, warm-hearted, good time girl – her, quite genuine, charity work much less publicised than Diana's. She was simply 'not cut out to be a royal princess in this or any other age', observed Martin Charteris, the last of the Private Secretaries of any stature. 'Vulgar vulgar vulgar,' he exploded in an extraordinarily frank interview with the *Spectator* after the revelation of her antics with one of her lovers. Indeed, this had been the public's reaction when she and Prince Andrew built themselves a pile in Surrey which was promptly christened South Fork after the Ewings' home in *Dallas*.

The single episode which did most damage to the royal image came in 1988 with the appearance of the younger members of the brood in an undeniably vulgar television game, *It's a Knockout*. By that time it was legitimate for the public to feel that it had been sold an increasingly false bill of goods with the presentation of the royal family as a model. By 1991 the majority thought the royal family an expensive luxury and that the Queen ought to be taxed on her income – a burden she accepted shortly afterwards. The next year, she admitted in her Christmas broadcast that it had been had been an *annus horribilis*, an unprecedented admission and one due not only to family problems but

* In that archetypal 1980s publication, *The Official Sloane Ranger Handbook*.

also to a horrendous fire at Windsor Castle. That same year, the historian David Cannadine declared, quite rightly, that the monarchy was 'passive, philistine, bewildered, anachronistic, obsessed with protocol and tradition and smothered in a courtly embrace redolent of quarter-deck attitudes and saddle soap'.[13] By then Julie Burchill, the wittiest of the new school of punk chic, could describe the royal family as 'life imitating soap imitating life', for royalty, like soaps, 'was a tranquilliser ... Monarchies are not a hallmark of classiness, but a brand of lack of confidence'. Naturally, republicanism came out of the closet. In the 1960s, said Stephen Haseler, a life-long anti-monarchist, 'you could never say it then. People would faint at the idea until the late 1980s.'

The fallout from Princess Diana's death led to a rethink, not before time and even then not fundamental enough, about the sheer size of the royal family and number of, in Philip's phrase, 'the firm's' subsidiaries. By the turn of the Millennium, many of the minor royals had settled down into an almost Scandinavian respectability. The example had been set by the Queen's cousin, the Duke of Gloucester, who had long worked as an architect (an enormous contrast with his father, whose chief public occupation had been the inspection of Commonwealth war graves). Her nephew, Margaret's son Lord Linley, was a talented carpenter – or rather *ébeniste*. But others had problems, like Prince Michael of Kent, who was unable to cope even as a non-executive director of the Tote. The comments of his chairman, that staunch royalist, the late Woodrow Wyatt, on his performance make it clear just how incapable such minor royals are of coping with life outside the gilded cage.

But problems with minor royals are the least of the monarchy's troubles. Charles has still seemingly not understood what was happening. 'The Prince's sense of the past,' wrote David Cannadine 'is, like that of most royals, romantic, escapist and superficial ... Like many of his predecessors, [he] is unable to come to terms with the limitations (and the privileges) of his own position ... He may genuinely care, he may seem sympathetic, but the care is vitiated by his romantic and outmoded outlook – one most obviously shown in his attitude towards architecture. Moreover it is dissipated, he is apparently unable to concentrate for long on a single subject.'[14]

Even more fundamental is the Bourbon-like attitude of the family. In the words of the playwright David Hare: 'It is this basic turn of mind – the country is not theirs in trust but by right – which has lately given the monarchy its peculiarly sullen character. The House of Windsor has not bothered to be generous because, literally, it does not see why it needs to be.' In 2000 the journalist Edward Pearce charted the decay of the monarchy, which, as he pointed out, 'rests upon deference, the instinct to cringe. Its opposite is the association of free autonomous citizens thinking for themselves. Monarchy, once despotism, has dwindled by way of crowd control into a sickly cult of the hereditary celebrity' – and a cult increasingly relying on a new superstar, the apparently stable, allegedly intelligent William.

Yet, unbelievably, the British respect for the monarchy had enabled the old firm to survive its worst crisis for a long time, one that was far more profound than the Abdication and which called into question its very legitimacy, its capacity to cope with a changing world, its willingness to justify itself other than by being royal. Which leaves unanswered and perhaps unanswerable the most fundamental question about life in Britain: is true democracy possible under so obstinately unlovable a monarchy, above all one so hedged with ceremonial as ours? To me the answer must surely be a definite no.

Notes

1. Quoted in the *New Statesman*, September 4 1998.
2. *Political Review*, July 1998.
3. *Economist*, August 7 1999.
4. *Guardian*, May 5 1998.
5. *Financial Times*, January 23 1999.
6. *New Statesman*, March 27 2000.
7. *Independent*.
8. *New Statesman*, July 26 1999.
9. *New Statesman*, March 5 1999.
10. *The Abolition of Britain*, Quartet Books, 1999 – an entertaining and, in this case anyway, justified rant.
11. *Guardian Weekend*, October 21 2000.
12. *Independent*, February 20 2001.
13. *Financial Times*, February 8 1992.
14. *History in Our Time*, Yale University Press, 1998.

Acknowledgements

To say the least, this book has had a troubled history, rejected as it was by a dozen or more publishers. As a result I have depended on the encouragement of a handful of friends to see me through a tense few years. I first realised that I could write the book and not just dream of its while staying in Portugal with Michael Pye and Professor John Holm. Much of the writing was done while staying with Sam Arnold-Forster and at the house in Talmont near Royan of my friends Michel & Catherine Guillard. Lady Marie-Louise Legg, Gina Alexander and Peter Cropper helped to fill in some of the many gaps in my knowledge. Other friends who were enormously supportive included Juliet Gardiner, John Torode, Sophia Gilliatt and Susie Morgan, all of whom showed forbearance beyond the call of duty at my frequent spells of angst and tension. Peter Ingrey of Lloyds TSB showed a full understanding of my problems by organising the loan which helped me to finance the publication of the book.

Professionally I have relied on the ever-friendly and professional staff at the London Library, the production skills of Michael Brown, the editing talents of Angus MacKinnon and the eagle eye of my friend and lawyer Rhory Robertson.

Thank you all.

Michelene Wandor's poem quoted on page 40 comes from *Gardens of Eden Revisited*, published by Five Leaves Publications in 1999. Tony Harrison's poem quoted on page 39 comes from *Punchline* in his *Selected Poems* published by Penguin in 1987. Ted Hughes poem *The Beach* quoted on page 17 comes from *Birthday Letters* published by Faber & Faber in 1988. *By the Seaside* and *How to Get On in Society* by Sir John Betjeman on pages 35 and 80 come from his *Collected Poems* published by John Murray. The poem by Philip Larkin on page 5 is taken from his *Collected Poems*, published by Faber & Faber and the Marvell Press in 1988. All are reprinted with the kind permission of the publishers – and, in the case of Ted Hughes, his estate.

Select Bibliography

Martin Adeney & John Lloyd, *The miners' strike*, Routledge & Kegan Paul, 1986.

Andrew Adonis & Stephen Pollard, *A Class Act*, Hamish Hamilton, 1997.

Kenneth Allsop, *The angry decade*, Peter Owen, 1958.

Noel Annan *Our Age, Portrait of a Generation*, Weidenfeld & Nicolson, 1990.

The Dons, mentors, eccentrics and geniusses, HarperCollins, 1999.

Julian Barnes, *Letters from London 1990–1995*, Picador 1995.

Francis Beckett *The Enemy within – the Rise and Fall of the British Communist Party.* John Murray, 1995.

Vernon Bogdanor and Robert Skidelsky (ed), *The Age of Affluence*, Macmillan 1972.

Christopher Booker, *The Neophiliacs*, Collins, 1969.

Sarah Bradford, *Elizabeth – a biography of HM the Queen*, Heinemann, 1986.

Asa Briggs, *History of Broadcasting in the UK*, OUP, 1995.

Brian Brivati, *Lord Goodman*, Richard Cohen Books, 1999.

Julie Burchill, *Diana*, Orion, 1999.

David Butler, *The 1975 Referendum*, Macmillan, 1976.

David & Gareth Butler, *British Political Facts*, Macmillan, 1994.

David Cannadine. *History in Our Time.* Yale University Press London, 1998.

Humphrey Carpenter*, Robert Runcie*, Hodder & Stoughton, 1996

Brian Cox, *An English Curricululm for the 1990s*, Hodder & Stoughton, 1991.

Susan Crosland, *Anthony Crosland*, Jonathan Cape, 1982.

Richard Crossman, *The Diaries of a Cabinet Minister vol 1,* Hamish Hamilton & Jonathan Cape, 1975.

Ralf Dahrendorf, *On Britain*, BBC Books, 1982.

Bill Deedes*, Dear Bill: Deedes reports*, Macmillan, 1997.

David Dimbleby & David Reynolds, *An Ocean Apart*, Hodder & Stoughton, 1988.

Bernard Donoughue, *Prime Ministers: the conduct of policy under Harold Wilson & James Callaghan,* Jonathan Cape 1987

Margaret Drabble, *The Ice Age*, Weidenfeld & Nicolson, 1977.

Stephen Fay, *The Collapse of Barings*, Richard Cohen Books, 1996.

Monica Furlong, *The Church of England: The state it's in*, Hodder & Stoughton 2000.

Juliet Gardiner, *From the Bomb to the Beatles*, Collins & Brown 1999

Jonathon Green, *All Dressed Up – the Sixties and the counter-culture*, Jonathan Cape 1998.

Germaine Greer, *The Female Eunuch*, MacGibbon & Kee, 1970.

A. H. Halsey, *Change in British Society*, Oxford University Press, 1995.

Willy Hamilton, *My Queen and I,* Quartet Books, 1975.

David Hargreaves, *Social Relations in a Secondary School*, Routledge & Kegan Paul 1967.

Adrian Hastings *A History of British Christianity 1920–1990*, Collins, 1991.

– *Robert Runcie*, Mowbray 1991.

Patrick Higgins, *Heterosexual dictatorship – male homosexuality in post-war Britain,* Fourth Estate, 1996.

Lord Hill, *Both Sides of the Hill*, Heinemann, 1964.

Peter Hitchens, *The abolition of Britain*, Quartet, 1999.

Godfrey Hodgson, *Lloyd's of London, A reputation at risk*, Penguin, 1986.

Richard Hoggart, *The Uses of Literacy*, Chatto & Windus, 1957.

John Hoskyns, *Just in time – Inside the Thatcher revolution*, Aurum Press, 2000.

Ted Hughes, *Birthday Letters*, Faber & Faber, 1998.

John Humphrys, *Devil's Advocate*, Hutchinson, 1999.

Richard Ingrams, *Muggeridge: the biography*, Harpercollins, 1995.

Bryan Johnson (ed), *All Bull: the national servicemen*, Quartet Books, 1972.

Anthony King, *Does the United Kingdom still have a constitution ?* Sweet & Maxwell, 2001.

Paul Lashmar, *Britain's secret propaganda war 1948–77*, Sutton, Stroud 1998.

John le Carre, *A small town in Germany*, Heinemann, 1968.

James Lees-Milne, *Ancient as the Hills Diaries 1973–74*, John Murray, 1997.

Trevor Lloyd, *Empire, Welfare State, Europe English History 1906–1992*, OUP 1993.

M McKie and C Cook (ed), *The Economy a study in Failure*, in *The Decade of Disillusion: British Politics in the Sixties*, Macmillan, 1972.

Colin MacInnes, *England half English*, Macgibbon & Kee, 1961.

Alistair McAlpine, *Once a Jolly Bagman*, Weidenfeld & Nicolson, 1997.

Brian Macarthur, *The Penguin Book of 20th century protest*, Viking, 1998.

Ross McKibbin, *Classes & Culture England 1918–51*, OUP 1998.

Kenneth O Morgan, *The People's Peace 1945–1989*, OUP1990.

Bryan Moynahan, *The British century*, Weidenfeld & Nicolson, 1997.

Like it was: the diaries of Malcolm Muggeridge, ed John Bright-Holmes Collins, 1981.

Tom Nairn, *The Enchanted Glass, Britain and its monarchy*, Radius Books, 1988.

– *The Break-Up of Britain*, New Left Books, London 1977.

Howard Newby, *Green and Pleasant Land*, Hutchinson, 1979.

Bernard Nossiter, *Britain: a future that works*, Deutsch, 1978.

Ben Pimlott, *The Queen, A Biography of Elizabeth II*, HarperCollins, 1996.

John Plender, *A Stake in the future*, Nicholas Brealey, 1997.

Anthony Powell, *The strangers all are gone*, Heinemann, 1992.

Geoffrey Robertson, *The Justice Game*, Chatto & Windus, 1998.

Lord Roll, *Crowded Hours*, Faber & Faber, 1985.

Paul Routledge, *Scargill, the unauthorised biography*, HarperCollins, 1993.

Trevor Royle, *The Best Years of their Lives*, Michael Joseph, 1986.

Anthony Sampson, *The Anatomy of Britain*, Hodder & Stoughton, 1962.

– *The New Anatomy of Britain*, Hodder & Stoughton, 1971.

– *Macmillan*, Allan Lane Penguin Press,1967

Clancy Sigal, *Weekend in Dinlock*, Secker & Warburg, 1960.

Michael Shanks, *The Stagnant Society: a warning*, Penguin, 1961.

Peter Shore, *Separate Ways – The Heart of Europe*, Duckworth, 2000.

Marion Shoard, *The Theft of the Countryside*, Temple Smith, 1980.

Diana Simmonds, *Di the national dish*, Pluto Press, 1984.

Andrew Shonfield, *British economic policy since the war*, Penguin, 1958.

Sir Michael Tippett, *Moving into Aquarius*, Routledge & Kegan Paul, 1959.

Nick Tiratsoo (ed), *From Blitz to Blair*, Weidenfeld & Nicolson 1997.

Hugh Thomas, *The Suez Affair*, Weidenfeld & Nicolson, 1967.

Mary Warnock, *A memoir, people and places*, Duckworth, 2000.

Alan Watkins, *A Short Walk down Fleet Street*, Duckworth, 2000.

Charles Webster, *The National Health Service: a political history*, OUP, 1998.

Philip Whitehead, *The writing on the wall, Britain in the 1970s*, Michael Joseph 1985.

David Widgery, *The Left in Britain 1956–68*, Penguin, 1976.

Martin Wiener, *English culture and the decline of the industrial spirit*, Cambridge University Press, 1981.

Peter Wildeblood, *Against the law*, Weidenfeld & Nicolson, 1954.

The Journals of Woodrow Wyatt, 3 vols, Macmillan, 1998–2000.

Hugo Young *This Blessed Plot*, Papermac, 1999.

Michael Young, *The rise of the Meritocracy, 1970–2033*, Thames & Hudson, 1958.

Index